Micro-Church Families on Mission

How to start small spiritual families that love God, one another, and their neighbors.

Dr. Timothy Johns

WHAT OTHERS ARE SAYING:

The International House of Prayer of Kansas City is an evangelical missions organization that is devoted to 24/7 worship and intercession for a global harvest of souls (Revelation 7:9). We join the prayers of millions across the nations in asking the Lord for at least a billion new born-again followers of Christ. There are already signs that the Lord is answering these prayers. Therefore, it is essential that we also develop biblical strategies to help these new believers become mature disciples of Jesus. This *Micro-Church Families on Mission* is an essential training manual to do just that. It provides very helpful practical insights and action items to help the body of Christ reach the lost and make disciples. Jesus was focused on raising up 12 disciples as his top strategy for advancing the kingdom. My friend, Tim Johns, has captured the essential elements necessary for starting and multiplying small spiritual families on mission. I recommend this training manual as a practical resource to help you launch missional communities and/or to improve the effectiveness of your small groups.

Mike Bickle
Director of the International House of Prayer

Once in a while a timeless "Life Manual" comes along that you will refer to for years to come. This is what Dr. Timothy Johns has given the Body of Christ in *Micro-Church Families on Mission.* Each section reads with liberating life wisdom and building-blocks to empower you and your church family. You can feel the prayer, research and experience that went into its making by the "Ah – ha's" of the Holy Spirit that you enjoy through its pages. I have known Tim for many years as a friend and brother-in-arms. What you will read in the content to follow is not just theory, but spiritual life in practice. These insights and methods have been forged in the fires of human trials while embraced in the loving arms of a wonderful God. From the DNA knitting of small groups to the foreign mission field everything is up and running. It works! Enjoy the journey ahead.

Dr. M. John Cava
President: World Outreach Center, Fort Mill, SC

Timothy Johns, *Micro-Church Families on Mission* training manual adds an important perspective on missions. This is a very practical manual and one which gives guidance to those who take a less traditional approach to church and mission. I have known Timothy for quite a few years and respect his commitment to the advancement of the Kingdom of God and his ability to communicate important training materials. He is passionate about global revival and has worked to present a biblical strategy of saturation communities through micro-church planting.

Dr. Randy Clark, D. Min.
Overseer of the Apostolic Network of Global Awakening, founder of Global Awakening.

We have been aggressive pursuers of relationships for as long as we can remember. We think that deep inside each one of us, God has embedded a drive to know and be known, to love and be loved, to connect and be connected. The most wondrous expressions of the image of God the Father come out of human inter-personal relationships. The most glaring failures and flaws of the human heart also show up most poignantly as we struggle to connect, belong, love, and live with one another. Tim Johns has drilled down into the ever-living hallways of interpersonal relationships and has discovered some forgotten rooms and pathways that help us live together in harmony, unity, healing, peace and life as they relate to our lives in the Brotherhood of Believers, and our functioning as ambassadors in the Kingdom of God. Unity is perhaps the number one recurring theme in the Bible and is the focus of the prayer that the Lord Jesus prayed for all of us to be one as He and the Father are one. The focus of "Micro-Church Families on Mission" is empowerment to enable us to live together, work together, and thrive together, thus being the living answers to Jesus' prayer!

Britt & Audrey Hancock
Founders & Directors of Mountain Gateway, Author of "Apprehended"

Shortly after His resurrection, Jesus left his followers with a final commandment: "go and make disciples of all nations…surely I am with you always." As believers, we have inherited both this empowering commission and the promise of His abiding presence. But the need to carry out this mandate can be overwhelming. In this training manual, *Micro-Church Families on Mission*, Dr. Johns has compiled numerous resources with practical tools to help us fulfill this extremely important assignment. This manual is filled with biblical insights, firsthand experience, and pragmatic advice to help us in building sustainable communities of believers who are empowered to impact culture for God's kingdom.

Bill Johnson
Bethel Church, Redding, CA
Author of *God is Good* and *Hosting the Presence*

Micro-Church Families on Mission is a training manual that assists others in developing an effective model for evangelism and in producing effective, life-giving disciples. Jesus called all of us to be life-giving and produce "fruit that remains." I had the opportunity to visit Dr. Timothy John's ministry and see first-hand the fruit this model and type of training produces in leaders of varying ages.

Dr. Tom Jones
Executive Director, overseer of the Global Awakening Apostolic Network (ANGA), and an international speaker.

Captured by the "heart and mind of Christ...possessed by the passion of Christ...and reaching forward with a passion for Christ" describes Dr. Tim Johns. I have sensed a link in The Spirit with him for several years and he consistently radiates a deep and abiding commitment to Jesus Christ! He is a true follower and disciple of Christ. *Micro-Church Families on Mission* Is a fruit of a life and labor of love for Christ and for people! This Manual is a Biblically based, academically sound, and extremely practical blueprint of a new wineskin that is destined to change the landscape of doing church!

Years of perseverance, patience, practice, and love have been condensed into a resource that can show you the way forward.

Christ likeness...oneness with Christ is the very heartbeat and the center piece of all that you will read. We all know that this is the goal, but sometimes it is elusive at best. Dr. Tim Johns is one of the most relational people that I know.

He found that in Jesus life! He experienced that with Jesus! He passionately desires to see this worked out in the lives of people in the nations of the earth! We all know that doctrine, teaching, organizations, and meetings do not accomplish what Jesus did with His disciples and apostles. Jesus accomplished it by being with His followers. They did life/ministry together!

We know that Jesus passionately wants it with us and through us! Dr. Tim Johns breaks this down step by step and makes it doable for all of us! Read it...do it...and reach the nations with real Christ-like disciples!

Dr. Sam Matthews, D. Min
Senior Pastor, Family of Faith Church, Shawnee, Ok
President, Family of Faith Christian University
Apostolic Company Leader, International Christian Leadership Connections (ICLC)

Micro-Church Families on Mission covers the waterfront for establishing "Christ Bodies." Most significant is the way Dr. Tim Johns includes chapters by contemporaries in sister organizations to fill in gaps in the manual. Why? He sees the Rock Tribe movement not as a castle being built within the Kingdom, but focused on building the Kingdom itself. He clearly endorses what most movements have missed: leadership vested in the fivefold Gifts of Christ for His Body, as expressed in Ephesians. The Rock Tribe points to what the Last Days body of Christ will be like.

Dr. Ralph Neighbour
Founder of Touch Ministries, Author of many books like "Where Do We Go From Here?"

Dr. Timothy Johns is a dear friend with a huge heart for God and people. He has a unique blend of a devoted heart, a brilliant mind, a winsome way and a naturally supernatural lifestyle all wrapped up in the deep joy of Jesus Christ. His infectious joy always stirs our hearts whenever we get the chance to be with him and the affectionate and vibrant communities of faith that he has pioneered. Tim, and his amazing wife, Janet, are dedicated and resilient practitioners of what they profess. This manual is laced with God's wisdom and practical applications of the Good News that can inspire and inform lasting transformation into the image of Jesus in personal lives and whole communities of Christ-followers. It has been shaped and reshaped by private prayer, long hours of study, careful meditation, trials and errors and especially by engaging in authentic ministry on the front lines of human need within broken neighborhoods. Thank you Papa Tim for who you are and your faithful worship and service for the honor of our beautiful Savior and King and on behalf of His Body that is in need of another global reformation!

Michael & Terri Sullivant
Senior Pastors of New Hope Community Church
Michael authored "The Romance of Romans", "Prophetic Etiquette", "Thy Kingdom Come"
Terri authored "The Divine Invitation: Entering The Dance of Becoming Fully Alive"

Anyone who knows Timothy Johns, realizes that he is a man committed to the task of world evangelism. This work is not only a balanced and thorough approach to that task but a carefully thought-out plan for the stages of telling the world of Christ, leading people to Christ and training them for Christ. He agrees that evangelism is more than changing a person's destination from hell to heaven and presents the whole picture of a total takeover of a person's life with the purpose of forming a Christ-indwelt display of heaven on earth. The timing of this work is doubtlessly the result of an all-knowing God and a fully committed instrument co-laboring to form a helpful guide for the greatest harvest of souls and bringing them into Christlikeness history has ever seen.

Jack Taylor, President
DIMENSIONS MINSTRIES
Melbourne, Florida

Tim is a true spiritual father – a man of deep passion for God and self-giving love for His people. A father's heart knows both joy and anguish. From a lifetime of serving in the beauty and the pain that is the Bride of Christ, Tim now gives us a wonderful manual for church life that is both big picture and visionary, and detailed and tactical. Filled with deep insight and practical tools, this is a must read for all those on the journey towards the corporate fullness of God, the mature image of Jesus in His people.

Dr. Malcolm Webber, Ph.D.
Founder and Executive Director
LeaderSource SGA

I have known Tim Johns since he was a bright young student at Fuller Seminary. Being personable, fun and athletic, he attracted young people to Jesus Christ. He found a true teammate in his wife Janet and they began to build a model Christian family. He was a dynamic denominational pastor, but his creativity and inspiration was too much for their system. By the power and wisdom of the Holy Spirit he rediscovered the secrets of building the family of God and proved them in a rundown old city neighborhood. Tim is an exciting communicator, has a transformative message, is a master at building the body of Christ and has a vision that motivates and enables us to be all we can be for the glory of God.

Rev. Bob Whitaker

Change into the character of Christ is much talked about and seldom seen. Dr. Timothy Johns has combined the two elements needed for sustainable transformation – the active presence of God and communities of loving attachment. It is one thing to have both ingredients needed by change agents who want to impact the world and another thing to combine these elements wisely. Dr. Johns provides a framework that is rich in Biblical models and personal experience for leading the people of God.

Dr. E. James & Kitty Wilder

Founders of The Life Model. Jim has authored books like "Living From the Heart Jesus Gave You", "Joy Starts Here", "Rare Leadership", "Joyful Journey".

MICRO-CHURCH FAMILIES ON MISSION

A TRAINING MANUAL

How to start small spiritual families that love God, one another, and their neighbors.

By Dr. Timothy Johns

Micro-Church Families on Mission

A Training Manual

How to start small spiritual families that love God, one another, and their neighbors.

Published by Jesus Tribes Publishing
PO Box 472
Fort Collins, CO 80522

To order additional copies please contact us at:

www.JesusTribes.com
1st printing July 2017

2nd printing, August 2017

3rd printing – January 2018

TABLE OF CONTENTS

ACKNOWLEDGEMENTS

This "training manual" represents a lifetime of learning. But one cannot learn and grow into Christ's likeness apart from unconditional love in relationships. Therefore, I want to thank the person who has been the most loving, merciful, and supportive person in my life – my wife Janet. We describe her as the ultimate "golden retriever," loyal and consistently helpful to the highest degree. She married a pioneer and entrepreneur, which comes with a difficult "suffering package."

Big vision calls for many challenging learning curves, trial and error, recovery, and resilience. Who Father designed me to be, and what He has asked me to do as a change agent has required Janet to come out of her comfort zone time and time again. Because of her strong sense of oneness with me, she has felt every painful sting that has come from negative, judgmental, and critical people, along with the disappointing setbacks that come from starting churches and businesses. Yet she has never quit, never gotten bitter, and has stayed by my side for over 42 years of marriage. This capacity to keep going is directly related to her love for God, and a very healthy fear of the Lord. Janet, you are my hero and I love you beyond words.

I also want to thank all of the precious family members in the Rock Tribe over the years who have come into unity with God's Kingdom core values, vision, culture, and strategies. You, too, have paid a high price to go on this incredible and challenging journey into authentic Biblical Christianity. We have had no road map, no training manual, for how to become an "apostolic tribe" which develops into a catalyst for revival, the restoration and reformation of the Church, and the transformation of society. But you keep moving forward, keep growing in your faith, and are now realizing real eternal fruit in the kingdom. There is something very special about "early adopters" of a God-breathed vision. They have to see and believe that something is really from God, even when there is no evidence in the natural realm. I am constantly amazed at how willing you are to keep learning, growing, and following Christ. I am grateful beyond measure to all of you.

Finally, I would like to thank Sue Reding for her tremendous partnership and support in publishing this Micro-Church Training Manual. Sue is my administrative assistant, but so much more – a sister in Christ, spiritual daughter, and friend. She helps lead our personal prayer shield. Sue is also a Micro-Church Leader, who is constantly assimilating the skills necessary to help others grow as disciples of Christ. Thank you, Sue, for being a radical lover and follower of Jesus. Your faithful partnership has helped us come closer to actualizing Christ's Kingdom vision.

Micro-Church Families on Mission

INTRODUCTION

I came to Christ in 1971 at the height of the Jesus Movement. Young people by the millions encountered Jesus, became His disciples, and never looked back. Jesus and the Bible were central to this explosive move of God. Instinctively we found ourselves gathering in small informal groups for prayer, Bible study, discussion, and personal ministry. It was these small groups of friends that helped keep the fire of God's love burning in our hearts.

Today there is another, even bigger, Jesus Movement breaking out around the world. God is pouring out His Holy Spirit on unreached people groups, on university campuses, in the marketplace, and in some of the most unlikely and difficult places of the earth. Life-on-life small groups of bonded friends will be the key to reaching the lost, healing them from life's trauma, and transforming them into Christ's likeness.

I believe that God is changing the understanding and expression of Christianity in this generation. One way He is doing this is by recovering the Biblical paradigm of heart-connected relationships in family. We cannot become like Christ in isolation or just in meetings or programs. We need loving relationships to heal and mature. As Graham Cooke stated, "It is God Himself who changes our sin nature, but it is our spiritual family that helps eradicate our sin habits."

We were made in God's image. Therefore, our primary reason for existence is relational love. Every person was designed by God to be loved and to love, to be known and to know, to be heard and to hear, to belong and to help others belong, to grow and help others grow, to be served and to serve. The best setting for this to happen is natural and/or spiritual family. The Church must rediscover that it can only advance God's kingdom if it becomes a true spiritual family of love. God only builds His kingdom according to the pattern of the Trinity which is Family: Father, Son, Holy Spirit. The Church has tried many institutional and programmatic methods to make disciples, but where is the fruit? How much are people really getting healed and transformed into Christ's image? Programs don't love and mature people. Only people love and disciple people. Therefore, I am not proposing another programmatic strategy. I am contending for a lifestyle of love in the kingdom of God. We are simply trying to learn how we can enjoy four directions of love: 1.) receiving the love God pours out upon every person, 2.) reciprocating God's love back to Him, 3.) exchanging God's love in a bonded family, 4.) sharing and demonstrating God's love with our neighbors. Relational love in family can be messy and painful. Therefore, relationships will only work if we deny ourselves, pick up our crosses, and follow Jesus.

One of the most underdeveloped and overlooked factors in creating a healthy bonded family is cultivating the relational skills necessary to facilitate love. Therefore, I devote a chapter to introducing The Life Model, which I believe is the best relational training available today. I am indebted to my friend, Dr. Jim Wilder, a neuro-theologian who is the primary innovator of breakthrough technology aimed at maturing relational brain skills.

The Holy Spirit is extending an invitation to the Church to enter into the fullness of all the promises of God in the Bible. There is an unlimited supply of grace to become the authentic Body of Christ described in the New Testament. We really can do God's will, God's way, by God's Spirit, for God's glory. Christ and the kingdom are on earth and they are ever advancing. We can maintain the status quo, or we can enter into everything Christ purchased with His blood. Let's become catalysts for revival, restoration, and transformation!

I believe we are at the beginning of a second great reformation of the Church. The key to advancing this move of God's Spirit, this next Jesus Movement, is to merge three kingdom realities: 1. Christ Himself – His Immanuel Presence inside fiery hearts of love. (**Revival**) 2. Christ's Body organically connected heart-to-heart through covenant love. (**Restoration** of the church into family) 3. Christ's Kingdom advancing in every area of life (comprehensive **Transformation** of cities and nations).

This next Jesus Movement, this second reformation, must have both the "Wine" of the Spirit and the right "Wineskin." Jesus Tribes made up of small spiritual families on mission is that "Wineskin". Father wants to gather His sons and daughters into bonded love relationships, connected in mind, heart, and life as an extended family to help each other become more like Christ. As Christ's literal body, we can then advance Christ's kingdom. This *Micro-Church Family on Mission* training manual is a tool to help you make disciples of Christ in the context of Christ's family and then advance Christ's Kingdom on earth.

There are seven relational settings in the spiritual family that are essential for personal growth into Christ's likeness and for advancing Christ's Kingdom.

1. Relationship with God our Father through Christ by the Holy Spirit.

2. DNA groups (a gender specific group of 2 or 3) designed for Discipleship, Nurture, Apostolic Mission.

3. Micro-Church (small Missional Kingdom Family).

4. Local congregation led by Biblical elders.

5. Families-of-churches led by APEST teams (Jesus Tribes).

6. Interconnected Jesus Tribes (Tribes Middle T).

7. The whole Body of Christ – Father's Tribe Big T.

This training manual focuses largely on how to make disciples in 2's and 3's (DNA Groups) and in Micro-Church Family-Platoons (5-15). However, it is critical that these two relational and missional settings are integrated into local church families that are a part of a larger family-of-churches (Jesus Tribe). Every living thing will only thrive if it is integrally connected to something greater than itself. Stand alone, isolated small groups or independent local churches are not God's highest way of building His kingdom. God is a Father, Son, and Spirit, a Family of Three, yet One. God must build His kingdom according to who He is - a Family. God is relational and He created us for relationships with Himself and His larger family. Love is why we exist! Receiving and giving love brings God glory, our highest core value.

The word "Tribe" is used because it is the best word we could find in the Bible that describes extended trans-local families-of-church families that are also spiritual armies on mission. An example of a trans-local international family-of-churches, which also acted like a spiritual army, can be seen in the book of Acts and the epistles written by the apostle Paul. Paul led an APEST (Apostles, Prophets, Evangelists, Shepherds, Teachers) leadership team made up of people such as Barnabas, Timothy, Titus, Silas, Aquila, Priscilla, Simeon, Lucius, Manaen, Phoebe, Andronicus, Junias, Sosthenes, Tychicus, and Epaphroditus. This APEST leadership team planted inter-connected churches in many cities and regions (Corinth, Rome, Ephesus, Philippi, Colossae, Thessalonica, and the Galatian region). They also provided on-going governmental oversight, correction, training, and support for those local churches, in partnership with the local elders. Finances and human resources were exchanged between this family-of-churches (Jesus Tribe), so that they could mutually build up one another in the Lord and reach a lost and dying world. Family language is laced throughout Paul's letters. He referred to himself as a "father" and to his partners as "sons".

The Church is to be a family that helps each believer to discover their new identity as a son/daughter of God, be saturated in the unconditional love of God, and fulfill their calling and destiny. At the same time, the Church is to corporately function as a spiritual army that equips people to advance Christ's Kingdom in neighborhoods, cities, and nations. A Micro-Church is not just a small spiritual family; it is also a small "platoon" that mobilizes effective mission.

One of my biggest passions is to encourage leaders to become change agents who will have the courage to upgrade the culture, paradigm and practices of the businesses and/or churches they lead. Imagine creating an atmosphere and strategy that helps people discover their true identities, enables love and belonging, provides healing and growth, and creates a kingdom model of business and church that empowers every person to have meaningful impact. Think of the incredible possibilities if we would shift local churches into "apostolic equipping centers" that train and send fiery people into neighborhoods, cities, and nations to spread the gospel and advance the kingdom. We need thousands of "Antioch-type Equipping and Sending Centers" around the world that make disciples and leaders who move in the presence and power of Christ. (Acts 13:1, 14:26-27) This apostolic strategy must include small spiritual family-platoons, Micro-Churches on mission. Small Micro-Church Families (Missional Kingdom Families) were modeled by Jesus with His twelve disciples, and carried on in house-to-house gatherings. Micro-Churches are Biblical and they work if they have the benefit of good leadership and strategic prayer.

I pray that this "Micro-Church Family on Mission" training manual serves as an effective tool to make disciples of Christ, and to mobilize God's people for effective gospel mission.

In Christ and for the advancing of Christ's Kingdom,

Dr. Timothy Johns

LET'S BUILD WISELY: THE ESSENTIALS FOR HEALTHY MICRO-CHURCHES

The apostle Paul referred to himself as a "wise master builder". 1 Corinthians 3:10 He wasn't bragging, just being truthful. It is quite possible to know if you are a good builder or not. Apostle Paul had acquired insights from God about how to start interconnected church families – most of which were micro-churches. We, too, can become wise master builders. Better to build according to the specifications of heaven than to build poorly. We want to do what it takes to produce fruit that remains, and keeps on reproducing into eternity. John 15:16

Let us understand all the essentials necessary to build obedience-based, disciple-making movements, utilizing healthy DNA Groups and interconnected Micro-Churches. Every component mentioned in this training manual is essential for starting and multiplying life-giving small spiritual families. In order to build a real micro-church, then all of the ingredients need to be added. Many small groups get started but then lose momentum, lack effectiveness, or fail altogether because an essential component is left out. If it is in this training manual, then it is very important. We are going after full-service micro-church families that make real disciples of Christ and reach the lost.

Our end goal determines how we build. God makes it quite clear what He desires. He wants new creation sons and daughters to be transformed into Christ's likeness, connected in loving family, and empowered to advance Christ's kingdom on earth. God is "bringing many sons to glory". Hebrews 2:10. That level of purpose requires high quality relational discipleship in the context of small spiritual families. A casual fellowship group alone will not achieve this. Single emphasis small groups have their place, but they are not what we are learning to build in this training manual. There are small groups devoted to just Bible study, or just prayer, or just a mission, fellowship, or a simple recovery group. While they are helpful, they are also limited. A full-service Micro-Church Family integrates all of those elements and more. We are learning to build small reproducing spiritual families that make disciples, heal the broken hearted, and reach the lost.

Building according to God's standards will bring great results. Building poorly, taking short cuts, will produce bad fruit. People can get hurt if leaders are not competent. However, do not shrink back from going through the difficult learning curve necessary to be a "wise master builder". There is a great need for loving spiritual parents, and healthy leaders. You can do this by God's grace. All things are possible to those that believe. Mark 9:23

The Essentials for Building Healthy Micro-Church Families

Making disciples and building spiritual families is all about forming high quality relationships. Creating love bonds in a small group requires relational skills only learned in the setting of healthy relationships. We can learn relational concepts in a training manual. However, the way we really apply the principles of love is through relational mentoring and practice. The ideal is to have relational coaching, experiential learning, with written out biblical principles. Ideally, the best use of this training manual is as a supplemental resource, a reference guide, as you seek to create small micro-churches with DNA Groups. This training manual plus relational coaching is the ideal combination for learning how to raise up Micro-Church Families on mission.

I am going to lay out the key ingredients necessary to be a wise builder of both DNA Groups and Micro-Church families. Every point I make has more expanded explanations in the training manual. Think of this as an introductory overview. Or you can see these points as a flight check list. When pilots are ready to fly an airplane, they go through a detailed protocol to insure the takeoff goes smoothly.

Wise master builders....

1. Pray without ceasing. 1 Thessalonians 5:17. Every step forward in the kingdom requires the supernatural grace of God. Romans 5:17. We access that grace by faith through intercession. There are many things only God can do, but there are also many responsibilities humanity has been assigned. When God said, "Let them rule" He desired our full cooperation. Genesis 1:26 Without God we cannot, without our prayers God will not. Advancing the kingdom of God involves immense spiritual warfare. Praise, worship, and prayer (with frequent fasting) is essential for winning this cosmic spiritual battle. The only way to realize victory is fervent unified believing prayer.

2. Always start by focusing on beliefs, worldview, and core values. In the kingdom, we build from the inside out. This means that we must first aim at the inner motivations of the heart and upgrade people's belief systems. Renewing the mind, transforming the heart will cause lifestyles to change. People must understand the "Big Why", so that the strategies make sense. One of the worst mistakes leaders make is to start by introducing strategies, programs, and methods. Your followers must know, understand, and believe the larger narrative. What is the big God story and how do we fit into that story? Be a values-driven leader. This is how Jesus and the apostle Paul initiated their ministries. The Sermon on the Mount is an example of how Jesus leads with kingdom values as his foundation. Change starts internally with a shift in beliefs and values. Start from the macro story and move to the micro. The big will define and contextualize the little.

3. Learn and practice how real transformation takes place. Here is the formula for the traditional Western approach to discipleship: True Information + Right Choices + Plus Commitment = Transformation. While this may appear like the right strategy for change, it isn't effective for changing the inner-heart motives. Nor does it follow the Biblical strategy. God's way of changing people goes like this: New Identity as a Child of God + Belonging to a Bonded Loving Family + The Power of the Indwelling Christ and the Holy Spirit = Transformation. To build a healthy small spiritual family, make sure every person has received the revelation of their new identity as sons/daughters of Father. Romans 8:16 Learn how to recognize orphaned behavior and how to bring healing to areas that are still wounded. Cultivate bonded relationships of trust and love. The building of bonded family relationships must involve mature believers and relational brain skills that develop in the right front side of the brain. Bonded love relationships are not formed by simply agreeing with right information or doctrine. The classic strategies for building small groups have emphasized information over intimate personal encounters with God and

others. Please become a wise master builder in the areas of emotional and relational intelligence. Most real transformation occurs as a result of death to the false self. Be prepared to support people going through the painful dynamics involved with changing.

4. As one who is taking responsibility for the lives of others, make sure you have a substantial level of emotional, relational, and spiritual health. There are necessary levels of relational, spiritual, and emotional maturity to be an effective leader of a small spiritual family. Do what it takes to be prepared. Become competent, mature, and healthy.

5. Get submitted and relationally connected to a larger family-of-churches. It is dangerous to accept responsibility for the lives of others without the benefit of all five ministry gifts helping you to succeed: apostles, prophets, evangelists, shepherds, teachers. Be a part of a legitimate New Testament church that is governed by a plurality of elders. Satan has been effectively dividing relationships since humanity was created. Therefore, do not go into battle without the support of a larger trans-local church family who will fight with you and for you. It is presumptuous to attempt this level of relational discipleship without a "Jesus Tribe" – an international family of churches. There is safety in numbers and being accountable to others. God gives grace to the humble. James 4:6, 1 Peter 5:5-6

6. Pray for committed partners who will build with you on the foundations of Christ and the kingdom. Create strong bonds of love and trust with them. Jesus sent out the disciples by two's for a reason. Find at least one other person who loves you, feels a calling to this vision and these values, culture and strategies. You need a battle buddy.

7. Stay relational. Making disciples of Christ in small families does not occur simply by teaching information. It happens when we bond relationally with one another at a deep heart level. The current model for church life tries to unify people around Bible knowledge, doctrine, church government, and ministry programs. None of these are bad, just inadequate for the kind of love and intentional discipleship described in the Bible. We are to "love each other deeply from the heart." 1 Peter 4:8. We are to "maintain the unity of the Spirit and the bond of peace". Ephesians 4:3

8. Understand how the brain was hardwired by God for relational bonding and love. God created our physiology to enable us to fulfill our reasons for existence. The King and the kingdom are all encompassing. Everything matters in the kingdom, and all parts of our body, souls, and spirits need to be well stewarded. This challenges us to be holistic in our approach to life, including both hemispheres of our brain. The cultural church appeals largely to the left side of the brain, which is designed to organize thoughts into logical patterns. This is why we have put such a great deal of emphasis on Bible Colleges and Seminaries that exchange information in classrooms. The graduates then become instructor-pastors whose primary job description is to teach information to the left side of the brain. Again, teaching truth is a good thing, but our mandate is to love. It is the right frontal cortex of the brain that is designed to connect relationally, to love God and

people, to dream and imagine. The right side of the brain has relational circuits that can be switched on, allowing us to connect relationally with God and others. The right front of the brain is a faster processor and gathers information through impartation, revelation, and relational encounters. It is the right front side of our brain that was designed by God to be our leader. The left side was created to be the manager. The left side of the brain is to serve the right side of the brain in the same way truth exists for love. Loving God, each other, and our neighbors is the Great Commandment. Truth tells us how to love. Truth is the means to the end of love. The forming of healthy spiritual families will only be done if the leaders learn how to lead from the right side of their brains and live from their hearts. The Apostle Paul was so relationally intelligent that he was able to discern if his family members had opened and connected their hearts to his. 2 Corinthians 6:11- 12 He could detect if the affection of Christ Jesus was being exchanged through connected hearts or not. Therefore, it is essential that those starting and leading small spiritual families have matured in relational skills. Getting people into close proximity to one another can be like heaven on earth or it can be a disaster. It will be the maturity and relational skills of the leaders, who then model relational love skills to the family, that will determine the quality of the micro-church.

9. Develop the culture of the kingdom, which are all the fruit of the Holy Spirit. Galatians 5:22-23 Culture is an atmosphere or weather pattern. Plants grow best when they are in the perfect environment, as in a green house. People also grow best when they are surrounded by an atmosphere of love, affection, joy, and grace. If there is an atmosphere of negativity, criticism, legalism, performance orientation, then the members of the family will not be safe.

10. Encourage transparency. We call this "fellowshipping in the light". 1 John 1 Transparency is the freedom to share our inner conversations with other members of the family. Healing and growth occur when we live in the light. Transparency will only occur if a clear understanding and application of the gospel of grace is in operation.

11. Emphasize the lordship of Christ - His kingly ownership and rule over all creation. Develop an obedience-based discipleship culture. Encourage people to so love and trust Jesus Christ that they become passionate about obeying him in every area of life. The Micro-Church needs to be a Missional Kingdom-advancing Family centered on the Person of Jesus Christ as King. We call this a "pray, hear, obey" lifestyle. Love for God, overflowing into obedience, will be the catalyst for an unstoppable kingdom revolution. I believe it is possible to inspire people to love Jesus so much that obedience becomes a delight. Let us go after happy holiness.

12. Make sure everyone is having a daily Face Time with God. Teach your spiritual family how to hear God's voice through the Word of God, the Spirit of God, and through the people of God. Coach them how to know God's voice, His will and ways, and inspire them to obey Him quickly, completely, and cheerfully. Emphasize interactive gratitude and journaling

as powerful tools to experience an Immanuel lifestyle. Practicing and experiencing God's presence all the time, everywhere, will be our Source of eternal life.

13. Clearly orient each person, and the entire spiritual family together, on a regular basis as to the values, vision, culture, and strategies of the micro-church. Communicate the expectations and commitments upfront, and review them often. People should know what they are being invited to be and do. Then, they should be given the freedom to respond without pressure.

14. Know and respect boundaries. There are five spheres of government in the kingdom: Personal, Marriage and Family, Church, Marketplace, Civil. Do not allow family members to illegally encroach upon or cross boundaries. This could result in manipulation and control which are not part of the kingdom of God. Freedom is necessary for true love. Therefore, avoid all attitudes or actions that put inappropriate pressure on others.

15. Every person has been wounded in this fallen world. People are broken and fragile. Therefore, learn how to heal the broken hearted. Become competent at inner-healing and deliverance. Luke 4:18 The practice of healing people from trauma, both omission and commission, needs to be woven into the lifestyle of the micro-church family.

16. Be gospel centered and grace oriented. Teach the group to view each person through the loving eyes of Father and the finished work of the cross. In other words, know each person by the Spirit and not the flesh. People will be tempted to give expression to their "old man", their "false self". Our response could keep them in prison or help them become their true self in Christ. The best way to help people grow is to consistently tell them who they really are as new creation sons or daughters of God. Create a culture of sharing the good news of God's grace to one another. The best strategy for removing something negative is to displace it with the good. Focus on the "new man" or "true self" in Christ. 2 Corinthians 5:16-17

17. Debrief, evaluate, and process how the DNA Group and Micro-Church is doing. Facilitating this time of reflection will produce tremendous learning and growth.

18. Make sure joy is a high value. Weave fun and celebration into micro-church life. The degree of our love and intimacy determines the level of our joy.

19. Leadership development is a high priority. Create many opportunities for others to grow in their calling, gifts, and talents. The key to multiplication is raising up leaders who raise up leaders.

20. Develop a "prayer, care, share" lifestyle in all family members. Identify those you are trying to reach with the gospel. Initiate ways to get into their worlds to build a bonded friendship. Cultivate gospel fluency and gospel mission as a way of life.

JESUS CHRIST AND THE SUPERNATURAL POWER OF THE GOSPEL

For in Him all things were created: things in heaven and on earth, visible and invisible, whether thrones or powers or rulers or authorities; all things have been created through Him and for Him. Colossians 1:16

For I am not ashamed of the gospel, because it is the power of God that brings salvation to everyone who believes: first to the Jew, then to the Gentile. Romans 1:16

To them God has chosen to make known among the Gentiles the glorious riches of this mystery, which is Christ in you, the hope of glory. Colossians 1:17

But seek first His kingdom and His righteousness, and all these things will be given to you as well. Matthew 6:33

I have been crucified with Christ and I no longer live, but Christ lives in me. The life I now live in the body, I live by faith in the Son of God, who loved me and gave himself for me. Galatians 2:20

What are the key ingredients to successfully starting and multiplying small spiritual families on mission? The answer, "Build on the centrality and supremacy of Jesus Christ and His kingdom." Jesus Christ is King. He is worthy of our love and obedience. Our goal is to help people know Jesus Christ as Lord, so that we can teach them to obey Him from hearts overflowing with love. We want to cultivate a pray, hear, obey lifestyle among all believers in response to the Lordship of Christ. That is the kingdom revolution we are after. The key is drawing life from the indwelling Christ, who is our all-powerful King.

The secret to the Christian life is Christ Himself. Contend for each member of the family to love Jesus with all their hearts. Build the family around Christ and His presence. Cultivate a "pray, hear, obey" and a "prayer, care, share" lifestyle that advances Christ's Kingdom everywhere, all the time. Obedience-based discipleship will unleash the expansion of Christ's kingdom on earth.

Life in the Kingdom of God is 100% naturally supernatural. We are animated by Jesus Christ, who is a "life-giving Spirit". 1 Corinthians 15:45 "For in Him we live and move and have our being." Acts 17:28 The Christian life is allowing Christ to live His life in and through us. Connecting with one another mind-to-mind, heart-to-heart, life-to-life can only happen if Jesus Christ is at the center of our relationships. Acts 4:32-35

Another key to success is for each person to clearly understand and apply the pure gospel of grace. Acts 20:24 It is the undiluted, unmixed gospel of grace that is the reason we are made right with God through Jesus Christ. It is also the ongoing grace of God that is the enabling power of God to become like Christ and advance His kingdom.

How we understand and apply the gospel will determine how we relate to people. The gospel enables us to see people "by the Spirit" through the lens of the finished work on the cross. 2 Corinthians 5:16 "For it is by grace you have been saved, through faith – and this not from yourselves, it is the gift of God – not by works, so that no one can boast." Ephesians 2:8-9

The safest and most loving place on earth is a healthy spiritual family. What makes that family healthy will be determined by how much each member understands and applies the pure gospel of grace. If we see each other through Father's eyes, through the person of Jesus and His finished work on the cross, then we will be the "skin of heaven" – the incarnation of Christ -- to each other. We will love people the way Christ loves them. We will view and treat people the way Christ does because Christ is loving others through us.

On the other hand, there is no more dangerous place on earth than a group of people who say they are gathering around Jesus Christ but who live under the law and use it as a justification for judgment, criticism, condemnation, offense, performance orientation, and ultimately destruction and relational division. Serious emotional, mental, and relational damage has been done by some members of the body of Christ because they have vacillated between old covenant religion and new covenant gospel.

It is the pure gospel of grace, proclaimed and demonstrated by the family of God that helps each person to walk in their gospel identity as "sons/daughters" of God. Romans 8. It is a gospel-centered family that continues to reinforce the gospel every day by imparting the affection and joy of Christ Jesus through one another. It is a gospel-centered, "good news" spiritual family, that enables each child of God to receive inner-healing from life's traumas. It is gospel-applying families that enable each child of God to mature into the likeness of Christ. Romans 8:29

Loving Jesus Christ, living as a unified family as Christ's body, and reclaiming Christ's Kingdom on earth are the reasons for our very existence. All of this flows from Jesus Christ, who is the embodiment of Grace. John 1:14

NOTES:

GOD'S BIG FAMILY STORY

In the beginning, God was and always has been a Family: Father, Son, Holy Spirit. Therefore, He created the human family to bear His Trinitarian image. Family is God's model for relationship. We have physical families and spiritual families. For their own glory, God the Father, God the Son, and God the Holy Spirit created, and then redeemed through Christ, a covenantal spiritual family. This family is made up of "new creation" sons and daughters to advance God's Kingdom on earth. God said, "Let them rule". Genesis 1:26 In other words, He builds His kingdom through sons and daughters.

God self-disclosed as a family of three, yet one. Therefore, He builds His kingdom relationally in and through family.

The core values and purpose of the Trinity are the glory of God, centrality and supremacy of Christ, covenant and kingdom, Father and family, and the Great Commission to disciple the nations.

All reality and truth flows from the Trinity. Therefore, as sons and daughters, we get to enjoy these same heart motives and live in Father's epic story, His primary vision and purpose.

Everything, all reality, starts and flows from the Trinity: Father, Son, Holy Spirit – three persons, yet one God. As Family, God self-discloses with family language. Relationships are key. You cannot have Father without Son, or Son without Father. We, along with God, are defined by our relationships – never in isolation. Thus, relational separation is the very definition of sin.

GOSPEL POWER IN FAMILY

God builds His Kingdom according to who He is – Father, Son, Holy Spirit, i.e. Family. The Gospel starts with the Trinity, comes from the Trinity, and is for the Trinity. Roman 11:36. The gospel is adoption into a spiritual family. The content of this amazing reality must be contained in the context of family.

It takes a family to share and demonstrate the gospel because the gospel is the story about adoption into a family.

Total congruence means that the medium is the message as much as the message is the message. You cannot have the message without the medium (context) for that message. Wine and wineskin are inseparable. Because the gospel is a good news story about adoption into family, it takes a family to fully communicate and reveal the gospel.

The gospel is the good news of a Father and Son who created an extended family, lost that family due to sin, bought back that family through the sacrificial death of the Son, adopted sons back into that family through blood, restored the family back to its original mandate to glorify God and advance His Kingdom. We must understand the epic gospel story in the exact terminology and intent of the Father & Son & Spirit or we will reduce its power.

The true and full gospel story has total power of restoration if it is:
- Told accurately, because words have power to create reality. Religion redefines words and their meanings.
- Understood clearly, totally, and comprehensively.
- Believed totally both in the mind and from the heart. True faith accesses and activates the power of the gospel.
- Loved passionately. The gospel is a Triune Person, a people, a purpose. It's not just information that we can agree with or not. It is a Person that we both love and trust or don't.
- Lived. It should be applied every minute of every hour of every day in every situation in all parts of life. The gospel is holistic and comprehensive.

What is our why, our purpose, our mandate?

Image Bearers. We reflect the glory of another – God Himself. We are not God but we are physical manifestations of a spiritual being. We cannot bear the image of a Triune God while isolated and independent.

Intimacy. We were to live in unbroken communion with God in the Garden, and in total intimacy with each other, just like the Trinity.

Impact. We were given dominion over the entire earth. We are called to be fruitful, multiply, steward, and oversee the Kingdom of God on earth in every area of life.

Remember, everything is spiritual. The physical and the spiritual world are deeply intertwined. Everything about the physical is to reveal something about its source from the spiritual.

The natural world reveals, glorifies, and extends the spiritual.

Spiritual family (Universal Church) reveals the Trinity

Natural family (marriage between husband and wife) reveals Christ and the Church

Covenantal relationships are:
- Deeply unified, loving, and demonstrate communion through Christ and the Cross = "that they may be one"
- Designed to bring glory to God
- The greatest means of advancing Christ's Kingdom
- The most difficult thing to achieve on earth
- The most offensive to our flesh
- Opposed by Satan

FAMILY BUILT ON THE ROCK

Throughout Scripture, God teaches us about who He is and who we are through the symbol of a rock, or stone. We are all invited to build our lives upon the Rock – Jesus Christ. The Rock speaks of our identity in God/Christ, who is our source of life and our foundation. The Bible illustrates the need for individuals to be in proper relationship with one another by calling us "living stones". ROCK also speaks of our purpose, which is the **R**eclaiming **o**f **C**hrist's **K**ingdom.

It is a name for God in the Old Testament. Genesis 49:24; Deuteronomy 32:4; Psalm 19:14, 92:15

It is a name for Jesus Christ in the New Testament. Christ is our foundation and source of life. He is The Rock from which Living Water, which represents the Holy Spirit, is released. Exodus 17:6; 1 Corinthians 10:4

We are "living stones" placed together to build a living temple in which God dwells. 1 Peter 2:5

Peter, a representative man, was also a "rock," a foundational person, upon which the church was built. Matthew 16:18

It is an acronym for our purpose, which is the **R**eclaiming **o**f **C**hrist's **K**ingdom. Matthew 6:33

We are called to build our lives upon the "rock," that which is immovable and unshakeable. Matthew 7:24

God exhorts us to be careful how we build our lives and the lives of others. We can build wisely or poorly. 1 Corinthians 3:10-15. All building, including the laying of foundations, requires an architectural plan, a clear picture or vision of what is being built.

Our core values are the foundation of what we are building. They include:

> ➤ God's glory and supremacy spread throughout all the nations
> ➤ Christ –The King and the Kingdom of God
> ➤ God, the Father and the Natural and Spiritual Family
> ➤ The Great Commission – going into all the world and making disciples of Christ

FAMILY DESCRIBED AS TRIBES

Tribes are the family model seen in the Old Testament through the 12 tribes of Israel. In the New Testament, we see interconnected and interdependent churches led by the apostle Paul and apostolic team. Tribes are started and led by apostolic fathers with five-fold ministry leadership which serve as spiritual parents.

Jesus Tribes:
> ➤ Are trans local extended family-of-families
> ➤ Are designed by God to illustrate, inspire, and equip the whole Family of God (Church) for its purpose
> ➤ Give each "son" a Biblical context, through a spiritual family, to be and do their purpose on earth.
> ➤ Provide the practical day-to-day context to walk out the larger mandate given to the entire Church of Jesus Christ.

➢ Almost all references in the New Testament to spiritual fathering and sonship are used in the context of trans-local church-planting tribes.

THE VALUE OF VISION IN GOD'S FAMILY

Vision is a picture, a concept, or an idea of a future reality. Vision describes **what** we are doing while values describe **why** we are doing it. A vision statement is a form of mission statement by an individual or organization in which its intentions for the future are stated.

Vision is important because everything that exists starts with vision. Everything you see, touch, taste, and experience came from vision. Creation started with a vision. God envisioned creation and said, "Let us make..." and everything began.

Knowing and believing in the vision God has for our lives:

➢ Keeps us focused and on track. Without vision we drift and live without restraints.

➢ Inspires discipline and sacrifice.

➢ Motivates us to get into covenant relationships for the sake of building relationships with fellow believers who can help us to achieve our vision.

➢ Helps us determine how to live our lives, spend our money, steward our time, talents, and gifts.

➢ Results in eternal rewards when we keep faithfully working toward the vision/plan God has for our lives. Ephesians 6:7-8; Proverbs 29:18. Every invention, every manmade object originated with vision. Every company, school, institution, government, and organization started with vision. God-inspired imagination and creativity are the starting points for all the good that has ever been accomplished.

God has an overall vision and purpose for all that He creates. Knowing the big vision will help us understand the framework and context for all other vision. The big vision is the overarching reality that God is making happen. Every other vision must fit within and underneath God's vision.

Four General Stages of the overall story of God's unfolding vision:

1. Paradise (God's Kingdom) Created. The dominion mandate given to mankind to co-create with God utilizing His life (symbolized in the Tree of Life).

2. Paradise Lost. Due to deception, unbelief, and pride mankind disconnected from God by relying on the Tree of the Knowledge of Good and Evil.

3. Paradise Recovered and Expanding. Thy kingdom come on earth as it is in heaven. Matthew 6:10, 33. The establishment of the Jewish people. The incarnation, life, death, shed blood, crucifixion, resurrection, ascension, outpouring and empowering, and return of Christ are all unto the end of restoring God's original vision – His glory and kingdom on earth as it is in heaven. This involves "bringing all things under one head, Jesus Christ." Ephesians 1:11-12

4. Paradise Restored. Completed at Christ's second coming. See the book of Revelations.

The culmination of God's epic narrative will be the creation of a New Heaven and a New Earth. These two realms of reality will be mystically connected. Those in Christ will be given new bodies, exactly like the body Christ received at His resurrection. These new bodies will have the capacity to move seamlessly between the New Earth and the New Heaven.

Everything we become and everything we do has significance into eternity. When we are faithful stewards in little, we will be given exponentially much greater responsibilities in the age to come. Because we are in eternity now, everything we say and do matters. Each and every attitude, action, and relationship has significance. Reward and judgment are real. It would be a terrible tragedy to live in a lesser story, one that accentuates self-absorption and mere survival. We are called to be a part of an eternally significant story of the Kingdom of God on earth as it is in heaven. Revelation 21:1-8; Luke 19:11-27; 2 Corinthians 5:10. Please consider reading: "Surprised by Hope" by N. T. Wright

The **whole body of Christ** is commissioned to help achieve God's vision of establishing His kingdom and expanding His glory.

Each **spiritual family**, which is part of the whole family of God, has a specific vision from God which will help achieve the overall vision of bringing the Kingdom of God (restoring Paradise) to the earth.

Each **individual** also has a specific vision from God to help reach the vision given to their spiritual kingdom family. Every person was created for good works. Ephesians 2:10. Every personal vision must fit, support, and serve the bigger vision given to each spiritual family. Ephesians 4:16. All vision, however, involves other, it is always corporate. Anything that comes from God will always be too great for just one person to achieve.

Kingdom Vision Examples:
  ➢ Adam and Eve - Genesis 1:26-3:24
  ➢ Abraham - Genesis 12-15; Hebrews 6:13-15, 11:10
  ➢ Moses - Exodus 2-6
  ➢ David - I Samuel 16:1-13
  ➢ Jesus - Matthew 1:20-25
  ➢ Paul - Acts 9:1-19, 13:1-3, 26:1
  ➢ Saints of old had the vision of "another country/city" - Hebrews 11:13-16
  ➢ Timothy - Philippians 2:19-24
  ➢ All Disciples - Matthew 28:18-20

How does one get vision for their life?
  ➢ From the Word of God - Psalm 119; 2 Timothy 3:16
  ➢ From visions, dreams, and prophecy - Acts 2:17-21
  ➢ From intuition, connecting with your inner blueprint - Ephesians 2:10
  ➢ Seeing from the "eyes of your heart" - Ephesians 1:18-23
  ➢ Delighting yourself in the Lord and then His desires get downloaded into your heart becoming your desires - Psalm 37:4

- Passed down from natural and spiritual parents and grandparents - Colossians 1:12, 3:24; Deuteronomy 4:20; Proverbs 13:22
- Through others, especially prophetically and apostolically gifted leaders. Every spiritual family that is properly based in kingdom vision, values, strategy and leadership should have a clearly defined vision that has been confirmed prophetically, through other leaders, and proven fruit. - Acts 9, 11:27, 13:1-3; Ephesians 2:20
- Hinted at throughout one's childhood and young adulthood
- Circumstances
- Tangible results of one's life point to one's vision -- our fruit can be an indicator of our calling
- Feedback and affirmation of others
- In the context of fasting, prayer, praise and worship - Acts 13:1-3

And He made known to us the mystery of His will according to His good pleasure, which he purposed in Christ, to be put into effect when the times will have reached their fulfillment – to bring all things in heaven and on earth together under one head, even Christ. Ephesians 1:9-10

Our ultimate value is to bring God glory by bringing all things in heaven and on earth under Jesus Christ. Therefore, we want to be absolutely sure that our motives and methods are pleasing to God.

God is moving on the hearts of many followers of Christ, inspiring them to devote their lives to fight for the authentic kind of Christianity they read about in the Bible. They have heard a sound from heaven, and received a vision in their hearts for a kingdom reality that can be experienced on earth. Loving and ministering with people of like passion from around the world builds our faith and results in high-level kingdom impact.

We are called to gather around our love for the person of Jesus Christ. He is central and supreme. We also want to build Christ's Kingdom, not a man-made enterprise.

FATHER'S FAMILY & CHRIST'S KINGDOM: COVENANT RELATIONSHIPS & KINGDOM RESPONSIBILITIES

Jesus Christ started THE movement of all movements thousands of years ago. We might call it the "Kingdom of God on Earth" movement. As both God and man, He clearly announced His intentions to bring all things back under His kingly rule. He shed His blood. He died on the cross to pay the penalty for the sin of humanity. After His resurrection, He has been infiltrating the hearts of those who place their faith in Him, changing their very nature back to its original condition before Adam's fall.

He has been pouring out His Holy Spirit upon all "sons of God," giving them gifts, and empowering them to reclaim His Kingdom on earth in every area of life. He is the head of the church, and is preparing her to be His eternal bride. He is bringing all things under His government.

At the end of the age, we will experience a new heaven and a new earth. Our new bodies, like Christ's resurrected body, will have the capacity to interact with both realms of reality – the earth realm and the heavenly realm. God's family will rule and reign with Him into eternity. All sin, sickness, self-worship, and satanic influence will be destroyed. God's perfect Kingdom will be the only reality. Every created being will voluntarily do God's will, God's way, by God's Spirit for God's glory, and do so with the deepest gratitude and highest praise. 2 Timothy 2:12; Revelation 20:6, 21:1-5, 22:5.

God's Kingdom is an ever-expanding reality on earth. The Kingdom is here, but it is not yet. The manifestation of Christ and His Kingdom is increasing decade by decade and will come to a crescendo when heaven splits open, trumpets blast, and Christ returns on His white horse as Warrior-Judge King. Revelation 19:11.

What we do now, the degree of our love and faithful stewardship, will determine the level of reward and responsibilities we receive in the age to come. Luke 19:17-19; Ephesians 6:7-8. Therefore, it is essential that we understand exactly what God wants, how He is building His Kingdom, so that we can perfectly comply with His will and ways.

There are two central Biblical themes, two necessary realities, for experiencing the Kingdom of God on earth.

Covenant Relationships

The word "covenant" in the Bible is defined as "relational oneness." It is a loving, unified connection of mind and heart between God and us, and us and other people. When we are relationally one, God's life can be organically exchanged between connected hearts. We were made in God's image with a capacity for intimate relationships with God and each other. The Hebrew word for "covenant love" is "chesed" or "hesed". It can be translated as "sticky love", "bonded love", "mercy", "lovingkindness", "steadfast love", "compassion", and "goodness".

Kingdom Responsibilities

Kingdom means the dominion of the King. It is a combination of divine life flowing through divine order. Matthew 9:17   Life in the kingdom involves accepting responsibility for doing God's will, God's way, in every area of life. God delegates His authority to His people, so that they have the ability and power to carry out their responsibilities. We can see in the first few chapters of Genesis that humanity was made to fellowship with God and one another in the garden. That is all about relationship. They were also given the mandate to be fruitful and multiply, ruling, reigning, subduing and stewarding the earth (responsibility).

REVIVAL, RESTORATION/REFORMATION, TRANSFORMATION

Jesus Christ is strategically building and purifying His church in both categories: covenant relationships and kingdom responsibilities. In order to either correct a problem in the church or re-insert an important component that has been lost, Jesus often initiates a sub-movement. Sub-movements help to inject critical components of the Kingdom into the church, so that the church can more effectively advance THE Kingdom Movement on earth. A sub-movement is a powerful combination of specific Biblical truths, the Holy Spirit's endorsement, and an enthusiastic response from a large segment of the body of Christ. Sub-movements have leaders who champion the emphasis, but they are much larger than any one personality or group. Within the last few hundred years, the church has benefitted from some of the sub-movements listed below. Each sub-movement has so much truth to absorb, and so many new skills to learn, that it could take more than a life time just to gain competency in the kingdom emphasis brought through only one movement. Even whole denominations have been formed around the truths and practices brought through a sub-movement. Unfortunately, those who have embraced the elements of one sub-movement often diminish the importance of other sub-movements, or even oppose them altogether.

While sub-movements are highly important for the revitalization and reformation of the church, they are not the ultimate Person or Purpose. That would only be Christ, The King and His Kingdom. Sub-movements cannot fully answer the deepest heart cry of the people of God. Only God and God's Kingdom can do that. The people of God sense that there is much more to Jesus and His Kingdom Movement than they have experienced. They are growing less tolerant of the narrow limitations found in just one or two sub-movements, and especially the restrictions experienced in religious systems. There is much less attraction to denominational brands, and very little interest in the depersonalization that often occurs when they are institutionalized in religious structures. There is a passionate longing for more relational love with God and others, and more kingdom responsibility-authority on earth.

We believe that God is now providing both the grace and leadership to the body of Christ, so that the essential kingdom "nutrients" found in each sub-movement can be merged together in order to allow for the whole gospel to be enjoyed by the whole church in order to impact whole cities, regions, even nations. The convergence of all the powerful elements in each sub-movement as well as appropriating all the promises in God's Word will result in a much purer and more powerful church. This revitalized and reformed church can then be a dynamic catalyst which transforms culture.

A big step in reforming the church is helping God's people experience a shift of identity into sons of God who are members of a spiritual family. God revealed Himself as a Father, Son, and Spirit. He is one God, yet expresses Himself in Three Persons. God is a Family of Three in One. Therefore,

He builds His kingdom relationally through natural and spiritual families. Ultimately, there is only one spiritual family – the Church. The Bible refers to all those who have been truly transformed into sons of God as members of the universal family of God. We could call this the family big "F" – Family. (Or Big "T" – Tribe) Ephesians 3:14. We also believe that a child of God must walk out the reality of their universal spiritual family with specific people Father assigns. We could call this specific group of people our spiritual family little "f" – family. (Or Little "t" – tribe) A Biblical example of a Tribe little "t" is the apostle Paul and his relationship with spiritual sons like Timothy, Titus, and other spiritual children. Titus 1:4; 1 Timothy 1:2; 1 Corinthians 4:14-17 It is in the spiritual family little "t" (or "f" – family) that we practically apply all the Biblical "one another" admonitions like loving one another, bear each other's burdens, confess sin to one another, have all things in common, etc.

Here are some of the most prominent sub-movements in the last 400 years of church history:

> ➢ Praise and Worship
> ➢ Prayer
> ➢ Biblical Authority/Orthodox-Reform Theology/Spiritual Formation
> ➢ New Apostolic Reformation (includes the Prophetic Movement)
> ➢ Pentecostal, Charismatic, Third Wave (includes baptism and filling of the Holy Spirit, spiritual gifts, visions and dreams, signs, wonders, miracles)
> ➢ Discipleship/House Church/Missional Communities/Cell Groups
> ➢ Men's Gender Roles and Fathering
> ➢ Compassion/Justice/Social Action
> ➢ Marketplace Ministry
> ➢ Cultural Transformation/City-reaching
> ➢ Global Missions/Cross-cultural Missions/Church Planting
> ➢ Israel Mandate/Messianic

Often, a group will combine the valuable contribution of one, two, or even three sub-movements. Merging the emphasis of even two movements can have amazing results. For example, the current prayer sub-movement has also connected with the praise & worship sub-movement. One of the Biblical passages used as a reference is Revelation 5:8-9, *"Each one had a harp and they were holding golden bowls full of incense, which are the prayers of the saints. And they sang a new song."* The combination of praise, worship, and intercession has helped to fuel the global prayer sub-movement, and up-graded a culture of prayer in many local churches.

The "Word-Faith" wing of the church combined Biblical truth with the explosion of faith inspired by the Pentecostal-Charismatic sub-movement. As a result, many people have more effectively appropriated the vast promises of God.

Often, within each sub-movement there are excesses or imbalances that arise. These impurities become a stumbling block for the rest of the church, tempting them to discount all the benefits of the sub-movement because of the errors.

The time has come for mature leaders to glean from all the best truths found in each sub-movement and then to merge these Holy Spirit inspired realties in such a way that the church can impact whole cities. It will take that depth of humility and mutual submission in the body of Christ to produce this level of unity. This level of unity is what it will take for city-wide impact.

We want to appropriate all the best elements of each sub-movement, the valuable contributions from each denomination and ministry, along with all the other promises in God's Word. Ultimately, we want our point of reference to be the Person of Christ and our allegiance to be THE Movement of all Movements – The Kingdom of God on earth!

SEVEN LEVELS OF GOD'S VISION

Personal transformation into Christ's likeness as sons of God in the context of natural and spiritual families. Romans 8:29; 1 Corinthians 15:48-49

Marriages & Families experiencing divine order and divine life through Christ and the Kingdom of God. Ephesians 5:21-6:4

Micro-Church Families - small micro-church families on mission, groups of 5 to 25 people connected and submitted to a local church, led by Biblical elders composed of DNA Groups which are Discipleship, Nurture, Apostolic Mission Groups (See DNA Groups: Introduction & Overview). Acts 2:42-47

Local Churches which start and oversee Micro-Church Families and other ministries. Luke 10:1-21; Acts 14:21-28

City-wide and Regional Churches with five interconnected ministries:

- Worship & Prayer
- Interconnected, Multiplying Micro-Church Families
- Comprehensive Equipping & Training
- Compassion, Justice, Marketplace Ministries
- Cross-cultural & International Missions. Acts 11:19-30, 14:26, 20:17-21

Unified Body of Christ in cities and regions working together for reformation and transformation through Christ and the Kingdom of God in every sphere of life:
- Marriage & Family
- Marketplace
- Education
- Media
- Arts
- Religion
- Civil Government & Social Services. Revelation 1:4, 2:1, 8, 12, 18; 3:1, 7, 14

All nations glorifying God and under Christ's kingly rule. Matthew 28:18-20; Revelation 7:9-10

HIGHEST BIBLICAL-KINGDOM CORE VALUES AND HEART MOTIVES

Core values answer the question, "**Why** do we do what we do?" They supply the reasons behind our vision.

We value the glory and love of God. Bringing glory to God is the ultimate goal of God and man. 1 Corinthians 10:31; Isaiah 43:7

We value:

➢ God's centrality and supremacy, therefore all life exists to bring Him glory, honor, and pleasure. Colossians 1:15-23

➢ Receiving God's love, returning love back to God, and extending God's love to others. Matthew 22:37-39; 1 John

➢ Passionate praise and worship as a lifestyle and the Biblical ways we get to express our love for Him. Psalm 29:1-2, 150; Acts 13:2

➢ God's Word as written in the 66 books of the Bible as our authority for Truth in all areas of faith and life. 2 Timothy 3:16

➢ Knowing and obeying God's written Word because we love Him. Luke 11:28; John 14:15-24

➢ Hearing and obeying Holy Spirit's voice because we know and love Him. Romans 8:12-17

➢ Holiness. Hebrews 12:10-14; 1 Corinthians 1:2; 2 Corinthians 7:1; 1 Peter 1:13-16

➢ The fear of God. Proverbs 1:7; Luke 12:5; 1 Peter 1:17; Revelation 14:7

➢ The reality of God's eternal judgments and rewards and, therefore, we seek to live our lives in the light of eternity. Acts 17:31; Romans 2:16, 14:12; Hebrews 12:23; Revelation 20:4; Ephesians 6:8

We value the Gospel - The person and work of Jesus Christ and the reclaiming of Christ's Kingdom on earth by declaring and displaying the Gospel. John 1; Ephesians 1:9-10; Colossians 1:15-23, 2:6-7; Matthew 6:33; 1 Thessalonians 2:8; Philippians 1:27; Luke 8:1; Acts 8:12

We Value:

➢ Relating to Jesus Christ as our King and Lord. Luke 6:46-49

➢ Complete, quick, and cheerful obedience to Christ with Holy Spirit's help. Romans 1:5; Matthew 28:20

➢ Doing God's will, God's way, by God's Spirit, for God's glory. Proverbs 22:6; Isaiah 30:21; Colossians 1:10

➢ Divine order, plus divine life, in every sphere of life, perfectly combined and balanced. Matthew 9:17

➢ Being baptized and continually filled with the Holy Spirit for ministry, the demonstration and proclamation of the Gospel, power, boldness, spiritual gifts, signs, wonders, and miracles. Luke 24:49; Acts 1:4-5, 1:8, 4:31; 1 Corinthians 2:4-5, 4:20, 12:4-11; Romans 12:4-8

- ➢ Liberating and empowering men and women through distinct, Biblical, complimentarian gender roles. Genesis 1:27
- ➢ Ruling and reigning in all areas of life as royal sons of God. 2 Timothy 2:12; Revelation 20:6, 22:5

We value loving God as Father and living in covenant love with His family so we can demonstrate Father's love to a lost and dying world. John 14:6-14, 14:18-21, 17:20-26; Romans 8:1; Ephesians 3:14-21; 1 John 1:3

We Value:
- ➢ Relating to and loving God as our Father through Christ, the source of all life. John 17:1-26
- ➢ Living by faith, trusting in and depending on our good, loving, and powerful Father. Matthew 9:29, 17:20, 21:21; Romans 1:17; Galatians 3:8-26; Ephesians 3:17
- ➢ Receiving our identity from Father as sons of God through Christ by the witness of the Holy Spirit to our human spirits. John 1:12-13; Romans 8: 12-17; Galatians 3:26-29
- ➢ Receiving our sense of love, worth, value, and esteem from Father rather than from people and performance. Mark 1:11; John 14:20-21; 1 John 4:7-21
- ➢ Exchanging the love, wisdom, and life of Father through heart-to-heart covenant relationships within the context of natural and spiritual family. This includes valuing unity, communication, conflict resolution, and transparency, speaking the truth in love, honoring one another, and demonstrating godly affection to one another. Acts 4:32-34; 2 Corinthians 6:11-13; 1 Peter 1:22
- ➢ Loving one another and our neighbors as ourselves, and having faith expressed through love as indispensable for pleasing God, and fulfillment of the greatest commandments. Galatians 5:6; Hebrews 11:6; Matthew 22:37-40; 1 Corinthians 8:3
- ➢ Mercy and forgiveness. Matthew 5:7, 6:12-15, 9:13, 18:35
- ➢ Enjoying and celebrating life through Christ. John 6:40, 10:10; Ephesians 3:19; Colossians 2:6-7
- ➢ Being every expression of the church described in the Bible:
  - ‑ Ekklesia - The Greek word used for "Church." The word for a group of people who has been given authority to make governmental decisions and to act on their ruling.
  - ‑ People - 1 Peter 2:9; Luke 1:17
  - ‑ Family - Galatians 6:10; Ephesians 3:15; 1 Timothy 5:1-2
  - ‑ Bride of Christ - Revelation 21:2,9; Luke 1:17
  - ‑ House of Prayer - Matthew 21:13; 1 Peter 2:5; 1 Timothy 3:15; Ephesians 2:19-21; 1 Corinthians 3:9-15; Matthew 16:18; Romans 15:20; 2 Corinthians 10:8, 13:10
  - ‑ Pillar of Truth - 1 Timothy 3:15
  - ‑ Field - 1 Corinthians 3:5-9; James 1:21
  - ‑ Fellowship of the Holy Spirit - 2 Corinthians 13:14; Acts 2:42; 1 John 1:7
  - ‑ Flock - 1 Peter 5:1-5; John 10:16; Acts 20:28
  - ‑ Body of Christ - Romans 12:4-8; 1 Corinthians 12:12-27; Ephesians 4:1-16

- Salt of the Earth - Matthew 5:13
- Light of the World - Matthew 5:14-16; Revelation 1:20
- Holy Royal Priesthood - 1 Peter 2:5,9
- Holy Nation - 1 Peter 2:9; Hebrews 11:16; 2 Corinthians 5:20; Ephesians 6:10-20

We value devoting our entire lives to fulfilling Christ's great commission to make disciples who make disciples of all nations through the powerful proclamation and demonstration of the gospel of Christ and the Kingdom of God. We value being missionaries as a lifestyle. John 20:21; Matthew 28:19-20

We Value:
➢ Prayer and fasting. Acts 13:2; Mark 9:29; Matthew 21:13, 21:22
➢ Equipping and training leaders and all followers of Christ. Matthew 28:18-20; 2 Timothy 2:2; Colossians 1:28-29
➢ The utilization of all spiritual gifts. I Corinthians 12, 14; Romans 12:4-8
➢ The restoration of apostolic and prophetic gifting and ministry. Ephesians 2:19-22, 4:7-16; Acts 2:17-18; Romans 12:6; 1 Corinthians 14:1; Acts 19:6, 21:9
➢ Healing and deliverance. Matthew 10:1; Luke 10:1-24; James 5:13-16
➢ Signs, wonders, and miracles from the Holy Spirit. 2 Corinthians 12:12; Acts 2:19; Romans 15:19; 1 Corinthians 12:28
➢ Serving others as a demonstration of God's love. Matthew 20:26; Philippians 2:7
➢ Biblical leadership and administration. Hebrews 13:7; Romans 12:8
➢ Starting, growing, multiplying and sustaining new churches. All of Acts
➢ Advancing Christ's Kingdom in every sphere of life: marriage & family, church, marketplace, media, arts, education, civil government & social services. Matthew 6:33
➢ Social and cultural transformation. Matthew 5:13-16
➢ Compassion and justice, especially toward youth, poor, widows, orphans, and foreigners. Jeremiah 22:16; Matthew 11:5, 19:21, 25:31-46; Luke 14:13; Galatians 2:10; James 1:27
➢ Extravagant giving. Romans 12:8; 2 Corinthians 9:6-15; Galatians 6:7-10
➢ Cross-cultural and international missions. Matthew 28:18-20; Revelation 14:6-7

Great
Commission

Father & Family

King & Kingdom

God's Glory in the Nations

Core Values

Flow Questions:

1. Summarize the big God story.

2. Why is knowing and believing this story so important?

3. How is your life story a part of God's larger epic story?

NOTES:

JESUS TRIBES: FAMILIES-OF-FAMILIES ON MISSION LED BY FATHERLY APEST LEADERSHIP TEAMS

For their own glory, God the Father, God the Son, and God the Holy Spirit created, and then redeemed through Christ, a covenantal spiritual Family, made up of new creation sons/daughters, to advance God's Kingdom on earth. God self-disclosed as a Family of Three, yet One. Therefore, He must build His Kingdom relationally in and through Family. The glory of God, centrality and supremacy of Christ, covenant & kingdom, Father & Family, great commission to disciple the nations, are the core values and purpose of the Trinity. All reality and truth flows from the Trinity. Therefore, as sons/daughters we get to enjoy these same heart motives, and live in Father's epic story, His primary vision and mission.

APOSTOLIC TRIBES - GOD'S STRATEGY TO DEFEAT SATAN & BRING ALL THINGS UNDER CHRIST
Trans-local Spiritual Families/Armies

He made known to us the mystery of His will according to His good pleasure, which He purposed in Christ....to bring all things in heaven and on earth together under one head, even Christ. Ephesians 1:9-10

The Lord says to my Lord: "Sit at my right hand until I make your enemies a footstool for your feet." Psalm 110:1

You are no longer foreigners and aliens, but fellow citizens with God's household, built on the foundation of the apostles and prophets, with Christ Himself as the chief cornerstone. Ephesians 2:19-20

It was He who gave some to apostles, some to be prophets, some to be evangelists, and some to be pastors and teachers, to prepare God's people for works of service, so that the body of Christ may be built up until we all reach unity in the faith and in the knowledge of the Son of God and become mature, attaining to the whole measure of the fullness of Christ. Ephesians 4:11-13

God has appointed first of all apostles, second prophets, third. I Corinthians 12:28

The reason the Son of God appeared was to destroy the devil's work. I John 3:8

Introduction: A cosmic spiritual war is raging! Satan is attempting to resist the spread of God's glory across the earth and keep all life from coming under the Lordship of Christ. God is restoring Biblical Christianity in this age in order to defeat His enemy and bring about His ultimate intentions. God is changing the understanding and expression of Christianity in this generation back to its original form. This means a restoration of all the ministries and gifts mentioned in the Word such as apostles and prophets. Under the leadership of these spiritual parents/soldiers, extended spiritual families/armies will be equipped and mobilized to powerfully expand the Kingdom of God into every sphere of life. God only uses a paradigm, context, or wineskin which reveals who He is and is consistent with His nature – a Father and Son. Thus, Father builds His Kingdom relationally in the context of natural and spiritual family. The church must be changed at the most foundational levels back into a true covenant family and army. This is a much more dramatic paradigm shift than most of us can imagine, and it will take many years of hard work and spiritual warfare to experience this reality.

The Biblical pattern for church planting is apostolic teams, Acts 13:2-3,13; I Corinthians 1:1; II Corinthians 1:1; Galatians 1:1-2,2:8-10; Colossians1:1; I Timothy 1:1-2; Titus 1:1, 4. Apostolic teams are led by spiritual fathers and mothers who raise up an extended spiritual family of sons and daughters. The spiritual parents are responsible for receiving the values, vision, mission and general strategies from Father and communicating and modeling them to the family members. Generational transfer of God's love and ways through discipleship within natural and spiritual families is how Father chooses to expand His Kingdom. The family is Father's chosen paradigm and context for His life and love to be exchanged. These trans-local spiritual families also function as spiritual armies which powerfully advance the Kingdom of God in every sphere of life (personal, natural family, market place, civil government, etc.). God sovereignly joins all His children into a natural and/or spiritual family in order to reveal and advance the Kingdom of God in tangible ways, through skin. These covenantally connected sons and daughters will model kingdom love by enjoying relational intimacy. They will help to reveal the relationship of The Father and The Son (The First Family) through spiritual family. And they will forcefully advance the Kingdom with the efficiency of a modern army. Many people have never experienced life and love within a healthy natural or spiritual family. This deprivation will require significant healing and discipleship. Others need additional teaching and coaching to help them move from good family life to excellent. Everyone, no matter their background, has a need to be taught how to communicate and behave in Biblically healthy and positive ways. Describing and contrasting the attitudes and actions of those who are true spiritual fathers, mothers, sons and daughters with those who are connected programmatically, institutionally, politically, religiously, or just around purpose will help us all move toward the incredibly rich life Christ's blood has purchased. We do not want to live beneath the promises of God or fall short of His glory. True healthy apostolic spiritual families are being raised up by our Father. Every Christian needs to find their tribe and enthusiastically contribute to the quality of loving relationships and the successful achievement of its vision. Let us all strive to enter this reality called the "unity of the Spirit and the bond of peace", Ephesians 4:3, and experience loving each other deeply from the heart, I Peter 1:22.

The word "salvation" in the scriptures is a relational term. It means to be reconnected and restored back into relationship with our Father in heaven and adopted into His Family. Biblical salvation is both "vertical" (i.e. relationally reconnected to Father through His Son Christ) and horizontal (i.e. placed in the spiritual family composed of created people). All Christians are expected to walk out their spiritual lives in a specific spiritual family.

The Bible teaches that all believers (those who place their trust in Christ for salvation and obey Him as Lord) are adopted into the family of God through the shed blood and sacrificial death of Jesus Christ. However, the Bible also teaches that every believer is to walk out the reality of their salvation in the context of an identifiable spiritual family with legitimate church government. The Family "big F" speaks of the whole and universal body of Christ on earth and in heaven. The family "little f" are the real live human beings that God calls us to experience covenant relationships with. Bonding in a specific family group identity is crucial for inner-healing, maturity, and impact.

Be concerned and cautious with those who identify themselves as members of the universal family of God (big "F" Family) but will not bond, connect, commit, and submit to a specific spiritual family-tribe (little "f" family). This may initially sound noble and spiritual but is, in fact, a smoke screen and a deception concealing deeper issues. These are signs of deeper issues:

- Not covenantally connect at the heart in a specific spiritual family
- Will not commit long term to the values, vision, mission, strategies, leaders and family members through time, energy, tithe, affections, talents, gifts
- Not coming into accountability and submission, could be evidence of:

  a.) Not truly saved

  b.) Not under the Lordship of Christ revealed in unwillingness to connect righteously to His Body

  c.) Rebellion or compromise

  d.) Fear and/or unbelief

  e.) "Mommy or daddy" wounds from the past manifesting in self-protection

  f.) Lack of understanding God's ways

  g.) Spirit of control, manipulation, pride, selfish ambition

A specific little "f" (or "t" – tribe) spiritual family has Biblical government and is led by apostles, prophets, pastors, teachers, evangelists, elders, and deacons. Apostolic leaders, those ultimately responsible for families-of-churches, always seek to be accountable to other apostolic leaders. True apostles love submitting to other apostles and leaders.

Heavenly Father wants all His children to prosper and receive the full rights, privileges, and blessings that Christ's blood has purchased. However, He requires that we receive and experience these blessings on His terms, according to His ways. As a Father and Son, God invented the natural and spiritual family. Family is God's context for love, discipleship, empowerment, blessings, wealth, success, callings, destinies, the discovery and contribution of spiritual gifts and talents, promotion and more. Anyone attempting to experience God's will and blessings outside of God's ways (natural and spiritual family) will not only miss His promises but actually experience His resistance. God resists the proud.

 God's primary way to mediate His grace is through human beings submitted to one another. Ephesians 6:1-3; I Peter 5:5-6; Roman 1:11

The way we relate to people, especially natural and spiritual family and those in authority, indicates the depth and health of our relationship with God. I John; I Peter 3:7.

Due to broken covenants, unfulfilled promises, moral failure, and abusive leadership styles, credibility and trust are at an all-time low. This has produced serious distrust and skepticism towards authority. The temptation for many people is to diminish or even eliminate the necessity and role of parents/leaders. There are subtle ways that we can minimize the place natural and spiritual parents are to have in our lives. We can appear open and connected at the heart, while maintaining walls, self-protection, independence and self-reliance. People think, "If I cannot rely on or trust parents/leaders, I cannot trust anyone". "I'll just trust myself and take matters into my own hands." The equation becomes, it is better to have no leadership than bad leadership.

This ultimately leads to isolation, independence, and anarchy and leaves people depleted and ineffective.

One of the results of the breakdown of spiritual parenting is the formation of religious institutions run by hirelings. Church organizations can easily become institutional orphanages run by program directors, social workers, and hired staff.

The answer to bad leadership is not NO leadership. It is recovering healthy spiritual parents and family.

A healthy spiritual father or mother has the following attributes:

➢ The word "father" in Hebrew means "source". Father in heaven delegates authority and responsibility to natural and spiritual parents to be conduits of His life. In that sense, they are a source for the Source. Spiritual parenting is all about bringing forth life, training that life, sustaining life, protecting life, etc. It involves profound self-sacrifice in order to help another mature and fulfill their destiny. Parents exist to serve offspring, not the other way around. A true parent will always be a resource of life to others. As a result, the positive impact or fruit from their lives will be evident everywhere.

➢ Spiritual fathers are the communicators and guardians of Biblical kingdom values. They model and train on the basis of character and values, and they create mechanisms for those values to be reinforced, instituted, and guarded.

➢ Spiritual fathers are the communicators of God-inspired faith vision.

➢ Spiritual fathers birth and raise spiritual families, through new births and spiritual adoptions.

➢ Spiritual fathers create a context and setting for the family members to be trained and discipled. Family members are encouraged to grow to their maximum potential.

➢ Spiritual fathers create a culture and atmosphere for people to be loved, encouraged, valued, and utilized.

➢ Spiritual fathers create and enforce boundaries. They facilitate church discipline in love.

➢ Spiritual fathers cover their families in prayer.

➢ Spiritual fathers impart blessings, spiritual gifts, and help gather resources for the family vision.

➢ Spiritual fathers model godliness, and kingdom lifestyle.

➢ Spiritual fathers rally and motivate their family to love and serve children, youth, poor, widows, orphans, aliens, and the unreached in the nations. They call the family to lose its life for those outside itself in order to gain its life.

➢ Spiritual fathers train and model covenant life. They are not just professional ministers, hired church workers, who maintain a pastoral persona and are moving from church to church to expand their careers.

➢ Spiritual fathers create an atmosphere of love, acceptance, forgiveness, mercy, kindness, and fun.

> Spiritual fathers are accountable to other spiritual fathers. They are easily corrected, admit their sin, failures, and weaknesses, and work hard to improve themselves for the sake of the family.

> Apostolic fathers will not be able to have a direct relationship with everyone in the tribe they lead due to the natural limitations of space and time. However, their fathering can be experienced indirectly through the leaders they raise up, the vision they cast, the values they teach and sustain, the ministries they launch, the loving atmosphere their leadership produces, etc.

It is critical to understand what constitutes a true healthy spiritual family. Just because a group calls themselves a church or spiritual family does not mean it is one.

> A true spiritual family is connected at the heart and mind covenantally. This means that the basis of their relationships is the cross of Christ, acceptance, love, forgiveness, mercy, and relationships based on "being" versus "doing/performance". They do not judge or reject one another based on performance. Relationships involve deep commitment, sacrifice, and care. Conflicts are resolved through up front communication, Biblical due process, forgiveness, reconciliation, and mercy. Gossip and slander are unacceptable forms of communication. People are encouraged to influence the group through appeal versus political power moves.

> A true spiritual family has a clear set of values, a vision and mission, strategies, and goals that come from God and delivered through the point leader. All the members own the same values, vision, and mission as the point leader and thus enjoy great unity and oneness.

> A true spiritual family has identifiable spiritual parents (government) who have accepted the responsibility of giving account for the souls of the members of the family. These spiritual parents/leaders are committed long term to the people. Because of calling and sovereign joining, not because of a pay check, a position, a certain level of power and authority. These spiritual parents lead by example, do not try to influence through control or manipulation and are not abusive or dominating.

> A true family has identifiable membership.

> A true spiritual family has created an atmosphere and opportunity for all its members to grow in their character, gifts, callings, and responsibilities. They have placed no ceiling of growth on its members.

> A true spiritual family exercises spiritual discipline within Biblical guidelines.

> A true spiritual family encourages people to celebrate their own unique personality, temperament, and interests. They do not try to clone their members to be like a few of the leaders. They encourage their members to think for themselves, to own what is in their hearts. They do not try to force or coerce people to certain attitudes and actions. People can be themselves, yet are being encouraged to be their best self through Christ.

> A true spiritual family laughs and plays together.

> A true spiritual family has created a culture of affection, safety, transparency, and trust.

- A true family encourages people to express their differing opinions and ideas because it values the notion of total ownership.
- A true family has "all things in common" which means it voluntarily makes its time and resources available to one another.
- A true spiritual family reproduces new babies and has a means to raise those new believers into mature Christians.
- A true family is concerned about the well-being of the whole person – their individual body, soul, and spirit, their natural family, their spiritual family, their job, their government.
- A true healthy spiritual family gets feedback, coaching, and correction from leaders outside itself. It refuses to be ingrown, isolated, or to cultivate an elite, superior attitude.
- A true healthy spiritual family feels a responsibility and call to youth, poor, and the unreached in the nations. They will exist for something and someone outside of themselves. They will lose their life in order to gain it.
- A true healthy spiritual family avoids all forms of dysfunctional behavior like co-dependency, insecurities, viewing and connecting to people and community as the source of life instead of drawing on God as the Source.
- A true spiritual family pools and sacrifices its money and resources through tithes and offerings in order to worship God and achieve its mission.

What is an Apostolic Father?

Apostles are "sent ones". They have a commission from the Trinity to expand the Kingdom of God by planting churches and providing ongoing support, accountability, and relational connection for the churches they plant or adopt. "Apostle" is a military term. The King delegates His authority to another, commissions and sends him out to expand the Kingdom.

Seven demands that define apostles. (taken from David Cannistraci's *The Gift of Apostle*)

1. Apostles must have a definite call from God. This should be confirmed by the prophetic.
2. Apostles are required to have special intimacy with Christ. I Corinthians 9:1
3. Apostles must qualify as elders. I Timothy 3:1-7; Titus 1:5-9; I Peter 5:1-4
4. Apostles must qualify as five-fold ministers who equip people for the work of ministry. Ephesians 4:11-17
5. Apostles must be confirmed and recognized by peers. They are not self-proclaimed, but sent out by credible leaders. Galatians 2:9; Acts 13:1-3
6. Apostles must have specific fruit. I Corinthians 9:1-2
7. Apostles must maintain their ministry by submission to Christ, Divine and human accountability structures. Acts 1:25

Two aspects of Apostolic Ministry: Planting & Watering. I Corinthians 3:5-9

Seven Responsibilities of an Apostle:

1. Planting Churches. Acts 13:4 - 14:26
2. Overseeing and strengthening churches. II Corinthians 11:28
3. Develop leaders through spiritual fathering. II Timothy 2:22
4. Ordaining Ministries. Titus 1:5; Acts 6:1-6
5. Supervising and coordinating ministry. Acts 16:1-4; Philippians 2:19-20; Colossians 4:7-12
6. Managing Crisis. Acts 4:24-37; 11:29-30
7. Networking with other ministries. Acts 15

Apostolic character:

➤ Humility: Apostles saw themselves as slaves of Christ. Romans 1:1; James 1:1; I Peter 1:1; Revelation1:1
➤ Apostles glorify God and never themselves. I Corinthians 9:16; Acts 3:12; 14:11-15; I Thessalonians. 2:6
➤ Apostles understand their need to submit. I Corinthians 16:12

Apostles have the top governmental authority over the churches they plant or adopt. II Corinthians 10:8- 18; I Corinthians 12:28

Apostles have vision and are most responsible for stewarding the vision of the trans-local spiritual family. II Corinthians 12:1

Apostles establish divine order in all spheres of life.

Apostles are spiritual fathers who encourage their spiritual family to connect covenantally from the heart. I Corinthians 4:15-17; Philippians 1:8; I Thessalonians 2:7-8

Apostles are for today.

➤ The original 12 pre-ascension Apostles have a unique place in church history. They were given authority to form the cannon of New Testament scripture. They will rule perennially.
➤ Post ascension apostles are gifts given by Christ to extend His government and bring divine order in all spheres of life.

"The Biblical evidence strongly supports the continuity of the gift of apostle. The original twelve apostles have a unique place in Christian history and they will be commemorated permanently in the New Jerusalem (see Revelation 21:14), but they were not the only apostles. I Corinthians 15 mentions that after the resurrection Jesus appeared to "the twelve" and then also to "all the apostles," indicating that there were apostles other than the twelve. I Corinthians 15:5, 7 Furthermore, the warnings against "false apostles" would be nonsense if apostles were limited to the twelve. II Corinthians 11:13, Revelation 2:2"
C. Peter Wagner

Examples of apostles mentioned in scripture other than the 12 & Paul: Silas, Timothy in I Thessalonians 1:1, 2:6-7, Andronicus and Junias in Roman 16:7.

Apostles are to exist and function **until** the church reaches unity and maturity. Ephesians 4:12

The Devil's primary attack was leveled against apostles. "Strike the shepherd and the sheep will scatter". Zechariah 13:7 In early church history, the gift of apostle was the first to be lost. The apostle is the last governmental gift to be restored. This is the most exciting development in 1500 years of church history. **We will not have New Testament Christianity without valid Apostolic Fathers!**

Apostles are at the point of the spiritual battle and thus are the first target in spiritual warfare. See Acts 16:16; 19:23-40

How the modern-day apostle gets called and released.

> ➢ He receives a specific call from Jesus by way of personal revelation. He sees and hears the Lord. Acts 9:4-7
> ➢ The prophetic ministry confirms this calling. Acts 9:10-19; 13:1-3
> ➢ The character of Christ is built into their lives. Visible in personal, family, work, and church life.
> ➢ They begin carrying out apostolic ministry with obvious fruit. They make disciples, cast vision, train and enforce values, plant churches, impart gifts, raise up leaders, etc.
> ➢ Other mature ministries recognize and affirm their calling and gifting.
> ➢ They stay accountable to seasoned and established ministries.
> ➢ Signs, wonders, miracles and favor from God accompanies their lives and ministries.
> ➢ Significant spiritual warfare and suffering are attached to their lives.
> ➢ The vision, values, mission, promises and anointing that is given to the point apostle comes onto all those who are placed in his spiritual family. Romans 1:1-5; Roman 16:20-24. The same calling to the gentiles which came to Paul was extended to his apostolic team.

THE IMPORTANCE OF INTERNATIONAL FAMILIES OF AFFECTION

Why we all need to be a vital part of an international family-of-churches on mission.

God has several Big Purposes. Two of them are:

1. Transform each son/daughter into the likeness of Christ, which involves healing and discipleship in the context of family. Romans 8:29
2. Create the literal Body of Christ on earth to advance Christ's Kingdom for the glory of God. 1 Corinthians 12:27

To achieve these Big Purposes, God has His responsibilities. But Father has also given His sons/daughters their responsibilities. We are to make disciples. 2 Timothy 2:2; Matthew 28:18-20

God's work/responsibilities:
➤ Creation
➤ Salvation
➤ Sanctification
➤ Spiritual adoption
➤ Supernatural power of the Holy Spirit to heal and deliver

Our responsibilities as sons and daughters: It is our job, assigned way back in the Garden of Eden, to be fruitful and multiply, to help raise and mature others, and to rule and reign on earth. Genesis 1-3 *"We proclaim Him, admonishing and teaching everyone with all wisdom, so that we may present everyone perfect in Christ. To this end I labor, struggling with all His energy, which so powerfully works in me."* Colossians 1:28.

➤ Be fruitful and to multiply. For example, it is our job to make babies and raise them.
➤ Proclaim and demonstrate the gospel.
➤ Make disciples of all nations. We teach others to hear and obey Christ. We help them mature.
➤ Heal the sick and cast out demons (with the power of the Holy Spirit).
➤ Bear one another's burdens.
➤ Teach, train, rebuke, and correct others entrusted to our care.

We make disciples relationally in family. People don't grow by simply reading a book or watching a YouTube video. We all need healthy relationships in loving community, a family, to heal and mature. It takes healthy families, made of relationally skilled and mature parents to raise up healthy people. This points to a huge problem in both society and the Church. Compared to the entire population, few people are relationally skilled enough to heal and mature others. We strongly believe that, *"The absence of key relational skills and maturity are almost always behind failures of ministers, ministries and missions. Sadly, the lacking skills are rarely identified, and when the lack of skill is seen, no one knows how to restore the skill. Relational skills are the basis for expressing godly character and identity to others around us when the 'heart Jesus gave us' seeks expression."* Taken from: *Living From The Heart Jesus Gave You. An introduction to the Life Model*

God's solution to this massive relational problem is to change the understanding and expression of Christianity in this generation by paradigm shifting the Church into international families of affection i.e. "Jesus Tribes". These families-of-families will be led by humble, mature, and relationally skilled APEST leaders who reveal Father's heart. A Jesus Tribe will create the smaller spiritual families that heal and mature each individual family member. Each Jesus Tribe will establish a self-perpetuating and easily transferrable model (Biblical strategy) to help bring as much healing and growth to as many as possible. God is raising up early adopter pioneers who will accept the daunting task of allowing their minds to be renewed, their hearts to be healed and transformed, their lifestyles to be "kingdomized", their relational skills to be upgraded, and their entire beings to mature so they can bear real responsibility in the kingdom for the lives of others. Will you accept this profound invitation from God? Will you become a vital and active member of an international family of affection – a Jesus Tribe?

THE FIVE STAGES OF MATURITY: TAKEN FROM THE BIBLE AND THE LIFE MODEL

Maturity is about reaching one's God-given potential. It means maximizing our skills and talents, and using them effectively, while growing into the full capability of our individual designs. Maturity involves growth in many areas: relational, emotional, spiritual, mental. Our brains were designed to help us mature. While most of the brain stops growing at certain stages of development, the brain's 'joy center', located in the right orbital prefrontal cortex, is the only section of the brain that never loses its capacity to grow! It is the one section of the brain that retains the ability to grow our entire lives, which means that 'joy strength' can always continue to develop! What makes it grow? It grows in response to real, joy-filled relationships. We are not talking about casual, superficial relationships here. When people are engaged in authentic, bonded relationships showing real joy, this section of the brain will grow at any age! (Taken from: *Living from the Heart Jesus Gave You*)

1. **Infant (0-3)** – the fundamental need is to receive unconditional love and care. If these needs go unmet, we will spend the rest of our lives trying to get others to take care of us.

2. **Child (4-12)** – a child still needs unconditional love and care. They also start learning how to care for themselves. They must master several personal tasks: a. A child must learn to say what he thinks and feels and appropriately ask for what is needed. b. Children must learn what brings them satisfaction. c. Children need to learn how to do hard things. d. Children

need to develop their personal talents and resources. e. Children need to learn self-care. f. Self-care requires knowing yourself and making yourself understandable to others. g. Children need to understand how they fit into history as well as the big picture of life. When they understand the big picture of life, they realize they have the ability to personally impact the world.

3. **Adult (13-birth of first child)** – a shift from being self-centered child to a both-centered adult. While a child needs to learn me-centered fairness, an adult learns we-centered fairness (how do I make it fair for us). Mutuality is the trademark of an adult because he can take care of two people at the same time. Adults know how to remain stable in difficult situations and can return self and others to joy. Adults contribute to and are a part of vital community. They are a part of something bigger than "me" – which is empowering and inspiring. Adults express the characteristics of their heart in a deepening personal way. Once people know who they truly are and understand the power and beauty of their God-given characteristics, their passion, purpose, talents, and pain will all come together and begin to define specifically who they are. The better they can express their unique identities in their words and actions, the more positioned they will be for speaking and living truthfully.

4. **Parent (first birth until youngest child becomes adult)** – one is at the parent stage when they can sacrificially care for their children without resenting the sacrifice or expecting to receive anything for their efforts. Parents know how to protect, serve and enjoy their families. Parents are wise in allowing and providing spiritual family members – other important people in their children's lives who will help their children become the persons they were designed to be. Mature parents will be able to bring their children through difficult times and return to joy from all unpleasant emotions.

5. **Elder (beginning when youngest child becomes an adult)** – one who has raised children to maturity and completed all the prior maturity tasks. True elders can act like themselves in the midst of difficulty. They can also establish an accurate community identity by finding out what their community has been designed by God to be, rather than imposing what they would like it to be. True elders prize all community members and see them as God sees them – looking past their flaws and facades to see the persons they have been designed to be. True elders are also well and able to parent and mature the community. They are qualified to do this because they have learned from a lifetime of experiences. Taken from *Living From The Heart Jesus Gave You*.

SEVEN CRITICAL RELATIONAL SETTINGS

There are seven critical relational settings described in the Bible that are essential for facilitating healing, maturity, and transformation into Christ's likeness - settings in which we freely receive and freely give. All seven settings are essential. Leave one or more of these relational settings out of your life and you will not fully develop into a mature son.

1. **Face time with Father: You with God**. Freely receive from Father through Christ by the Holy Spirit. You freely give glory, worship, praise, and love back to God. Mark 1:35, 6:45; Luke 5:16, 6:12 Face time reaches God! He is the One who needs to receive our ministry as first priority. Do you consciously minister to the Lord? 2 Chronicles 3:10; Revelation 1:4-6

2. **2's – 4's: You with 4 plus God.** (DNA Group – Discipleship, Nurture, Apostolic Mission) You freely receive from God directly and through other disciples with the same gender. You freely give back to Go and then to each other: love, wisdom, revelation, and healing power. You also demonstrate and share the gospel with one or two friends. They can come right into your DNA Group. Matthew 18:19-20; Luke 10:1; Mark 9:2; Matthew 17:1; Luke 9:28; Ecclesiastes 4:12. DNA's reach one or two people.

3. **5's – 15ish: You with 12 plus God** (Micro-Church Family or "Missional Kingdom Family") that is part of a larger local church which could gather in a house, business, school, coffee shop, park, under a tree, wherever, whenever, because it's a family on mission. Four directions of love: down, up, in, and out. We freely receive from God and give back to Him. We freely receive from each other and give back to each other. We freely give out to those who do not know Jesus as Lord. We are all are on mission in our neighborhoods, school, work, friends, family, wherever, whenever, because we are always sons who are soldiers who advance Christ's Kingdom with no limits or constraints. Micro-Church Families (MCF's) reach neighborhoods, businesses, schools, etc. Exodus 18:21-25; Matthew 10:1; Roman 16:5; Philippians 1:2; Acts 2:42-46; Colossians 4:15; 1 Corinthians 14:26, 16:19

4. **70 – 5,000ish: You with 100's-1000's plus God** (Local church led by elders connected to APEST leadership team) We freely receive from others in different DNA's and MCF's. We freely receive from the elders and APEST ministries like apostles, prophets, teachers, evangelists, etc. We also give through regular prayer, tithing, offerings, serving, etc. Local churches reach their city. Luke 10:1-23; Acts 1:4, 13-15, 2:41, 2:46, 4:4, 11:21-24

5. **International family of churches** i.e Jesus Tribe: You with family-of-churches led by loving fatherly APEST leadership, plus God. (Tribal Gatherings, Regional Tribal Gatherings, Discipleship Training, Leadership Training, All Nations College, Mission Trips, Micro-Church planting, etc). We freely receive from God directly, and also through trans-local five-fold ministry gifts like apostles, prophets, teachers, evangelists, pastors. We freely give through prayer, offerings, connecting relationally with family from other cities and nations, participation in events, serving through missions, church planting, etc. Jesus Tribes reach new cities, regions, and nations. There is "apostolicity" in every son of God, a capacity to send and be sent. Apostles are called to equip the people for the work of ministry. Apostles equip by instilling faith-vision to pioneer, take new ground, bring something out of nothing, and go into your neighborhood or to the nations. They impart the revelation of Father's heart, create the family context for you to flourish as a son, and mobilize the family-army with a Biblical strategy to advance the Kingdom of God holistically in cities, regions, and nations. Christ in you wants to use you to bring Him glory in the nations!

A. Antioch was a hub for trans-local church-planting and mission. Apostolic people BOTH send and are sent. It takes senders and sent out ones. Acts 11:19-30, 13:1-14:28

B. No matter what role you play in a Tribe, everyone can receive the same level of reward. 1 Samuel 30:24

C. Each local church family had the benefit of trans-local support, gifts, training, and accountability. Acts 15:22-35, Ephesians 2:19-22, 4:7-16, 1 Corinthians 12:28

D. People with different ministry gifts served in other local churches besides their own. Every person in every local church supported the trans-local vision and mission. Acts 17:14-15, 18:18-23, 20:4-6; 1 Corinthians 4:17

E. Finances where received and then distributed by the apostolic team to help fulfill their international mission. 1 Corinthians 16:1-4; 2 Corinthians 8:1-9:15; Philippians 2:19-30

F. Apostles raised up other younger apostles who were then commissioned to help appoint elders in the new church plants. 1 Timothy 3:1-7; Titus 1:5-9; 1 Timothy 1:3

G. Apostolic leadership teams planted new churches and then had an ongoing responsibility to help support and grow those local churches. Acts 15:36-16:5

H. Loving and supportive relationships were formed between people from other local churches in other cities. Acts 21:7-9; Roman 16:1-24; 1 Corinthians 16:5-24; 2 Corinthians 8:16-24

I. A great deal of the Book of Acts and the Epistles described the dynamic of an interconnected family-of-churches or a tribe. Galatians 1:1-2

J. Paul describes himself as a spiritual father, who has spiritual sons, and the members of the churches as family, and constantly uses familial language. Roman 16:17; 1 Corinthians 4:14-17, 2 Corinthians 6:11-13; Philippians 2:19-30 Paul even describes his relational sphere of apostolic authority. 1 Corinthians 9:2; 2 Corinthians 3:2-3

K. Different tribes were all to be considered a part of only one Tribe in the order of Melchizedek. Hebrews 5-7, 7:11-17

L. Roland Allen, in his book "Missionary Methods: St. Paul's or Ours?", wrote:

> In like manner the churches of which they were members were not separate and independent bodies. They were not independent of the Apostle who was their common founder, they were not independent of one another. In St. Paul's mind the province was a unit. So, when his churches were established, he distinctly recognized the unity of the Church in the province. He constantly spoke of the churches of Macedonia, of Achaia, of Galatia, of Syria and Cilicia, of Asia as unities. For the purpose of the collection which he made for the poor saints at Jerusalem, the churches of Macedonia, Achaia, and Galatia were each treated as a separate group, and officers were appointed by each group to act

on behalf of the province which they represented in the administration of the collection. This unity was more than a convenient grouping. The same bonds which united individual Christians one to another united the churches. They were not simply groups of Christians who, for mutual assistance and convenience, banded themselves together in face of a common danger. They were all alike members of a body which existed before they were brought into it. They could not act as if they were responsible to themselves alone. The churches were in frequent communication one with another. Visitors passed easily from one to another and prophets soon began to spend their lives journeying from place to place preaching and expounding the faith.

6. **Tribe Middle "T"** – Larger segments of the Body of Christ that have common core values, theological perspective, doctrines, or church government. Examples: Orthodox (like Eastern, Russian), Roman Catholic, Reformed, Anglican, Evangelical, Fundamentalists (cessationists), Pentecostals, Charismatics.

7. **Tribe Big "T"** – the entire Body of Christ.

APOSTOLIC FATHERING

By Bill Johnson

For centuries, the people of God have gathered together around specific truths. Denominations and organizations have been formed to unite these groups of believers. Having common belief systems has helped to build unity within particular groups and define their purpose. Historically these groups were formed from people who were usually newly saved, or were asked to leave whatever denomination they were previously a part of. [1]

Unity based on common doctrines has a measure of success. But there is an inherent problem with this approach – unity of this nature is based upon uniformity. When God is saying something new, [2] those who are listening are usually asked by their leaders to leave the group they were a part of. [3] Their newfound convictions and beliefs are considered threatening and divisive. If the whole group doesn't move in step with what God is saying, there will be a break in fellowship. When agreement in nonessential beliefs are considered necessary for fellowship, then division is natural and to be expected. While doctrine is vitally important it is not a strong enough foundation to bear the weight of His glory that is about to be revealed through true unity.

Change is in the Air

There are major changes in the "wind" right now. For the last several years' people have started to gather around fathers instead of doctrine. In the natural, it would be easy to imagine a father with two very different children – one politically liberal and the other conservative. While discussions would probably be quite lively at the evening meal, they would not bring an end to the family. Gathering around fathers gives a stability that enables people to endure differences in opinion without falling under the influence of the spirit of offense. Fathers bring an element of peace that is impossible without them.

Spiritual Fathers

Apostles are first and foremost fathers by nature. True fathers continually make choices for the well-being of their children with little thought to personal sacrifice. They are not jealous when their children succeed, but instead are overjoyed because of those successes. It is normal for a father to desire his children to surpass him in every way. Brothers compete - fathers do not.

In the same way that a father and mother are to bring stability to a home, so the apostles and prophets are the stability of the church. The Apostle Paul calls them the church's foundation.[4] Good foundations bring stability. The concept of team ministry starts with these two. Stability is the primary fruit of the ministry of the apostolic team.

Team Makeup

Apostolic teams are not necessarily made up of just apostles and prophets. They are a group of people that carry the 'family mission' without selfish agendas. They are sent by their leadership, and entrusted with delegated authority to establish God's rule in their realm of experience and expertise. When they go with that heart they carry an apostolic anointing because they function under the umbrella of the apostle's authority.

We can't be co-missioned until we're in sub-mission to the primary mission. This is true of every believer before God. But it is especially true of apostolic teams. Setting aside personal agendas is a big part of the success of team ministry. Many teams have failed in their mission because of an individual who wanted his/her gift or opinion to be recognized.

Measure of Rule

A big misunderstanding occurs when apostles think they have the same measure of authority in every geographical location. When Paul went to Jerusalem to participate in the first Apostolic Council, [5] he submitted his experiences to the other apostles who had also gathered there. It wasn't until James, the apostle in Jerusalem, spoke, that there were any conclusions. A true apostle carries their apostolic authority wherever they go, but it is foolish for him to not recognize local authority. The same is true with apostolic teams. It is their respect for the local church and the Biblical authority that helps them to serve effectively.

Authority, like favor, is for the benefit of others. It is not a title to help in building one's own self-esteem, and is never for personal gain. For that reason the Apostle is at the 'bottom of the stack' . . . the 'least of all'. The title simply recognizes function. And that function is to make others better and more complete in their walk with the Lord.

The Purpose of the Title

Throughout history there have been many ordinary individuals who have become desperate for God in unusual ways, and have sought God with reckless abandon. The encounters they had with God made them appear extraordinary. Their breakthrough made them household names with remarkable gifts and ministries. But when God gives someone an unusual gift, it is never for the purpose of acquiring admiration and fame, or even drawing big crowds. Those things are normal byproducts, but they are not the purpose. The place of favor that one gets as a result of God's unusual touch on their lives is a God given position to equip others. It is God's heart to take those high points of human experience in the man or woman of God and make them the new norm for the believer. Equipping the saints becomes the focus of true fathers.

The Spirit of Revelation

One of the things that helped to keep the early church strong and healthy was their continual devotion to the apostle's doctrine. [6] However, you'll notice that there is no mention of a list of beliefs that the Bible declares to be the official record of important doctrines. It is safe to say the "apostle's doctrine" is referring to something other than a specific list. Peter understood this when he exhorted the church concerning 'present truth'. [7] That phrase is to direct our attention to that which the Lord is emphasizing for this season. That is the apostle's doctrine. The word coming from apostles is to bring clarification of the Father's focus for the church, and in turn strengthen our resolve to His purposes. Fresh revelation carries fresh fire, which helps us to maintain the much needed fire in our souls.

Apostles carry a blueprint in their hearts concerning the church and God's purposes on the earth. They are used to bring fresh revelation to the church. Apostolic teams are sent to represent their spiritual father, and carry the word that has been entrusted to their 'tribe'. They help bring an understanding and establish an order needed in the particular location they were sent to.

The Need for Others

God never gives the whole picture of His plan for the church to one father/apostle, or even to one tribe. Scriptures declare that "we" have the mind of Christ, [8] not "I". Dependence upon the whole is essential for us to grow up in a way that pleases Christ. As the various "tribes" learn to work together we will see a more complete picture of the Father's intent for planet earth.

The revelation carried by Apostles and the five-fold ministry will result in a church coming to a common knowledge of the Son of God. [9] Much division presently exists in this area. He is our common focus. A study of the scriptures without the Holy Spirit giving understanding creates much religious conflict. Division exists because people are committed to different levels of truth that appear contradictory. Fathers are necessary to sort these things out. Variety, without uniformity, is important. These teams carry revelation to help the church to live out of a common revelation of Jesus – who He is, and who we are because of Him. God's aim is to fulfill His word in John 4:17 - "As He is, so are we in this world." We are to become like the Jesus revealed in Revelation chapter one – resurrected and glorified. We are not headed for the cross – we live 'from' the cross. Apostolic revelation has that in mind.

The Day of Power

One of the more notable prophets of our day recently told me that he wouldn't be able to come into all that God had created him for until the apostles came forth to their appointed place. The apostles help release the prophet into their destiny, and vice versa. In a sense they complete each other.

Apostolic order without apostolic power is to be questioned. Order based on Biblical principle that is lacking Biblical power is tragic at best, and deceptive at worst. Order does not exist unto itself. The wineskin exists for the wine. The wine is the focus. All order exists to house God Himself – not to restrict Him, but to accurately express Him. Wineskins need to flex in order to be useful, because of the expanding nature of the wine in the fermenting process. The Holy Spirit brings constant change, and to house Him means to embrace flexibility as a way of life. The goal is not to create a perfect structure or government. It is to create one that recognizes Him, and flexes with His changes.

Last Days Assignment

All of this serves one purpose – Jesus is returning for a bride. For this to happen the harvest must be brought in, and must be "cleaned." He's not returning for a bride that He has to heal up and put together like a puzzle in heaven. He is returning for a bride whose body is in equal proportion to her head, and whose parts work together in coordination. It's called a "glorious church, without spot or wrinkle" [10] in scripture. Anything less is an illegitimate vision.

The bride is to make herself ready for that day. [11] As Larry Randolph puts it, "it is a perversion to think that Jesus will dress the bride before the wedding." Our assignment is clear, and the gifts are in place. And they are all expressions of Jesus Himself. But they are simple in purpose. Represent Jesus to the world!

The fire of God must rest in the souls of men. Christians without passion are almost as great a mystery as Christians without purpose. Apostolic teams carry fresh fire with divine purpose. They enlist men and women to God's dream, and in the process the church steps into her destiny.

Reprinted by permission from Bill Johnson. BJM.org

Support Footnotes:

1. There are three basic levels of Biblical doctrine. 1. There are doctrines that are essential to the Christian faith – For example, Jesus is the eternal Son of God. 2. Then there are doctrines that are important, but not essential – For example, how we use the gifts of the Spirit in a church service. 3. And finally, there are doctrines that are good but not essential – For example, the exact nature and timing of Christ's return.

2. This is never in addition to scriptures. Instead He unveils what is already there.

3. This is far from an absolute rule, as many leaders are in tune to what God is saying. However, some are more concerned with preserving past accomplishments over and above the advancement of the kingdom. This creates a weakness that tends to miss God's present word.

4. Ephesians 2:20

5. Acts 15

6. Acts 2:42

7. 2 Peter 1:12

8. 1 Corinthians 2:6

9. Ephesians 4:

10. Ephesians 5:27

11. Revelation 19:7

Apostolic Team Leadership

By Floyd McClung

Leadership in church is like steering a ship

One person cannot single-handedly sail a ship much less guide a fleet of ships! If our dream is a movement of simple churches, it will take a fluid team, moving from community to community to give it direction and input. Different communities will have members with a variety of gifts and strengths. As these men and women move among the church, they are connected organically rather than by policies or rules. It takes a crew of people to navigate, set the sails, clean the decks, and cook the food, etc., for such a movement. In fact, it will take many crews for many ships. That means team effort. It means creating a culture that encourages people to take initiative while learning to work with others to sail in the same direction. The role of each person in a team is vital for a ship to reach its destination. The responsibility of the helmsman is to point everyone in the same direction by involving the entire crew in the task at hand. Though each person on the crew has equal value, not everyone has the same responsibility. It is the captain/helmsman who steers the ship, who brings the crew together and who inspires each person on board to fulfill his or her duties. Others can do the same thing from their place of serving on the ship.

God has provided the gift of leadership to the church. This gift is mentioned in I Corinthians 12:28, and comes from the Greek word *kubernesis*, which literally means to steer or pilot a sea going vessel. While it is having a servant heart that qualifies a person for leadership, it is from words like *kubernesis* that we learn more about the responsibilities of those who step forward to lead. The same spiritual gift is referred to in Romans 12:8. In the Romans passage Paul uses the word *proistimi*, which is often translated *to govern* or to *give oversight*. We call this the gift of leadership. The exercise of this gift should not be to the exclusion of others leading as well, from their area of strength.

Three responsibilities of those who lead

Those that are given spiritual leadership are called to lead from underneath, not on top. The purpose of leadership is leading, but there are ways to do that that encourages simple church and ways that do not.

The exercise of spiritual authority differs according to the culture, gifts and personality of a person. While our culture will influence how we lead, it is our spiritual gifts that motivate what we do when we lead (teachers teach, evangelists evangelize, etc.). The spiritual authority of a teacher flows from right use of the Scriptures to persuade and convince, whereas the prophet warns about sin in people's lives and asks penetrating questions. Apostolic authority is derived from the faith and vision the person has for new pioneering efforts.

When Paul appeals to his authority as an apostle in correcting the believers in Corinth and Galatia, he is not thinking in terms of institutional or positional authority, but of his relationship to the believers as a spiritual father to them. He was not thinking in terms of hierarchy, but relationship and responsibility.

With these caveats and conditions in mind, it might be helpful to review the three primary responsibilities of those who lead in a local ecclesia. They are:

To guard:
- Against 'wolves' from within – Acts 20:28-30
- Against false doctrine – II Timothy 4:1-5
- Against deceivers – II John 7-11
- Against those who cause divisions – Romans 16:17- 18, Titus 3:10
- Against influences of sexual promiscuity – I Corinthians 5:9-13

To govern
- By caring for people – 'I have a special concern for church leaders. I know what it's like to be a leader, in on Christ's sufferings as well as the coming glory. Here's my concern: that you care for God's flock with all the diligence of a shepherd. Not because you have to, but because you want to please God. Not calculating what you can get out of it, but acting spontaneously. Not telling others what to do, but tenderly showing them the way. 'I Peter 5:1-5 The Message
- By teaching God's word – 'Elders who do their work well should be paid well, especially those who work hard at both preaching and teaching.' 1Timothy 5:17
- By correcting people in error – 'And the Lord's servant must not be quarrelsome but kindly to everyone, an apt teacher, patient, correcting opponents with gentleness. God may perhaps grant that they will repent and come to know the truth.' 2 Timothy 2:24
- By appointing other elders – Paul modeled and taught that elders appoint elders: 'I left you behind in Crete for this reason, so that you should put in order what remained to be done, and should appoint elders in every town, as I directed you.' Titus 1:5
- By making decisions – 'Command and teach these things…James spoke up: brothers, listen to me, it is my judgment…then the apostles and elders, with the whole church, decided…' I Timothy 4:11, Acts 15:13-22

To guide:
- By teaching the word – 'I solemnly urge you: proclaim the message; be persistent whether the time is favorable or unfavorable; convince, rebuke, and encourage, with the utmost patience in teaching… Now an overseer must be above reproach… able to teach…' 2 Timothy 4:1, 1 Timothy 3:2
- By discipling and equipping others to lead – 'And what you have heard from me through many witnesses entrust to faithful people who will be able to teach others as well…the gifts He gave were that some would be apostles, some prophets, some evangelists, some

pastors and teachers, to equip the saints for the work of ministry...' 2 Timothy 2:2, Ephesians 4:11

- By imparting passion for God's glory to others – 'It has always been my ambition to preach the gospel where Christ is not known...I urge you, brothers...to join me in my struggle...so that all nations might believe and obey Him– to the only wise God be glory forever through Jesus Christ! Amen.' Romans 15:20, 30, 16:26

Leadership styles need to change

By understanding and being able to adapt one's leadership style, the dexterity of a leader increases. Such a person recognizes that different circumstances and different cultures call for different approaches to how we lead. We should always be servants in our attitude and character, but that does not mean we should always lead in the same manner. Jesus' style of leadership when He entered the temple in outrage at the injustices done by the temple priests and money changes was directive. He told people what to do, to say the least:

"Jesus went straight to the Temple and threw out everyone who had set up shop, buying and selling. He kicked over the tables of loan sharks and the stalls of dove merchants..."[1]

But when the disciples were disputing about their place of honor in His Kingdom, Jesus was kind to them, coaching them in the right attitude and understanding. He welcomed little children to sit on His lap as He illustrated what it meant to be great in His kingdom.[2]

Many leaders make the mistake of thinking leadership is equal to being able to give directives. That is true if it is about task authority in the work place, or has to do with dealing with an emergency, such as airline pilot when there is a crisis, but it does not work that way with spiritual authority.

Simple church by its size and nature needs a coaching and supporting leadership style, not a directing or delegating manner of leading.

People have a natural style, according to their personality and culture and family upbringing. To not be aware of one's natural leadership style will in a person becoming a prisoner of their own personality. Self-awareness allows a mature person to adjust their leadership style to be able to serve people more effectively. My natural style is directive. Though I love to inspire people, I naturally lean towards accomplishing tasks and getting things done. I have both ingredients in me. It is how I was wired in my personality and makeup. While giving orders would enable me to be a good boss on a chain gang, it does not work well in inspiring people to be part of organic church. I have had to learn to adopt a coaching and supportive style of leading to be the servant leader I want to be. That has meant dying to myself, more times than I like to think about. But it

---

[1] Matthew 21: 12 The Message

[2] Luke 9:46-48

is the right thing to do. It has made me more effective, and more sensitive to others. It has allowed me to connect to people's hearts, and to coach and support those I lead. That doesn't take away the responsibility from others to be appropriately submissive, but it does make it easier for them!

Three kinds of authority

The dominant value in our culture today is freedom, usually accompanied by a big dose of cynicism and mistrust towards authority figures. Freedom is certainly the greatest value among post-moderns. It is not surprising, therefore, when young adults come to Christ that they struggle with being 'under authority,' particularly where there is no relationship with the one leading. Different generations in the church think differently about spiritual authority. While baby boomers in America have a history of challenging authority, preceding generations have questioned the need for any authority.

It is important to teach new believers the true nature of spiritual authority, i.e., servanthood, and the value of allowing themselves to be served by godly leaders. A father in the Lord, Tom Marshall, once wrote, 'We live in freedom only within the constraints of divine order in all of our relationships.' What is the divine order Tom wrote about, and how does it work?

We live in freedom only within the constraints of divine order in all of our relationships.

It seems the easiest way to deal with the issue of spiritual authority is to avoid it, or to shy away from a church that expects submission and accountability. The answer is not found in either extreme.

Being part of a simple church community includes submission to true spiritual authority. Some have erroneously taught that there is no need for spiritual authority in a simple church. In fact, submission to a person or a group of people who follow Jesus is a sign of spiritual maturity. That includes submitting to those who lead. However, there is a difference between submission and blind obedience. Obedience for the sake of obedience is not good. We can obey evil as well as good; we can obey man when we ought to obey God. Nor is obedience that produces conformity Biblical obedience. Obedience to spiritual leaders to gain acceptance feeds an unhealthy need for approval.

It was Tom Marshall that taught the difference between three different kinds of authority and the obedience that is appropriate to each one:[3]

1. Task authority
2. Teaching authority
3. Spiritual authority

_____

[3] Understanding Leadership, published by Regal

Submission to authority is to be exercised differently in each of these categories. Many of the problems regarding submission to leaders arise from not understanding these differences, or confusing their use and application. Let's take a look at each one of them.

Task authority

This is the simplest and easiest to understand. This kind of authority has to do with a job that is to be done. A person put in charge of a task or projects gives assignments and direction; under him or her is a group of people whose responsibility is to comply as promptly and efficiently as they can with the leader's instructions. It may or may not be appropriate to be 'creative' in fulfilling those responsibilities, or to take time to discuss the pros and cons of how to do the tasks assigned to us. In a work situation, sometimes we just need to be told what to do and do it. Kindly, of course!

Task authority is a legitimate and effective form of leadership. It wields a group of individuals into a single operating unit, and allows work to be done efficiently. The New Testament uses the Greek word *peitharcheo* (to obey a chief or ruler) to describe the obedience that is appropriate in response to those in charge in work situations.[4] This word is also used to describe the kind of obedience we are to give to government leaders.[5]

Teaching authority

When we consider submission to teaching authority, the purpose is much more than simply accomplishing a task. Teaching authority is not about something to be done, but truth to be learned. What is of greatest importance is that the one learning has the opportunity to internalize what is being taught and make it part of themselves. In these situations, unlike task authority, questions and answers, reasons, explanations and dealing with objections and misunderstandings are all part of the learning process. The Bible uses the Greek word *peitho* (to be persuaded) to describe the kind of response God is looking for to someone teaching the Bible. God wants obedience to truth *with understanding*. God wants us to respond from the heart. When the writer to the Hebrews says, 'obey your leaders,'[6] *peitho* is the word he uses. This passage is about teaching authority, not task or spiritual authority. Unfortunately, this passage is often quoted to support dominating leaders.

Teaching authority is based on the ability to persuade. We can convince others by appealing to God's word and to our story, with the aim that those who are taught have revelation for themselves. Paul said 'Therefore, knowing the fear of the Lord, we try to *persuade* others...'[7] Remember, 90% of what people remember and apply to their own lives comes through self-

---

[4] Titus 3:1
[5] Romans 13:1
[6] Hebrews 13:17
[7] 2 Corinthians 5:11

discovery. The teacher may teach, but there has to come a moment when the light goes on in a person's mind by the work of the Holy Spirit. Those 'aha' moments are what effective teachers live for.

Teaching authority is based on the ability to persuade...

Teaching authority in the church is often confused with task and spiritual authority. The pastor or leader who balks at being asked legitimate questions needs to understand the difference between the different types of authority. Applying task authority to teaching authority will not produce true learning. It actually does real harm by hindering true learning, and tempts people to say what is expected of them to stay in good standing with their leaders.

Spiritual authority

The aim of spiritual authority is different from teaching and task authority. The purpose of spiritual authority is not passive compliance, but for people to be motivated from the heart to Jesus commands. Those with spiritual authority have responsibilities to guard, govern and guide those they are given authority to lead. Their task is made easier if those they lead submit to their leadership. If their leadership is exercised in a mature manner they will seek to influence those they lead to hear God for themselves and obey Him from the heart. Spiritual growth happens through self-discovery, not imposed obedience. The purpose of spiritual authority is to inspire people to obey the commands of Jesus and to equip them for service, not command or control people's lives.

The purpose of spiritual authority is to inspire people to obey the commands of Jesus and to equip them for service, not command or control people's lives.

The essence of Christian maturity is a response from the heart to the will of God and to the direction given by spiritual leaders. If a person alters their behavior for any other reason than a loving response to God, e.g., to please their leaders, it is not obedience that pleases God nor does it make for healthy community.

The word for spiritual authority is *hupakouo*, 'to listen under'. This does not mean to listen under to others, but to listen from under the surface in one's heart, to hear God from deep within. Hearing and obeying God comes from under the surface, from deep within the heart. A spiritual leader may be a channel of God's Spirit motivating a person, but that person still needs to internalize what God is saying *to them*. Telling a person what they must do, and why they should not do something else, may get a leader the immediate results he or she wants, but it doesn't produce spiritual maturity in others.

The exercise of spiritual authority in relation to this kind of obedience should be aimed at helping a person discover the will of God by hearing God themselves. If people know how to hear God themselves, then spontaneously reproducing movements of simple churches is much more likely to happen. Top down spiritual authority stifles a movement, making the leaders the bottleneck through which all decision must pass. But when people hear God for themselves, they can get on with the work God has called all of us to do.

Perhaps it is helpful to summarize the nature of spiritual authority this way:
- Derived authority: this is the authority that has to do with earning the right to lead others. Derived authority is the consequence of godly character, wisdom, servanthood, humility, and recognition by others of a person's gifting and calling.
- Delegated authority: Delegated authority has its place. This is the authority given to a person by someone else. A person with delegated authority must also earn the right to lead people spiritually.
- Distributed authority: Distributed authority is given by Jesus to all those who know, love and obey Him. It is distributed to everyone in the church but is only effective if it is exercised in wisdom and humility. All those who are Christ-like share in the spiritual authority that Jesus gives to all His children.

There are conditions and qualifications in order for spiritual authority to be exercised properly. For example, the Bible is careful to distinguish between spiritual authority in the church and the authority of government leaders. The authority that Paul speaks about in Romans 13 is the *right* and *power* to enforce obedience by government officials. But the authority Peter speaks about in I Peter 5 is the *responsibility* spiritual leaders have to serve God's people with love and integrity, not the power to command or control those they lead.

Below are a list of scriptures that clarify the scope of authority spiritual leaders have been given by God, with clear conditions and restrictions:
- 1 Peter 5:1-5 Now as an elder myself and a witness of the sufferings of Christ, as well as one who shares in the glory to be revealed, I exhort the elders among you to tend the flock of God that is in your charge, exercising oversight, not under compulsion but willingly, as God would have you do it —not for sordid gain but eagerly. Do not lord it over those in your charge, but be examples to the flock. And when the chief shepherd appears, you will win the crown of glory that never fades away. In the same way, you who are younger must accept the authority of the elders. And all of you must clothe yourselves with humility in your dealings with one another, for God opposes the proud, but gives grace to the humble.
- 1 Timothy 5:17 Let the elders who rule well be considered worthy of double honor, especially those who labor in preaching and teaching.
- Titus 1:5 I left you behind in Crete for this reason, so that you should put in order what remained to be done, that you should appoint elders in every town, as I directed you.
- Acts 20:28-30 Keep watch over yourselves and over all the flock, of which the Holy Spirit has made you overseers, to shepherd the church of God that He obtained with the blood of His own Son. I know that after I have gone, savage wolves will come in among you, not sparing the flock. Some even from your own group will come distorting the truth in order

to entice the disciples to follow them. Therefore be alert, remembering that for three years I did not cease night or day to warn everyone with tears.

- <u>1 Thessalonians 5:12-13</u> And now, friends, we ask you to honor those leaders who work so hard for you, who have been given the responsibility of urging and guiding you in your obedience. Overwhelm them with appreciation and love!
- <u>Hebrews 13:17</u> Obey your leaders and submit to them. Let them do this with joy and not with sighing —for that would be harmful to you.
- <u>2 Timothy 4:1</u> In the presence of God and of Christ Jesus, who is to judge the living and the dead, and in view of His appearing and His kingdom, I solemnly urge you: proclaim the message; be persistent whether the time is favorable or unfavorable; convince, rebuke, and encourage, with the utmost patience in teaching.
- <u>2 Timothy 2:24</u> And the Lord's servant must not be quarrelsome but kindly to everyone, an apt teacher, patient, correcting opponents with gentleness. God may perhaps grant that they will repent and come to know the truth.

The real question concerning spiritual authority is not whether it exists, but how is it to be exercised and our response to it. Jesus made it abundantly clear that what He meant by authority was different from what the spiritual leaders of the day thought was their authority. Jesus defined authority as influencing people by serving them. If we serve we have influence, and if we influence people, we have spiritual authority in their lives.[8] In this way, authority is defined as the privilege of influencing others by exercising one's spiritual gifts in a Christ-like manner.

If we serve we have influence, and if we influence people, we have spiritual authority in their lives.

But how do we know if we are exercising spiritual authority the Jesus way did? The following 'authority' tests may help:

- Does it liberate or does it enslave?
- Does it lead to conformity or does it bring creativity?
- Does it bring dependence on man or God?
- Does it produce servility or servant hood?
- Does it depend on law or grace?
- Does it destroy or does it build a person's confidence?
- Does it equip people to function in faith or does it produce fear?
- Does it produce accountability or anarchy?
- Does it equip people for ministry or does it make them spectators to the ministries of others?

---

[8] Luke 22:26-27

Working in teams

I believe in teams. Teams are the most ideal way to pioneer new churches. Jesus sent out His disciples in small teams. Team ministry, even if it is just two or three functioning as the team, is the best way to lead a simple church or network of simple churches. When it comes to leadership in church communities, I believe in appointing elders who lead together under the leadership of a recognized team leader. Elders in the New Testament served as peers, and as peers, they cared for those in the community they served. I believe there was not just one pastor in the early church, as is common today.[9]

Just how does diversity on a team glorify God? There is a unique honor God receives from a team of people who subordinate their individual personalities and perspectives to work together. It requires each team member to work through his or her differences and fears. The glory God receives from a team learning to work in such a way is much greater than that which comes from one-person ministry models. Each team member has to go to the cross with each new challenge the team faces, dying to one's rights, preferences, mistrust, and old ways of relating.

Team members must speak truth to other members of the team. Biblical principles of speech must be followed, forgiveness given, and personal trust developed. Such trust is not based on performance or perfection, but on growing together in truth and grace.

Harnessing the gifts and callings of a group of strong-willed, gifted, and opinionated team members takes a major work of grace on the part of each member of the team. It can be done but not without the team getting involved in each other's lives, spouses included. It takes years of sacrifice, humility and continuing growth on the part of team members for it to work.

I am zealous about team ministry because working together in unity is just as important to God as what we do for him. How we treat each other, the depth and honesty of our relationships, is a reflection of our ultimate team leader, the Lord Jesus. If we are obedient followers of Christ, then we do ministry the way He modeled for us to do it.

Here are a few more reasons why teams are important at every level of church life, including leadership:

I believe in team ministry because it gets at the very heart of what it means to be and do simple church. We are the family of God, and as such we are designed and called by God to function in family units. One-man leadership models do not fulfill what we are taught in the Scriptures nor do they glorify God as much as leading in teams. Team leadership is a form of simple church; it is a group of men and women sharing their lives with each other in order to fulfill the great commission and the great commandment.

---

[9] See Team Ministry, by Dick Iverson, City Bible Publishing, for more on this topic.

I believe in team ministry because I believe the journey of building relationships is as important as the end goal.

I believe in team ministry because it helps us grow spiritually. It confronts our flesh patterns and exposes our brokenness. Working with a team of strong willed people pushes all our 'buttons'. When we work side by side, making decisions, initiating projects, supervising people, gathering small groups, discipling and evangelizing, acting and reacting to each other, we get to know one another at a deep level. We can't hide our flesh in the close spiritual quarters of team life. We have to open up our hearts to each other if we are to lead as a cohesive unit. Building such a team takes time and transparency. It means working through conflicts privately and openly as a team. We have to be willing to open our hearts to each other, learn to trust, be open to adjustment, and get used to humbling ourselves a lot. If you are willing to not get your way on occasion, to give in to others, die to the flesh often, then you will enjoy team ministry!

I believe in team ministry because I believe the journey of growing together is as important as the end goal. If all Father wants from us is results, He would have created robots. But He wants a spiritual family, not a well-oiled machine. He wants to build redeemed people into a community of connected hearts and lives, not just well run programs that reduce church life to watching others do their thing. Team ministry is contrary to Western, goal-oriented, individualistic ways of doing things. We have come to believe in the West that inefficiency is the sin against the Holy Ghost. If we run churches like corporations, and church programs like assembly lines, we can get results, but at what price?

We have come to believe in our Western culture that inefficiency is the sin against the Holy Ghost.

Modern evangelicals have mastered the techniques of building big churches, but is it New Testament churches they are building? They know how to manage church growth, but if someone took away the buildings and the programs, what would be left? Technique-oriented Christianity takes the soul out of church. And who needs a soulless Christianity in a postmodern world?

I believe in team ministry because it gets us to the soul of what church is all about. It is a way of building community by modeling church as family. It imparts to a church or movement the spirit and values of what it means to be ecclesia. God designed the church to function as a body, as a family, and naturally that requires genuine relationships. The organs of our body cannot function alone and fulfill their purpose. Nor can prophets or apostles or teachers function that way either. We are made to work together, 'individually members of one another.' [10]

I believe in team ministry because it calls us to deep levels of trust. Trust is vital for a healthy team. Absence of trust stems from an unwillingness to be vulnerable with one another, of taking time to work through differences and conflicts in an open and humble fashion. Team members who are not open with one another about their fears, their hurts and their sinful tendencies make it

---

[10] Romans 12:4-5

impossible to build a foundation of trust. Patrick Lencioni, in his brilliant book *The Five Dysfunctions of a Team*, defines trust as 'believing the other members of the team have my wellbeing in mind'. [11] Trust means I want people to help me by speaking into my area of ministry, my personal performance, and into the deep places of my heart. It means inviting and welcoming input from others on the team. Trust means I submit the important decisions I make to my co-workers in an open and direct manner.

Failure to build trust in a team is damaging because it hinders healthy debate, resulting in little or no heart-felt commitment to decisions, avoidance of mutual accountability, and getting sidetracked from our mission. Without trust a team cannot be a team, certainly not a team that reflects the love that exists between the Father, Son and Holy Spirit. A team without trust and mutual submission cannot experience the oneness of heart and mind that Paul calls the 'mind of Christ.' [12]

I believe in team ministry because it facilitates mutual accountability. I don't believe in top down accountability, where the leader is responsible to get everyone to toe the line. Mutual accountability is the natural result of uncensored debate, waiting on God together, healthy patterns of truth talking, meeting with 2-3 three others to share burdens and confess sins, and owning the decisions that are made by the team.

Having shared why I believe in team ministry, I also need to say very clearly that team ministry is not an end in itself. Below are several caveats about team ministry:

- Team ministry is not a panacea for all the challenges facing a simple church community. Don't idolize it or allow it to be a bottleneck to what God wants to do.

- When a team leader inherits team members, there is little likelihood the team will be able to function without a profound work of God in the team member's hearts.

- Team ministry can easily become a hindrance to the work we are called to do if the team becomes ingrown, particularly in cross-cultural efforts. Teams have to die and be reborn within the host culture to be effective in birthing church planting movements.

- Team leaders need to be empowered to make decisions in a crisis.

- The people we thought we were going to work with on a team may end up leaving the team - and God brings new people to join us. As the team forms around those who are proven and faithful, then the team becomes cohesive.

---

[11] Patrick Lencioni and Jossey Bass, *The Five Dysfunctions of a Team*, page 30.
[12] Philippians 2:1-3

Leadership and friendship

God said it is not good for a man to be alone.[13] In fact, God said this before Adam and Eve fell into sin. He does not want us to be alone in marriage or ministry. Friendship with loyal team members and a few close friends keeps us alive.

Jesus did not trust himself to the crowds, or the followers who came out of the crowds.[14] He knew the difference between a follower and a friend. And we must, as well.

A warning: crowds of people who want to speak into your life don't equal quality friendships. Having numerous people in your life can actually prevent the development of significant friendships. Jesus modeled the solution for us. He preached to the crowds, but He built His friendships with a few close associates. He invested most of His time and energy in the lives of those He worked most closely with, and they became His friends.[15] Jesus did not trust himself to the crowds, or the followers who came out of the crowds.[16] He knew the difference between a follower and a friend. And we must, as well.

We can and should build friendships with those we disciple. Every effective leader invests in the lives of a few people at a time. In-depth personal discipleship takes the sting out of the 'lonely leader' syndrome and creates a culture of friendship and community. As I write these words, I am thinking about a few friends I am investing in on a regular basis. I love hanging out with Nelis, Danny, Juergen and Monika, Matt and Elizabeth, Robert and Renee, Cobus and Marlize, Gawie and others in our movement. I trust them, and because I trust them, they are my friends. Discipleship involves friendship. You can't invest yourself in someone's life without becoming friends. Paul said, 'We loved you so much that we gave you not only God's good news, but our own lives, too.'[17]

This gets a little complicated for me personally because I wear multiple 'hats'. I am a spiritual leader, at times a project manager, and a friend. Because I am someone's project supervisor doesn't mean I have to be their best friend. But quality friendships must be part of a team if it's to be effective. There are times when I have to say no to a co-worker. When that happens I sometimes must take off my friend hat, and speak firmly about what I believe is right for everyone involved. That kind of talk is a test for friends and co-workers, but talking truth with each other is absolutely essential if we are to grow together as real friends and healthy co-workers.

Is this too difficult to do? Not for Jesus, and not for us either if we are willing to grow in the love and honesty it requires. There came a point in His relationship with His disciples where Jesus

---

[13] Genesis 2:18

[14] John 2:24 says, 'But Jesus did not commit Himself to them, because he knew all men...'

[15] John 15:15

[16] John 2:24 says, 'But Jesus did not commit Himself to them, because he knew all men...'

[17] 1 Thessalonians 2:8

called them friends.[18] That doesn't mean we have to be best friends with everyone we work with, but we should work towards good friendships with all those we work closely with. It's not possible if there is a lack of trust, but where there is humility and transparency, there will be growing friendships.

Apostolic teams

The primary difference between elders serving in a simple church community and an apostolic team, is vision and function. Elders serve by equipping and discipling the members of a church, or network of churches. Apostolic teams focus on pioneering amongst those who have not yet heard the good news. Apostolic teams give oversight to pioneering movements; they cultivate a set of core values that empower such a movement. Local church elders care for the flock under their charge; an apostolic team does the same thing but also cultivates a church planting culture of faith and vision for those who have never heard the good news.

Apostolic teams give oversight to pioneering movements; they cultivate a set of core values that empower such a movement.

Apostolic teams are focused. They are not satisfied with just overseeing the affairs of a local church. They burn with a desire to plant churches and reach those outside the influence of the gospel, especially those who have never heard of God's love in Christ. Apostolic teams are not apostolic because the team members are prophets or apostles. They are apostolic because they have a vision to plant churches where the gospel has not yet been proclaimed. You can be an apostle by gifting and fail to fulfill the purpose of your gift. Apostles are pioneers by calling, but they start new churches to fulfill their calling.

I have a very simple way of defining apostolic teams: they do what apostles did in the book of Acts. They preach the gospel, make disciples for Christ, plant churches and appoint and coach elders of local churches. They believe God for the impossible and pull down Satan's strongholds amongst the unreached and the unchurched. They suffer and sacrifice for what they believe in. In short, they win, gather, and multiply disciples and churches for Jesus – *especially* where people are unchurched and unreached.

You can talk about being apostolic until you're blue in the face, but if you don't plant and reproduce churches you're not apostolic.

Apostolic teams typically are linked to a leader with an apostolic gifting, although sometimes it is the combination of gifts on a team that makes it apostolic. The key to being an apostolic team is that you do the stuff early church apostles did! Paul said, '... I make it my ambition to preach the

---

[18] John 15:15

gospel, not where Christ has already been named...'[19] If your team has that ambition, you can function as an apostolic team.

You can talk about being apostolic until you're blue in the face, but if you don't plant and reproduce churches you're not apostolic. If you worship and fast together to hear God's plans and strategies for the lost, and then lay hands on those God appoints to be sent out,[20] you have the beginnings of an apostolic team.[21]

Death benefits: The price of leading a dry-bones army

Death benefits. I heard that term once when someone was trying to sell me insurance. I didn't buy the insurance, but I do buy the concept. I believe in death benefits. There are huge benefits to dying to self. One of the best ways to reap those benefits is to serve others. Leading in the simple church model I have presented in this book is not complicated.

Do you want to stand out? Then step down.

Leading in the 'dry bones' army of simple church is not complicated – if we are not doing it for recognition. That's the death benefit. We get to die to ourselves. Leading is not about us finding our ministry. It's about bringing life and hope to others. God calls people to lead for His sake, and the sake of others, not ours. Practically speaking, that means equipping and releasing those we serve into a life of 'skilled servant work'. Paul understood this concept of leading as a doorway to death benefits. He called it a 'sentence of death'. He described in this way:

> *"We felt like we'd been sent to death row that it was all over for us. As it turned out, it was the best thing that could have happened. Instead of trusting in our own strength or wits to get out of it, we were forced to trust God totally – not a bad idea since he's the God who raises the dead!"*

We are called to die. Not just once to sin, but as a way of life. By dying to 'our' rights, we find life. That means dying to our opinions, dying to the right to be understood, the right to be represented, the right to be loved, the right to be treated justly, and all our other rights. Very few leaders understand this truth. They strive to find their role, their ministry, how they fit on the team, etc. It is sad to watch men and women strive to keep what they have to give up anyway if they are to be part of God's mission. Jim Elliot wrote in his journal, 'He is no fool who gives up what he cannot keep to gain what he cannot lose.'

It would be easy at this point to go on without considering the implications of this truth. But would you mind pausing for a moment and reflecting with me on God's invitation to die? It is an

---

[19] Romans 15:20

[20] A study of the missionary journeys of Paul makes it abundantly clear that the one thing he consistently accomplished was the preaching of the gospel and the establishing of new churches.

[21] Acts 13:1-3

invitation. We are not forced to live like this. We don't have to serve others. We can hide in the dry bones army and not volunteer. We can be a super star type leader and avoid dying to self. We can go to heaven without getting to this place in our walk with God. Serving is key to the new way of doing church. The old way is about rights, about position, about 'running the church.' But to be part of the dry bones army we learn to live for His glory, not ours. That means serving from underneath, not on top.

Paul accepted being sent to 'death row' because he learned that it put him in a place where he had to trust God. As you take this time to pray about the 'death benefits' in this new way of doing church, consider the following:

- Death benefits means giving up control over my time. Am I willing to make a commitment to set aside time each day to read God's word and pray? Not just driving time, or walking around the house prayer time, but time I give up something else to be alone with Jesus?

- Death benefits means purity. Am I willing to make a pledge to God and others to live a life of sexual and moral purity, including the kinds of music I listen to and the movies I watch? Will I stay away from all forms of pornography, including the Internet?

- Death benefits means dying to my rights. Am I willing to give up all personal rights?

- Death benefits means accountability to others. Am I willing to invite others to speak into the important decisions of my life before I make them? That includes decisions that will affect my church community and co-workers? Am I willing to be known in areas of personal holiness?

- Death benefits includes being committed and loyal to a small community of people that invest in one another's lives through personal discipleship and accountability – are you willing to accept this death benefit in the Kingdom of God?

- Death benefits include telling people about Jesus without regard to personal reputation or ambition. Am I willing to share Jesus with my neighbors, family members and others in my sphere of influence a way of life?

- Death benefits mean embracing sacrifice and suffering. Am I willing to live sacrificially, even suffer for Him so others can hear about Jesus? Am I willing to give up my country, my comfort, what is familiar, so others can know Jesus?

Used by permission Floyd & Sally McClung

THE BIG "WHY" OF MICRO-CHURCHES: HOW THEY HELP FULFILL THE PURPOSE OF GOD

For Their own glory, God the Father, God the Son, and God the Holy Spirit created, and then redeemed through Christ, a covenantal spiritual Family, made up of "new creation" sons/daughters, to advance God's Kingdom on earth. God self-disclosed as a Family of Three yet One and therefore must build His Kingdom relationally in and through Family. The glory of God, centrality and supremacy of Christ, covenant & kingdom, Father & Family, great commission to disciple the nations, are the core values and purpose of the Trinity. All reality and truth flows from the Trinity. Therefore, as sons/daughters we get to enjoy these same heart motives, and live in Father's epic story, His primary vision and mission.

Father is bringing many sons/daughters to glory in the context of family. Hebrews 2:20 He is transforming His sons/daughters into the likeness of Christ. Romans 8. We are called to make disciples who make disciples in the setting of small families on mission. Matthew 28:18-20 No one can be healed or grow without consistent relational love, affection, and joy. Small spiritual families on mission are a key strategy Christ employs to heal the broken hearted, mature His sons/daughters, and to reach the lost, placing them in loving families. They are a great setting for people to receive support as they establish faith-goals which appropriate the grace of God. Micro-Church families offer a safe environment to discover one's gifts and calling, and to grow as a leader. Micro-Church Families on Mission also help to advance Christ's Kingdom in all seven spheres of influence in society: 1.) Marriage & Family, 2.) Religion & Church, 3.) Marketplace, 4.) Education, 5.) Media, 6.) Arts, 7.) Civil Government & Social Services.

THE BIG "WHY'S"

 ➤ Bringing many sons/daughters to glory in the context of family
 ➤ Transformation into the likeness of Christ.
 ➤ Making disciples who make disciples
 ➤ Raising up and training leaders
 ➤ Healing the broken hearted
 ➤ Loving family which proactively enables sons/daughters to mature
 ➤ Reaching the lost
 ➤ Generational transfer
 ➤ Impacting neighborhoods & communities
 ➤ Bringing the kingdom in the seven spheres of influence: 1.) Marriage & Family, 2.) Religion & Church, 3.) Marketplace, 4.) Education, 5.) Media, 6.) Arts, 7.) Civil Government & Social Services

Why Start, Grow, And Multiply Micro-Church Families?

1. Both Moses in the Old Testament and Jesus in the New Testament chose the small group model and format (twelve disciples) as their method of making disciples, caring for people, and spreading and reproducing the Life and ways of God.

2. They are the most effective form of evangelism. An authentic loving community is the most convincing argument for the reality of God and reveals the basic meaning of life. John 17:20-23

3. Multiplying Micro-Church Families are the most effective structure to facilitate both the quality and quantity of connected caring relationships. The purpose of life is love. Kingdom Families create the very best organic setting for the highest quality of love, in the most efficient way, with the greatest number of people.

4. They create the best setting for mentoring and training people at the heart and life level because the life of Christ is more "caught" than taught. Consistent, loving, transparent relationships allow hidden weaknesses and sins to come into the light, so they can be eliminated and replaced with the attributes of Christ.

5. They are the best way to develop leaders because everyone is expected to contribute that which Christ has given to them and to experiment with their gifts and callings.

6. They are the most effective way to enable the participation and ministry of every member.

7. They have the most flexibility and the quickest response time for providing pastoral and practical care among the members.

8. They can easily infiltrate every human situation and setting.

9. They allow "church" to take place all the time, everywhere, and through everyone.

10. They are the only "structure" that can absorb a massive influx of people in a short amount of time when genuine revival occurs.

11. They allow the church to grow even during persecution.

12. No building costs.

NOTES:

WHAT'S & HOW'S OF MICRO-CHURCHES: A SMALL SPIRITUAL FAMILY ON MISSION

What is a Micro-Church Family on Mission and why are they important in the Kingdom of God? What are the essentials for being a healthy Micro-Church family? What are the stages of growth in the life of a micro-church? How do children and youth fit into the micro-church family? What are DNA Groups? How important is inner-healing and deliverance to the life of the small spiritual family? We will constantly encourage ongoing sensitivity to the voice of God and the leadership of the Holy Spirit. That is because there is no formula or program that will ever replace the Person(s) of the Trinity, the Presence of God, and the ongoing leadership and empowerment of the Holy Spirit. Everything in the kingdom is supernatural, especially starting and multiplying a Micro-Church Family on Mission.

WHAT IS A MICRO-CHURCH FAMILY ON MISSION?

Micro = Small (between 5 and 25)

Church (Ekklesia) = legitimate sons & citizens in God's Kingdom authorized to initiate the intent of the King on earth, making disciples and displacing hell with heaven.

Family = sons/daughters of Father, covenantally connected in Jesus Christ: mind, heart, and lifestyle. Families exchange God's life, love, affection, joy, wisdom, revelation, and power through the Holy Spirit.

On Mission – sent out by God Himself, with His authority, to demonstrate and share the gospel to a lost and dying world.

MICRO-CHURCH FAMILIES: AN INTRODUCTION & OVERVIEW

"So whether you eat or drink or whatever you do, do it all for the glory of God."1 Corinthians 10:31

Acts 2:42-47, 4:32-37; Romans 16:5; Matthew 6:10, 33

Introduction:

God has always longed to have a people whose heart motives, passions, and commitments accurately reflect and reveal His nature, a holy people devoted to expanding His glory in the nations. He wants a people who, like King David in the Old Testament, have "a heart after God". This will occur when God's people have a profound revelation and experience of Father's intense mercy, love and grace. Father wants a people committed to doing His will, His way, by His Spirit, for His glory. He wants to pour out His fatherly emotions toward us as His children even when we are immature and sinful. When the impact of God's love demonstrated in the cross and shed blood of Jesus touches us in the core of our being, and Father has convinced our minds, won our hearts, and healed our inner life, God's family will reciprocate that love back to Him. His sons and daughters will enjoy a pleasure in glorifying Father that ultimately reforms the church and brings kingdom transformation to society.

There is immense pleasure in a self-denying, self-sacrificing love for God and others. Losing our lives really does result in the gaining of our lives. Only a people who have died to themselves and live unto God can fully enjoy this reality. It will take a people who deny themselves, pick up their crosses and follow Jesus completely who will be used of God as "points of release" for revival, reformation, and transformation. Only those committed to a love which is self-sacrificing can understand what it means to fellowship in the sufferings of Christ. The kind of Micro-Church Families (Missional Kingdom Families) we have been assigned to start and multiply are to promote a high degree of Christ's life and love, so that they positively impact the church and help to transform cities one person at a time. However, this is to be done without being "religious", programmatic, or exclusive. On the other hand, because we have an assignment to be pioneers and change agents, we must not compromise on our expectations. We will battle in prayer and personally encourage and disciple anyone who is willing to respond to Christ with their whole hearts, but we cannot enable lukewarm Christianity or allow ourselves to be mixed with the spirit of the world. We will have to humbly and wisely live with the tensions that come from wanting both quality and quantity.

Because the church worldwide is struggling in its mission to be "salt and light" in the world, and in some areas is even losing ground both in quantity and quality, we cannot afford slow incremental progress. The extreme suffering among youth, poor, and lost, and the acceleration of evil requires a rapid and radical invasion of God's glory. We must have a catalytic explosion, a massive outpouring of God's manifest presence, love, mercy, grace, wisdom, power, compassion and justice. This dynamic eternal life of God (the wine of the Holy Spirit) must be conducted through an equally dynamic Biblical conduit (wineskin) in order to maximize and preserve the impact. God's Divine Order (His will and ways) must be the conduit of God's Divine Life (His Holy Spirit). God is a Father, Son, and Spirit, so the only wineskins capable of revealing who He is and what His is like are healthy natural and spiritual families. Apostolically and prophetically led international spiritual families or tribes are the new yet ancient Biblical human agency for expanding God's glory in the nations in a rapid and qualitative way. When an apostolic people come into profound unity around Father's love and glory in the nations, the supremacy and centrality of Christ as Lord over all, in the advancing of God's Kingdom in every area of life, and will totally abandon themselves for these values and purposes, we will witness a staggering expansion of God's Kingdom and glory resulting in the salvation of millions and the transformation of culture.

The starting and multiplying of Micro-Church Families must occur under these heart motives in order to receive the full enabling presence and power of the Holy Spirit. It takes the supernatural Life of Christ to sustain Christ-centered relationships. It is almost as if a warning label should be attached to any document which tries to explain or instruct people about Kingdom Families. **Warning: Do not attempt to start, grow, or multiply Micro-Church Families as another church program or evangelistic strategy. Micro-Church Families will only work to the degree each individual and the group as a whole have died to themselves and are governed and empowered by the indwelling Lord, Jesus Christ, and His Word by the Holy Spirit.**

One more key point must be made regarding the reason for writing down the purposes, expectations, and commitments of Micro-Church Families. All of the contents included in this overview should be understood as instructions on "how to love God and people in a way that advances Christ's Kingdom." It should not be viewed as a rule book or religious document that has to be mechanically applied. This overview is to help coach people in the "science and art" of relationships and love. Every requirement or recommendation has Biblical wisdom, truth or reasoning, with the ultimate intention that the greatest amount of love occurs among the most people in the highest quality way in the least amount of time. Because people are suffering and dying, our mission is time sensitive. Truth exists for love. So many people come from dysfunctional families and/or unhealthy churches (or no church background at all) that it takes clear teaching and constant coaching to help people walk in God's ways of truth and love combined. Most people have very little understanding as to the etiquette of relationships and group life within the context and government of a healthy spiritual family. The "spirit" of this document is to promote the life and love of Christ within individuals and Micro-Church Families, and should in no way be used legalistically, so that people are judged or rejected. Micro-Church Families should be the safest, most loving, life-giving settings on earth. But true safety involves accountability and discipline along with unconditional affection and love, just like a healthy family. Bottom line, Micro-Church Families should feel as much like heaven on earth as possible!

The key to advancing the Kingdom of God on earth is for those who love and follow Christ to exchange His life between each other in the context of heart connected Christ-centered relationships. Because the Kingdom of God involves coming under the Lordship of Christ in every sphere of life, those in Micro-Church Families learn to submit to the Christ in one another and assist each other to follow Christ completely.

1. **Definition:** A Micro-Church Family is made up of at least five people but no more than twenty-five (one of whom is a qualified leader and the other one is their assistant) who connect around the Lordship and Person of Christ and His manifest presence and glory (as a lifestyle, plus meet once a week minimum) for the purpose of enabling one another to be radical disciples of Christ, reach the lost, advance the Kingdom of God in all areas of life in their cities/communities, and multiply more Micro-Church Families. Christ, God's manifest presence and glory, spreading the love of the Father by the Holy Spirit, and the advancing of Christ's Kingdom are the passions and purpose of a Micro-Church Family.

   A. Micro-Church Families are a spiritual family – people connected covenantally heart-to-heart around Christ in order to advance His kingdom. I Corinthians 4:15-17; Ephesians 3:14

   B. Micro-Church Families are a group of friends unified around Christ's love and mission. Matthew 11:19; John 15:12-17

   C. Micro-Church Families are a healing community that prays for the sick, counsels the confused, carries out inner healing, sets people free from curses and demonic bondage, and creates such an atmosphere of acceptance and love that rejection and insecurities are displaced automatically over time. James 5:16; Matthew 10:1, 8

   D. Micro-Church Families are a training and equipping center, a safe setting for people to practice leadership, management, preaching, teaching, creative ministry, spiritual gifts, and all forms of servanthood. Matthew 28:18-20

   E. Micro-Church Families are a missionary team and spiritual army – a flexible, spontaneous, organized platoon capable of reaching those who do not follow Christ and are not in a spiritual family. They are dedicated to seeking and saving the lost, delivering people from demonic bondage, doing justice, and serving youth, poor, widow, orphan, and alien. Luke 19:10; Ephesians 6:10-18

F. Micro-Church Families are a lifestyle of deep, intentional, meaningful relationships that connect any time and place with an ultimate goal to reach lost people, and transform communities through Christ and the Kingdom of God. Acts 2:42-47, 4:32-35.

2. **Perspective:** For Micro-Church Families to be viewed and experienced as the primary context for church life, it will take a significant paradigm shift in the hearts and minds of people. Being in a true "Book of Acts" Micro-Church Family (house church) is really a major shift of perspective, values and lifestyle. Usually this does not occur unless there is

- High degrees of discontentment, dissatisfaction, and internal and external pain and pressure
- High degrees of promise and pleasure that come from both the manifest presence of Christ and authentic covenant love between the members
- A willingness to make the sacrifices necessary to reach the lost and transform communities

God is transitioning the church in the West. He is raising up forerunners or "early adopters" who will help to pioneer what C. Peter Wagner calls "the new apostolic paradigm/reformation". The word "apostle" means "sent ones". It is a military term used in the Bible to describe certain individuals and those they lead who have been mandated and empowered by the King to expand His kingdom through new pioneering efforts in families, church, business, civil government, and all of society. An apostolic people will know themselves as weak and dependent for they will have been broken and humbled by God. This is the necessary backdrop for God to display His love, wisdom, power, and glory. He will share His glory with no other. Ephesians 4:7-13

Apostolic people are merciful having themselves been saved through the shed blood and sacrificial death of Christ. They also place their faith in God's grace because it is His power, provision, and goodness alone that sustains all creation.

Apostolic people embrace a set of core values that act as the foundation for their life together and guide their mission. Here are some essential apostolic core values:

A. Apostolic people don't live for themselves but for the glory and pleasure of God. Integrity, humility, holiness and the fear of the Lord are the foundational attributes of their character. They live to see God's glory and presence manifested in the nations, so that He will be worshipped universally. 2 Corinthians 5:9; Revelation 14:7; Psalm 96:3; 2 Corinthians 5:14-15

B. Apostolic people are totally empowered by the Life of Christ within them versus their own strength. Abiding in Christ and His Word is a 24/7 lifestyle. Totally trusting and depending on Christ is evidenced by a life of prayer and fasting. They put a high value on faith and obedience to Christ. John 15:1-17; Colossians 1:27; Ephesians 3:17; Luke 17:21

C. Apostolic people receive their identity, worth, and approval solely from their heavenly Father and not from people, success, or the world. John 1:10-13; Ephesians 1:3-14

D. Apostolic people are committed to bringing everything into divine order, under the Lordship of Christ: their personal lives, marriages & families, churches, businesses, and civil governments. Luke 6:46-49; Ephesians 5:21-6:9

E. Apostolic people submit first to the objective truth of the Word and also to the Christ living inside other believers, especially the leaders and members of their spiritual family. They understand that Christ mediates His grace through God-ordained and appointed human vessels like natural and spiritual parents/leaders. Matthew 4:4; Hebrews 13:17; 1 Peter 5:1-6

F. Apostolic people deeply value intentional committed relationships. They understand the power of being connected in heart and mind, and to "have all things in common" as in the early church. God's glory is poured out to create unity, so the world will be able to see and experience Father's love through His authentic family. Thus, they are active contributing members of a spiritual family. Church is a 24/7 family lifestyle carried out at work and in homes, not only in church buildings and programs. Starting, growing, and multiplying house churches is the agenda of all apostolic people because that is the Biblical strategy capable of allowing relational intimacy but expandable enough to absorb a large surge of new believers. Ephesians 2:21, 4:3; John 17:20-26; 1 John 4:7-21

G. Apostolic people are highly committed, sold out, and abandoned for the expansion of Christ's Lordship, glory, and kingdom. This is evidenced in their use of time, energy, and money. Lifestyles are radically adjusted and simplified for the sake of the gospel. Tithing, for example, is a beginning level spiritual discipline. Matthew 6:33, 10:32-39; Matthew 6:21; Malachi 3:10

H. Apostolic people are aggressive spiritual warriors who work in harmony with other members of a spiritual "army". They are committed to destroying the works of the evil one, to seek and save the lost, to be used as vessels for healing and deliverance, to make disciples of all nations, to plant and multiply house churches, to start kingdom businesses, to be godly citizens who insist on kingdom values, and to bring all of society under Christ and His ways. Everyone is a minister possessing spiritual gifts and a "call" from God. They fight for justice and demonstrate God's love and compassion to youth, poor, oppressed, and unreached people. They are ground taking pioneers who are constantly expanding the boundary lines of heaven on earth. Matthew 10:1-42; Ephesians 6:10-20; I John 3:8

I. Apostolic people live in the reality of eternity, the judgment seat of Christ, eternal reward, the spiritual realm and the supernatural, and have as their point of reference and resource "the heavenly realm", God's "throne of mercy and grace". They believe that all the spiritual gifts described in the Bible are for today, and they exercise these gifts to build up the body of Christ and to reach the lost. Signs, wonders, and miracles are expected and normative, though not necessarily predictable. Ephesians 1:3, 2:6, 3:23-25; Matthew 5:3-12; 2 Corinthians 5:9-10; Roman 15:18-19; John 14:12-14; 2 Corinthians 12:12

J. Apostolic people understand that love means self-sacrifice and inconveniencing themselves as servants for the sake of others. Father may even ask them to love so extremely that it might involve risking their lives or even dying in order to reach other's for Christ and bring them into the family of God. Luke 14:25-35; Revelation 12:11-12; Philippians 1:20-21, 2:1-11

3. **Accountability:** Each Micro-Church Family will enjoy the benefits of being connected with and accountable to the local elders of their church. The Micro-Church Families in each city will be relationally connected to one another through the local elders, and they will also be connected to the other Micro-Church Families in their city.

4. **Standards:** What are the expectations for being an "official" Micro-Church Family?

A. There is a trained, approved, qualified and commissioned Micro-Church Family leader who is in unity with and submission to the values, vision, strategies, and leadership of the elders who lead their local church. There is a qualified assistant leader who functions as a covenant partner and co-laborer with the Micro-Church Family leader. Besides evidencing the qualifications described in the New Testament for elders and deacons I Timothy 3:1-13; Titus 1:5-9, these leaders have demonstrated that they are "life-giving" people John 7:38. They have consistently conducted the Life of Christ in such a way that others have come into a relationship with Christ as Lord and are enthusiastic followers of Christ themselves. A person who conducts the Life of Christ consistently has a way of helping people experience the fruit of the Spirit Galatians5:22-23, the wisdom of the Spirit Ephesians 1:17-18, and the power of the Spirit, Acts 1:8, and makes sure that God gets all the glory.

The Micro-Church Family leader accepts responsibility (in part) for the spiritual well-being of its members, making sure that they are growing as disciples of Christ. Matthew 28:18-20; 2 Timothy 2:2

i. The Micro-Church Family leader encourages, trains, and facilitates outreach, evangelism, and ministry among its members.

ii. The Micro-Church Family leader and its members are actively raising up new leaders who can plant, grow and multiply new Kingdom Families.

iii. There are at least three other members who are in unity with the Micro-Church Family leader around Christ and His Kingdom (one of whom is the assistant leader), and the values, vision and leadership of their family-of-churches (Jesus Tribe).

iv.   The Micro-Church Family leaders and members give tithes and offerings to God through their local church.

5. **Expectations and qualifications of Micro-Church Family leaders:**

C. They are born again Christians, baptized in the Holy Spirit, radical followers of Christ, with consistent evidence of the fruit of the Holy Spirit in attitude, actions, and impact in other people's lives. They actively and consistently conduct the Life of Christ (fruit, wisdom, and power of Holy Spirit) into other people to such a degree that there is obvious impact. They are life-giving, loving, serving, positive, faith-filled people.

D. They meet the Biblical qualifications for an elder in the area of character, personal life, marriage, and family management, with proven integrity and fruitfulness in their families, church, neighborhoods, workplace, and community. Titus 1:5-9; 1 Timothy3:1-13 They evidence godly character such as truthfulness, honesty, integrity, obedient to corporate and civil laws. They properly steward their body in the following ways: sexual purity, no illegal drug usage, does not use alcohol as means of escape (such as relaxant) to get high or intoxicated, not gluttonous, etc. Their relationships are healthy and in divine order with parents, children, spouse, employers, and civil authorities.

E. They evidence good stewardship in the areas of money (including tithing), time, and talents.

F. They demonstrate order and management in the care and maintenance of living space, automobiles, etc.

G. They have appropriate relational and "people" skills, such as communication (listening and talking), conflict resolution, gentleness, kindness, patience, tactfulness, ability to correct, confront, and rebuke in a way that is respectful, gentle and restorative.

H. They have been able to consistently apply and incorporate spiritual disciplines into their life. 1 Timothy 4:7. Some spiritual disciplines include: prayer, worship, evangelism, serving, fasting, silence & solitude, learning the Bible with application/obedience, frugality, confidentiality, doing acts of service secretly, confession, submission.

I. They have the ability to interpret, understand, apply, and teach the Word of God as given to us in the Bible.

J. They have the ability to provide the beginning levels of pastoral care to members of the house church: prayer, listening, inner healing, deliverance, godly counsel, encouragement, comfort, exhortation.

K. They have the basic leadership and management skills necessary to rally people, keep unity, resolve conflict, equip others for ministry and leadership, facilitate Kingdom Family gatherings, and reach mutual ministry and mission goals together. They have the capacity to initiate love, relationships, ministry, and outreach.

L. They have the understanding and ability to make good decisions based first upon objective truth like: Word of God, godly counsel from mature believers, utilizing wisdom, research, and common sense, taking into consideration circumstances, resources, limitations and opportunities, pros and cons, risks versus rewards. And secondarily by utilizing the subjective imputes of the Holy Spirit: such as the inner intuitive "small voice" of the Lord, the prophetic indicators and revelations such as dreams, visions, etc.

M. They are willing and able to facilitate discipleship, evangelism, kingdom advancing ministries, and house church multiplication with the members of their Kingdom Family.

N. They accept responsibility (in partnership with the local elders) for the spiritual well-being of the members of the Kingdom Family, keeping watch over them, knowing that they will give an account before God. Hebrews 13:17

O. They pray for and connect with their members regularly throughout the week.

P. They are constant learners who participate in the regular training and support which comes from the other Kingdom Family leaders, local elders, and apostolic team.

Q. They are in unity with and in submission to the agreed upon values, vision, strategies, and leadership of their family-of-churches (Jesus Tribe).

R. They participate in the expansion of the kingdom by giving tithes and offerings to God through their local church.

6. **Commitments** and **expectations** of Micro-Church Family members: These commitments and expectations should be presented in writing and discussed with each person at the beginning of their involvement in the Micro-Church Family. They should also be reviewed regularly with all the members. One becomes a member of a Micro-Church Family and local church by becoming son or daughter of Father through Christ by the Holy Spirit and becoming an active member of a Micro-Church Family and local church. **Remember: These commitments and expectations are not rules and regulations. They are to be used as helpful guidelines and principles which enable us to love Christ, one another and unbelievers more effectively.**

A. We are sincerely seeking to know God through Christ unto the end that we become born again Christians, Spirit-filled, radical disciples of Christ. By joining the Micro-Church Family, we are inviting the leaders and other members to help us follow Christ and grow into Christ's likeness.

B. We are in unity with and submission to the values, vision, strategies, and expectations of the leaders of this Micro-Church Family, and the local elders.

C. We attend and participate weekly in the life and activities of the Micro-Church Family, and regularly attend the celebrations and training of our local church. We honor and worship God and help advance His kingdom by giving tithes and offerings through our local church.

D. We contribute to the discipleship of the other members in the Micro-Church Family, engage in evangelistic outreach, and help to advance the Kingdom of God in the settings and with the people God has placed them. We enthusiastically embrace the multiplication of our Micro-Church Family.

E. We are committed to grace affirmation: (Unconditional Love, Agape Love) Colossians 3:5-14 *"I will choose to love you, up build you, and accept you, my brothers and sisters, no matter what you say or do. I will choose to love you in whatever form you come. There is nothing you have done or will do that will make me stop loving you. I may not agree with your actions, but I will love you as a person and do all I can to hold you up in God's affirming love."*

F. We are committed to honesty: Ephesians 4:25-32 *"I will not hide from you what I feel about you or coming from you, good or bad, but I will see, in the timing of the Spirit, to deal openly and directly with you in a loving and forgiving way so that you are affirmed when in need, and so that our frustration with each other does not become bitterness. I will try to mirror back to you what I am hearing you say and feel. If this means risking pain, realizing it is in 'speaking the truth in love' that we grow up in every way into Christ who is the head, then I will take the risk. I will try to express this honesty in a sensitive and controlled manner and to meter it, according to what I perceive the circumstances to be."* Ephesians 4:15

G. We are committed to openness: Romans 7:15-25 *"I will try to strive to become a more open person, disclosing my feelings, my struggles, my joys and my hurts to you as well as I am able. The degree to which I do so implies that I cannot make it without you. This is to affirm your worth to me as a person. In other words, I need you!"*

H. We are committed to prayer and fasting: 2 Thessalonians 1:11-12 *"I commit to pray for you in some regular fashion, believing that our caring Father wishes His children to pray for one another and ask Him for the blessings we all need. I will not be merely a passive listener. Rather, I choose to be a spiritual participant, willing to enter into your situation and prayerfully helping to shoulder your burden."*

I. We are committed to sensitivity: John 4:1-29 *"Even as I desire to be known and understood by you, I commit to be sensitive to you and your needs to the best of my ability. I will try to hear you, see you, and feel where you are and to draw you out of the pit of discouragement or withdrawal. I will earnestly avoid giving 'simplistic' answers to the difficult situations you may find yourself in."*

J. We are committed to availability: Acts 2:43-47 *"Here I am if you need me. Anything I have--time, energy, insight, possessions--is at your disposal, if you need it, to the limit of my resources."*

K. We are committed to confidentiality: Proverbs 10:19; 11:9,13; 12:23; 13:3; 15:4; 18:6-8 *"I will keep whatever is shared within the confines of the Micro-Church Family in order to provide the atmosphere of trust necessary for openness. I understand, however, that this confidentiality does not prohibit my Micro-Church Family leader from sharing either verbally or in written form any pertinent information with the elders. I understand that Micro-Church Family leaders function under pastoral/elder oversight, having delegated authority as an extension of the pastoral care ministry of this congregation. As a result, they are accountable to the elder(s) of this church, who are themselves accountable to others in ministry and the Chief Shepherd, Jesus Christ, my Lord. "* Hebrews 13:17

L. We are committed to accountability, transparency, and confession of sin: Ezekiel 3:16-21 and Matthew 18:12-30. The Bible calls this "fellowshipping in the light". I John 1:5-10 *"I commit to growth, maturity and discipleship using the Bible and other equipping materials that each of the Micro-Church Family in our church are progressing through as part of their equipping times, and in doing so will make myself accountable weekly to my accountability partner in the Micro-Church Family. I give you the right to question, confront, and challenge me in love when I seem to be falling in any aspect of my life under God--family, devotions, general spiritual growth, etc. I trust you to be in the Spirit and led of Him when you do so. I need your correction and reproof so that I may ever better fulfill God-given ministry among you. I will try not to be defensive."* Proverbs 12:1, 15; 13:10, 18

M. We are committed to following the Biblical process of conflict resolution. Matthew 18, Galatians 6:1-5 *"We will not triangulate, gossip, or slander our brothers or sisters in Christ. We will deal with offenses with truth and love. Disagreements or conflicts should in no way divide our hearts or justify a breech in our relationship."*

N. We are committed to time regularity: Luke 9:57-62 *"I will regard the regular time which my Micro-Church Family spends together weekly as time under the disciplining hand of Jesus in our midst. I will not grieve the Spirit or hinder His work in the lives of my brothers and sisters by my absence, except in an emergency. By His permission, and through prayer alone, will I consider being absent. If I am unable to attend for any reason, out of consideration I will call my Micro-Church Family leader in order that the Micro-Church Family members may know why I am absent, will be able to pray for me, and will not worry about me."*

O. We are committed to outreach: Matthew 25:31-46 *"I will find ways to sacrifice myself for those outside our Kingdom Family and local church in the same way that I have committed to sacrifice myself for you, my brothers and sisters. I will network in prayer and relationships with my fellow Micro-Church Family members to bring two or more unbelievers or unchurched friends to my Micro-Church Family outreach gatherings during the course of its life. I will do it in Jesus' Name so that others are added to the Kingdom of God in His love. I will join and/or lead a DNA Group because that is one of the most effective strategies for discipleship and evangelism."* (See chapter entitled "DNA Groups")

7. **Discipleship and Leadership Development track** for each Micro-Church Family member (the 5 C's): We will help each other establish and achieve faith goals in the 5 C's using the 4 Dynamics of transformation (instruction, relational, experiential, and spiritual).

    A. **Christ**: Helping each member know, love and experience Father through Christ. To know and experience the joyful reality of being a child of God. To help each member become a lover and follower of Christ who advances His kingdom in every area of life. This involves helping each member know and experience Christ through His written Word, and to enjoy praise, prayer and worship as a lifestyle. It includes teaching people to be "prophetic", knowing how to hear and obey God's objective and subjective voice. It means being a "priestly" people who minister to the Lord and intercede for others. And it involves being a "kingly" or "apostolic" people who proactively advance Christ's Kingdom and facilitate divine order (God's will and ways) in all of life.

    B. **Community**: Helping each member connect organically and covenantally (head to head, heart to heart, hand to hand, house to house) with the family of God. This involves learning the ways of forgiveness, mercy, and Biblical conflict resolution. It involves the proper use of the tongue for blessing, affirming, and prayer. It is the ability to exchange the life and love of Christ organically 24/7.

    C. **Character**: Helping each member to become like Christ in their heart motives, attitudes, personal integrity, and actions.

    D. **Call**: Helping each member discover their calling from God, their spiritual gifts and talents, their destinies, ministries and purpose in life.

    E. **Competence**: Helping each member to gain the skills, abilities, and resources they need to carry out their life's purpose and mission.

8. The **essential activities** of a Micro-Church Family gathering: Up, Down, In, Out

    A. Welcome: Food, Fun, Fellowship, Communion, Checking In.

    B. Worship: Communing with Jesus in praise and worship, collecting offering.

    C. Word: Hearing from Jesus through the written Word. Also releasing teaching and prophetic ministry to one another.

    D. Discipleship, prayer, encouragement, and support throughout the week.

    E. Works:

        i.   Ministering to one another through prayer, healing, inner healing, deliverance, personal discipleship, etc.

        ii. Doing baptisms.

        iii. Confessing sin, releasing forgiveness, holding each other accountable.

iv.   Strategically planning evangelism or kingdom advancing ministry with a person, neighborhood, or city.

v.   Praying for the lost. Doing acts of service or outreach.

9. **Micro-Church Families as a family & "army" lifestyle.** Here are some of the things that will happen:

A. Food, fun, and fellowship.

B. Lightly and deeply connecting: keeping our ongoing internal and external "story" current.

C. Praise & worship: Connecting with Father through Christ by the Holy Spirit.

D. Hearing from Father/Christ through His Word (Bible).

E. Sharing victories and struggles. Communicating transparently for the sake of support, training, and accountability.

F. Ministry to one another utilizing spiritual gifts: prophetic communication (words from Holy Spirit of encouragement, comfort, and exhortation), words of knowledge (supernatural insight), healing, tongues and interpretation of tongues, miracles, helps, intercession, etc. It may involve meeting each other's needs in practical ways.

G. Special training so that we can more effectively advance Christ's Kingdom in our families, at work, and in our communities.

H. The sacraments: Lord's Supper and water baptism.

I. Informal hanging out.

J. Special gatherings: retreats, adventures, picnics, game nights, outreaches, mission trips.

K. Strategic planning for outreach to the lost and missions in the community.

L. Actual corporate evangelism. Love expressed through spiritual family touches the longing of every human heart.

10. **Why Start, Grow, And Multiply Micro-Church Families?**

A. Both Moses in the Old Testament and Jesus in the New Testament chose the small group model and format (twelve disciples) as their method of making disciples, caring for people, and spreading and reproducing the Life and ways of God.

B. They are the most effective form of evangelism. An authentic loving community is the most convincing argument for the reality of God and reveals the basic meaning of life. John 17:20-23

C. Multiplying Micro-Church Families are the most effective structure to facilitate both the quality and quantity of connected caring relationships. The purpose of life is love. Kingdom Families create the very best organic setting for the highest quality of love, in the most efficient way, with the greatest number of people.

D. They create the best setting for mentoring and training people at the heart and life level because the life of Christ is more "caught" than taught. Consistent, loving, transparent relationships allow hidden weaknesses and sins to come into the light, so they can be eliminated and replaced with the attributes of Christ.

E. They are the best way to develop leaders because everyone is expected to contribute that which Christ has given to them and to experiment with their gifts and callings.

F. They are the most effective way to enable the participation and ministry of every member.

G. They have the most flexibility and the quickest response time for providing pastoral and practical care among the members.

H. They can easily infiltrate every human situation and setting.

I. They allow "church" to take place all the time, everywhere, and through everyone.

J. They are the only "structure" that can absorb a massive influx of people in a short amount of time when genuine revival occurs.

K. They allow the church to grow even during persecution.

L. No building costs.

11. What is a recommended **use of time and ministry** "flow" in a Micro-Church Family gathering? **No two Micro-Church Family gatherings will ever be alike because they should all be led by the Holy Spirit.** Jesus is very creative and fun. Everyone should be trying to discern His presence and leadership throughout the gathering. There will be some consistent elements week in and week out that point to a pattern. There are hundreds of formats the Holy Spirit can direct. **Here is just one:**

6:00 P.M. – Food & Fun. The meal and hang out time. Consider including the Lord's Supper during the meal.

7:00 P.M. – Praise & Worship. Guitars, key boards, small drums are great to assist the singing. Praise tapes or CD's work as well. Also, take some time to wait on the Lord and be silent. Always invite the Holy Spirit to manifest His presence and lead the time together. Include reading scripture passages that praise the Lord. Allow people to offer prayers of thanksgiving and praise as well.

7:30 P.M. – Time in the Word. Start with reading a chapter of the Bible aloud. Designate (usually at least a week in advance) someone to give an expository teaching of the passage for about 10 minutes. Follow up the teaching with "flow" questions (a question that cannot be answered with a "yes" or "no" and presses people to understand and apply the passage). The Serendipity Bible has flow questions included in the margins beside the Bible verse. Encourage the members to systematic Bible reading through the same book of the Bible, and have them study the same passages on their own so they will have familiarity with the scripture.

8:00 P.M. – Share. Take time to have people share their hearts, life situations, give testimonies, and ask for prayer requests. If the house church is too large to allow everyone to share, it can be divided into groups of 3 to 4 people for this time of personal ministry. Do personal ministry with one another.

8:30 P.M. – Reach. Do some planning and prayer for the people the group is trying to lead to Christ.

8:45 P.M. – Prayer. End with a short time of prayer.

8:50 P.M. – Linger. People can hang around and visit longer, but release those who need to go. Some folks start work early the next morning, so be sensitive. Also, be sensitive to the people hosting the house church gathering. If people linger late into the evening, over time this could create an emotional and physical weariness and lead to "burn out".

9:15 P.M. – Reflect. Spend some time processing and evaluating how the Micro-Church Family gathering went that night with those you are developing as leaders. Ask questions like: "In what ways was Christ and His presence evident in our gathering?" "In what ways did our house church members connect with and minister to each other?" "How could we improve our ministry to each other?" "How did our time in Scripture go?" "How is our discipleship doing?" "In what ways are we being effective in reaching the lost and how can we improve on evangelism?" "In what ways can we encourage relationally connecting with our house church family throughout the week?" "How are we doing with children?" "What was the level of participation from each person?"

12. **Stages of the life of a Kingdom Family.** We can easily observe developmental stages in both individuals and even marriages. Knowing these general stages helps us to understand and prepare for the positive and negative aspects of each period of the group's life.

A. The initial birth or planting stage. Forming.

B. The honeymoon period. Forming.

C. The conflict stage. Storming.

D. The true community phase. Norming.

E. The reproductive stage. Performing.

F. The multiplication stage. Transforming.

13. **What about children in the Micro-Church Family?**

A. In a fragmented and mobile culture, children need the benefit of spiritual fathers and mothers, aunts and uncles, brothers and sisters, etc. When they connect relationally at the heart, the deepest needs of affection, belonging, identity, and affirmation get met.

Children love Micro-Church Families as long as they aren't done like a strict religious program.

B. Children can and/or should be included in almost every part of the Micro-Church Family gathering. The meals, times of praise, checking in, sharing, personal ministry, Bible study, outreaches are all opportunities for children to experience church life. In fact, they add a great deal of fun, love, entertainment, and excitement. Children keep things real. Besides all this, children are much more capable of ministry than we might imagine. They can enter in to praying for the sick, contributing during the sharing, and expressing compassion for those who are struggling.

C. There are segments of time in a Micro-Church Family gathering when it may be best for a couple adult members to take the children to another part of the house and especially focus on the children, so that the other adults can share deep struggles and confess sin. During this time, age sensitive Bible study and training can occur, or kids can minister to and pray for each other, or they can enjoy recreation, games, crafts, etc.

D. Since being in a Micro-Church Family is a 24/7 lifestyle, members of the Micro-Church Family should include the children in their lives outside the gatherings. Mentoring and relationship opportunities can be woven into everyday life.

14. **What about intergenerational Micro-Church Families?**

A. There is a notion that youth prefer being in groups with just youth, or that singles prefer only being with singles. This is often not the case. There is a rich exchange of life that occurs when people from different generations come together in a meaningful way.

B. The keys to making intergenerational Micro-Church Families work are the same for more homogenous groups – humility, transparency, and the exchange of affection. When people are valued, received, and desired, and humbly and openly give and receive life, great personal advances are made in people's lives.

C. Oddly enough, it is those who are older who usually need to be pursued and invited. Those from the "Senior" generation (born in 1926 and earlier) and the "Builder" generation (born between 1927 to 1945) are not as use to smaller settings where people share personal information. Yet, with enthusiastic encouragement, coaching, and positive affirmation, they will become stable pillars in a spiritual family. The "Boomer" generation (born between 1946 to 1964) needs to be encouraged to make relationships and spiritual family a priority in addition to their inclination towards the successful reaching of goals and financial independence. If their idealism and "can do" approach to life are utilized, powerful victories for the Kingdom of God can be won. They must be encouraged to "keep it real" and avoid condescending attitudes and superficial advice giving. They will also need to let go of control and positions of power in order to be approachable to the younger generations. The "Busters or Gen-Xer's" (born 1965 to 1983) are more skeptical (often cynical) of pat answers and cultural norms, and don't usually have much respect for institutions (especially the traditional church) or authoritative positions. They are won over by love, relationships, tangible care giving, fun, and quality time, not logical arguments or structured programming. Millennials or Mosaics (born 1984 to present) are a very eclectic and creative group. They will pull all kinds of information and experiences together in what feels like a random way, but is exciting and meaningful to them. They borrow from all areas of life to piece together meaning and experiences that are important to them. Relaxed but meaningful relationships, especially friendships, are very important to Millennials. And by all means, don't forget having fun with them.

D. Fun, in-depth relationships/friendships, exciting adventures, and experiential learning are of utmost importance to GenXer's and Millennials. For the generations to connect, the older (and often more powerful due to their positions, education and finances) must regularly defer to the younger. That means the Kingdom Family experience must include lots of hanging out time, goofing off, laughing, and what older people will consider experiences and activities that are unproductive, silly, and even meaningless. Nothing could be further from the truth. These generations must find each other if the fullness of God's purposes are to be realized.

E. Each generation has been created in such a way as to accent a kingdom value. Often, these values seem paradoxical and mutually exclusive. However, they are all complimentary if we will look more deeply into what each generation values. Those born after 1965 tend to lean toward relational intimacy, toward "being" more than "doing". Is that not a kingdom value? Those born before 1965 have a tendency to lean toward "doing" and desire to make impact. They really want to build something that lasts, and produce something of worth. Leadership, management, and discipline are highly valued because they enable the successful achievement of important goals. Is that not also a kingdom value? If we take a fresh look at the situation, we will realize that we all need each other. Mutual humility and respect are essential for actualizing the fullness of Christ. Let us submit to the Christ in one another.

15. Watch out for distractions.

A. Many people have never been in a setting like a Micro-Church Family where people are being vulnerable and sharing issues that are in some cases life and death. Because of this, they may not be sensitive to the damaging effects of distractions. A cell phone ringing and getting answered right in the middle of gut level sharing could damage the heart of the one sharing and cause them to never open up again.

B. Lots of spiritual warfare will be occurring before, during, and after a Micro-Church Family gathering. Leaders and members should be on the alert for demonic distractions.

C. Practical advice:

    i.   Have all cell phones and pagers turned off. Only keep one phone line open for emergencies and designate a person to answer the phone.

     ii.   Keep pets locked up and out of the way.

     iii.   Help people to be aware of themselves and the ways they may be distracting, so that they will self-correct. Some people have habits like rapping their fingers on tables, or clicking ballpoint pens in and out. Little things like this can produce distracting annoyances that the enemy uses to reduce the impact of the time together.

16. **Teaching visitors and members basic Micro-Church Family "manners".** The etiquette of conduct in a spiritual family gathering.

    A.   Without being too rigid or programmatic, the leaders should help the visitors and members understand that there are ground rules that are important to keep so that everyone can have a meaningful experience.

    B.   Here are some examples:

     i.   When someone is talking, do not interrupt, or judge them with your words or body language. Don't talk to someone else while another is talking, make eye contact with the person sharing, and be an active listener.

     ii.   When someone is finished sharing, don't jump in and offer advice. Respond with acceptance, affirmation, and affection.

     iii.   Don't make speeches or sermons. Share personally from the heart, and do it in short segments of time. Don't dominate the discussion.

     iv.   Correcting and/or redirecting the house church is the responsibility of the leader and, therefore, if someone has input at this level it should first be brought to the leader in private.

     v.   Avoid debates and arguments. They can result in threatening the sense of acceptance and safety in the group. This is a place for heart connecting, and dialogue.

17. **How big should a Micro-Church Family get and why?**

    A.   Minimum number: five people.

    B.   Maximum number: best is twelve, should keep beneath twenty-five people. Too many people, begins to compromise the ability to connect meaningfully from the heart. The bigger the group the lesser the intimacy. Also, shy and reserved people tend to slip into the background the bigger the group becomes. Always encourage, plan for, and celebrate Kingdom Family multiplication.

18. **The relationship of Micro-Church Families to the Local Church and Trans-local "Tribe":**

Every living thing must be connected to and a part of something greater than itself. Each person needs to be organically and relationally connected to a spiritual family which gathers as a Micro-Church Family. Each Micro-Church Family needs to be connected to their extended family which is other Micro-Church Families in their city or region (a local church led by Biblical elders), so they can strategically advance the Kingdom of God in that geographic area. Each group of Micro-Church Family's needs to be connected to an even larger spiritual family we call a "Jesus Tribe". A Jesus Tribe is a family-of-families that is strategically reaching other cities, regions, and nations. Each Jesus Tribe (apostolic/prophetic family-of-families) needs to be in relationship with and submission to the leadership of other Jesus Tribes. The unifying of resources, influence, gifting, and strategies among the whole Body of Christ will result in the transformation of cities. Apostolic/prophetic leaders are called to help connect the hearts and minds of believers in such a quality way around Jesus that there is a seamless flow of His life and love out to the poorest and most unreached in the nations. This allows each member of their tribe the eternal rewards of contributing to those Christ mentions in Matthew 25:31-46.

19. **How each individual becomes a member of a Micro-Church Family and Local Church**:

There are five steps to membership in a Micro-Church Family and local church. We understand and believe that whenever anyone becomes a child of God through Christ, that they automatically become members of the universal family of God. We also believe that identifying with and becoming members of a specific group of believers (local church) is God's ordained strategy for helping His children become mature disciples of Christ. Every specific spiritual family (local church) should have a clear understanding and set of expectations for membership. This enables the highest quality of pastoral care, training, and mobilization.

Step 1: The person repents from trying to "save" themselves. They place their faith in the blood and sacrificial death of Christ. They place their faith in Christ as Savior and Lord asking Him to come and live in their heart and baptize them with the Holy Spirit. In other words, they become a born-again Spirit-filled member of God's family and a follower of Jesus Christ. They experientially receive the Spirit of adoption. The outward sacrament of this inward reality is water baptism.

Step 2: They become an active member of an official Micro-Church Family.

Step 3: They go through a membership orientation training (OSV) put on by the elders of their local church. This helps each person know how to come into unity with the values, vision, strategy and leadership of their local church.

Step 4: They meet with elders and Micro-Church Family leaders to discuss and confirm becoming a member of the local church. Both parties agree that this is God's will.

Step 5: They enjoy being received into their local church publicly at a larger worship celebration. They receive water baptism if they are newly born again.

20. **The importance of evaluation, assessment, and processing:**

We have developed a simple evaluation process that allows all the members of the Micro-Church Family the ability to determine areas of strengths and weaknesses, so that together we can steadily grow in Christ's likeness and kingdom advancement. We have also developed assessment tools to determine the strengths and weaknesses of our Micro-Church Family. This tool helps us to make the necessary improvements.

Regularly assessing and evaluating our Micro-Church Families helps us to make constant adjustments and improvements in our life together. This process should be done with the utmost care and sensitivity. When people communicate about the Micro-Church Family, its leadership and members, it should be done with great love, respect, sensitivity, mercy, and kindness. The truth is not really the truth if it is not immersed in mercy and love. The process of assessment should produce increased faith not discouragement. It takes true humility to honestly evaluate our lives together. However, the rewards of this exercise are staggering because God gives grace to the humble. (See "Assessing Our Micro-Church Family" at the back of the manual under Discovery & Discipleship Tools)

FOUR ESSENTIALS OF A MICRO-CHURCH FAMILY

Four Essentials: For a small group of Christians to be considered a legitimate Micro-Church Family, we believe it is essential that four "directions" of God's love be exchanged as a lifestyle among the members.

1. **Down Love:** First, each individual and the group as a whole must be constantly receiving into their hearts, their Father's mercy, grace, love, glory, truth, power and life through Christ by the Holy Spirit. They must all be in regular communion with Christ who dwells in their hearts as Lord. Obedience to the Lordship of Christ is a supernaturally natural result of their faith and love for Him. The individuals and the group should enjoy the manifest presence and power of the Holy Spirit in their midst. Both the Word of God and the Spirit of God are the means by which Father's life flows into the house church.

2. **Up Love:** Second, the members must be constantly reciprocating the love and glory they receive from God back to Him, in the form of praise, worship, and obedience. Bringing glory to God as a lifestyle and expanding His glory in the nations is their top value. The full expressions of praise and worship described in the Bible should be practiced when they gather.

3. **In Love:** Third, the family members must exchange Christ's love, wisdom, and power between one another through covenantally connected hearts and minds. This includes an ongoing lifestyle of acceptance, encouragement, forgiveness, affection, affirmation, discipleship, correction, accountability, inner healing, personal prayer ministry, communion (Lord's supper/agape meal), bearing one another's burdens, helping meet each other's needs especially during difficult times, and having lots of fun. The point is to help facilitate the formation of Christ within each other's minds, hearts, and lifestyle. It is to help each member become like Christ.

4. **Out Love:** Fourth, a Micro-Church Family is a small spiritual family, but it is also a spiritual army (platoon) which has a kingdom-advancing mission. God's life and love must be flowing out through the group to those who haven't experienced Father's love through Christ. As the body of Christ, the group needs to be a corporate and tangible expression of Christ to those it is called to serve. Christ is alive in us and wants to do through us today what He did while He was a man 2000 years ago. He wants to bring the kingdom of heaven to earth, seek and save the lost, heal the sick, cast out demons, and bring compassion and practical help to those in need. The Micro-Church gets to be the voice and hands of Jesus. This most effectively occurs when each member discovers and selflessly shares their spiritual gifts, talents, time, money, and other resources. In addition, each Micro-Church should embrace the exciting opportunity of multiplying into other Micro-Churches. Just as the children of a natural family are expected to mature and start their own families, so the members of the spiritual family should grow to the point they can reach others with Christ and start another Micro-Church. Growth and multiplication is the evidence that a Micro-Church has Christ as its Center and Source and is "organically" connected to the Body of Christ. We believe Micro-Churches are

the best strategy for evangelism, pastoral care, discipleship, leadership development, and kingdom-advancing missions.

OTHER ESSENTIAL DYNAMICS OF A MICRO-CHURCH:

1. **Father's Heart of Love:** The Father heart of God needs to pervade the group's life, causing everyone to help each other discover their identities as sons or daughters of God, enabling everyone to experience the affection of Jesus Christ, and facilitating the calling and destiny of each person. In a healthy family, there is no room for control, manipulation, jealousy, envy, bitterness, selfish ambition, undermining, gossip, rejection, insecurity, judgment, competition, co-dependence, or the concealing of sin. Sin blocks the blessings of God, stunts the maturing process, and hinders God's people from fulfilling God's eternal purpose for their lives. The Father and His family (natural and spiritual) is the platform for bringing heaven to earth. For this reason, we encourage inner-healing to be practiced.

2. **Expanding Christ in One Another through Transparency, Accountability and Truth:** The members must practice coming into the light of God's love and truth by living transparently, confessing sin, and revealing their inner conversation to selected accountability partners. Especially in matters of marriage, sexual issues, or other intimate content, mutual accountability should be done with those of the same gender. Confidentiality has to be practiced, but house church members and house church leaders must be allowed to disclose complex, weighty, or life-threatening issues "upward" with their Micro-Church leaders or elders.

3. **Submission And Accountability to the Christ in One Another, Unity, and the Benefits of Delegated Authority:** The Micro-Church leaders and the members must value and practice a.) Mutual submission and accountability with each other under Christ, b.) Unity and submission with those who are their elders and the overseeing apostolic leadership of their "Jesus Tribe". Mutual submission and accountability are God's provision to protect us from lukewarm or imbalanced Christianity, compromise, abuse, incompetence, doctrinal error, or moral misconduct. Also, the Micro-Churches need to enjoy the rich benefits of remaining relationally connected and mutually submitted to other Micro-Churches regionally, nationally, and even internationally. It is highly recommended that each Micro-Church leader be a part of a closed group of other Micro-Church leaders, so they can receive personal ministry and equip one another for more effective ministry in their Micro-Churches. Every Micro-Church should be connected to a local church for mutual edification, equipping, and strategic partnership to impact the region for the kingdom.

4. **Conflict Resolution God's Way:** Due to our sin, immaturity, personality clashes, disagreements, and Satan's top commitment to divide natural and spiritual families, conflicts will occur between church members. We must all follow the Biblical model for conflict resolution described in Biblical passages like Matthew 18:15-29 and Galatians 6:1-5. Every

member *"should make every effort to keep the unity of the Spirit through the bond of peace"* Ephesians 4:3.

5. **Honoring Delegated Authority, Spiritual Etiquette, and Godly Transition:** There is kingdom etiquette when entering into and leaving a Micro-Church. Try not to leave due to offense or relational conflict. Apply the principles in Matthew 18:15-17. Call on other leaders to help arbitrate and resolve conflict. Hurt feelings are a wonderful opportunity to grow in grace. Applying God's ways in these situations should be a high priority, because it determines whether we receive His blessings or experience His correction & discipline.

6. **Consistency with Diversity:** Even though each Micro-Church will have all four essential elements necessary to be a healthy family and platoon, no two Micro-Churches will ever be the same. God's consistency with diversity is illustrated throughout creation. Every snowflake has the same elements, but each one is different in size and shape. Every Micro-Church needs to find its own life and mission together under Christ. Some groups will focus on whole families and include children, others will be gender specific and may focus on one particular age group. Some Micro-Churches will never even meet in a house. They may target co-workers and meet in the company cafeteria on break or after work. The Holy Spirit will inspire creativity and diversity, yet with the four basic ingredients necessary to receive and give Life.

7. **Holy Spirit's Leadership:** We highly encourage each group to be led by the Holy Spirit. We believe God is unleashing a world-wide revival that will result in a massive ingathering of souls into His kingdom. This will be an organic and grassroots move of God that cannot be contained by institutional or corporate programming. Hearing and obeying Jesus in a present and ongoing way is essential for each house church. This will help them avoid becoming co-dependent on one another, exalting a certain leader, or coming under the influence of "religious spirits". We must totally trust and obey Jesus all the time.

8. **Developmental Phases of MCF's:** The times and seasons of each Micro-Church must be discerned and accommodated. Even though all four elements of an MCF are essential, there may be times when the Holy Spirit emphasizes a certain focus. For example, birthing a Micro-Church will involve lots of intercession and evangelism. At the beginning, the "members" may just be seeking truth and love and have not yet placed their faith in Christ. Another example, at some point in the group's life, the emphasis may be developing deep and quality relationships with Christ and one another, so that there is a substantial level of unity and maturity to absorb new believers later. Groups also move through developmental stages just like individuals or a marriage. The stages of group life are 1. Forming, 2. Storming, 3. Norming, 4. Performing, 5. Transforming, 6. Reforming, 7. Multiplying

9. **Connection to a local church:** We highly encourage each Micro-Church to be actively involved in a healthy local church, which is part of a trans-local church-planting family-of-families (Jesus Tribe). Each believer needs the benefits of receiving the leadership, teaching, and other

ministries that come from those who have "five-fold" gifts (apostles, prophets, evangelist's shepherds, and teachers).

10. **Shared Life and Economics For The Purpose Of International Missions:** Father has called His sons/daughters to be a part of an international apostolic tribe gathered around Christ, His glory and kingdom, common core values, clear vision, some general strategies. Micro-Churches with DNA Groups are clearly one of God's strategies. Having a shared life and mission with members of an international family builds a relational bridge of love that can reach to people groups and nations that are without Christ. North Americans and Western Europeans enjoy water, food, shelter, medical benefits, education, and other provisions far beyond the rest of the world. A bona fide Jesus Tribe will want to help close the gap between the "haves" and the "have-nots" who live in urban centers and third world nations. Therefore, we want to encourage dispersing of tithes and offerings so that a large percentage of finances goes for local and international missions. The spirit of this is shared life together in order to reach the most people for Christ. Dispersing tithes and offerings locally and internationally should not be perceived as an imposed requirement, membership dues, or denominational taxation. We are part of a larger spiritual family, so we have the joy of building a relational bridge of love to the nations. We want all God's people to see themselves as missionaries who are partnering together for the highest level of kingdom impact. Everyone gets to benefit from the eternal rewards that come from our shared sacrifice and unified efforts. All financial expenditures in Micro-Churches, local churches, and a Jesus Tribe should be discussed and prayed through by the APEST leaders, utilized with the highest integrity, responsibly accounted for, and reports made available to members.

11. **Trans-Local Relationships and Hospitality:** We highly encourage each Micro-Church to establish supportive relationships with other churches that are a part of their Jesus Tribe. Often, entire Micro-Churches will travel to other cities or countries to help love, serve, and support another Micro-Church and its mission. This greatly benefits and enriches the lives of each member. We also want to practice hospitality with those who are traveling through our area on vacations or ministry trips. The members of an international spiritual family do not have to be limited in their ability to pray for and love one another because of geographical distance.

12. **Warning:** Our Father would have us realize that Micro-Churches may be dangerous to our spiritual, emotional, and relational health if they are not based in the love, presence, and power of Christ, help each member become more like Christ, and are committed to advancing Christ's Kingdom in every sphere of life. Many people have been seriously wounded in small group settings. Being in a Micro-Church does not guarantee a positive, life-giving, Christ-exalting reality. It is the quality and spirit of the Micro-Church which facilitates Life. Abusive, dysfunctional, passive, or immature leadership can open the door to many negative and damaging experiences. Disruptive, unhealthy, or inexperienced members who haven't learned to be led by the Holy Spirit and practice healthy family etiquette need to be trained

and corrected. While Micro-Churches can be very unsafe and even damaging, they have the best chance of revealing what heaven is like. Just as marriage can be the closest thing to hell on earth or the greatest expression of heaven depending on the couple's willingness to deny themselves and come under the centrality and supremacy of Christ's Lordship. In the same way, Micro-Churches can be a disaster or they can be one of best most Biblical strategies for bringing the Kingdom of God to earth.

NOTES:

PREPARATION FOR MICRO-CHURCH LEADERSHIP

Father goes to great lengths to prepare humble sons & servant leaders in the kingdom. This is because they are entrusted with the precious hearts and lives of others. God is raising up healthy, mature and skilled servant leaders who have His heart, values, vision, culture, and strategies. God qualifies leaders in many ways, sometimes using very painful experiences to renew minds and shape character. There are internal heart motives and external skills God upgrades resulting in these kingdom attributes: 1.) a new identity in Christ, 2.) an ongoing intimate relationship with Father through Christ by the Holy Spirit, 3.) a capacity to establish and grow intimate, positive, joy-filled relationships with others, 4.) a renewed mind, 5.) a transformed heart, 6.) a pray, hear, obey lifestyle, 7.) healing and maturity in Christ & Christ's Body with ever-growing maturity in the 19 brain skills necessary to be effective relationally. Healthy identity and intimacy as sons/daughters of God is the foundation for being an effective spiritual parent and leader.

Introduction: The key to successful leadership in the kingdom, especially pioneering a Micro-Church plant, is to be sure that you are personally ready for this responsibility. We do realize that it is not as much "what we know" but "Who we know" that counts. We will never be perfect, or have all the wisdom and skills necessary, but there are some basic foundations that one needs to have in place. Here are some suggestions for how you can prepare for Micro-Church Leadership:

1. Have a solid relationship with Jesus Christ, God as Father, and the Person of the Holy Spirit. Have you cultivated a Pray, Hear, Obey lifestyle with God? Do you read and apply the Bible on a nearly daily basis? What is your understanding and practice of FaceTime with God? Have you cultivated the ability to hear God's voice, and then do you obey Him quickly, completely, and cheerfully? Do you have an understanding and practice of prayer & fasting? Have you learned the dynamics of advancing the Kingdom and the spiritual warfare involved?

2. Embrace the process of inner-healing from trauma. Make sure your mind, heart, and soul are whole and well. Are you free from besetting sins, addictions, a destructive (bad) habits? Have you personally gone through inner-healing and deliverance?

3. Develop maturity and skills in relationships. What level of maturity are you in the kingdom? Can you handle conflict, pressure, and crisis and maintain stability? Are you a life-giving person? Do you impart Father's love, affection, and joy to others? Consistently? How well developed are all 19 relational brain skills?

4. Cultivate in-depth transparent relationships with a DNA Group, Micro-Church Family, local church, and trans-local Jesus Tribe. Fellowshipping in the light, enjoying intentional community is key to healing and growth.

5. Develop Christ's core values, motives, fruit, and character. Be a person of integrity. People buy into the leader more than the vision or strategies. Be a person others can trust because you are actually trustworthy.

6. Have you received clear confirmation regarding your calling? Do those around you believe that you are called to be a Micro-Church leader?

7. Have you developed the initial leadership skills to start, grow, and oversee a Micro-Church? Have you lead a DNA Group? Have you been an assistant leader of a Micro-Church Family?

8. Do you have shepherding skills and gifts: a.) ability to carry out inner-healing & deliverance, b.) ability to make disciples who make disciples, c.) understand and apply the gospel of grace, d.) can teach the Word of God, e.) have a father's/mother's heart for people.

9. Is humble, teachable, and demonstrates a submission to the Christ in others as a servant of Christ.

10. Do you have an ability to cast vision, rally & gather people, take initiative in evangelism, run a Micro-Church gathering?

11. What is the health of your marriage and children? Is your spouse in unity and partnership regarding your calling?

12. What is your reputation at work? Do you have a solid source of income?

13. Do you have the benefit of more experienced and mature leaders to help you? Are you in partnership with and submission to more seasoned leaders in the kingdom? Are you a vital and active member of a local church family, a Jesus Tribe?

14. Do you have an identifiable people and location that God has called you to reach? Where and who?

NOTES:

DNA GROUPS: DISCIPLESHIP, NURTURE, APOSTOLIC MISSION

DNA Groups Defined:

A DNA Group is a small gender specific (men with men, women with women) gathering of 2 to 4 disciples of Christ who are helping each other become transformed into Christ's likeness, and advance Christ's Kingdom in every area of life. Utilizing the power of God's Word (Bible), God's Spirit, and God's Family, a DNA Group emphasizes the three major practices of a disciple:

1. **Abiding** relationally with Christ

2. **Hearing** God's Word and Spirit

3. **Obeying** God's Word and Spirit

Each person will help the others to abide with Christ, hear His voice, and obey God's Word in the two main areas of the Kingdom of God:

1. **Covenant Relationships** - covenant means high quality relational unity and oneness

2. **Kingdom Responsibilities** - fulfilling the original dominion mandate by doing God's will, God's way, by God's Spirit, for God's glory. Genesis 1-3

DNA Groups are not a religious program. They are a way of life. When two, three, or four sincere believers come together for the purpose of helping one another become like Christ and advance His Kingdom, supernatural transformation will occur. Roman 8:29; 1 Corinthians 15:48-49; Luke 10:1-24; Matthew 6:33, 10:7-8

There are five purposes for a DNA Group:

1. To help each other love, follow, and obey Jesus Christ

2. To read and apply the Word of God to our everyday lives

3. To pray for those who do not have Christ living in them as Lord and/or who are not in a Biblical church, i.e. healthy spiritual family

4. To build loving relationships with those who are not in Christ for the purpose of sharing the good news of the Kingdom of God in word and deed

5. To follow-up and disciple those who have just come to Christ

A small committed group of two to three people has a much better chance of digging into the deep root issues that are blocking personal transformation. In the safety of unconditional love, trust, and confidentiality, people can truly open their hearts. They are more apt to let their inner conversation and personal issues come into the light. In the light and love of Father's Spirit and Father's Family, we can fight for one another's transformation into Christ's likeness. 1 John 1:1-7

DNA Groups meet at least once a week to help each member become like Christ, love God, share the gospel, advance Christ's Kingdom, and make disciples that make disciples. **D**iscipleship, **N**urture, **A**postolic Mission

DNA (deoxyribonucleic acid) contains the genetic instructions which are used in the development and functioning of all living organisms. DNA is the essential code for life that determines exactly how each cell will live and reproduce. In the same way, for us to **be** and **do** what God intends, we must have His DNA in every part of our life: such as the stewardship of our bodies, our minds, hearts, attitudes, desires, motives, actions, relationships, lifestyle, work, and ministry. Following Jesus Christ means that His very Personhood, His Presence, dwells inside us as our Savior and King. It involves **hearing** and **obeying** His voice as a lifestyle 24/7/365. Let us make sure we have the right DNA of Christ: **Christ** Himself, Christ's **Community** – His Church, Christ's **Character**, Christ's **Calling**, and Christ's **Competency**. Luke 6:46-49; 1 Thessalonians 5:23-24; Colossians 1:28

No one can become like Christ, apart from supportive, loving, and accountable relationships. When 2-3 men (or women) fellowship in the light, opening their hearts with safe and loving friends, they can help each other hear and obey Jesus. 1 John 1:3-10

GOD'S DNA: CHRIST'S CHARACTER

Jesus teaches that it is the inner character of one's heart that determines the quality of one's life. Did you know that we can have the mind of Christ? Roman 12:2 We can also have the same attitude and motives of Christ. Philippians 2:5 Our passion can be to glorify God in everything we do. 1 Corinthians 10:31 If we are cultivating an intimate relationship with the Trinity, fellowshipping in the light with God and the body of Christ 1 John 1:1-10, humbly submitting ourselves directly to Christ and the Christ in others, then our internal character will be transformed into the likeness of Christ. This process is not easy because our flesh, our false self that prefers self-worship, does not want to die. If we want to be *"transformed into Christ's likeness with ever-increasing glory"*, we cannot hide from God and His people. 2 Corinthians 3:18 It is quite possible to daily read our Bibles, attend church meetings and programs, but still not open our hearts and lives to our brothers and sisters. By remaining isolated and independent, we will never have the power to defeat our false sinful self, the power of sin, the spirit of the world, or Satanic influences. Rightly living in true community is absolutely necessary for obtaining Christ's character. Having Christ's character is the basis for fulfilling Christ's calling. That is because we minister from who we are, the quality of Christ's life which flows from our inner most being. John 7:37-39; Matthew 5:8, 15:19-20

BECOMING CHRIST'S DISCIPLE

Did you know that Jesus is still making disciples today? This is true, and He wants you to be one of them! Because He is in His resurrected body, invisible to our natural eyes, He has commissioned us to be His "skin". We are to teach each other what He taught in His Word, and help one another obey everything He commanded. As we help make disciples of Christ, He promises to always be with us, to never leave our presence. Matthew 28:18-20 In fact, when invited, He comes to dwell in the very core of our being – our hearts (spirits). Ephesians 3:17 Christ also baptizes us with the Holy Spirit and Fire. Matthew 3:11. This enables us to have the fruit of the Spirit Galatians 5:22, the wisdom and revelation of the Spirit Ephesians 1:17-18, and the power of the Spirit. Acts 1:8

Making disciples, who make disciples, in the context of small DNA Groups is a basic Biblical strategy that comes straight from our King - Jesus Christ.

DNA GROUPS - EKKLESIA GROUPS OF 2-4

Gender specific groups of two to four people who carry out authorized legislative purposes in the Kingdom of God, help each other love God, love people, become like Christ, advance His kingdom, and make disciples that make disciples. (DNA – Discipleship, Nurture, Apostolic Mission)

Divine Truth & Spirit, **N**urturing Relationships, **A**postolic Mission
Discipleship, **N**urture, **A**ct

I am not ashamed of the gospel, because it is the power of God for the salvation of everyone who believes: first for the Jew, then for the Gentile. For in the gospel a righteousness from God is revealed, a righteousness that is by faith from first to last, just as it is written: "The righteous will live by faith." Romans 1:16-17

For those God foreknew He also predestined to be conformed to the likeness of His Son, that He might be the firstborn among many brothers. And those He predestined, He also called; those He called, He also justified; those He justified, He also glorified. Roman 8:28-30

We proclaim him, admonishing and teaching every one with all wisdom, so that we may present everyone perfect in Christ. To this end I labor, struggling with all His energy, which so powerfully works in me. Colossians 1:28-29

You then, my son, be strong in the grace that is in Christ Jesus. And the things you have heard me say in the presence of many witnesses entrust to reliable men who will also be qualified to teach others. Endure hardship with us like a good soldier of Christ Jesus. 2 Timothy 2:1-3

Again, I tell you that if two of you on earth agree about anything you ask for, it will be done for you by my Father in heaven. For where two or three come together in my name, there I am with them. Matthew 18:19-20

Jesus replied: "Love the Lord your God with all your heart and with all your soul and with all your mind. This is the first and greatest commandment. And the second is like it: 'Love your neighbor as yourself.' All the Law and the Prophets hang on these two commandments." Matthew 22:37-40

Then Jesus came to them and said, "All authority in heaven and on earth has been given to me. Therefore go and make disciples of all nations, baptizing them in the name of the Father and of the Son and of the Holy Spirit, and teaching them to obey everything I have commanded you. And surely I am with you always, to the very end of the age. Matthew 28:18-20

"After this the Lord appointed seventy-two others and sent them two by two ahead of Him to every town and place where He was about to go. He told them, 'The harvest is plentiful, but the workers are few. Ask the Lord of the harvest, therefore, to send out workers into His harvest field. Go! Heal the sick who are there and tell them, 'The Kingdom of God is near you.'" Luke 10:1-24

"Though one may be overpowered, two can defend themselves. A cord of three strands is not quickly broken." Ecclesiastes 4:12

THE IMPORTANCE OF GOD'S DNA

Christ in you, the hope of glory! Colossians 1:27

I pray that out of His glorious riches He may strengthen you with power through His Spirit in your inner being, so that Christ may dwell in your hearts through faith. Ephesians 3:16-17

DNA (deoxyribonucleic acid) contains the genetic instructions which are used in the development and functioning of all living organisms. DNA is the essential code for life that determines exactly how each cell will live and reproduce. In the same way, for us to **be** and **do** what God intends, we must have His DNA in every part of our life: such as the stewardship of our bodies, our minds, hearts, attitudes, desires, motives, actions, relationships, lifestyle, work, and ministry. Following Jesus Christ means that His very Personhood, His Presence, dwells inside us as our Savior and King. It involves **hearing** and **obeying** His voice as a lifestyle 24/7/365. Let us make sure we have the right  "DNA" of Christ: Christ Himself, Christ's Community – His Church, Christ's Character, Christ's Calling, and Christ's Competency. Luke 6:46-49

God's "DNA" For Life: The Gospel

The Trinity (Father, Son, and Holy Spirit) redeems and restores the human race back to its original intention through Christ's sacrificial death on the cross. Our sins are forgiven, enabling us to have  a right relationship with our heavenly Father. When Jesus enters our hearts as Lord, we literally become a new creation, a son of God. Rather than have the same nature as the Adamic race, we are given a radically new heart, a new nature. We are transformed into an entirely new species with totally new capacities. 2 Corinthians 5:17 Christ's Spirit lives inside us, and with our ongoing cooperation and faith, He transforms us into His very likeness! He gives us His mind, His heart, and His life. God relationally connects His children, so they can become a loving Family – Christ's body, the Church. God's people, in unified loving relationships, become saturated and overflowing with the Person of the Holy Spirit empowering them to demonstrate and proclaim the gospel, advancing Christ's Kingdom on earth.

God's DNA: Divine Truth

God has an intelligent Mind. It was His Mind that produced an orderly creation. Chaos cannot create order. Order is illogical apart from Mind. The reason we experience the benefits of scientific process is because Mind created order. God created other conscious minds, in His image, who could also observe and create order. God reveals His Mind, His absolute Truth, in His Word – the Bible. His Word, revealed in the 66 books of the Bible, is to guide every part of our lives. With the Holy Spirit's help, we can understand and apply God's Truth. However, we cannot comprehend and apply the Bible unless our hearts are pure. That is because we do not just commune with God through our intellect alone, but through our hearts. Our minds have the ability to justify what our hearts desire, even perverting the Bible to support our sinful agenda. Our hearts cannot be pure unless we have the inspiration and power of the Holy Spirit. Satan knows the information in the Bible, but He does not have a love relationship with the God of the Bible. One can know facts in the Bible, but because of pride and unbelief, not utilize the Bible for the purpose it was written, which is to help us love God and people. In fact, a person can accumulate a great deal of Bible knowledge, and wrongfully think they are spiritual. However, their knowledge has "puffed them up" and distanced them from God and others. The Bible is God's absolute and inspired objective Truth which is THE authority for faith and life. The Truth, as revealed in the Bible, is the basis and standard for determining the authenticity of our love relationship with God and others. Knowing the Bible and sound doctrine is a means toward communion with God and others, never an end. Truth without love is not real truth. The Bible is also the constitution of the Kingdom of God, stating clearly the governing laws and principles that guide us to establish the Kingdom of God within us, between us, and upon the earth. Believing Truth involves doing truth, which is wisdom. Truth is not just believing the right doctrines. It is holistically applying God's wisdom in every area of life. Psalm 24:4, 119; Joshua 1:8; Matthew 5:8; 1 Timothy 4:16; 2 Timothy 3:16; Titus 2:1; John 5:39; 1 Corinthians 8:1

God's DNA: Divine Spirit

The Bible was written under the inspiration of the Holy Spirit. The Holy Spirit will never contradict His own Word. The Bible is not intended to replace the Holy Spirit, but guide us into a vibrant relationship with the Person of the Holy Spirit. Experiencing a direct love relationship with Father, through Christ, by the Holy Spirit is the gospel. Those who lean toward structure and orderly concepts, like engineers and mathematicians, can be prone to only loving God with their minds. People who are more imaginative, intuitive, feeling-based, like artists and musicians, can be prone to only valuing experiences over objective Truth. **Both** the Word **and** the Spirit are available to believers. We can love God with our mind **and** experience Him in our heart. The Person of the Holy Spirit has been poured out upon sons of God. He fills us and flows from within us. The Holy Spirit leads, empowers, teaches, and comforts. We can actually quench and grieve the Person of the Holy Spirit, diminishing His manifest presence and power in our lives. As we fellowship with the Holy Spirit, there will be supernatural experiences that occur. Supernatural should be natural for all sons of God. However, all supernatural encounters should be judged through the lens of objective Truth revealed in the Bible and the fruit evaluated by the Body of Christ. The fruit of the Spirit and fruitfulness will be the by-product of the Spirit-filled, Spirit-led, Spirit-empowered life. We must be careful not to fall in the two ditches on each side of "The Way". John 14:6; Acts 9:2 One ditch is coming under the influence of secular humanistic, naturalism of the age in which supernatural manifestations are viewed with suspicion. Even well-intentioned Bible-believing people can subtly undermine a dynamic experiential relationship with God, often promoting this cold-hearted distance from Him with theological rationalizations. One must never disdain or minimize the importance of the Holy Spirit, nor His influence and gifts. The other ditch is to define spirituality primarily on the basis of mystical experiences. Good people, desperate for an encounter with God, can open themselves to deceiving spirits or emotionalism. They can also be more enthralled with revelation and/or power gifts than the character of Christ revealed in the fruit of the Spirit. This tempts them to be attracted to sensational manifestations, reducing their ability to accurately discern authentic and substantial kingdom reality. The Holy Spirit will always move us to be holy, as our God is holy. He will help us to become more like Christ every day. The ongoing baptism (means "full immersion") and filling of the Holy Spirit is one of the greatest benefits of Christ's death on the cross. Because of Christ's shed blood, forgiveness of sin, we are cleansed vessels who can now be a living temple of the Holy Spirit. 1 Corinthians 3:16. Let us also desire and utilize all the spiritual gifts described in the Bible, in divine order: 1.) Fruit of the Spirit, Galatians 5:23 2.) Wisdom and Revelation of the Spirit, Ephesians 1:17 3.) Power and Gifts of the Spirit. Matthew 3:11; Acts 1:4-8, 19:4-7; Ephesians 5:18-21; John 7:37-39, 14:15-21; 1 Corinthians 12-14; Roman 12

God's DNA: His Family, Body – The Church

God's DNA includes coming into a new family, the body of Christ. Christ has formed an authentic, radiant, tangible expression of Himself on earth and in heaven, His Church. When His Body comes into unity, loves each other deeply from the heart, the world will know that God is real. Christ's life is best transferred through life-on-life loving relationships. Living in transparent and loving community is the context for shaping our character. 1 Corinthians 12

God's DNA: Christ's Character

Jesus teaches that it is the inner character of one's heart that determines the quality of one's life. Did you know that we can have the mind of Christ? Romans 12:2. We can also have the same attitude and motives of Christ. Philippians 2:5. Our passion can be to glorify God in everything we do. 1 Corinthians 10:31 If we are cultivating an intimate relationship with the Trinity, fellowshipping in the light with God and the body of Christ 1 John 1:1-10, humbly submitting ourselves directly to Christ and the Christ in others, then our internal character will be transformed into the likeness of Christ. This process is not easy because our flesh, our false self that prefers self-worship, does not want to die. If we want to be transformed into Christ's likeness with ever-increasing glory, we cannot hide from God and His people. 2 Corinthians 3:18 It is quite possible to daily read our Bibles, attend church meetings and programs, but still not open our hearts and lives to God's people. By remaining isolated and independent, we will never have the power to defeat our false sinful self, the power of sin, the spirit of the world, or Satanic influences. Rightly living in true community is absolutely necessary for obtaining Christ's character. Having Christ's character is the basis for fulfilling Christ's calling. That is because we minister from who we are, the quality of Christ's life which flows from our inner most being. John 7:37-39; Matthew 5:8, 15:19-20

God's DNA: Reclaiming Christ's Kingdom on Earth

God's DNA involves a wonderful combination of God's mercy and grace, enabling us to do His will, His way, by His Spirit, for His glory. As sons of God, in unity with His family, we can actually bring Christ's Kingdom to earth. His kingdom is the "dominion of the King", the realm of reality in which He is uncontested Lord. We can experience kingdom marriages, kingdom families, kingdom businesses, even kingdom neighborhoods. The Kingdom of God is a combination of Divine Order with Divine Life under Christ's rule which is evidenced by observable peace, righteousness, and joy in the Holy Spirit. Matthew 6:33, 9:17, 10:9; Roman 14:17

God's DNA: Christ's Calling

The word 'vocation' comes from 'voice'. When we hear God's voice, His passion and purposes, are downloaded into our heart. Our vocation is the specific and tangible way we extend God's love to others. Our occupation is the way we fund and even give expression to our vocation. Every child of God has a calling on their life. We need to listen and practice our faith as it pertains to discovering God's will for our lives. Our Father has a special purpose and plan for each one of His sons. Have you heard God's voice, His call? Ephesians 2:10

God's DNA: Christ's Competency

Christ baptizes His disciples in the Holy Spirit and Fire! Matthew 3:11; Acts 1:4-8, 2:1-4, 15:8-9, 19:1-7 When the Person of the Holy Spirit comes upon us and flows from within us, we receive gifts from the Holy Spirit that supernaturally enable us to build up the Body of Christ and advance the Kingdom of God. In addition to spiritual gifts, the Spirit also helps us grow in wisdom, faith, hope, and love, increasing our ability to influence and serve others. John 7:37-39

DNA GROUPS DEFINED

A DNA Group is a small gender specific (men with men, women with women) gathering of 2 to 4 Disciples of Christ who are helping each other become transformed into Christ's likeness and advance Christ's Kingdom in every area of life. Utilizing the power of God's Word (Bible), God's Spirit, and God's family – the church, a DNA Group emphasizes the two major practices of a disciple: 1. **Hearing** God's Word and Spirit, 2. **Obeying** God's Word and Spirit. Each person will help the others to hear and obey God's Word in the two main areas of Kingdom of God: a. Covenant Relationships - covenant means high quality relational unity and oneness), b. Kingdom Responsibilities - fulfilling the original dominion mandate by doing God's will, God's way, by God's Spirit, for God's glory. Genesis 1-3 DNA Groups are not a religious program. They are a way of life. When two, three, or four sincere believers come together for the purpose of helping one another become like Christ and advance His kingdom, supernatural transformation will occur. Roman 8:29; 1 Corinthians 15:48-49; Luke 10:1-24; Matthew 6:33, 10:7-8

DNA Groups: One of God's Strategies to Make Disciples Who Make Disciples

Ideally, DNA Groups are a strategic part of a small Micro-Church Family (also called house church, missional community, or missional kingdom family). A Micro-Church Family is made-up of men, women, and children, a spiritual family of 5 to 20 people on gospel mission together. Micro-Church Families (MCF) should be interconnected with other MCFs and submitted to Biblical elders of a local congregation. MCFs gather weekly, most often in homes, to do the four essentials of the church: **Up** – worship & praise God; **Down** – hear and obey God's Word & Spirit; **In** – minister to one another; **Out** – demonstrate and share the gospel to the lost. MCFs are led by those who have the attributes and character of a Biblical elder. A primary strategy Jesus used to advance the Kingdom of God was to gather 12 disciples, and focus on mentoring them in all areas of life: beliefs, character, motives, relationships, lifestyle, and ministry. This same strategy of making disciples and doing evangelism by gathering believers into groups of 5 to 20 has been utilized by the church from the very beginning see Acts 2:42-47. Every Micro-Church Family (MCF) is called to help each member become like Christ through discipling relationships and to carry out the great commission. Matthew 28:18-20 DNA Groups can add an effective discipleship and evangelism dimension to any MCF or local church.

The Strategic Benefits of DNA Groups

When believers gather in small groups of two or three, dynamic kingdom impact can occur. Jesus sent out small DNA Groups made up of only two people in order to impact whole cities! They were commissioned to advance the Kingdom of God through prayer, proclamation, and power, such as healing the sick. Luke10:1-24 In order to help make disciples of Christ and advance His Kingdom, God's Word encourages people to relationally connect with one or two others in order to enhance and extend discipleship, focused prayer, and evangelism. Sometimes being deliberate, even to the point of naming an activity like discipleship, prayer and evangelism, can inspire God's people to be more proactive. This is why we form DNA Groups, to more effectively carry out **D**iscipleship by submitting to **D**ivine Truth (God's Word) and the Person of the Holy Spirit, **N**urturing relationships, plus **A**ccountability & **A**postolic mission. Hebrews10:24-25

We encourage DNA Groups to be part of a Micro-Church and local church (Jesus Tribe). The exception is that a DNA Group might need to be the core "seed" of an emerging Micro-Church Family, if there is no Micro-Church in a geographic area. DNA Groups might even be a way to start a new local church. There are five purposes for a DNA Group: 1.) to help each other love, follow, and obey Jesus Christ, 2.) to read and apply the Word of God to our everyday lives, 3.) to pray for those who do not have Christ living in them as Lord and/or who are not in a Biblical church, i.e. healthy spiritual family, 4.) to build loving relationships with those who are not in Christ for the purpose of sharing the good news of the Kingdom of God in word and deed, 5.) to follow-up and disciple those who have just come to Christ. A small committed group of two to three people has a much better chance of digging into the deep root issues that are blocking personal transformation. In the safety of unconditional love, trust, and confidentiality, people can truly open their hearts. They are more apt to let their inner conversation and personal issues come into the light. In the light and love of Father's Spirit and Father's family, we can fight for one another's transformation into Christ's likeness. 1 John 1:1-7

At the same time, two's and threes are highly effective outreach teams. They are flexible, spontaneous, and naturally relational. They can go into the everyday world of those who don't know Christ and meet them on their turf. This is in contrast to valid church strategies that try to draw the unbeliever into church meetings in order to hear the gospel. Attractional evangelism attempts to bring unbelievers into church gatherings where they can hear the gospel. Apostolic evangelism and mission is about **going out** into **all** the world in order to proclaim the gospel and make disciples. The word apostle means **'sent ones'**, people who **go** to where lost people live, demonstrating and proclaiming the gospel in their setting.

Five Activities of a DNA Group

1. Helping each other become like Christ involves opening up our hearts and lives, so we can exchange the life of Christ between one another. Transformation occurs when we help one another: a.) renew our minds so that we have the mind of Christ, b.) get our hearts

transformed into Christ's heart, c.) take on a kingdom lifestyle which is complying with God's will, God's way, through God's Spirit. The key is submitting to Christ through His written Word, to Christ's Spirit, and to the Christ who dwells in our brothers and sisters. There are several questions that we will each answer truthfully every time we meet. Everything said during this time will be held in the strictest confidence, creating a safe environment for confession of sin and honest conversation about our common struggles. In this process we will become known as we truly are, and invite one another to keep us accountable for our progress. Prayer over the issues raised will be our only response to sin confessed. Another way we grow in Christ is to set faith goals in one of the 5 C's (Christ, Character, Community, Calling, Competence) using the 4 dynamics necessary for change: instructional, relational, experiential, spiritual.

Two Key Questions We Regularly Ask Each Other:

A. What are you **hearing** God say to you through His Word and Spirit?

B. How are you specifically **obeying** God's Word in your relationships and in your responsibilities?

2. **Reading of Scripture:** We believe that there is power in the scriptures to transform lives, if we are humble and hungry to actually know and obey Christ. Each week our group will select chapters from the Bible to read. Our goal is that we will read about 14 to 30 chapters each week. It may take us a while to develop an appetite for this much scripture, and that's OK. This isn't about skipping through the Bible in one year. If one or more of us are unable to finish the agreed upon reading, then we'll just try again with the same scriptures the following week. The Bible actually gets better when read repeatedly. There are many good Bible-reading strategies that will help you to read the entire Bible every year.

3. **Harvest Praying:** We will endeavor to pray new people into the Kingdom of God, and also pray that God will add to our number in this group enabling us to multiply. We will strategically pray for those who are not yet in Christ. Prayer releases the Holy Spirit to convict unbelievers that they can get right with God. It unleashes the Spirit of wisdom and revelation causing blind eyes to see the glory of God. It moves people and circumstances to positively influence unbelievers. It brings us before Christ's face and keeps us focused on who we are and why we exist. Matthew 6:9-13. *"My house will be called a house of prayer for all nations."* Mark 11:17 Prayer moves God who moves the world. Pray specifically for a person bringing their name before God. Ask God for these five things to occur in their life:

A. Pray that the Father would draw them to Jesus. John 6:44 Include fasting. Mark 9:27 *"This kind can come out only by prayer and fasting".*

B. Bind the spirit that blinds their minds. 2 Corinthians 4:4

C. Loose the Spirit of adoption (sonship). Romans 8:15

D. Pray that believers will cross their paths and enter into positive relationships with them. Matthew 9:38

E. Loose the Spirit of wisdom and revelation on them so they may know God better. Ephesians 1:17

4. **Reaching Out to Those Who are Not Followers of Christ:** There are several great places to meet and influence friends to become followers of Christ. Co-workers, neighbors, schoolmates, and relatives are some of the places to reach out. You could even start a DNA Group at work, meeting during your lunch break or after work. Build loving relationships with those who are not yet in Christ. They open their hearts to us because we have loved and served them. The gospel will flow out of us and affect their hearts, causing them to open and receive Christ for themselves. Listen to their life story and respond with affirmation, acceptance, and affection. Do not hesitate to operate in the gifts of the Spirit as well. Healing and deliverance should be practiced regularly. Matthew 10:7-8; Mark 16:15-18

5. **Discipling New Believers:** There are several ways to follow up a new believer: 1.) get them a well-translated easy-to-understand Bible, 2.) have them start meeting in your DNA Group, 3.) introduce them to your Micro-Church Family and make sure they get baptized in water and the Holy Spirit, 4.) give them regular calls throughout the week to see how they are doing, 5.) lead them through inner healing and deliverance, 6.) teach them to hear Christ's voice objectively in the Word and subjectively in their spirit, 7.) make sure they have experienced the revelation of sonship, Romans 8, and know their authority as a child of God. 8.) teach them how to meet with Jesus every day. Here is an easy acronym to remember strategy for meeting with God: *2Proapt* - Pray, Preview the passage, Read, Observe, Apply, Pray, Tell others.

Reviewing the DNA Group's Purpose

We are two or three brothers or sisters who covenant to meet weekly for the purpose of being mutually accountable for our personal struggles and sin, and in turn offering each other prayer and support. In addition, we will pray for and reach out to those who do not know our Heavenly Father through Christ. When those we reach invite Christ to live in their hearts as Lord, we will follow-up and disciple them to become followers of Christ, to join our DNA Group, and come into our Micro-Church Family and local church.

- **Same Sex Only:**

  Some of the things we need to talk about most are less likely to be dealt with in a coed group.

- **Two or Three and Then Multiply:**

  Size is a critical element that can help or hinder our group purpose. While limiting our size to two or three people, we still continue looking for opportunities to include others. When the fourth person shows up we multiply and become two different groups. In this way there is no limit to the number of people who can become involved. A group of two or three has increased opportunity to achieve intimacy in sharing. Reproducibility is one of our stated goals, and one of the hoped-for results of our harvest prayers. Fewer moving parts means more flexibility in planning our times together. Of course, we can maintain relationships with those who were once in our DNA Group, either informally or through our Micro-Church Family and local church.

BECOMING A BOND SLAVE: THE KEY TO ACCURATELY HEARING GOD'S VOICE

In the Bible, there are two kinds of "slaves". A hired slave was in this predicament to either work off a debt or as the only option for survival. Exodus 21:2-6; Deuteronomy 15:12-18; Leviticus 25:35-46; John 10:12-13 A hired slave/servant retained some measure of personal rights. For example, they could chose who they married or where they lived after their 6 years of indentured service was fulfilled. The bond slave, our second option, made a personal choice to give up their rights and become bonded to their owner for life. This voluntary submission of love was sealed by the piercing of the ear. In other words, the ears were pierced as a symbol of total consecration to **hearing only the voice of the master. They dedicated their entire lives to only hearing one voice, so they could cheerfully fulfill their master's requests.** Pleasing the master, doing his will, was the bond slave's only life mission. Exodus 21:2-6; Deuteronomy 15:16-17. The apostles referred to themselves as bond slaves to Christ. Roman1:1; Titus 1:1; James 1:1; 2 Peter1:1; Jude 1; Revelation 1:1. Because bond slaves were motivated by such a high degree of love and loyalty, they often became the most trusted people in the family and were given large amounts of responsibilities and oversight. Genesis 24:1-4 Therefore, the clarity of God's voice and your ability to hear His voice will be determined by the inner condition of your heart. Because of gratitude and love, are you a bond slave to Christ? Have you given up your rights, your will and ways, in order to follow Him? Death to self is the key to experiencing eternal life in Christ! We gain our lives by losing our lives. John12:24; Luke9:23-27

Christ's Invitation plus Your Total Commitment = Transformation into Christ's Likeness

Jesus Christ has done everything necessary for you to become just like Him. He paid the penalty for your sin with His own blood. He died your death. Now He wants you to let Him come into your heart (spirit), so that He can transform you from the inside out. Ephesians 3:14-21; Colossians 1:27; Galatians 4:19 If you completely give yourself to having a love relationship with Jesus Christ, and let Him be your King, He will pour His Holy Spirit upon and within you, causing three supernatural things to happen. Mark 1:8; John 14:26, 16:3; Acts 1:8; Ephesians 5:18 First, the fruit of the Spirit will start forming in your heart and manifest in your lifestyle: love, joy, peace, patience, kindness, gentleness, self-control. Galatians 5:16-26 Second, you will start having the mind of Christ, thinking His thoughts, gaining His wisdom, and receiving revelation from Him. Roman 12:2, Ephesians 1:17-18 Third, you will receive supernatural power and gifts to advance Christ's Kingdom on earth. Acts 1:4-8; 1 Corinthians 12-14; Roman 12:4-8

You are being invited, by Jesus Christ, to follow Him. Turn away from being your own god, and from conformity to the world. Don't stay a prisoner to your false self. You can be your true self as a son of God. John 1:12-13; Roman 8:15-17; Galatians 3:26-29; Hebrews 2:10 Christ will change your very nature, turning you into a new creation man or woman. 2 Corinthians 5:17

Putting to Death Your "Old Man" or "False Self"
(With the Holy Spirit's Help) – So That Your True Self Can Fully Live - Roman 8:5-17

When Christ comes to live in our heart as God, He begins to help us "put to death" anything and everything that does not bring glory to God. This often confuses new believers because the process of dying to their false self is painful. How could a loving God allow me to suffer? But when the false self is put to death, the true self is liberated. God made us to be a son of God, our true self.

Initially, new believers can be disoriented by Satan's attempt to kill the true self and exalt the false self. While at the same time, God wants us to cooperate with putting to death the false self, so the true self can fully live in Christ. Roman 8:13 Both God and Satan are trying to facilitate a death process. One is death unto life, the other is death unto death. The death our Father God is encouraging is death to self-worship, so we can fully receive His eternal life. Satan promotes death unto death by making sin look good, tempting us to make choices that only result in destruction and death.

Practices & Activities of a DNA Group

Each DNA group should have a designated facilitator who makes sure that the group fulfills its mission to make disciples of Christ. The emphasis is becoming disciples of Christ, not disciples of a human being.

A DNA Group should gather for at least one hour each week. However, the relational connection, friendship, personal support and encouragement should also become a lifestyle, life-on-life, throughout each week.

During the DNA gathering each person should answer these two questions: a.) what have you been hearing from God's Word and Spirit this week? b.) how are you obeying what you hear? The two questions need to specifically point to the two central themes of Scripture: a. loving covenant relationships (with God, family, others), b. our dominion mandate to assume responsibility for advancing the Kingdom of God on earth. As trust increases in the DNA Group, you can add other questions which might foster more self-awareness, accountability, and growth. Here are three more support and accountability questions: a.) what do you see in my life that encourages you? b.) what do you see in my life that you would like to caution me about? c.) is there anything else you would like to tell me?

The Bible needs to be the central and most important reference. The DNA Group might select a book(s) of the Bible to read together. For example, the DNA Group might start by reading the gospels (Matthew, Mark, Luke, and John), a couple chapters each day. Every time the DNA Group gathers, those particular chapters can be the Word from God that we want to **hear** and **obey** in the areas of **relationships** and **responsibilities.**

New people can and should be added, after they receive clear orientation and the group agrees they are ready to actively participate. Make sure expectations are clear and upfront. There needs to be a verbalized commitment on the part of each DNA Group member that they have received the invitation and challenge to be a disciple and make disciples of Christ.

New facilitators should be identified and trained for DNA Group leadership.

The DNA Group should consider multiplying when one or two new people are added. Two to three people is the ideal number, allowing everyone to participate. This also helps create the opportunity for more leadership development and inspires reaching out to include more new disciples.

Apostolic mission – the word apostle means 'sent ones'. To be proactively "on mission" means that we pursue those who haven't placed their faith in Jesus Christ. We do this by taking initiative to demonstrate and declare the gospel. Apostolic mission is not primarily about attracting people to our group gatherings. It is about going to people where they live and work to share the love of God with them in their setting.

Culture & Etiquette

Culture is like a weather pattern. It is atmospheric and environmental. A Kingdom culture is one of the most essential ingredients for experiencing, absorbing, and transferring Christ's life. For example, Biblical truth may be present, but if it is not accompanied by love, then our context will undermine our content. There are many people who have been deeply hurt in small groups, even Bible studies, because the atmosphere was legalistic, judgmental and argumentative. Correct information with a toxic atmosphere is very dangerous. Remember, Satan is an accuser who uses right information in a wrong way to produce guilt and shame. A Kingdom culture is contagiously attractive and almost irresistible. Affection, kindness, and affirmation can penetrate our hearts in the same way fragrances of a bakery saturate our clothing. Timely laughter, for example, lets our emotions get a much needed lift. It is often said that being a disciple of Christ is more caught than taught. Kingdom culture provides the environment necessary to grow healthy, fully alive followers of Christ. Over the long haul, if we are consistently exposed to the affection of Christ Jesus through His family, our chances for transformation into Christ's likeness dramatically increases. A true kingdom culture is to a person's life what a well-monitored hot house is to plants. Climate and atmosphere are some of the most important elements which enhance growth and draw the lost to Jesus

There are actually four Greek words for "love" in the Greek language. Greek is the language in which the New Testament Bible was originally written. The four words are:

- *Eros* - physical, sensual, and romantic love
- *Storge* - natural affection and the kind of love exchanged in families
- *Philia* - friendship, loyal brotherly/sisterly love and also demonstrated natural affection
- *Agape* - committed and sacrificial love of God, covenant love, self-denial on behalf of others as a result of the supernatural enablement of the Holy Spirit - Romans 5:5

Most believers have intellectually agreed with the notion of God's Fathering love. However, many people do not experientially know, down in the core of their being where feelings and emotions operate, that God and God's people actually like them. God always has affection for us. He always likes us, even when we sin. He does not like our sinful thoughts, attitudes, and actions, but He always likes us. We need to experience the gospel through the body of Christ, which includes receiving affection, affirmation, encouragement. To be liked and affectionately loved is part of the gospel. The apostle Paul wrote to the church family in Philippi, *"God can testify how I long for all of you with the affection of Christ Jesus."* Philippians 1:8 DNA Groups are a wonderful setting in which we can like and affection God's people. In other words, we need to emit the gospel to one another with *storge*, *philia*, and *agape* love because we are whole people with feelings and emotions.

Transparency is when we share our inner conversation out loud with trusted friends. It is another way of describing what the Bible calls "fellowshipping in the light". See 1 John 1:1-10. Transparent communication opens the door of our hearts to Truth and Love, which displaces darkness with the Light of God's Life. If there is truth presented without love, it is not really the Spirit of Truth. Truth and Love are inseparable. Truth exists to teach us how to love.

What each person shares is sacred and should be kept in the strictest confidence. What is shared in the DNA Group, stays in the DNA Group. One's spouse should not even be told what is shared. There are exceptions to this rule. If the information points to problems beyond the groups capacities, church elders should be included. If what is shared reveals illegal activity or behaviors which could harm others, then proper authorities and licensed individuals should be notified.

Each person needs to participate and share. No one should take over the meeting or dominate the conversation. The facilitator needs to tactfully keep order.

Holding each other accountable without being critical or judgmental is an essential part of the DNA Group. The goal is to help one another acknowledge (confess) and repent for thoughts, attitudes, and actions that do not bring glory to God. Accountability is also about positively encouraging one another to obey what we heard from God. The focal point of accountability needs to be the thoughts of the mind and the condition of the heart, not just outward behavior. We don't want accountability to feel like behavior modification, so that we carry out "sin management" as though the Christian life is simply a matter of avoiding bad and doing good. We don't want our DNA Groups to be a place where we come to get scolded or lectured. It needs to be a group of merciful and kind friends, who are fellow advocates helping each other's internal heart wholeness, resulting in godly outward behaviors. All of us struggle with self-worship, sin, the spirit of the world, and demonic oppression. Therefore, the way in which we hold each other accountable and bring correction needs to be done with humble gentleness and surgically excellent tact. Galatians 6:1-2 A mature leader returns to joy quickly. The level of your joy will be proportionate to the quality of your relationship.

A generous amount of encouragement and affirmation should be expressed between the members of a DNA Group. The body of Christ is the "skin" of God, His hands, eyes, and voice. God wants each person to vocalize His pleasure, value, and appreciation for who we are and what we do that brings Him glory. We need to acknowledge and celebrate even the smallest victories. Small wins accumulate into habitual patterns of obedience. This results in greater confidence that God is good and compliance to His ways results in successful eternal impact.

Praying for one another needs to be a regular part of each DNA Group. Prayer is one of the most important ways God brings His Kingdom on earth.

Caution: Helping each other follow Christ involves militant spiritual warfare. Ephesians 5:10-20. There is a very real possibility that the members of the DNA Group will experience relational conflict, offenses, and disappointments. The hurts that occur will expose pride, unbelief, sinful strongholds, and insecurity, providing a great opportunity for growth, if we respond correctly. The remedy is a combination of humility, faith, Truth and forgiveness. Forgiveness is a way of life that keeps us moving forward in love after we have been hurt and betrayed. Forgiveness is not really a working option, it is a necessity! Matthew 6:12-15, 18:15-35; Luke 17:3-5; Ephesians 4:32

Kingdom Fruit

What could be more exciting, more relevant, than following Jesus Christ? The greatness of this privilege calls for the entirety of our lives. The stakes are very high for yourself and those you love. Who you become and what you do is of utmost importance. It is literally a matter of life and death. If you hear and obey Jesus Christ every day, together with your DNA Group, you will experience life-changing results. God's Word teaches that it is fruit which reveals whether someone is authentically following Christ. There are two types of fruit mentioned in the Bible. First, the fruit of the Spirit is the motives, character, attributes, and emotions of Christ (love, joy, peace, patience, kindness, goodness, faithfulness, gentleness, self-control, etc). The second kind of fruit refers to outward, tangible kingdom impact. We often describe fruit as "excess life" which automatically grows if all the conditions are right. If you closely follow the Biblical principles and guidelines spelled out in this booklet, you will truly bear much fruit, fruit that remains into eternity! Matthew 3:8-10, 7:16-20; Galatians 5:23; John 15:1-17

NOTES:

PHYSICAL HEALING, INNER-HEALING & DELIVERANCE

A Micro-Church leader functions as a shepherd who is entrusted with the well-being of others. Knowing how to pray for the sick, facilitate inner-healing & deliverance are important ministries in the Kingdom of God.

PRAYER FOR PHYSICAL HEALING

1. **Interview** To determine the condition for which prayer is sought and, if possible, the cause. If the cause is known, then go to: **3. Prayer Selection**.

●What is your name? ●How can I pray for you? ●How long have you had this condition? ●Do you know the cause?

2. **Diagnosis** The purpose is to determine the root cause of the infirmity or sickness. Possible roots: an afflicting spirit; sickness rooted in the soul (psychosomatic); or natural causes such as accident, injury, or disease.

●Do you have a doctor's diagnosis? ●Did someone cause this condition? Have you forgiven him? (Unforgiveness can be a major hindrance to healing.) ●Did any significant or traumatic event happen to you when (or within 6 months or a year before) this condition started? (Before praying for physical healing, you may need to help the person with unforgiveness, or with emotional wounds such as fear, shame, and rejection.)

Depend on the Holy Spirit – quietly ask Him if He has anything to show you about the condition or its cause. Listen to Him!

3. **Prayer Selection:** Petition: "Father, in Jesus' name I ask You to heal the inflammation in Joe's knee & take out the swelling & pain."

Command: "In the name of Jesus I command the inflammation in Joe's knee to be healed & all swelling & pain to leave"

Use commands when:

●Breaking a curse or vow. ●Casting out an afflicting spirit or other spirit. You have used petition prayers and progress has stopped. ●You are led by the Holy Spirit. ●A word of knowledge or other circumstances indicates that God wants to heal the person immediately.

4. **Prayer Ministry (Praying for Effect)**

1. Audibly ask the Holy Spirit to be present with His guidance & His healing power. 2. Ask the person not to pray but instead, to close his/her eyes & focus on his/her body. It's a time for him/her just to receive. 3. Ask him/her to interrupt you & tell you if he/she feels something: heat/electricity/trembling, etc. (About 50% of people being healed feel something.) 4. If indicated, have the person confess any sin (unforgiveness, anger, etc.) and/or pray for the person's emotional healing before praying for physical healing.

Tips: ●Keep your eyes open, to see God's touch. ●Follow any leading of the Holy Spirit ●If a specific prayer brings improvement, keep using it. ●Use your normal tone of voice. ●Always pray in the name of ●Pray for symptoms & cause, if the cause is known Use short, specific prayers ●Pray where God is working ●Periodically ask, "What is going on?" ●Try different kinds of prayer. ●Don't preach or give advice. ●Remember: trust the Holy Spirit, not the method ●**Be loving! Be persistent!** ●**Thank God for whatever He does (You cannot thank God too much!)**

- If pain moves around or increases during prayer or if a condition has existed a long time, consider casting out an afflicting spirit

- If you are not making progress, consider interviewing the person further:

●Would you try again to remember any significant event?	●Have any other members of your family ever had this condition?
●Do you have a strong fear of anything?	●Has anyone ever pronounced a curse over you or your family?
●Do you know of anyone who is very angry at you?	●Have you ever participated in any kind of Satanic or other occult activity?
●Has anyone in your family been a member of the Freemasons?	●Have you had other accidents? (He or she may be accident-prone.)

- Stop praying when:
  The person: ●is healed ●wants you to stop ●The Holy Spirit tells you to stop ●You are gaining no ground and receive no other way to pray.

5. **Post-prayer Suggestions -** After praying, it is beneficial to give helpful follow-up instruction or exhortations.

●Encourage the prayee from Scripture. ●Share appropriate lifestyle changes for maintaining healing and to prevent problem re-occurrence. ●If someone is not healed or is only partially healed, do not accuse the person of a lack faith or of sin in his or her life as the cause. Prepare the person to resist any further attack after healing.

PRAYER FOR DELIVERANCE

The objective is to expel any demons, close their avenues of access to the victim, and enable the victim to keep these avenues closed in the future. It is most effective to work as a team. One person is in charge, he or she does all the talking and, in steps 2, 6, 7 and 8, all the touching. Others pray silently and talk with the leader quietly. Leadership can rotate during ministry. Steps 6 and 7 can be extremely painful. Don't hesitate to stop, provide comfort, and pray for healing. If the person can't remember important details or identify the cause of feelings, you can interrupt the ministry time and have him go home and ask the Holy Spirit.

1. **Give the individual priority.** Maintain a loving attitude. Be encouraging. Move to a quiet place if possible. Invite the Holy Spirit to be present.

2. **If a spirit manifests, make it be quiet.** Repeat "Submit in the name of Jesus!" Be persistent, this may take time. Only the leader touches the person.

3. ***Establish and maintain communication with the person.** You <u>must</u> have his cooperation. "Joe, can you hear me? Look at me!"

4. ***Ask the person what he or she wants freedom from.** <u>Make sure he or she really wants freedom</u> from the bondage(s).

5. ***Make sure the person has accepted Jesus as Lord and Savior.** If not, lead him/her in prayer for salvation. If you can't, bless him/her but don't try deliverance.

6. **Interview the person to discover the event(s) that have led to the bondage(s).** Expose where forgiveness is required, and where healing, repentance and breaking of bondages are needed. Find all open doors. If there is no obvious place to start, begin with his/her parental relationships, then move to other areas. Be thorough, don't rush. Do not stir up demons, keep them quiet. List the spirits encountered and areas requiring forgiveness of others or repentance. Consider a curse if the person has persistent difficulty in an area of life. Fear is an entry point for different spirits and a problem in many illnesses.

Body	**Soul**	**Spirit**
Sexual sin of any kind, Uninvited sexual relationship, Long Illness/General weakness	Resentment/Anger - Despair/Hopelessness - Hatred (all forms) - Trauma & its effects - Pride/Arrogance –Criticism /Gossip - Rejection/Loneliness - Rebellion/Vengeance - Envy in all forms Unforgiveness/Bitterness - Fear in all forms - Greed	Any occult experience Witchcraft/manipulation Satanism/Freemasonry Curses/Inner vows

7. **Lead the person in closing the door(s) through which the spirit(s) entered.** (If there is no one to forgive, go to Steps B through D.) He should:

   a. ***Forgive whoever caused the hurt or led him into wrong conduct.** Be specific, item-by-item. The seeker should release the offender to God, and commit to take his hands off – to not try to change the offender, and ask God to bless him in every way. If the seeker is unable to forgive, explain the scripture to him. You can quietly bind any spirit of unforgiveness. If he is still unable to forgive, pray for healing and blessing but not deliverance.

b. **Repent of his specific sins in the situation(s).** "Father, forgive me for _____ (hate, bitterness, sharing my body with _____, reading horoscopes, etc.)"

c. **Renounce audibly & firmly all spirits involved, in the name of Jesus.** In the case of sex outside marriage, the person should renounce spirits taken in from every partner he can recall, individually by first names. Pacts with Satan & inner vows must be renounced & curses broken. "In the name of Jesus I renounce the spirits of ___ & ___." "In the name of Jesus, I renounce the vow I made never/always to ____."

d. **Break the bondage(s) caused by the sin, attitude, conduct, vow, spirit, curse, etc.,** in the name of Jesus. This closes the door. (You or the seeker can do this.) "In the name of Jesus I break the power of the spirit(s) of ___ over (Tom) so that when they are cast out, they will not come back." "In the name of Jesus I break the power of every curse over (Tom) from ____ (father's careless critical words, father's Freemasonry, etc.)"

8. **Cast out the unclean spirit(s) in the name of Jesus.** Some people cast spirits out one-by-one; some cast them out by groups. Do what works for you. With all doors closed, the spirits will leave quickly & quietly. If they don't leave promptly, go back to Step 6. Tell the person there may be other spirits to deal with. Re-interview. Ask the Holy Spirit to show you or the seeker or a team member what He wants to do next. He is very willing to help you!

9. **Have the person thank Jesus for His deliverance.** If he cannot, or if spirits manifest, more doors need to be closed. (Same for Step 10.)

10. **Have the person ask the Holy Spirit to fill him or her and all the places formerly occupied by the evil spirits.**

11. **Get into a Micro-Church Family for ongoing support and accountability.**

12. **Follow and obey Christ daily, advancing His Kingdom in every area of life.**

*Do not pray for deliverance without these items, because the person probably will not stay free.

Just pray for his/her healing, and for blessing.

PRAYERS THAT HEAL THE HEART

Introduction: Because we have a covenant with God through Christ's shed blood and sacrificial death on the cross, we can approach our loving Father, and ask for the mercy and grace we need to live in full obedience to Him. He will release the power of the Holy Spirit to give us the fruit, wisdom, revelation, and power we need to advance Christ's Kingdom on earth in the context of our church family. It is rebellion to Christ and the Kingdom, and broken covenants that cause sin, sickness, inner wounding, and demonic bondage. Faith, obedience, and reestablished covenant is the means to healing and deliverance. See these Bible passages that describe the power of prayer: Luke 18; Matthew 6; Ephesians 1:18; James 5:15; Philippians 4:6-7; Acts 1:14, 2:42, 6:4, 10:31; Ephesians 6:18; 1 Thessalonians 5:17

(The following paragraph is from Mark Virkler, "Prayers That Heal the Heart") To heal the heart, you must use the language of the heart, not the language of the mind! The language of the mind is analytical reason. Matthew 16:7 KJV The language of the heart is flow John 7:37-39 KJV, imagination Genesis 8:21 KJV, dreams and visions Acts 2:17, emotions Genesis 6:6 KJV and pondering Psalm 77:61 KJV. **Therefore, as you pray stay tuned to flowing thoughts, flowing pictures/visions, and emotions.** If you neglect this, your prayers will be coming from your head and they WILL NOT HEAL YOUR HEART! Constantly rely upon the Holy Spirit (i.e. Holy Spirit "flow") to guide you through this healing process. He can and He will respond to your faith.

If we confess our sins, He is faithful and just to forgive us our sins, and to cleanse us from all unrighteousness. I John 1:9

Three steps: Confession – Forgiveness – Cleansing

Prayer #1: The Prayer that establishes a covenant with Christ through His blood, enabling us to enter His Kingdom as sons, reconciling us to God and our Kingdom family. All covenants are made in blood which is why we will take communion (Lord's Supper) with this prayer.

> Dear Lord God, I acknowledge You as my Lord and my Savior. I repent and turn from going my own sinful way, and I acknowledge that You have the right to the reins of my life. I place my life back under Your control where it should have been from day one. I acknowledge my sinfulness and self-will and stubbornness, and I turn from these sins and from the many other sins which come from my independent living. I acknowledge You as the One to Whom I will come for direction for my life from this day on. I ask that the blood of Your Son, Jesus Christ, which was shed on Calvary, be applied to my sins and wash them away as far as the East is from the West. Let them be remembered no more. Teach me Your ways. Instruct me in the way that I should go. From this day on, I look to You as my Lord and my Savior. Thank You for Your gift of eternal life, of life both now and in eternity. Transform me into a "son of God" and bring me into your Family. I worship You, Lord. In Jesus' Name, Amen." See Roman 8, 10:9-10; John 3:16

- If you have not been baptized in water, you should do this as a sacrament of identification with Christ, dying to yourself and living by, for, and through Christ.
- You need to also receive the baptism of the Holy Spirit and fire.
- Make sure that you become an active member of an authentic Biblical church family

Prayer #2: Prayer that breaks the power of generational & current sins and curses

Diagnostic discovery prayer for God to expose lies, sins, and curses:

> God, will you reveal all sinful thoughts, attitudes, motives, desires, and actions that were in my ancestors and received by me?

1. I **confess** and repent of the sin of my ancestors, my parents, and my own sin of_____, and of my anger and resentment against You, God, for allowing this to happen in my life. This confessing prayer was left out before.

2. I forgive and release my ancestors for passing on to me this sin and for the resulting curses of_____(be specific). I ask You to forgive me, and I receive Your forgiveness. I forgive myself for participating in this sin.

3. I come under the blood of Jesus and place the cross of Christ between my ancestors and myself, as a baby in my mother's womb. I command the sin of _____ and all accompanying curses to be halted at the Cross of Jesus Christ, and for freedom and release to flow down from the Cross of Christ to that baby in the womb.

   - Has the Lord given you a picture of this scene? Ask the Lord if He has more to show you about yourself as a baby in the womb. Added this visualization—find that we always do this here—has been powerful

   - Curses are stopped at the Cross of Christ and covered by the blood of Christ. Galatians 3:13

   - It is most powerful to apply the grace of God at the point of need (i.e. when the child received the curses in his or her mother's womb). God lives in timelessness, so this is no problem for Him.

Prayer #3: Prayer that severs ungodly soul ties. (We cut off the sinful influences, but we do not reject the person.)

Questions for discovering the need to sever ungodly soul ties:
- With whom have I had a close committed relationship that was unhealthy, dominating, controlling, or manipulative?
- Lord, please remind me of everyone with whom I have had a sexual encounter of any kind.
- Lord, were there any sexual encounters in my early childhood that I was too young to remember?
- When have I given or received blood or eaten blood?

1. I confess and repent of my sin of an ungodly soul tie with _____, and of my anger and resentment against You, god, for allowing this to happen in my life.

2. I forgive_____ for their involvement in this sin. I ask You to forgive me, and I receive

Your forgiveness. I forgive myself for participation in this sin.

3. Lord, sever the ungodly soul tie between _____ and me and restore the broken or torn portions of my soul. Lord, destroy anything that has come into me through this soul tie and, Lord, bring back anything godly that has been stolen from me.

- Has the Lord given you a picture of this scene? Ask the Lord if He has more to show you about yourself as a baby in the womb.

Prayer #4: Prayer that replaces negative expectations with faith. Negative expectations are ungodly beliefs or systems of belief that become established in your heart. It may be a belief or expectation against you, others, authorities, institutions or God. Most of these are on an unconscious level so you are generally not aware that you are holding them. Yet these beliefs are sin and need to be repented of and replaced with God's truth in order to walk in freedom.

Questions for discovering the need to replace negative expectations with faith:

- Lord, what beliefs do I hold that do not line up with your truth? What negative confessions come out of my mouth or are in my heart? What expectations rob me of love, joy and peace, and what negative emotions trigger these beliefs?

1. Negative beliefs activate the <u>Law of Faith</u> in reverse. Matthew 9:*29 "According to your faith let it be to you."*
2. Negative beliefs activate the <u>Law of Judgment</u>, Matthew 7:2 *"For with what judgment you judge, you will be judged…"* Exodus 20:12 *"Honor your father and your mother, that your days will be long…"*
3. Negative beliefs activate the <u>Law of Sowing and Reaping</u>. Galatians 6:7 *"… for whatever a man sows, that he will also reap."*
4. Negative beliefs activate the <u>Law of Multiplication</u>. Hosea 8:7 *"They sow the wind, and reap the whirlwind…"* All NKJV **added from various sources, we find ourselves always having to explain these.**

Questions for discovering the need to replace negative expectations with faith:
- Lord, what negative confessions come out of my mouth?
- Lord, what negative expectations are in my heart?
- Lord, what things do I believe that do not line up with what the Bible and Spirit are revealing to me?
- Lord, what expectations rob me of love, joy, and peace?
- What expectations keep me from giving thanks for all things and in all things? Ephesians 5:20; 1 Thessalonians 5:18

1. I confess and repent of my sin (and if appropriate my ancestors' sin) of believing the lie that _____ and for the ways I have judged others and/or institutions based upon this negative belief.
2. I forgive _____ for contributing to my forming this negative expectation/belief. I ask You to forgive me, and I receive Your forgiveness. I forgive myself for believing this lie.
3. I confess these positive affirmations of faith and divine truth that counter my negative

expectations _____ Roman 10:17; Ephesians 1:17-18

Prayer #5: Prayer that renounces inner vows. See Matthew 5:34-37; Acts 19:21

Questions for discovering the need to renounce inner vows:
- Lord, what do I promise I will do?
- Lord, what do I promise I won't do?
- Lord, what do I promise about myself?
- Lord, what do I promise about others?

1. I confess and repent of my sin of vowing that _____.
2. I forgive _____ for contributing to my forming this vow and myself for making this vow.
3. Instead, I now purpose by the power of the Holy Spirit to _____. (It is appropriate to have Biblical, godly resolutions that solicit the help and power of the Holy Spirit.)

Prayer #6: Prayer that enables God to heal you from traumatic and negative pictures. Prayer that releases the Spirit of wisdom, revelation, divine pictures, dreams, and visions. Ephesians 1:17-18; Acts 2:17-18; 2 Corinthians 4:17-18; Hebrews 12:2. W e are not talking about making up scenes or visions ourselves.

Questions for discovering the need to heal traumatic/negative pictures:
- Lord, what negative pictures are in my mind?
- Lord, what traumatic pictures have I tried to block out?
- Lord, what negative pictures come up in my dreams?

1. I confess and repent of any anger and bitterness I have against You, God for allowing this event to happen in my life. I ask You to forgive me, and I receive Your forgiveness.
5. Lord, please take me back to the appropriate memory that is underlying this issue in my heart. (See the scene. If a rape or other extremely traumatic scene, you may go back to just after it is over.)
6. Lord, show me where You were in this scene. (Look and see where Jesus is/was.) Holy Spirit, take over this scene and give me a vision, showing me what Jesus was doing. (Respond to what the Lord is showing and doing.)
7. Lord, please enable me to see you and the revelations you have for me through the eyes of my heart.

Prayer #7: Prayer that breaks word curses

Question for discovering the need to heal word curses:
- "Lord, what word curses have I or others spoken over me, which contribute to the problem of _____.

  (For example, "You dummy! You'll never make it in the field of _____! You are such a loser! What a moron! You are just fat! You are so lazy! You'll never amount to anything! This is my lazy daughter. This is the computer nerd, or any negative nickname.)

1. In Jesus name, I break all these word curses _____ spoken over me. I forgive _____ for saying these things. I forgive myself for receiving these curses. I place all negative words spoken under the blood of Jesus. I bless all those who have cursed me.

Prayer #8: Prayer that casts out demons

Demons attach themselves to sin. When the roots of sin are removed, it is much easier to command demons to leave. The goal is to displace darkness with the light of God.

Questions for discovering the need for deliverance:
- Lord, what compulsive pressures are within me?
- Lord, what sins can I not defeat?
- Lord, what stumbling blocks occur over and over?

1. Make sure the demon's house is thoroughly dismantled and his anchors completely pulled up by praying through the above six prayers. If the demon does not come out, go back to the above six prayers – something has been missed. Ask god what has been missed and honor what flows back in response.

2. In the Name of the Lord Jesus Christ, I renounce and break all agreements with the demons and the strongholds of lies they have tried to embed in my mind and heart. Individually identify these demons and/or groups of demons and command them to leave.

3. I take authority over the demons of _____ and I bind you and command you to leave me now in the Name of the Lord Jesus Christ.

Prayer #9: Prayer that enables us to experience the power of the Holy Spirit in our lives Ro 8:2, 13

The goal is to overcome the power of the flesh and sin within you by turning your focus from laws and self-effort to the Holy Spirit and His power within you. The power of the Holy Spirit in your heart breaks the power of sin in your flesh. Your flesh cannot break the power of flesh and sin, only the indwelling Holy Spirit can. The blood of Jesus, His mercy, opens the door to the power of the Holy Spirit, God's grace.

Questions for discovering the need for freedom from enslavement to sin:
- Lord, what sins am I attacking with my will?
- Lord, what sins continue to trouble me?

1. God, the power to overcome the sin of _____ is in You, the One Who lives in me.

2. I turn away from my self-effort to overcome this sin, and embrace the power of the Holy Spirit Who flows within me.

3. Jesus, I release the flow of the power of the Holy Spirit out through me, to overcome completely the sin of _____. (May use vision, seeing this happen.)

Most of the content of these prayers were taken from "Prayers That Heal the Heart" by Mark & Patti Virkler.

Prayer of Witnesses: After the prayers the team prays together, blesses the person and witnesses everything that has been done for the person by the Holy Spirit to this point (we adopted this from the Sanford's)

- Give any follow-up homework/things to remember to do
- Make any follow-up appointments/arrangements necessary

THE BIBLICAL BASIS FOR INNER HEALING

By: Bob Whitaker

1. Biblical References

The Bible has some wonderful general promises where God speaks to the condition of our hurts and afflictions. One of the best is Isaiah 61:1-3, which is quoted by Jesus in Luke 4 when He describes the objectives of His ministry.

> *"The Lord anointed me to bring good tidings to the afflicted; He has sent me to bind up the broken hearted, to proclaim liberty to the captives, and the opening of prison to those who are bound;... and to grant to those who mourn in Zion – to give them a garland instead of ashes, the oil of gladness instead of mourning, the mantle of praise instead of a faint spirit;..."*

2. The Love of God

The greatest need of everyone is to be loved and to love. To know God's love for us and to be released to give it to others is the greatest of all. This is the foundation, initiative and context for all Christian healing. In emotional healing we begin by assuring persons that God loves them unconditionally.

Key scriptures are: Jeremiah 31:3, John 3:16-17, Romans 5:8, 8:38-39, and 1 John 4:10.

I'm indebted to my friend, Mike Flynn, for the insight that Jesus loves us as much as the Father loves Him (John 15:9, 17:23). The corollary is that the Father loves us as much as He loves Jesus (1 John 3:1). To contemplate and reflect on this as we study the New Testament is the most healing thing in the world.

3. God's Omnipresence and Eternity

A crucial emphasis in praying for the healing of past hurts is the Biblical emphasis about the Lord always being with us. Psalm 73:23 and 139, Isaiah 43:2, Matthew 28:20 My favorite is Hebrews 13:5, *"I will never leave you nor forsake you."* Most quoted is probably *"Jesus Christ the same yesterday, and today, and forever."* Hebrews 13:8 Because of these truths we emphasize that because Christ is eternally the same, and because He lives in time and is yet beyond time, He can take us back to hurts that happened decades ago, and manifest His presence and heal us as though it were today. This is phenomenal reality which happens over and over again.

4. Comfortable Words

All through the scriptures the Lord invites us to turn to Him and assures us He will respond and help and bless. Most hurting people need the encouragement of such words to ask for healing prayer and to open up to ministry.

Key verses are: Psalm 23, 27:11, 46:1-2, 103:13-14, Lamentations 3:22, Micah 7:8, Matthew 10:29 and 11:28; John 6:37, 14:1, and 18, Acts 16:31, Romans 10:13, Philippians 4:19, Hebrews 2:18 and 4:15, James 4:8 and Revelation 3:20.

5. **Forgiveness**

Central to Christian teaching is God's forgiveness in Christ and the call to forgive others from the heart. In emotional healing we pray that the Lord will so touch persons with His forgiving and healing love that their hearts will be melted and they will be released to forgive. Jesus' teaching on the Lord's Prayer Matthew 6:7-15, and especially the parable of the unforgiving debtor, is extremely important. Matthew 18

Based on these and other passages, I emphasize the following:

A. Reflect on the greatness of God's forgiveness of you.

B. We imprison ourselves and hand ourselves over to torment when we do not forgive them from our hearts. Failure to love and forgive is a withdrawal into the prison of self. The most bound and "locked in) people are those who lock others out.

C. Failure to live in forgiving love leads to guilt, which causes fear and anxiety, which makes us sick. It also causes emotional conflict involving loss of self-respect, anger toward others, self-hatred and all sorts of unhappiness.

> *God's love is like sunshine. It will light up not only our spirit but our mind and body as well. It is constantly available, but if we block it out by excluding anyone from our love, we should not complain if we soon begin to feel the effects mentally and physically." -George Montague*

D. We need to face and confess to God as sin our anger, hate and distaste for others.

E. We need to pray for a forgiving heart, trust the Lord to give us grace to forgive, and begin to act it out in graciousness and benevolence towards our enemies.[22]

F. We need to ask for others to pray for us to actualize A-E above.

6. **Importance of Parents**

I never realized how important love and respect for parents are until I started praying for emotional healing. Until people learn to respect, love and forgive their parent's life will not go well for them. The fifth commandment (*"Honor thy father and thy mother"*), and all such scriptures Exodus 20:12, Leviticus 19:3, Proverbs 1:8, 6:20, 7:1, 23:22 and 30:17, Ephesians 6:1, Colossians 3:20, and the examples of the great Biblical characters prove this cardinal truth. Most of life's hurts go back to the relationship with father and mother or their substitutes. The next most important sources of hurts are other family members and spouses.

---

[22] See *Restoring the Christian Family* by John & Paula Sandford.

We find that the ministry of inner healing is essentially a ministry of reconciliation, an Elijah ministry of turning *"the hearts of fathers to their children and the hearts of children to their fathers".* Malachi 4:6 We also find that the greatest marital difficulties are rooted in the spouses' unhealed relationships with their own parents.[1]

7. **The Value of Suffering**

   A positive view of suffering is 'writ large' in the Bible. Romans 5:1-5 sums up that view:

   A. Suffering produces endurance. We never learn patient endurance without going through great difficulty, and it usually is through interpersonal relationships.
   B. Endurance produces character. God allows and sends tests to produce character that can stand up to anything. Tests expose our weaknesses so that we can face them, repent and be healed.
   C. But tests also bring out the strength and beauty we never knew God had put in us, and they force us to rely on God more than ever and thus discover how good and sufficient He is.
   D. **Battle-tested character produces hope. Knowing how, when we were wiped out on the human plane, the Lord came to our rescue and showed us new resources and possibilities; knowing that by His grace, the worst things turned out to be the best things; knowing how He taught us to cope and overcome;** we face the future hopefully and confidently knowing that *"I can do all things through Him who strengthens me."* Philippians 4:13. See also Romans 8:28.
   E. Hope does not disappoint us. Even though we have little earthly visible success, God's love is poured into our hearts as the Holy Spirit strengthens us in all the ups and downs of life.

8. **The Heart of Biblical Teaching**

   The heart of Biblical teaching concerning inner healing, and specifically emotional healing, can be found in the word "heart" (*Kardia* in Greek).

   The word heart (or hearts) is found 938 times in the Bible. I once looked up all the references in Strong's Exhaustive Concordance and studied most of them. What follows is a short condensation of some findings.

   Heart Definition

   The heart is the innermost part of persons. It is the center and source of the whole inner life, including the spirit, mind, emotions and will. (This is a summary of concordance and lexicon definitions.) There are places in the Bible where the word "soul" is used to refer to the emotional or psychological aspect of persons. Hebrews 4:21, 1Thessolonians 5:23 This is appropriate because the Greek for "soul" is "psyche". But generally the word "soul" is used in a broader sense and refers to the whole person, or is a synonym for "spirit". The Biblical concept of "heart" is inclusive of all the forces and functions of "spirit" and "soul". Often, however, it is used to emphasize difference aspects of the inner life.

The Spirit

In Psalm 51:10 and 51:17 "heart" refers to the "spirit" of a person. This is where God meets us and makes Himself known to us. *"Create in me a clean heart, O God; and renew a right spirit within me." "The sacrifice acceptable to God is a broken spirit; a broken and contrite heart, O God, thou wilt not despise;" "I will put my law within them, and I will write it upon their hearts; and I will be their God and they shall be my people... they shall all know me;"* Jeremiah 31:33-34 *"A new heart I will give you, a new spirit I will put within you; and I will take out of your flesh the heart of stone."* Ezekiel 36:26. See also Jeremiah 17:9-10, Proverbs 4:23, Ezekiel 11:19, Romans 2:29 and 10:8-10, 1 Timothy 1:5, Hebrews 3:8 and 15, etc.

Mind, Thought, Understanding

Where we would speak of the illumination of the mind, the Bible often uses the word "heart" as in 2 Corinthians 4:6, Ephesians 1:18 and 2 Peter 1:19. *"Jesus, knowing their thoughts said 'Why do you think evil in your hearts?'"* Romans 1:21 in the RSV reads, *"their senseless minds were darkened."* The literal Greek is, *"their undiscerning heart was darkened."*

The Will

2 Corinthians 9:7, RSV, says, *"Each one must do as he has made up his mind."* The literal translation is, *"Every man as he purposes in his heart."* In Luke 21:14, RSV, Jesus says, *"Settle it therefore in your minds."* Actually He uses the word *"hearts."* See also Nehemiah 7:5, John 13:2, Acts 5:4, 8:20 and 11:23.

Moral Life

Matthew 5:8 says, *"Blessed are the pure in heart for they shall see God."* See also Psalm 22:4. 1 Thessalonians 3:13 speaks of *"hearts blameless in holiness."* See also Hebrews 10:22.

Emotions, Feelings, Desires

Luke 24:32, *"Did not our hearts burn within us while He talked to us on the way?"* John 14:1, *"Let not your hearts be troubled."* 2 Corinthians 7:3, *"you are in our hearts to die together and to live together."* See also Matthew 5:28, 6:21, 12:34, and 22:27; Acts 7:54 and 21:13; 2 Corinthians 6:11-12; Ephesians 6:22; Colossians 4:8; Romans 10:1; Philippians 1:3-7.

Memory

Emotional healing is often called "Healing of the Memories." Therefore, it is significant to remember that "heart" includes memory. Luke 2:19 *"Mary kept all these things, pondering them in her heart."* See also Luke 2:51 and Acts 7:23.

Imagination

Most important for our understanding of emotional healing and the use of active imagination (visualization) in its healing is to appreciate anew that the heart is the imagination center of our life. The rabbis taught this in olden times, and it is scripturally based. *"God saw that every imagination of the thoughts of his heart was only evil continually."* Genesis 6:5 and 8:21 This word for "imagination" is used in Deuteronomy 31:21, 1 Chronicles 28:9 and 29:18 and is derived from a word meaning "form".

The Genius of Jesus

The prophets had perceived that *"the heart is deceitful above all things and desperately wicked (sick)."* Jeremiah 17:9 Jesus saw even more deeply that the heart was the source and fountain of all pollution and that what was needed was a radical transformation. In the passages on defilement Matthew 15:1-20 and Mark 7:1-23, He said, *"For from within, out of the heart of man, come evil thoughts..."* The word translated *"thoughts"* is just as well translated *"imaginations."* The Greek word is so translated in the key passage of Romans 1:21 KJV. I believe Jesus headed the list of sins pouring out of the heart with the word "imaginations" because He knew that the image-making faculty is the author of the evil deed. This comes out forcefully in His teaching on adultery in Matthew 5:27-30 where the lustful thought/imagination is attacked as the root of the deed.

Jesus' Appeal to the Imagination

More importantly than perceiving the root problem, Jesus perceived the cure. Since the imagination was the trigger of any heart response, He sought to change hearts by appealing to the imagination. He vividly portrayed the Kingdom of God with word-pictures, parables and picturesque sayings. In Matthew 13 He called His listeners to picture a sower. (In the KVJ the parable is preceded by the word, *"Behold."* This can justifiably be translated, *Picture a sower going to sow."*)

Then He explained why He spoke in parables (word-pictures), *"This is why I speak to them in parables, because seeing they do not see, and hearing they do not hear, nor do they understand."* Matthew 15:13 Jesus wanted to captivate their hearts with a whole new vision which would displace the old evil imaginations. In this He was the fulfillment of the patriarchs and prophets. They had all spoken in pictures because they were inspired by God who knows the secrets of hearts and knows that the eye-gate is the way to heart change. He Himself spoke to them in dreams and visions and vivid speech.

Visualizing Jesus

Jesus did not tell people in Palestine to picture or see Him with them when they prayed for the healing of their hurts. He didn't need to because they could see Him in the flesh. But after His ascension, they learned very quickly to see Him by faith. Their models were the great heroes of the Old Testament. It is intriguing that on the day of Pentecost, after the Spirit was poured out, Peter reminded them of David's practice: *"I keep the Lord always before me;*

because He is at my right hand, I shall not be moved. Therefore my heart is glad and my soul rejoices …" Psalm 16:8 and 9. See also Acts 2:25-28.

The apostle Paul talks about the veil being taken away that obscures the Lord's glory. Then he says, *"…and we all, with unveiled faces, **beholding** the glory of the Lord, are being changed into His likeness from one degree of glory to another; for this comes from the Lord who is the Spirit."* 2 Corinthians 12:18 The writer of Hebrews describes the Old Testament heroes envisioning the city of God in chapter 11. Then in 12:2 he bids us to be *"fixing our eyes on Jesus"* (NAS) and run the race before us. These verses were originally heard by a people who were simple, poor, and childlike. With the help of John's first chapter of Revelation, they could readily picture the Lord of glory with them always and coming on the clouds of heaven.

When they talked about practicing His presence, they said they were *"seeking His face"* 2 Chronicles 7:14, Psalm 105:4 and 27:8 KVJ. Seeing Jesus, in their minds, as they prayed was natural. So common was the practice that in the sixth century Maximus the Confessor felt it necessary to justify praying without imaging.[23]

The disciplined practice of picturing the Lord with us when we pray about the past, present or future was specifically taught in the Catholic Church since the fifteenth century. We know this from the Benedictine tradition.[24]

Peter's Memory Healed

Granted the importance of visualization, the question arises: "Did Jesus have people relive their hurts in His presence?" You will remember the awful experience of Peter's denying his Lord three times. Remember also that it was in the courtyard of the high priest where a fire had been kindled. Luke 22:55 It must have been terrible after he apostatized to have Jesus look at him. Luke 22:61 *"He went out and wept bitterly."* He was crushed in his spirit.

Later, after the resurrection, Jesus took Peter back to relive his awful memory. John 21 He did it by building a fire on the shore of Galilee and inviting Peter and the others to have breakfast with Him. He set the scene, then three times He gave Peter an opportunity to reaffirm his love for Him. Nothing could be more healing!

The key methodology in emotional healing today is to relive the old hurts while calling upon Jesus to manifest His presence in healing love.

Relationship to Psychology

There are **certain similarities** between inner healing as practiced by us and psychotherapy. Both are empathetic in the approach to hurting people. Both seek to help the person get in

---

[23] This information comes from Sister Mary Milligan, former Prof. Of Spirituality at Loyola University, Los Angeles.

[24] Same as 2 above

touch with hurts rooted in the past, especially with parents. Both encourage honest facing of how we got to be where we are and why we react as we do. The two approaches share somewhat in terms of the use of imagination. Both desire insight to come which will result in a happier way of relating to self and life. Both encourage responsible action based on new understanding.

There are, however, **big differences**. We are not psychologically trained and we do not follow their disciplined counseling methodologies. Unless the psychologist is a Christian, we are very different in what we rely upon. We call upon the Lord to be present to guide us and to manifest His presence in healing power. The psychologist desires human understanding to grow in the patient, resulting in a better adjustment to life. We desire illumination to come with a healing encounter with the Lord, leading to a renewed and transformed life motivated by His love and truth.

Several of my friends are clinical psychologists, two are psychiatrists. I have also prayed for emotional healing for a number of therapists. Some of these people have told me that **more is achieved through Christian inner-healing than through psychotherapy**. Of course, there are good and not-so-good inner-healers, and the same is true of therapists. Consider also that Christian inner-healing is normally free.

But it should be said that many people, even Christians who have had some inner-healing, can often benefit from a good psychologist who will help them face and deal with things they need to face. Also, it is nice to know that the psychologists are there to handle tough cases that we can't handle.

Basic Steps in Ministering Emotional Healing

1. Church Context

   Normally we do not do emotional healing with strangers. We do it with persons involved with us in worship, teaching and ministry. It is an aid to total Christian maturation, not a cure-all. People will open up best with persons they've learned to trust in the fellowship. We, in turn, need to be in a position to see what is happening in the lives of those we pray for and to follow through on wounds that were opened up but not yet substantially healed.

   We make an appointment at the request of the person feeling a need, or we might have trained teams available to meet with persons after a worship or prayer service. The best times are after services because we have sensitized our hearts through worship. As Jesus said, *"Where two or three…"* If people request one of us to pray, we usually ask him or her who else we could invite that they would feel comfortable with. In that way, they have a Christian friend with them who can help pray and whom we begin to train informally by modeling. We encourage at least two, but no more than three, to be on the healing team.

   A. Desirability of a Team

1. To work in ministry teams is the method that Jesus used and instructed His disciples to use. Mark 1:16-20, Luke 10:l

2. It is Jesus who does the healing, not us! A team approach avoids one person's becoming prideful when people are healed. It also lessens the danger of those who are touched becoming dependent upon one person.

3. In inner healing, as well as physical healing, there is the need for the exercise of different gifts of the Holy Spirit for effective ministry. In a prayer team, many more gifts may be manifested. For instance, one person may have the gift of discernment, another may receive words of knowledge, and etc.

4. The team guards against unwise intimacy developing between a solo counselor and a needy supplicant.

5. God's love and glory are more manifested in Christian teamwork than in one person.

   We ask the person if he/she would feel comfortable if we meet in the sanctuary in a quiet corner or if he/she would prefer to go to an office or other private place. In either case, we assure them, and remind ourselves, of confidentiality.

B. Introductions and Invocation

We briefly introduce one another if we are not acquainted. One of us will pray, asking the Lord to be present, to minister to the person through us, and ask Him to give us His perception and healing power. Or, we begin with a brief statement of what we are about and then have a prayer of invocation.

The prayer is not routine. It is a sincere cry of faith. We know that everything depends upon the Lord's manifesting His presence. We know that without insight, discernment, wisdom and the leading of the Spirit, not much can happen. Sometimes we include confession and reading of scripture.

C. Preparation

If the person has obviously been touched in a service, not much is needed, but usually we want to assure him/her of the Lord's presence, His love for them, His desire to show His healing mercy to him/her and our readiness to help. Someone who is a friend may sit close or hold their hand if it's natural. We may begin with some comforting words, but they may blurt out their need before any of that.

D. Empathetic Listening

If they need help to start talking or explaining their need, we may ask a question or two to get them started. Basically, we listen understandingly and may echo back to them from time to time how we sense how they are feeling. We want them to share their problem and tell us how they think it began. We often invite them to describe their relationship with their parents and their family life and to reflect on how it connects with their hurt. We may do some teaching about the relationship of family life to hurts and give appropriate examples. If the basic root causes do not begin to emerge through this sharing, we might ask some questions to get at the roots.

E. Readiness to Pray

As we listen and observe we can, by the Spirit, sense whether the person is receptive to ministry. Sometimes they need several interviews. Sometimes they are so nervous and fearful that we have a quiet time and ask the Lord to come and grant them His peace and enable them to be receptive to ministry.

F. Beginning the Healing Prayer

1. If the person knows the roots of their hurt, or at least one of them, we will commence by asking them to relive the painful event and see the Lord present with them there while we pray. For example, "Lord Jesus, help Tom to vividly recall his mother severely whipping him, and as he does so, make your presence known, help him to see and feel you present there, and minister your healing love to him." Having prayed that aloud, we will pray silently, trusting the Lord to minister.

2. If they only remember an unhappy home, but cannot remember anything specific, we will ask the Lord to walk back through the years with them and bring to mind anything He wants them to remember, good or bad. Then we pray silently until a memory comes to mind. Often He starts them with a happy memory, which we ask them to share. That relaxes them and then He begins to bring key hurtful memories.

3. If neither of the above proves fruitful, there are other options; the most important is that we pray for a word of knowledge which is often given through a scripture, vision or a question to ask.

G. Active Imagination or Visualization

We find that the Lord brings certain key memories to mind which sum up the history of hurt. We don't have to pray about everything they've been through. We ask them to share the first one that comes and we encourage them to visualize the event by saying things such as: "See yourself as you were at that time and place, notice the room or surroundings, recall what the other person did that was so hurtful, see his/her face, hear his/her voice, feel your anger, etc., as you react." Then as they get into it we may ask them periodically to report what is happening so that we may pray for Jesus to minister to them appropriately, or we may exhort them, "Tell Jesus how you feel; let it all hang out; pour out your heart to Him." Then we might say, "See Him looking at you, see Him coming to you with eyes full of compassion; hear Him speaking to you; run into those arms, feel His arms around you, your face buried in His chest, feel His hair brushing the side of your face; listen to Him; receive His great healing love" etc. We say what we feel led to say.

We might say the same things in a prayer to the Lord instead of exhorting the person. We may pray silently. Sometimes the person gives us a running account of what they see happening. Usually within three to ten minutes they give us a full report. Often they are in tears or deeply moved. Often, after they report the encounter with Christ and what He said and did, we just worship.

H. Sensitivity and Timing

Through it all, we're praying silently to know when to speak, when to be silent, when to wrap up one episode and move on to another. Normally an hour to an hour and a half is the limit. Usually one to three key hurts can be dealt with in that time.

I. Forgiveness

After each episode we often coach the person to forgive the one who hurt them, but often they are not ready until we've gone through several key hurts involving the same relation. Whichever it is, we ask them to call on the Lord to give them the will and grace to forgive from the heart. Frequently we have them picture the wounder and imagine Jesus standing beside them or holding the hands of both, then as the person looks at the wounder, we ask Jesus to enable him/her to see that other as He sees them ... to give them a whole new perspective and perception. What they then report is often remarkable. The Lord often then and there changes their point of view, and often it is within a few weeks. Whether or not we pray for that, we certainly encourage them to **surrender all bitterness, hate and revenge, and with the use of visualization, to verbalize forgiveness and embrace the offending relation.**

J. Cultivating Gratitude

We may give them homework to pray every day for that person; to write down all the good that has come to them through that person; to develop a list of all that person's good qualities and deeds and to regularly give thanks to God for those things. We will ask them to continue to pray for a whole new perception of the wounder as one who is also wounded, and as one for whom Christ died.

K. Repentance and Reconciliation

Quite often we are led to ask the person to ask the Lord to show them what they may have done to provoke the hurt, or how they made it worse by their reactions. As they visualize the wounder, we may suggest that they ask, "Why did you do that?" Then we ask them to listen for the answer that comes or to find out from their relations the story of that person's struggles in life. This can be tremendously motivating in forgiveness. Often we lead them in a prayer of confession and then encourage reconciliation and also restitution where possible. Obviously, this whole dimension falls in the category of spiritual healing or sanctification (steps I, J, K). It shows the necessary relationship between emotions and spirit if we are to see maximum healing.

L. The Healing Vision

I never cease to be amazed at the variety of creative and redemptive visualizations people have of Jesus interacting with their wounding events. In most cases, I am convinced that it must be the Lord who is guiding the use of active imagination; it is too ingenious and beautiful for humans to conceive. In my experience, at least a third of the persons have a healing vision. Their use of active imagination is taken over by the Spirit and transmuted into a vision encounter. They experience the presence of the Lord as waves of loving kindness, resurrection life lifting them, and warmth enfolding them, illumination giving them a whole new positive perspective. The glory that breaks through is lovely and healing. In such cases, we have learned to encourage them to recall that vision every day for a while and simply to bask in it and soak it up. What began in the prayer circle continues to expand and penetrate. See 2 Corinthians 3:18.

M. How Often?

Depending upon the leading of the Spirit, we may counsel and pray for a person once because at the time it seems sufficient, and then ask them to keep us apprised. More often, we will see them once every week or two for three to five times. Where there is much deep hurt and progress is slow, we may see them every week for a few months or periodically over several years. We meet by agreement, and for as long as they feel they are being helped and need the support. Seldom does it become a burden because they are encouraged to read about inner healing, pray for themselves, and be faithful in the whole life of the church. Seldom have we had to tell a person that it is time for them to start praying for others. They usually look for opportunities to do for others what has been done for them.

IMMANUEL HEALING

God With Us
Condensed from *Share Immanuel*
By E. James Wilder and Chris M. Coursey

Used by permission of E. James Wilder and Chris M. Coursey, - joystartshere.com

Starting a good connection

Learn the practice of interacting with Immanuel (God with us) in a way that resolves painful life experiences. God is always present with us and always has been. Our life memories are incomplete when we lack the awareness of God's presence. Without this awareness our interpretations of life are distorted, bring pain and rob our peace.

We interact with God best from the memories of times we spent with God. From these memories we can better explore those times where we do not perceive God's presence. The memories of times when we had a close relationship with God are like open windows for seeing God's active presence again in the present.

Starting with a good connection produces:

- Less confusion, distortion and resistance.

- Less time in our pain because we do not begin our search for God's presence while we are sitting on our pain. Instead, we explore our pain while sitting comfortably close to God.

- Guidance from the starting moment.

- A spot to return quickly if we get lost.

- A place to pause an incomplete process without staying in pain.

- A shorter healing process.

Sitting with God

When the pain-processing pathway in the human brain cannot figure out how the painful event fits together, our mind will keep the painful memory active. Every time something similar happens, the unfinished memory gets mixed in with the current event. Trauma comes from events that leave us feeling alone. When we have God with us (Immanuel) we are no longer alone and discover how to recover.

Don't sit waiting in pain memory thorns! Most healing methods ask people to start in their pain and look for meaning or God from there. We do not recommend trying to climb the hill of awareness by starting in pain. Start at the top of the hill with God. God offers us hospitality. Begin where our minds remember God best - in either our appreciation memories or interactive memories. From either of these comfortable seats we can share a state of mind with God and feel God peace. These two seats face opposite directions but are both comfortable places to sit and hear God. From the interactive memories seat we can look toward God and sense His responses toward us. The appreciation memories seat faces the other way and, while we cannot see God or be directly aware if the responses come from God, we can see and appreciate the signs that God cares about us. Both appreciation memories and interactive memories need to be real times and places in our lives.

The appreciation memories seat will help us warm up our brains when we actively seek and focus on appreciation memories. Appreciation comes from the "ah!" moments: a baby's smile, a beautiful scene, kindness, special recognition and warm cozy moments –whether we give them or receive them. Most of the time our appreciation memories have no sense of God's presence in them. This is fine. Even if the appreciation memories seat faces away from God, God can still communicate to us. Our minds will be appreciative. You should have at least three appreciation memories that bring you a sense of warmth you can feel inside before we continue.

The interactive memories seat is the best place to stay for Immanuel experiences. These memories from our lives take us back to times when we could sense God's thoughts and feelings toward us. These times are filled with God peace. They will feel like we are relating to someone we know. We will have a sense that both God and I are there. We may not be clear about which thoughts were God's thoughts and which were ours - that is fine. The important point is that God is still there when we go back and remember the moment. Now we can interact again.

Stay seated at the top of the hill. Our goal, when looking at pain memories, is to stay in our appreciation or interactive memories seat and return to appreciation as soon as possible if we "fall off" due to pain, distraction or a blockage of some sort. It is most important that we get our minds synchronized with God in either an appreciation memories seat or an interactive memories seat before we look at thorny pain memories.

Sharing minds

An ancient example of sharing minds with God comes from the prophet Elisha and his servant. A large army had been sent to capture them and the young servant was badly frightened. The prophet said, "Do not fear" and prayed that the servant would see that God was with them (Immanuel). Then the servant saw the mountains were filled with horses and chariots of fire. Seeing what was on the mountains allowed the servant's mind to share what God's mind saw.

Asking questions of God - No matter which of the two comfortable seats we are sitting in, we ask questions and then look in our minds for responses from God. Responses can be words, pictures, thoughts, feelings in our bodies, desires, memories, emotions and internal shifts. Not all the things that come to our minds are God sending us a message. Often God shows us something we need to notice. When we do get "a message from God," so to speak, it will make things fit together in God peace. When something does not feel true, again we tell God, "This does not feel true. What do you want me to know about that?" These instructions are easier to follow when we have someone with us. We ask questions and examine the responses together. Sometimes these responses seem important but often they do not. If we notice a response that does not seem important we ask God out loud, "What do I need to know about that?" This is how we talk to God whether we can perceive God's presence or not.

If we are comfortably in the interactive memories seat we can often start by asking directly, "Where are You, God in the painful memory?" Sometimes that is all it takes. If we are in the appreciation memories seat, "What keeps me from perceiving You are with me?" or "What do You, God want me to know?" are good questions to ask. We may want to ask, "What keeps me from seeing You in the painful memory?"

So here is how the rounds of questions and answers and responses go:

1. Ask what God wants us to know (about that.)

2. Notice:

    a. In the appreciation seat, we notice our responses.

    b. In the interactive seat, we notice God's responses and our responses.

3. Tell God our reactions (this is the same in both seats.)

4. Check to see we are still in our seats.

5. If we do not have God peace we repeat.

We need to watch and see if we fall out of our seats. We need to notice when we stop feeling appreciation or don't feel God's presence. Every time this happens we go back to our appreciation memory or interactive memory and get back in our seat before going on. We don't want to fall down the hill and lay in the thorns.

When the *pain memories* are processed, we feel peace. If we ask the question, "Does that peace like to be with me?" there is a delightful discovery to be made about God. In God peace, we know where God is and everything now fits for us even when we can neither explain nor describe all we know.

Speaking telling

By this point we are half way through Immanuel and feeling much better. Our bed of thorny *pain memories* is now a picture in our minds. If we go back and try to feel how upset we were, we can't feel it.

Our minds do not yet understand what happened enough to change the way we view the future. Speaking the story of what changed when we perceived God's presence is what changes the way that our brain sees the future, giving us hope and joy instead of dread and despair. We do not get the same benefit from telling the story of life in the thorn patch BEFORE Immanuel. That story depresses others and us.

Speaking the Immanuel story takes observation and preparation.

1. What was the moment in our memory where we first became aware of God's presence? We give that moment a phrase like, "I was sitting in the dark hallway." Now speak your phrase out loud or write it down.

2. What did God do first? Give that activity a phrase like, "I sensed God's concern for me." Continue speaking or writing the phrases.

3. What reaction did we have? Give the reaction a phrase like, "I was surprised but my body still felt frozen."

4. What process did God take us through? Give a "play by play" description like a sports reporter would tell about a game. Tell each thing God did and our reaction to it. Speak or write each phrase.

5. Make a simple list of what we felt and thought before and after interacting with God's presence in our painful memory. Make a series of sentences like, "Before I knew God was with me I felt hopeless and stuck forever (next, what God did to make a change) but then Immanuel showed me that God was holding me next to His heart (last, a phrase about the result) now I realize it really is over and I have a future and I started to smile and relax." Speak this out loud or write it down. If we are in a group, we have the group repeat the sentences back and see if they sound and feel true.

6. What would we call the kind of changes we experienced with Immanuel? We can say or write, "I have always been afraid to get close to men but now that I can sense God is with me I have compassion for men that feels true and peaceful. I have become more loving." Speak or write about everything that changed and now feels true.

We can now tell the whole Immanuel story. First we tell our story to God. We start by describing how our seat on the hill with God felt to us. We do not tell what our thorns were like. Next we tell about discovering God was with us, what changed with that discovery, how God peace feels and what we appreciate. When we are done we stop and sense God's response to hearing our story. After telling God we speak the story to anyone who was with us for our Immanuel experience. We speak the Immanuel story to three people before we go to bed tonight. We tell others our Immanuel story in a way that helps them find an appreciation seat for their Immanuel healing.

Solutions when things go wrong

It is common to encounter problems while seeking interaction, avoiding falls into the thorny patches of pain or telling our Immanuel story.

I don't think the answers I am getting are from God - The lack of God peace is a good indicator that we should take a moment to investigate. Because Immanuel is a relational interaction it may bring up beliefs or fears about God that come from our previous interactions with people. All these feelings come from pain memories and, if we ask God about them, Immanuel will remove the fears one at a time. If we are not sure then we check with respected people who know Immanuel.

I can't do this on my own - There are three common reasons why we cannot finish Immanuel on our own:

1) difficulty observing ourselves

2) our brain lacks necessary brain skills and

3) our joy capacity is too low. Ask God to show you your next step and who can help you.

My story is hard to tell or people don't like to hear it - If our story is hard to tell or we notice people do not like to hear it most likely we are telling a thorny pain story instead of a top of the hill story. Our goal is to speak the change that happens when we perceive Immanuel's presence.

What should I expect will happen? - We should expect four things from God with us:

1) God will answer us.

2) God's peace will be exquisite.

3) Telling our Immanuel story will help us become the person we would have been if we had not been traumatized.

4) All parts of Immanuel, from the seating to the stories, lead to appreciation opportunities.

After telling the Immanuel story without the thorns three times we begin feeling and thinking differently about ourselves, our minds are renewed and we become the persons we would have been without the trauma. In the future we will be looking for Immanuel again.

NOTES:

KINGDOM CULTURE: LET'S BRING THE ATMOSPHERE THAT'S IN HEAVEN TO EARTH

Culture is the "atmosphere" and "energy" that emits out of our spirit and soul, individually and corporately. Culture is an environment, like a green house, that can either enhance or inhibit growth. Everybody participates in making culture. However, it is the leaders that have the greatest ability to influence the culture of a Micro-Church. Developing the atmosphere of heaven is essential for people to heal and mature. Consistent love, affection, joy, and a positive mercy-grace environment will saturate each family member with the gospel, helping to effecting change. Bill Johnson writes, "A culture is the system of beliefs, disciplines, practices, and relational boundaries that reveal how life is lived among a particular group of people. Movements of any kind succeed when they have created a culture that can sustain it."

The word "culture" refers to a combination of values, beliefs, attitudes, atmosphere, environment, behaviors, and practices created by a spiritual family. It is the life of Christ that radiates off His people. We want to create a Kingdom culture that reveals the heart of our Heavenly Father. Culture is like a weather pattern. It is atmospheric and environmental. A Kingdom culture is one of the most essential ingredients for experiencing, absorbing, and transferring Christ's life. For example, Biblical truth may be present, but if it isn't accompanied by love, acceptance, and humility then our context will undermine our content. A Kingdom culture is contagiously attractive and almost irresistible. Affection, kindness, and affirmation can penetrate our hearts in the same way fragrances of a bakery saturate our clothing. Timely laughter lets our emotions get a much needed lift. It is often said that being a disciple of Christ is more "caught" than "taught". Kingdom culture provides the environment necessary to grow healthy, fully alive followers of Christ. Over the long haul, if we are consistently exposed to the affection of Christ Jesus through His family, our chances for transformation into Christ's likeness dramatically increases. A true kingdom culture is to a person's life what a well monitored hot house is to plants. Climate and atmosphere are some of the most important elements which enhance growth and draw the lost to Jesus. Here are some of cultural expressions of the Kingdom of God we seek to create with the help of the Holy Spirit:

- A culture of praise, worship, and prayer because all life, all good things, all mercy and grace come from our Father through Christ by the Holy Spirit.
- A culture of hope which produces great faith in God and His Word. This includes a culture of expectancy and practice of the supernatural power and gifts of the Holy Spirit. It also includes a culture that embraces a positive perspective of life in the kingdom versus cynicism, skepticism, and unbelief.
- A culture of true fellowship, love, affection, and genuine caring.
- A culture of humility and honor in which we recognize each other by the Spirit as sons of God, submitting to the Christ in one another.
- A culture which is passionate about living out BOTH divine order with divine life holistically. This includes areas like gender roles, godly stewardship of our bodies, time, relationships, resources, finances, gifts, talents, callings.
- A culture of fathering & mothering sons of God in the context of Micro-Church Families (small family mission groups of 3-16). This involves fellowshipping in the light, speaking the truth in love, being open, vulnerable, and teachable, in order to grow into Christ's likeness. This includes a culture of accountability but without a religious spirit of performance orientation and legalism. It is a culture of making disciples who make disciples as a lifestyle.
- A culture of justice and compassion in which we help to reveal Father's heart to orphans, widows, the poor, alien, mistreated, and unreached.
- A culture of joy, gladness, and fun, enjoying and celebrating our humanity under Christ's Lordship.

- A culture of freedom, faith, and encouragement to explore, start and practice new kingdom enterprises and ministries.
- A culture which promotes genuine, authentic, holistic, and substantial kingdom reality versus hype, superficiality, and religious hypocrisy.

NOTES:

MAKING DISCIPLES WHO MAKE DISCIPLES

What is a disciple and how are we to "make disciples"? Making disciples in the context of small spiritual families involves the art of spiritual parenting. A disciple is a follower of Christ. Making disciples involves teaching others the truth of God's Word, actualizing the power of the Holy Spirit in order to obey Christ in every area of life. How do we help others access the grace of God through faith and the establishing of faith-goals? What are the 5-C's utilizing the 4-D's (Dynamics of Transformation). It is essential that we teach disciples how to develop facetime with God every day and throughout the day. This includes a relationship with God's Word & Spirit, which are keys to transforming into the likeness of life in Christ. We are teaching others to have a pray, hear, obey lifestyle in connection with God's Word, Spirit, and Body.

MAKING DISCIPLES OF CHRIST WHO MAKE DISCIPLES OF CHRIST: PRAY, HEAR, OBEY LIFESTYLE

Key Bible Passages: Matthew 28:18-20, 7:24-27; Mark 3:13-15; Colossians 1:27-29; Romans 8:28-30, 12:4; 2 Peter 1:3-11; 1 Corinthians 12:12-30, 15:45-49; Colossians 1:18; John 14:15

1. A disciple is a lover and follower of Jesus Christ. Christ has been permitted to dwell inside the heart of a disciple as King, and given authorization to transform the willing disciple into Christ's likeness. This activates the power of the Holy Spirit who helps the disciple obey Jesus in every area of life. As a result of one's love relationship with Jesus, a disciple obtains the mind of Christ, the heart of Christ, and the lifestyle of Christ. A disciple is totally committed to doing God's will, God's way, by God's Spirit, for God's glory. They give Jesus Christ what He wants, in the way He wants it. A disciple enthusiastically obeys God's Word quickly, completely, and cheerfully. While praying and hearing are essential, discipleship isn't complete until one obeys Jesus Christ as a lifestyle. There is only one kind of Christian described in the Bible, disciples of Christ who help make disciples of Christ.

2. The three main activities of a disciple are:

    A. Prayer - a word used to cover all categories of intimate communication with God
    B. Hearing
    C. Obeying.

    There are five areas of life involved in being a disciple:

    A. Christ Himself
    B. Christ's community – deep connection to a spiritual family
    C. Christ's character
    D. Christ's calling
    E. Christ's competency – the ability to carry out one's calling.

3. No one can be a disciple, a son of God, outside of a close and loving spiritual family. Discipleship is caught as well as taught. Disciples are made relationally. To live "in Christ" involves direct relational connection to the Head of the Church, Jesus Christ. It also includes a real heart-to-heart, life-on-life covenant relationship with members of Christ's Body, the Church. Christ and Christ's body are inseparable.

4. One needs to be a disciple to make a disciple. To be a disciple one needs to make a disciple. It is our responsibility to make disciples of Christ, influencing people to trust God as their Source, verses creating dependence on the disciple maker.

5. Making disciples who make disciples is supernatural, involving a great deal of spiritual warfare. Therefore, disciple-making disciples are people who pray and fast as a lifestyle.

6. Jesus wants everyone to make disciples who make disciples in the context of Micro-Church Families (5-15 believers gathered in a Micro-Church led by Biblical leaders). All Micro-Church Families need to be connected with other MCF's in a local church led by true Biblical elders, who are all mutually submitted to a five-fold leadership team (apostles, prophets, teachers, pastors, evangelists). Micro-Church Families are composed of gender specific DNA groups of 2-4 people. (see chapter entitled "What's & How's of Micro-Churches: A Small Spiritual Family on Mission")

7. The first Biblical number of relationships for disciple-making is 2's & 3's (DNA Groups), with one person serving the role of facilitator. DNA stands for Discipleship, Nurture, and Apostolic Mission. (See chapter entitled "DNA Groups – Ekklesisa Groups of 2-4")

WE ARE CALLED TO BE DISCIPLE MAKERS

1. As Christians, we are called to leadership, to lead a lost world to salvation. Where do we start, how do we implement leadership from theory to practice? When we have an eternal vision, when we really understand what Jesus did for us, we know we have been "saved" from the judgment by the blood of Christ, how can we not be prompted to action? We have the key to eternity, through our knowledge of Jesus Christ. How can we stand by while those around us die without Christ? The answer is we can't, Jesus wants us to take action.

2. In Matthew 28, He ordered the apostles to make disciples of all nations, teach them all things walking in His authority. This was the method of leadership used by the early church to reach the lost in pagan Greek and Roman society. Our society today is not much different, as the conflict between the secular and faithful grows.

18 And Jesus came and spoke to them, saying, "All authority has been given to Me in heaven and on earth. 19 "Go therefore and make disciples of all the nations, baptizing them in the name of the Father and of the Son and of the Holy Spirit, 20 "teaching them to observe all things that I have commanded you; and lo, I am with you always, even to the end of the age." Amen. Matthew 28:18-20

3. Jesus left instructions for the Church, first they were to wait at Jerusalem until they received power from the Holy Spirit. Once this occurred, they were to take the teachings (make disciples) of Jesus to the nations. That is our job, to bring the Gospel to the nations, Jesus gives us the authority, we need to act on the authority we have.

4. The knowledge the disciples bore was the light of the world. We bear this same light, we are the light bearers to the world, the Holy Spirit works through us. The Gospel message is the light to the nations as foretold by Isaiah, seven-hundred years before the birth of Jesus.

"Listen, O coastlands, to Me, And take heed, you peoples from afar! The Lord has called Me from the womb; From the matrix of My mother He has made mention of My name. 7 Thus says the Lord, The Redeemer of Israel, their Holy One, To Him whom man despises, To Him whom the nation abhors, To the Servant of rulers: "Kings shall see and arise, Princes also shall worship, Because of the Lord who is faithful, The Holy One of Israel; And He has chosen You." 8 Thus says the Lord: "In an acceptable time I have heard You, And in the day of salvation I have helped You; I will preserve You and give You As a covenant to the people, To restore the earth, To cause them to inherit the desolate heritages; 9 That You may say to the prisoners, 'Go forth,' To those who are in darkness, 'Show yourselves.' "They shall feed along the roads, And their pastures shall be on all desolate heights. 10 They shall neither hunger nor thirst, Neither heat nor sun shall strike them; For He who has mercy on them will lead them, Even by the springs of water He will guide them. Isaiah 49:6-10

5. The word Jesus uses in verse 19 is translated *disciple*; which comes from the Greek word, **Matheteuo** meaning a learner, one who follows the precepts of a teacher. Jesus calls us to go forth and make the nations *learn* His ways. This is our calling and purpose, when we as followers of Christ, follow this precept, we find fulfillment, in our assigned mission.

6. In the world, many people think they will find fulfillment through their profession or company, only to find an empty unfilled life. When we try to find our fulfillment outside of Christ, we will be left empty every time. Only when we allow the Spirit of God, who dwells in us to direct us, do we feel fulfilled. The Holy Spirit instructs us to do the will of Christ, which is to *make disciples of the nations*.

7. As Christians, we are called to be leaders, to lead people to Christ, to disciple and teach the nations, baptizing them in the name of Christ.

The Jesus Leadership Model

Jesus was a discipler, He trained men, He disciplined them to take His message to the nations. In the three and half years He ministered, Jesus chose twelve men, the apostles, as the leaders of the church. Through them, the light of the Gospel would be preached to the nations; today through a long line of disciples, the Church of Jesus Christ is world-wide, made up of many races and languages. However, the job will not be finished until the end of the age, one of the major signs of His coming is the preaching of the Gospel in all the world. *"And this gospel of the kingdom will be preached in all the world as a witness to all the nations, and then the end will come. Matthew 24:14*

Therefore, by following the leadership model of Christ, we are to reach the nations. Jesus made disciples by spending quality time with chosen people to bring the Gospel to the nations. Out of a larger group, Jesus chose twelve-men after He prayed to the Father. Jesus invested himself in these men; this was His plan of evangelism. Jesus had a method of leadership, first, He choose twelve men out of the greater body, second He invested in them to carry the work forward.

Reading through the Gospels, we can see the plan of advancing the Gospel, Jesus demonstrated this for the Church. Robert Coleman in his book, *The Master Plan of Evangelism* [1] breaks down the method Jesus used, a method for leaders to follow. He detailed this eight step process, for reaching the world, so we can follow in the footsteps of Jesus Christ.

	The Master Plan of Evangelism
1	**Selection:** Jesus operated through people; He selected men willing to learn and concentrated His disciple training on the twelve. He did not neglect the masses, but trained the twelve to reach them.
2	**Association:** Jesus stayed with the 12 disciples for the three-years of His ministry. They learned firsthand by being with Jesus the principles Jesus taught.
3	**Consecration:** The men were separated from the larger group; they sought after God and were obedient to Christ.
4	**Impartation:** The disciples followed Christ because the Holy Spirit was involved in their life, revealing the meaning His teachings.
5	**Demonstration:** Jesus demonstrated how to live the life He taught. They learned by observing, He made His life transparent to the disciples, He taught by personal demonstration.
6	**Delegation:** Jesus delegated work to the disciples; He sent them to the cities of Israel to preach the Gospel. All in preparation to their greater task, when He was gone.
7	**Supervision:** Jesus supervised their work and ministry, correcting areas and attitudes along the way. Looking for real life examples to demonstrate the right methods of ministry.
8	**Reproduction:** The process was designed for reproduction, the disciples were not to die with their knowledge by to reproduce themselves in others. They were to follow the model set forth by the Master.

[1] Robert E. Coleman, The Master Plan of Evangelism, Baker Book House, Foreword by Billy Graham.

- Paul did the same with Timothy and the Church at Ephesus. Paul spent three-years, discipling the leaders of Ephesus, the church he founded.

- Paul invested his time in people, teaching them how to live the Christian life; he instructed them on doctrine, he gave direction to the Church, even when he was not there, the Epistle to the Ephesians is the case in point. Remember, Paul's epistles were letters written by Paul to the Church's in the cities. The books of Ephesians, Corinthians, Philippians, Colossians, Thessalonians were to church and its leaders in the city, giving them spiritual direction and doctrine. Paul wrote to Timothy, his son in the faith, giving him instructions on how to lead. Paul was a leader of men, who taught leaders to lead. This is the role a leader provides to those he is leading, the goal being to reproduce leaders.

- Jesus, the disciples and Paul set an example for us to follow. They established a model of leadership, finding people and investing in them, establishing them in the faith. In city after city Paul used this model to establish churches in the pagan cities of the Roman Empire. Paul found people who were willing to invest their time in eternity, and he invested his life in them. Timothy and Silas are two people Paul addresses throughout his Epistles. In Acts 20, Paul is on his way to Jerusalem, on the way, he calls the leaders of the church at Ephesus to meet with him. He knows this will be the last time he sees them, so he gives them final guidance before he leaves.

> [31] "Therefore watch, and remember that for three years I did not cease to warn everyone night and day with tears. [32] "So now, brethren, I commend you to God and to the word of His grace, which is able to build you up and give you an inheritance among all those who are sanctified. [33] "I have coveted no one's silver or gold or apparel. [34] "Yes, you yourselves know that these hands have provided for my necessities, and for those who were with me. [35] "I have shown you in every way, by laboring like this, that you must support the weak. And remember the words of the Lord Jesus, that He said, 'It is more blessed to give than to receive.' " [36] And when he had said these things, he knelt down and prayed with them all. [37] Then they all wept freely, and fell on Paul's neck and kissed him, [38] sorrowing most of all for the words which he spoke, that they would see his face no more. And they accompanied him to the ship. Acts 20:31-38

- Paul used the model established by Jesus; he worked closely with specific people, not ignoring the masses. He trained people to continue when he was gone; they were not dependent on Paul's presence to minister. They were to reproduce after Paul was gone; the church was to grow by using the model of leadership established by Jesus.

This is what happened, the Church grew, even under persecution and finally the Roman Empire claimed itself a Christian kingdom.

Practical Ways to Follow the Jesus Leadership Model

This a model of leadership for us in the church today, to find people who want to grow in their faith, then invest their time and energy in other's life.

Find people: Selection, look for people who need to be discipled in the Christian walk today, many Christians fail simply because no one has spent the time to take them to the next level. Look for sincere people, who want to grow, help them by investing your time in their life.

Spend time with them: Association, you need to be willing to spend time with the people God has put in your life. Make the time count; invest your time in essential spiritual growth activities. Do a discipleship study together, such as *Practical Christian Living*, where their faith can be established.

Spirit led: Consecration, look for people who are willing to be led by the Spirit, who have been consecrated and are obedient to the Spirit's calling.

Lead by Example: Demonstrate the Christian walk, let them see you in action. Show them what it means to be a disciple of Christ. Use personal example to teach them.

Give them opportunities: Delegate and supervision, look for ways to introduce people to ministry. Such as co-teaching, involving them in an outreach event, etc. Introduce them to leading others to Christ.

Evangelism: Reproduction, stress to them the need to reach the lost, cast the vision of evangelism trough reproduction. Model for them, what they are to model to others to advance the Kingdom of God.

Steps to Being a Spiritual Leader

1. Do I know people who need to be established in the faith? _____

   _____

   _____

2. Do I have time to spend/invest in the lives of others? _____

   _____

   _____

   If not, where can I free up time in my life to invest in the Kingdom of God? _____

   _____

   _____

3. Has God put people in my life the Holy Spirit want me to work with? _____

   _____

   _____

4. Do I have what it takes to lead people, do I trust in my own ability or the power of the Holy Spirit? _____

   _____

   _____

5. Am I willing to go forward in leading people by trusting in the Lord's ability to transform me?

   _____

   _____

6. Am I willing to challenge myself to grow, will I invest the time to be equipped to lead people?

   _____

   _____

Plan of Action

- Pray for people to help
- Find people
- Ask them if they want to get together to grow in their faith
- Set aside time in your life to learn God's Word. Pray to lead others.
- Just do it, move forward with the plan.

BIBLICAL SUPPORT FOR DEVELOPING LEADERS THROUGH THE 5 C'S WITH THE 4 D'S

Everyone a Leader: The Word of God makes it very clear that everyone has been called to help others love and obey Jesus Christ. A leader helps someone move from where they are now to somewhere else, somewhere he/she would not go on their own. Leadership is influencing others to think, feel, and act differently. Making disciples, training others, spiritual fathering & mothering are other terms used to describe leadership in the Kingdom of God.

Bible Passages Which Encourage Everyone to Develop Leaders Who Develop Leaders: Matthew 9:35-38, 28:18-20; 2 Timothy 2:2; Ephesians 2:10, 4:11-13; 1 Thessalonians 4:1-2

Accessing Grace by Setting Faith-Goals Using the 5 C's: Helping others establish clear reachable goals is an essential part of leading others. A goal is a measurable result. Establishing Biblical goals and striving to reach those goals with the empowering help of the Holy Spirit is the way we change into Christ's likeness and advance His Kingdom. Read these Bible passages which inspire the establishing and reaching of goals: 1 Corinthians 9:25; Acts 24:16; 1 Timothy 4:10; Roman 14:19, 15:17-22; 1 Thessalonians 4:11; Luke 13:24; John 5:44; Ephesians 4:3; 1 Thessalonians 2:17; Acts 1:8; Hebrews 4:11, 12:14-16; Colossians 1:28-29

The Five C's:

Christ: 1 Corinthians 3:11-13; Colossians 1:18, 1:27-29, 2:6-7; John 6:57, 15:5, 17:3; Philippians 1:10-11, 3:7-11; Hebrews 3:1, 12:2; 1 John 1:3. Establishing a loving, close relationship with Christ is the reason for our very existence. Everything flows from our union with Christ, who dwells within the hearts of those who have placed their faith in Him. Abiding in Christ, following Him, obeying Him quickly, completely, and cheerfully will determine the quality of our relationships with others, our character, calling, and level of competence.

Community: 1 Corinthians 12:12-14; Ephesians 2:22, 3:16-19, 4:12-16; Colossians 2:10-19; John 13:34, 17:21; 1 John 4:12. We can only know God in fullness in the context of true Christian community. God is a Father, Son, and Holy Spirit, a family of One. He builds His church relationally through natural and spiritual families. Loving God and loving others are the two great commandments, and they are inseparable. "Effective spiritual communities achieve a balance between a single, overall community purpose AND the various purposes of the individuals with the community."[2]

Character: 2 Corinthians 6:3, Titus 2:7-8, Proverbs 10:9; Matthew 7:21-23; 1 Timothy 4:12-16, 6:11; Galatians 5:22-23. Character is formed as we abide in Christ. We become who we connect with. In close relationships with others, our strengths get affirmed and our weaknesses come into the light allowing God's Spirit to change us.

Calling: 1 Corinthians 3:9-13; Galatians 1:1; Ephesians 2:10, 4:11-16; Matthew 9:37. A "calling" is God's voice, His loving burden, downloaded into an individual and spiritual family. It is a God-inspired vision and mandate to fulfill an eternally important assignment which advances Christ's Kingdom. Every person and community has a calling from God to fulfill.

Competence: Psalm 78:70-72; Proverbs 22:29; 1 Timothy 1:7; 3:4-5; 2 Timothy 2:2, 2:15, 3:14-17, 4:2; 2 Corinthians 3:5-6; Philippians 3:4-11, 4:13; Colossians 1:10-12; 1 Peter 4:11; Zechariah 4:6; Roman 1:16, 12:6-8; 1 Corinthians 12:7; 1 Thessalonians 1:5 A leader must not only possess a burning vision and calling from God, not only have character, they must have the skills to carry out their calling.

The Four Dynamics of Transformation: 1.) Instructional, 2.) Relational, 3.) Experiential, 4.) Spiritual

---

[1] The 5 C's and 4 D's are integral components of "The ConneXions Model of Leadership Development" designed by Malcolm Webber, Ph.D. For more information about the ConneXions l of Leadership Development visit these websites: www.StrategicPress.org www.sgai.org

[2] Healthy Leaders: SpiritBuilt Leadership 2 by Malcolm Webber, Ph.D., Strategic Press.

NOTES:

NOTES:

FACE TIME WITH GOD: DEVELOPING AN IMMANUEL LIFESTYLE

God longs for each of his children to enjoy His presence throughout every day. Christ lived by the Life of His Father. He could only do what he saw his Father doing. In the same way, we are animated by Father's life through Christ who lives inside our hearts. When we abide in Christ, and enjoy an intimate relationship with God, the Person of the Holy Spirit flows through our hearts. An "Immanuel Lifestyle" is living with a conscious awareness that God is always with us and that He wants to be involved in every part of our lives. By staying relationally connected with God, we become like Him and are empowered to fulfill our calling.

FACE TIME WITH GOD: DEVELOPING AN IMMANUEL LIFESTYLE

Cultivating intimacy with God through gratitude, praise, worship, prayer, hearing, obeying.

Promises in God's Word:

- "Behold, the virgin shall conceive and bear a son, and they shall call his name 'Immanuel" which means 'God with us'. Matthew 1:23

- "I am the vine: you are the branches. Whoever abides in me and I in him, he it is that bears much fruit, for apart from me you can do nothing...If you abide in me, and my words abide in you, ask whatever you wish, and it will be done for you. By this my Father is glorified, that you bear much fruit and so prove to be my disciples. As the Father has loved me, so have I loved you. Abide in my love." John 15:5-11

- "Keep your life free from the love of money, and be content with what you have, for he has said, 'I will never leave you nor forsake you. So we can confidently say, 'The Lord is my helper; I will not fear; what can man do to me?" Hebrews 13:5-6

- "My sheep hear my voice, and I know them, and they follow me." John 10:27

- "All authority in heaven and on earth has been given to me. Go therefore and make disciples of all nations, baptizing them in the name of the Father and of the Son and of the Holy Spirit, teaching them to observe all that I have commanded you. And behold, I am with you always, to the end of the age." Matthew 28:18-20

Face Time defined: Face Time is BOTH 1.) specific times during the day in which you deliberately commune with God, 2.) a lifestyle in which you are aware that Christ's Spirit is "in" you, "on" you, all "around" you. God is always trying to "connect" with your spirit through the Word of God, the Spirit of God, and the people of God. God is Immanuel, which means "God with us". When you repent, believe, and receive Christ into your heart as savior and King, He comes inside of you and never leaves. You are "sealed with the Holy Spirit". The Baptism of the Holy Spirit is when God pours out His Holy Spirit upon you to empower you to be a witness. The Spirit of God within, upon, and between is a true reality that we want to cultivate all the time. (Ephesians 1:13, 3:17, Colossians 1:22; Romans 10:9; Galatians 2:20; Acts 1-2)

Why is Face Time so important? Abiding in Christ and living by the power of the indwelling Christ is what it means to be a Christian. Being a Christ-follower, a Christian, is 100% supernatural. We can do nothing apart from the power of God the Father, God the Son, God the Holy Spirit. It is God's Life that animates us to be like Christ: 1.) The Fruit of the Spirit, 2.) The Wisdom & Revelation of the Spirit, 3.) The Power of the Spirit. Face Time is the practice of staying relationally connected to God throughout the day and night. It is our ongoing relational connection with God that continually reinforces our new identity as sons/daughters of God, matures our relational intimacy with God and others, and enables us to make eternal impact by fulfilling our destiny – the good works God has prepared for us to accomplish. (Ephesians 2:8-10) Face Time is the key to accessing the supernatural power of God. When we practice the presence of God, hearing and obeying God's voice, we become healed from trauma and grow into a whole and mature person. Peace, righteousness, joy, love and affection emit out of our spirits and souls. We become Christ-infused, life-giving, love-radiating people. As each person in the family-of-God practices this "Immanuel Lifestyle", the presence and life of Christ grows exponentially. Together, we become the corporate Body of Christ, and can then reveal Christ's love, wisdom, and power to a lost and dying world. Each DNA Group, Micro-Church Family, local congregation, and "Jesus Tribe" will only be as effective in bringing about revival, restoration, and the transformation of culture IF each person cultivates a Pray, Hear, Obey Immanuel Lifestyle – FaceTime with God as a way of life.

FaceTime Essentials:

1. Go to a quiet and private place. Turn on your "relational circuits" in your brain, heart, soul, and spirit. (Psalm 37:7, 46:10) "Be still and know that God is God." Allow God's grace-filled voice to speak into your identity, your emotions, your circumstances, your relationships. God is always genuinely delighted to be with you! He loves you and likes you. God relates to you through Jesus Christ and the finished work of the cross, and the shed blood of Christ which covers your sin. Identify anything negative that is blocking your ability to hear God's loving voice. Here are some of the negative emotions that God's Word can dissolve: sad, anger, fear, shame, hopeless, disgust.

2. Practice Interactive gratitude. This is what the Bible calls praise, thanksgiving, and worship. Praise is when we thank God for what He has done. Worship is bringing glory to God because of who He is. Gratitude occurs when we realize that all good gifts come from God. (James 1:17) By acknowledging that all good things have come from God and thanking Him, you begin to turn on the relational circuits in the right side of your brain, which then gives you access to relationally connecting with God. We enter God's presence through thanksgiving. (Psalm 95:2, 100:4) Consider using both your memory and imagination to picture people, places, circumstances, events, tangible gifts, and other good things. Remember the times and places you felt closest to God. Then express your gratitude to God verbally, physically, or by journaling.

3. Meditate upon God's Written Word.

   Write: Copy the verse by hand onto a piece of paper or 3X5 card (Deut. 17:18) and keep it with me to meditate on, memorize and mutter throughout the day(s). I also record this verse in my meditation/journal (which can be written, typed or verbally recorded).

   Quiet Down: Become still in God's presence, loving Him through soft soaking music (2 Kings 3:15,16) and/or praying in tongues (1 Corinthians 14:14), or putting a smile on my face and picturing Jesus with me (Acts 2:25). I tune to His **flowing** thoughts, pictures and emotions (Jn. 7:37-39).

Reason: Reason together with God (Isa. 1:18), meaning the Spirit guides my reasoning process (i.e. through flow). "Lord, what do You want to show me about any of the following: the context of a verse, the Hebrew/Greek definitions of the key words in the verse, any cultural understandings." ("How to Meditate on a Topic" found below details these steps.)

Speak & Imagine: Ponder the Scripture, personalizing and speaking it to myself softy over and over again until I can say it with my eyes closed. As I repeat the Scripture, I allow myself to see it with the eyes of my heart. I note what the picture is in my mind's eye as I repeat the Scripture.

Feel God's Heart: While seeing the above picture ask, "Lord, what does this Scripture reveal about Your heart toward me?" Feel His heart and journal it out.

Hear God's *Rhema*: Put yourself in the picture of this Scripture in your mind. Ask, "Lord, what are You speaking to me through this Scripture?" Tune into the flowing thoughts and flowing pictures (God's voice and vision) and record this dialogue in your two-way journaling.

Act: Accept this revelation, repenting of any sin that is opposite of it and roaring at any obstacle that stands in the way of implementing it. I then speak it forth and act on it. *Our hearts burn within as He walks with us opening Scriptures to us (Lk. 24:32)*

4. **Two-way journaling** –Journaling is the process of hearing God's thoughts and matching your mind with God's mind. It is called "thought rhyming with God. "In Ephesians 2:10, Paul uses the Greek word 'poiema', which literally means God's poetry. When 'poiema' is translated as "handiwork" or "workmanship" it misses the following important point. Poetry in scripture does not rhyme sounds; it follows the Hebrew pattern and rhymes thoughts. This means that as God's poetry, our thoughts can rhyme with our Heavenly Father's. That is amazing! How can it work? We know that as we become intimate with someone, we begin to finish each other's sentences and thoughts. In a deep, authentic, mutual-mind state, we actually don't know where our thoughts stop and the other person's thoughts begin. This is exactly what can happen between God and us too. A mutual-mind state with God results in an emulation of His character and heart; we are sowing the world the poet behind the poetry. As our mutual-mind state becomes stronger, we are able to live out our purpose of being created for good works. It is important to note here that our 'good works' do not save us. Good works flow from thinking like our Creator; we rhyme God's actions and not just His thoughts." (Taken from "Joyful Journey: Listening To Immanuel" by James Wilder)

Four Keys to hearing God's voice as you write out the impressions that are coming from God's Mind into your mind. (Taken from the teaching of Mark Virkler)

A.) The first key to hearing God's voice is to go to a quiet place and still our own thoughts and emotions.

B.) The second key to hearing God's voice: As you pray, fix the eyes of your heart upon Jesus, seeing in the Spirit the dreams and visions of Almighty God. (Acts 2:1-4, 7)

C.) Fix your eyes upon Jesus and ask to receive visions. (Hebrews 12:2) So the third key to hearing God's voice is recognizing that God's voice in your heart often sounds like a flow of spontaneous thoughts.

D.) Journaling, the writing out of your prayers and God's answers, brings great freedom in hearing God's voice. I have found two-way journaling to be a fabulous catalyst for clearly discerning God's inner, spontaneous flow, because as I journal I am able to write in faith for long periods of time, simply believing it is God. I know that what I believe I have received from God must be tested. However, testing involves doubt and doubt blocks divine communication, so I do not want to test while I am trying to receive. (See James 1:5-8.) With journaling, I can receive in faith, knowing that when the flow has ended I can test and examine it carefully.

5. Prayer for self and others.

6. Set Faith-goals which access God's supernatural grace. A faith-goal is a specific manifestation of God's grace. Take the small steps of obedience that trigger the Holy Spirit's help. Acts 5:32

7. Share with your DNA & MKF what God is saying, asking, and how you are responding (obeying).

HOW TO HEAR GOD'S VOICE

By Dr. Mark Virkler

She had done it again! Instead of coming straight home from school like she was supposed to, she had gone to her friend's house. Without permission. Without our knowledge. Without doing her chores.

With a ministering household that included remnants of three struggling families plus our own toddler and newborn, my wife simply couldn't handle all the work on her own. Everyone had to pull their own weight. Everyone had age-appropriate tasks they were expected to complete. At fourteen, Rachel and her younger brother were living with us while her parents tried to overcome lifestyle patterns that had resulted in the children running away to escape the dysfunction. I felt sorry for Rachel, but, honestly my wife was my greatest concern.

Now Rachel had ditched her chores to spend time with her friends. It wasn't the first time, but if I had anything to say about it, it would be the last. I intended to lay down the law when she got home and make it very clear that if she was going to live under my roof, she would obey my rules.

But...she wasn't home yet. And I had recently been learning to hear God's voice more clearly. Maybe I should try to see if I could hear anything from Him about the situation. Maybe He could give me a way to get her to do what she was supposed to (i.e. what I wanted her to do). So I went to my office and reviewed what the Lord had been teaching me from Habakkuk 2:1,2: "I will stand on my guard post and station myself on the rampart; And I will keep watch to see what He will speak to me...Then the Lord answered me and said, 'Record the vision....'"

Habakkuk said, "I will stand on my guard post..." (Hab. 2:1). **The first key to hearing God's voice is to go to a quiet place and still our own thoughts and emotions.** Psalm 46:10 encourages us to be still, let go, cease striving, and know that He is God. In Psalm 37:7 we are called to "be still before the Lord and wait patiently for Him." There is a deep inner knowing in our spirits that each of us can experience when we quiet our flesh and our minds. Practicing the art of biblical meditation helps silence the outer noise and distractions clamoring for our attention.

I didn't have a guard post but I did have an office, so I went there to quiet my temper and my mind. Loving God through a quiet worship song is one very effective way to become still. In 2 Kings 3, Elisha needed a word from the Lord so he said, "Bring me a minstrel," and as the minstrel played, the Lord spoke. I have found that playing a worship song on my autoharp is the quickest way for me to come to stillness. I need to choose my song carefully; boisterous songs of praise do not bring me to stillness, but rather gentle songs that express my love and worship. And it isn't enough just to sing the song into the cosmos – I come into the Lord's presence most quickly and easily when I use my godly imagination to see the truth that He is right here with me and I sing my songs to Him, personally.

"I will keep watch to see," said the prophet. To receive the pure word of God, it is very important that my heart be properly focused as I become still, because my focus is the source of the intuitive flow. If I fix my eyes upon Jesus (Hebrews 12:2), the intuitive flow comes from Jesus. But if I fix my gaze upon some desire of my heart, the intuitive flow comes out of that desire. To have a pure flow I must become still and carefully fix my eyes upon Jesus. Quietly worshiping the King and receiving out of the stillness that follows quite easily accomplishes this.

So I used **the second key to hearing God's voice: As you pray, fix the eyes of your heart upon Jesus, seeing in the Spirit the dreams and visions of Almighty God.** Habakkuk was actually looking for vision as he prayed. He opened the eyes of his heart, and looked into the spirit world to see what God wanted to show him.

God has always spoken through dreams and visions, and He specifically said that they would come to those upon whom the Holy Spirit is poured out (Acts 2:1-4, 17).

Being a logical, rational person, observable facts that could be verified by my physical senses were the foundations of my life, including my spiritual life. I had never thought of opening the eyes of my heart and looking for vision. However, I have come to believe that this is exactly what God wants me to do. He gave me eyes in my heart to see in the spirit the vision and movement of Almighty God. There is an active spirit world all around us, full of angels, demons, the Holy Spirit, the omnipresent Father, and His omnipresent Son, Jesus. The only reasons for me not to see this reality are unbelief or lack of knowledge.

In his sermon in Acts 2:25, Peter refers to King David's statement: "I saw the Lord always in my presence; for He is at my right hand, so that I will not be shaken." The original psalm makes it clear that this was a decision of David's, not a constant supernatural visitation: "I have set (literally, I have placed) the Lord continually before me; because He is at my right hand, I will not be shaken" (Psalms 16:8). Because David knew that the Lord was always with him, he determined in his spirit to *see* that truth with the eyes of his heart as he went through life, knowing that this would keep his faith strong.

In order to see, we must look. Daniel saw a vision in his mind and said, "I was looking...I kept looking...I kept looking" (Daniel 7:2, 9, 13). As I pray, I look for Jesus, and I watch as He speaks to me, doing and saying the things that are on His heart. Many Christians will find that if they will only look, they will see. Jesus is Emmanuel, God with us (Matthew 1:23). It is as simple as that. You can see Christ present with you because Christ *is* present with you. In fact, the vision may come so easily that you will be tempted to reject it, thinking that it is just you. But if you persist in recording these visions, your doubt will soon be overcome by faith as you recognize that the content of them could only be birthed in Almighty God.

Jesus demonstrated the ability of living out of constant contact with God, declaring that He did nothing on His own initiative, but only what He saw the Father doing, and heard the Father saying (Jn. 5:19,20,30). What an incredible way to live!

Is it possible for us to live out of divine initiative as Jesus did? Yes! We must simply fix our eyes upon Jesus. The veil has been torn, giving access into the immediate presence of God, and He calls us to draw near (Luke 23:45; Hebrews 10:19-22). "I pray that the eyes of your heart will be enlightened...."

When I had quieted my heart enough that I was able to picture Jesus without the distractions of my own ideas and plans, I was able to "keep watch to see what He will speak to me." I wrote down my question: "Lord, what should I do about Rachel? "Immediately the thought came to me, "She is insecure." Well, that certainly wasn't my thought! Her behavior looked like rebellion to me, not insecurity.

But like Habakkuk, I was coming to know the sound of God speaking to me (Habakkuk 2:2). Elijah described it as a still, small voice (I Kings 19:12). I had previously listened for an inner audible voice, and God does speak that way at times. However, I have found that usually, God's voice comes as spontaneous thoughts, visions, feelings, or impressions.

For example, haven't you been driving down the road and had a thought come to you to pray for a certain person? Didn't you believe it was God telling you to pray? What did God's voice sound like? Was it an audible voice, or was it a spontaneous thought that lit upon your mind?

Experience indicates that we perceive spirit-level communication as spontaneous thoughts, impressions and visions, and Scripture confirms this in many ways. For example, one definition of *paga*, a Hebrew word for intercession, is "a chance encounter or an accidental intersecting." When God lays people on our hearts, He does it through *paga*, a chance-encounter thought "accidentally" intersecting our minds.

So **the third key to hearing God's voice is recognizing that God's voice in your heart often sounds like a flow of spontaneous thoughts.** Therefore, when I want to hear from God, I tune to chance-encounter or spontaneous thoughts.

Finally, God told Habakkuk to record the vision (Habbakuk 2:2). This was not an isolated command. The Scriptures record many examples of individual's prayers and God's replies, such as the Psalms, many of the prophets, and Revelation. I have found that obeying this final principle amplified my confidence in my ability to hear God's voice so that I could finally make living out of His initiatives a way of life. The **fourth key, two-way journaling or the writing out of your prayers and God's answers, brings great freedom in hearing God's voice.**

I have found two-way journaling to be a fabulous catalyst for clearly discerning God's inner, spontaneous flow, because as I journal I am able to write in faith for long periods of time, simply believing it is God. I know that what I believe I have received from God must be tested. However, testing involves doubt and doubt blocks divine communication, so I do not want to test while I am trying to receive. (See James 1:5-8.) With journaling, I can receive in faith, knowing that when the flow has ended I can test and examine it carefully

.So I wrote down what I believed He had said: "She is insecure. "But the Lord wasn't done. I continued to write the spontaneous thoughts that came to me: "Love her unconditionally. She is flesh of your flesh and bone of your bone."

My mind immediately objected: She is not flesh of my flesh. She is not related to me at all – she is a foster child, just living in my home temporarily. It was definitely time to test this "word from the Lord"!

There are three possible sources of thoughts in our minds: ourselves, satan and the Holy Spirit. It was obvious that the words in my journal did not come from my own mind – I certainly didn't see her as insecure or flesh of my flesh. And I sincerely doubted that satan would encourage me to love anyone unconditionally!

Okay, it was starting to look like I might have actually received counsel from the Lord. It was consistent with the names and character of God as revealed in the Scripture, and totally contrary to the names and character of the enemy. So that meant that I was hearing from the Lord, and He wanted me to see the situation in a different light. Rachel was my daughter – part of my family not by blood but by the hand of God Himself. The chaos of her birth home had created deep insecurity about her worthiness to be loved by anyone, including me and including God. Only the unconditional love of the Lord expressed through an imperfect human would reach her heart.

But there was still one more test I needed to perform before I would have absolute confidence that this was truly God's word to me: I needed confirmation from someone else whose spiritual discernment I trusted. So I went to my wife and shared what I had received. I knew if I could get her validation, especially since she was the one most wronged in the situation, then I could say, at least to myself, "Thus sayeth the Lord."

Needless to say, Patti immediately and without question confirmed that the Lord had spoken to me. My entire planned lecture was forgotten. I returned to my office anxious to hear more. As the Lord planted a new, supernatural love for Rachel within me, He showed me what to say and how to say it to not only address the current issue of household responsibility, but the deeper issues of love and acceptance and worthiness.

Rachel and her brother remained as part of our family for another two years, giving us many opportunities to demonstrate and teach about the Father's love, planting spiritual seeds in thirsty soil. We weren't perfect and we didn't solve all of her issues, but because I had learned to listen to the Lord, we were able to avoid creating more brokenness and separation.

The four simple keys that the Lord showed me from Habakkuk have been used by people of all ages, from four to a hundred and four, from every continent, culture and denomination, to break through into intimate two-way conversations with their loving Father and dearest Friend. Omitting any one of the keys will prevent you from receiving all He wants to say to you. The order of the keys is not important, just that you use them all. Embracing all four, by faith, can change your life. Simply quiet yourself down, tune to spontaneity, look for vision, and journal. He is waiting to meet you there.

You will be amazed when you journal! Doubt may hinder you at first, but throw it off, reminding yourself that it is a biblical concept, and that God is present, speaking to His children. Relax. When we cease our labors and enter His rest, God is free to flow (Hebrews 4:10).

Why not try it for yourself, right now? Sit back comfortably, take out your pen and paper, and smile. Turn your attention toward the Lord in praise and worship, seeking His face. Many people have found the music and visionary prayer called "A Stroll Along the Sea of Galilee" helpful in getting them started. You can listen to it and download it free at www.CWGMinistries.org/Galilee.

After you write your question to Him, become still, fixing your gaze on Jesus. You will suddenly have a very good thought. Don't doubt it; simply write it down. Later, as you read your journaling, you, too, will be blessed to discover that you are indeed dialoguing with God. If you wonder if it is really the Lord speaking to you, share it with your spouse or a friend. Their input will encourage your faith and strengthen your commitment to spend time getting to know the Lover of your soul more intimately than you ever dreamed possible.

Is It *Really* God?

Five ways to be sure what you're hearing is from Him:

1) Test the Origin (1 John 4:1)

Thoughts from our own minds are progressive, with one thought leading to the next, however tangentially. Thoughts from the spirit world are spontaneous. The Hebrew word for true prophecy is *naba,* which literally means to bubble up, whereas false prophecy is *ziyd* meaning to boil up. True words from the Lord will bubble up from our innermost being; we don't need to cook them up ourselves.

2) Compare It to Biblical Principles

God will never say something to you personally which is contrary to His universal revelation as expressed in the Scriptures. If the Bible clearly states that something is a sin, no amount of journaling can make it right. Much of what you journal about will not be specifically addressed in the Bible, however, so an understanding of biblical principles is also needed.

3) Compare It to the Names and Character of God as Revealed in the Bible

Anything God says to you will be in harmony with His essential nature. Journaling will help you get to *know* God personally, but knowing what the Bible says *about* Him will help you discern what words are from Him. Make sure the tenor of your journaling lines up with the character of God as described in the names of the Father, Son and Holy Spirit.

4) Test the Fruit (Matthew 7:15-20)

What effect does what you are hearing have on your soul and your spirit? Words from the Lord will quicken your faith and increase your love, peace and joy. They will stimulate a sense of humility within you as you become more aware of Who God is and who you are. On the other hand, any words you receive which cause you to fear or doubt, which bring you into confusion or anxiety, or which stroke your ego (especially if you hear something that is "just for you alone – no one else is worthy") must be immediately rebuked and rejected as lies of the enemy.

5)   Share It with Your Spiritual Counselors (Proverbs 11:14)

We are members of a Body! A cord of three strands is not easily broken and God's intention has always been for us to grow together. Nothing will increase your faith in your ability to hear from God like having it confirmed by two or three other people! Share it with your spouse, your parents, your friends, your elder, your group leader, even your grown children can be your sounding board. They don't need to be perfect or super-spiritual; they just need to love you, be committed to being available to you, have a solid biblical orientation, and most importantly, they must also willingly and easily receive counsel. Avoid the authoritarian who insists that because of their standing in the church or with God, they no longer need to listen to others. Find two or three people and let them confirm that you are hearing from God!

The book *4 Keys to Hearing God's Voice* is available at www.CWGMinistries.org.

YOU CAN HEAR GOD'S VOICE!

By Mark Virkler

I tossed and turned in bed, unable to fall asleep. The thought kept going through my mind: "What if I died tonight? I'm not ready to go to heaven." Since I could not shake the thought, I got up, went downstairs and waited for my parents to come home from their meeting. When they did, I announced that I wanted to get saved, and they took me straightway to the pastor's home where he explained the plan of salvation and led me in the sinner's prayer. I was 15 years old when I accepted Jesus Christ into my heart as my Lord and Savior.

It was God's voice that was speaking to me that night, calling me into His kingdom. His voice came as a spontaneous thought inside my head. However, I didn't define this as the primary way God's voice is heard until I had completed a desperate 10 year search to hear Him clearly.

Christianity is unique among religions, for it alone offers a **personal relationship** with the Creator beginning here and now, and lasting throughout eternity. Jesus declared, "This is eternal life – that they may *know God*" (John 17:3). Unfortunately, many in the Church miss the great blessing of fellowship with our Lord because we have lost the ability to recognize His voice. Though John 10:27 promises us that "My sheep hear My voice," too many believers are starved for that intimate relationship that alone can satisfy the desire of their hearts.

I was one of those sheep who was unable to identify the voice of my Shepherd. I hungered for deeper spiritual intimacy with God, but I could not find it. Then on the eleventh year of my Christian life I had the spontaneous thought that "I should take a year of my life and focus on learning to hear God's voice." I decided to act on that thought and devote a year to focused effort, learning to hear His voice. Unbeknown to me, it was the Lord calling me to invest that time.

That year the Lord revealed four simple keys, all found in Habakkuk 2:1, 2, which unlocked the treasure of His voice. Using the four keys together allowed me to easily hear God's voice on a daily basis. It was the most transforming step I have taken in the 45 years of my Christian life! I would like to share them with you so you can try them and see if they do the same for you.

<u>Key</u>: God's voice in your heart often sounds like a flow of spontaneous thoughts.

Habakkuk knew the sound of God speaking to him (Habakkuk 2:2). Elijah described it as a still, small voice (1 Kings 19:12). I had always listened for an inner audible voice, and God does speak that way at times. However, I have found that usually, God's voice comes as spontaneous thoughts, or flowing thoughts.

For example, haven't you ever been driving down the road and had a thought come to you to pray for a certain person? Didn't you believe it was God telling you to pray? What did God's voice sound like? Was it an audible voice, or was it a spontaneous thought that lit upon your mind?

Experience indicates that we perceive spirit-level communication as spontaneous thoughts, impressions and visions, and Scripture confirms this in many ways. For example, one definition of *paga*, a Hebrew word for intercession, is "a chance encounter or an accidental intersecting." When God lays people on our hearts, He does it through *paga*, a chance-encounter thought "accidentally" intersecting our minds. We consider it chance encounter in that we didn't reason it up, however it is purposeful, because God sent it to us.

Therefore, when you want to hear God's voice, you tune to chance-encounter, spontaneous or flowing thoughts. Even satan's thoughts come to us as spontaneous thoughts, which is why we are commanded to "take every thought captive" (2 Corinthians 10:5). I am sure all of us have experienced spontaneous evil thoughts coming to us, even attacking right in the middle of our prayer and worship times. So I conclude that analytical thoughts are mine, spontaneous good thoughts come from the Holy Spirit, and spontaneous evil thoughts come from evil spirits.

- **God's thoughts** line up with Scripture and with His various names: Comforter, Counselor, Teacher, Giver of Life, Healer and Deliverer. His thoughts edify, exhort, and comfort. They are pure, peaceable, gentle, reasonable, full of mercy and good fruits, unwavering (James 3:17).

- **Satan's thoughts** line up with his various names: accuser, adversary, thief who comes to kill, steal and destroy. His thoughts condemn and bring despair, rejection, fear, doubt, unbelief and in general, misery. Satan's thoughts bring jealousy and selfish ambition (James 3:14, 15).

Key: Become still so you can sense God's flow of thoughts.

Habakkuk said, "I will stand on my guard post..." (Habakkuk 2:1). Habakkuk knew that to hear God's quiet, inner, spontaneous thoughts, he had to first go to a quiet place and still his own thoughts and emotions. Psalm 62:5 encourages us to silence our souls before God. There is a deep inner knowing (spontaneous flow) in our spirits that each of us can experience when we quiet our flesh and our minds. If we are not still, we will sense only our own thoughts.

Loving God through a quiet worship song is one very effective way to become still. (Note 2 Kings 3:15.) After I worship and become silent within, I open myself for that spontaneous flow. If thoughts come of things I have forgotten to do, I write them down so I can do them later. If thoughts of guilt or unworthiness come, I repent thoroughly, receive the washing of the blood of the Lamb, putting on His robe of righteousness, seeing myself spotless before God (Isaiah 61:10; Colossians 1:22).

Clear focus provides the purest flow: To receive the pure word of God, it is very important that my heart be properly focused as I become still because the intuitive flow comes out of the vision being held before one's eyes. If I fix my eyes upon Jesus, the intuitive flow is pure and comes from Jesus. But if I fix my gaze upon some desire of my heart, the intuitive flow is affected by that desire. To have a pure flow I must become still and carefully fix my eyes upon Jesus (Hebrews 12:2).

Again, quietly worshiping the King, and receiving out of the stillness that follows quite easily accomplishes this. Beginning my prayer time as Jesus taught us to pray is expedient: "Our Father Who art in heaven, hallowed be Thy name…" Jesus taught us to begin prayer by lifting our eyes up to our Father and beholding Him. We don't start prayer with our issues. We start our prayer by gazing upon Him!

Key: Fix your eyes upon Jesus and ask to receive visions.

Habakkuk said, "I will keep **watch to see**," (Habakkuk 2:1, 2). Habakkuk was actually looking for a vision as he prayed. Since I believe the Bible is meant to be lived, I decided that I, too, would begin looking with the eyes of my heart into the Spirit world to see what I could see.

Do what King David did! A good way to begin using the eyes of your heart is by doing what King David did: *"For David says of Him, 'I SAW THE LORD ALWAYS IN MY PRESENCE; FOR HE IS AT MY RIGHT HAND, SO THAT I WILL NOT BE SHAKEN"* (Acts 2:25 NASB). The original Psalm makes it clear that this was a decision of David's, not a constant supernatural visitation: "I have set (literally, I have placed) the Lord continually before me; because He is at my right hand, I will not be shaken" (Psalms 16:8). Because David knew that the Lord was always with him, he determined in his spirit to see that truth with the eyes of his heart as he went through life, knowing that this would keep his faith strong.

We say, "A picture is worth 1000 words." I believe that is because pictures are the language of the heart. We notice that Jesus used pictures constantly as He taught (Matthew 13:34). When I use pictures in my prayer time, fixing my eyes on Jesus, I am speaking the language of my heart and that moves me quickly into heart/spirit realities getting me beyond my mind.

Use godly imagination: So I choose to do what King David did and I develop "godly imagination," which I define as "picturing things God says are so." Obviously if I am picturing that Jesus is NOT with me that would be picturing a lie, which is unwise. I can't imagine any reason I would want to picture unscriptural things. So I see Jesus at my right hand, always. I add to this Paul's prayer for God to enlighten the eyes of my heart (Ephesians 1:17, 18). Then I tune to the flow of the Holy Spirit, and He brings the scene alive. I find I can step from these godly imaginations, into a divine vision.

It is amazing, simple and child-like! Of course it would need to be, as we are told that to enter the kingdom we must become as little children. My 6-year-old granddaughter can do this and she shares with me her journaling and the visions of the angels standing on both sides of her protecting her and watching over her. You will find your young children can do these four keys easier than you can! Try it with them and see.

From Genesis to Revelation God gave dreams and visions, and He specifically said that in the last days He would pour out His Spirit and **we would** see dreams and visions (Acts 2:1-4, 17).

We must look if we want to see! Daniel saw a vision in his mind and said, "I was looking…I kept looking…I kept looking" (Daniel 7:2, 9, 13). So I needed to repent for not looking, and begin presenting the eyes of my heart to the Lord, and looking. As I pray, I look for Jesus, and I watch and listen as He speaks to me, doing and saying the things that are on His heart. Many Christians will find that if they will only look, they will see flowing pictures, in the same way they receive flowing thoughts.

Jesus is Emmanuel, God with us (Matthew 1:23). It is as simple as that. You can see Christ present with you because Christ *is present with you*. In fact, the vision may come so easily that you will be tempted to reject it, thinking that it is just you. But if you persist in recording these flowing pictures, your doubt will soon be overcome by faith as you recognize that the content of them could only be birthed by Almighty God.

A lifestyle: Jesus demonstrated the ability of living out of constant contact with God, declaring that He did nothing on His own initiative, but only what He *saw the Father doing, and heard the Father saying* (John 5:19,20,30). *What an incredible way to live!*

Is it possible for you to live out of divine initiative as Jesus did? Yes! It is called "abiding in Christ" (John 15). Fix your eyes upon Jesus. The veil has been torn, giving access into the immediate presence of God, and He calls you to draw near (Luke 23:45; Hebrews 10:19-22). "I pray that the eyes of your heart will be enlightened" and you will see His visions. They are His gift to you, freely given (Acts 2:17).

Key: Journaling, the writing out of your prayers and God's answers, brings great freedom in hearing God's voice.

God told Habakkuk to record the vision (Habakkuk 2:2). This was not an isolated command. The Scriptures record many examples of individual's prayers and God's replies (e.g. the Psalms, many of the prophets, Revelation).

I call the process "two-way journaling," and I have found it to be a fabulous catalyst for clearly discerning God's inner, spontaneous flow, because as I journal I am able to **write in faith** for long periods of time, simply believing it is God. I know that what I believe I have received from God must be tested. However, testing involves doubt and doubt blocks divine communication, so I do not want to test while I am trying to receive (Hebrews 11:6). With journaling, I can receive in faith, knowing that when the flow has ended I can test and examine it carefully, making sure that it lines up with Scripture (1 Thessalonians 5:21).

Remove doubt: Doubt may hinder you at first, but throw it off, reminding yourself that recording God's words and visions is a biblical concept, and that God is present, speaking to His children. In the Bible, satan is constantly casting doubt by saying, "Did God really tell you...?" (Genesis 3:1 GNB).

Learn to relax! When we cease our labors and enter His rest, God is free to flow (Hebrews 4:10). Sit back comfortably, take out your pen and paper (or computer or iPad), smile, and turn your attention toward the Lord in praise and worship, seeking His face. Write down, "Good morning, Lord! I love You. What do You want to say to me?" Then become still, fixing your gaze on Jesus. You will suddenly have a very good thought. Don't doubt it; simply write it down. Later, as you read over your journaling, you will be blessed to discover that the content is *amazing* and that you *are* indeed dialoguing with God!

Hear God through illumined Scripture: Knowing God through the Bible is a vital foundation to hearing His voice in your heart, so you must have a solid commitment to knowing and obeying God's written Word. We are commanded to meditate on Scriptures (Joshua 1:8). As we pray over Scripture, we find verses leap off the page and hit us between the eyes. This is another very powerful way that God speaks to us. Regular scriptural meditation is commanded by God and is a must for the effective Christian life.

Utilize spiritual advisors: It is also very important for your growth and safety that you be related to solid, spiritual counselors. All major directional moves that come through journaling should be confirmed by your counselors before you act upon them. The Bible says in the mouth of two or three witnesses every fact is to be established (2 Corinthians 13:1). Also, in the multitude of counselors, there is safety (Proverbs 15:22). So make sure you walk in meekness and seek out and receive input from your spiritual advisors. This step must not be skipped!

The four keys appear again in Revelation: John used the same four keys that Habakkuk did. In Revelation 1:9-11 we find he was in the spirit (stillness), he heard a voice behind him (tuned to spontaneity), saying, "Write in a book (journaling), what you see (vision)." So in both Old and New Testaments we find the same four keys being used to receive God's voice. Don't worry about the order of the keys. Just make sure you are using all four keys.

As a <u>PACKAGE</u> these four keys work (Stop! Look! Listen! Write!): They get the job done! People hear. We guarantee that if you will use these four keys **together**, they will work for you and you will hear God's voice. Try them as a bundle, and see how they work for you. We have free downloadable music you can listen to as you journal. It is available at www.cwgministries.org/galilee. The first part of the recording takes you for a visionary walk with Jesus along the Sea of Galilee, and guides you into using all four keys together. We encourage you to give it a try! May you be restored to taking walks with the Lord in the garden in the cool of the day. May you experience the fullness of a personal relationship with our Lord and Savior, Jesus Christ. May communion with God be deepened in your life, and may His healing and creative rays fill you through and through.

THE LIFE MODEL: AN INTRODUCTION AND OVERVIEW

The Life Model is a "unifying approach to ministries of counseling, recovery, pastoral care, prayer ministry, deliverance, inner healing, child rearing, body life and health. It is a multi-generational model of redemption and maturity from conception to death. It has been developed from a Biblical worldview in order to produce identity, character, and culture. The Life Model is a self-propagating model of recovery that will allow people to spread good relationships in low-joy places of the world." Taken from "Living from the Heart Jesus Gave You" by E. James Wilder

We want to integrate the insights and practices of The Life Model into Micro-Church Families and DNA Groups. www.JoyStartsHere.com

Three distinct features of the Life Model:

1. Depends on a multigenerational community for the formation of maturity.

2. It depends upon an Immanuel Lifestyle where God's interactive presence informs all we do and creates "shalom".

3. There are specific, learned, relational skills needed for a mature human identity. While everyone is born with the brain wiring needed to be a predator, training in the gentle-protector skills are needed to form godly character. These skills have been identified by brain studies and writings beginning about the year 2000. These brain skills are needed in all humans and are only acquired by joyful interactions and relationships with other people who already have the skills. The absence of key relational skills and maturity are almost always behind failures of ministers, ministries, and missions. Sadly, the lacking skills are rarely identified, and when the lack of skill is seen, no one knows how to restore the skill. Relational skills are the basis for expressing godly character and identity to others around us when the "heart Jesus gave us" seeks expression. We must restore and propagate gentle-protector, relational brain skills." (taken from "Living From The Heart Jesus Gave You")

The Goals of the Life Model:

The Life Model seeks to test and distribute Life Model technology to as many existing networks as possible. We are planting seeds that will change whole cultures, alter generational heritages and equip people with the skills they need to thrive.

1. The dream is to see self-propagating recovery as the normal function of the church around the world.

2. The Challenge is the spread of evil which produces trauma in both individuals and groups.

3. The two attempts at solutions:

    A. Clinical solutions which require professionals, but is not enough to stem the tide of relational destruction.

    B. Healthy spiritual families that can provide self-propagating recovery that transforms culture. The best delivery system is the church of Jesus Christ. Basic conversion alone does not heal or mature, we need all the elements of transformation in the kingdom such as loving family:

    "Simple conversion does not provide the missing brain skills they need for healthy relationships any more than salvation will make them suddenly literate."

4. Self-propagating healing can be accelerated through the Immanuel Process (intimately relating with our ever-present God).

5. But self-propagating relational skills are not as easy to transfer. The relational skills take community, bonded relationships and time. Let's reduce and even prevent some trauma and addiction as well as provide healing and improve relationships.

6. Relational joy is at the heart of the Life Model:

    A. Gentle-protector brain skills.
    B. Immanuel awareness of God with us
    C. Transformation of character
    D. Growth of maturity
    E. Nurturing a multigenerational community
    F. Recovery from trauma
    G. Development of resilience
    H. Prevention of predatory personality development
    I. Hope for the low-joy places of the world all require joy
    J. Relational joy starts with knowing who we really are meant to be, when we see ourselves and then others through the awareness and discernment of the heart Jesus gives us. "Living From The Heart Jesus Gave You"

Elements of the problem that require elements in a solution:

1. Trauma and addictions change our identities; therefore the solution must also change identities.
2. Trauma self-propagates; therefore the solution must self-propagate.
3. Trauma blocks the development of maturity and character; therefore the solution must restore maturity and godly character.
4. Trauma encourages people to reject others; therefore the solution must create belonging.
5. Trauma and addictions spread without needing education; although the solution should be based on the best science, it should not require a Western education or medical model.
6. Violence and terrorism traumatize whole groups at once; therefore the solution must heal whole groups at once.
7. All human cultures, races and ethnicities have the same nervous systems and the same spiritual needs. A solution based on solid neurology and Biblical spirituality would be a solution as universal as the causes for trauma.
8. The recovery model must be high-tech design with a low-tech implementation.
9. Abuse usually spreads through unhealthy relationships. The 19 relational brain skills through THRIVE materials in bonded relationships, train and encourage people towards joyful relating.
10. The identities formed by the solution must match God's design for us.

Life Model – It's for leaders and the wounded in church community.

1. Leaders need to know how to serve. People's hearts are easily wounded.

2. Jesus heals the broken hearted.

3. Synergy is what happens when two agents are combined, and they increase each other's effectiveness. Wounded mixed into and with family-community creates synergy.

4. "While you are living from your hurt, you may not be able to discover characteristics of your heart. As God heals hurt...we will discover nature of the heart."

5. Avoid isolation. You cannot overcome obstacles alone.

6. Living from the heart Jesus gave you is about receiving and giving life. This process only happens in family and community.

Wholeness:

1. People need to know who they are...and be reminded who they are frequently by those who love and know them.

2. People need repaired, healed, recovered.

3. It takes belonging to community to achieve wholeness in a fractured world.

4. It takes a lifetime of work.

5. Traumas are the wounds or injuries left in our identities that render us less than what God had in mind when He created us. Traumas block or slow growth.

6. Traumatic wounds can be caused by adding something to us we should not have...like a bullet to the body. Trauma B.

7. Traumatic injuries can be caused by the absence of what the soul needs – like malnutrition. Trauma A.

Relational Joy:

"In a child's first two years, the desire to experience joy in loving relationships is the most powerful force in life. In fact, some neurologists now say that the basic human need is to be the 'sparkle in someone's eye.' When you catch a glimpse of a child's face as she runs toward an awaiting parent with arms outstretched in unrestrained joy, you can witness firsthand that incredible power that comes from 'being the sparkle in someone's eye.' When this joy is the strongest force in a child's world, life makes sense, because children look forward to moments when they can reconnect to joy-by being with their beloved. Wonderfully enough, that innocent, pure desire that begins in childhood continues throughout life. Life makes sense and is empowered by joy when people are in relationship with those who love them and are sincerely glad to be with them.

Because joy is relational, it is also a contagious experience. Joy is produced when someone is glad to see me, which stirs up a bit of joy in me. Then my joy is returned and the giver's joy is increased as well. This experience goes back-and-forth at amazingly fast rates – six cycles per second in a nonverbal, face-to-face exchange – all that time growing stronger joy between both people.

Joy also comes from being in relationship with God. Throughout the Bible it is established that a powerful joy comes from a relationship with God who knows everything about me and is still as-glad-as-glad-can-get to be with me. Now, when ancient Biblical authors inspired by God, and 21st century neuroscientists propelled by knowledge all agree that joy comes through powerful relationships, we know there is something profoundly important to be learned from this.

In fact, when the joy strength is properly laid, just the knowledge that someone would be glad to be with me, even if not physically present at the moment, is enough to return me to joy. Images of faces, the memory of their responses, and the presence of God can all sufficiently return us to joy.

Having enough joy strength is fundamental to a person's will being. We now know that a joy-center exists in the right orbital prefrontal cortex of the brain. It has executive control over the entire emotional system. When the joy center has been sufficiently developed, it regulates emotions, pain control and immunity centers; it guides us to act like ourselves; it releases neurotransmitters like dopamine and serotonin; and it is the only part of the brain that overrides the main drive centers – food and sexual impulses, terror and rage. (From "Living from the Heart Jesus Gave You")

Relational Bonds:

Becoming healed and mature requires bonds between people – they are the foundation upon which maturity is built. Bonds are the connections that energize us, motivate our actions and establish our identities. The receiving-and-giving exchange in our bonds shapes our view of what is important. There are two essentially different and incompatible types of bonds – one based on fear and the other on love.

Fear Bonds: Fear bonds are formed around avoiding negative feelings and pain. Fear bonds energize people to avoid pain – like rejection, fear, shame, humiliation, abandonment, guilt or even physical abuse.

Love Bonds: Love bonds are formed around desire, joy and seeking to be with people who are important to us. Love bonds motivate people to live in truth, closeness, joy, peace, perseverance, kindness, and authentic giving.

The Five Stages of Maturity:

Maturity is about reaching one's God-given potential. It means maximizing our skills and talents, and using them effectively, while growing into the full capability of our individual designs. Maturity involves growth in many areas: relational, emotional, spiritual, mental. Our brains were designed to help us mature. While most of the brain stops growing at certain stages of development, the brain's joy-center, located in the right orbital prefrontal cortex, is the only section of the brain that never loses its capacity to grow! It is the one section of the brain that retains the ability to grow our entire lives, which means that joy strength can always continue to develop! What makes it grow? It grows in response to real, joy-filled relationships. We are not talking about casual, superficial relationships. When people are engaged in authentic, bonded relationships showing real joy, this section of the brain will grow at any age!

1. Infant (0-3) – the fundamental need is to receive unconditional love and care. If these needs go unmet, we will spend the rest of our lives trying to get others to take care of us.

2. Child (4-12) – a child still needs unconditional love and care. They also start learning how to care for themselves. They must master several personal tasks: a.) a child must learn to say what he thinks and feels and appropriately ask for what is needed, b.) children must learn what brings them satisfaction, c.) children need to learn how to do hard things, d.) children need to develop their personal talents and resources, e.) children need to learn self-care. f.) self-care requires knowing yourself and making yourself understandable to others. g.) children need to understand how they fit into history as well as the big picture of life. When they understand the big picture of life, they realize they have the ability to personally impact the world.

3. Adult (13-birth of first child) – a shift from being self-centered child to a both-centered adult. While a child needs to learn me-centered fairness, an adult learns we-centered fairness (how do I make it fair for us). Mutuality is the trademark of an adult because he can take care of two people at the same time. Adults know how to remain stable in difficult situations and can return self and others to joy. Adults contribute to and are a part of vital community. They are a part of something bigger than "me" – which is empowering and inspiring. Adults express the characteristics of their heart in a deepening personal way. Once people know who they truly are and understand the power and beauty of their God-given characteristics, their passion, purpose, talents, and pain will all come together and begin to define specifically who they are. The better they can express their unique identities in their words and actions, the more positioned they will be for speaking and living truthfully.

4. Parent (first birth until youngest child becomes adult) – one is at the parent stage when they can sacrificially care for their children without resenting the sacrifice or expecting to receive anything for their efforts. Parents know how to protect, serve and enjoy their families. Parents are wise in allowing and providing spiritual family members – other important people in their children's lives who will help their children become the persons they were designed to be. Mature parents will be able to bring their children through difficult times and return to joy from all unpleasant emotions.

5. Elder (beginning when youngest child becomes an adult) – one who has raised children to maturity and completed all the prior maturity tasks. True elders can act like themselves in the midst of difficulty. They can also establish an accurate community identity by finding out what their community has been designed by God to be, rather than imposing what they would like it to be. True elders prize all community members and see them as God sees them – looking past their flaws and facades to see the persons they have been designed to be. True elders are also will and able to parent and mature the community. They are qualified to do this

because they have learned from a lifetime of experiences. (Taken from "Living from the Heart Jesus Gave You")

HOW RELATIONAL BRAIN SKILLS ARE DEVELOPED

1. The part of the brain that guides our relational and emotional intelligence (right frontal cortex) operates faster than the part of the brain that gathers regular information (left side of brain). The "left side" of the brain can learn by gathering information through more traditional forms of education like lectures, reading, memorization, etc. However, the right frontal cortex of the brain, the location of relational and emotional intelligence, absorbs content at such high rates of speed that it depends on essential elements like culture, atmosphere, and positive relational encounters. For example, when someone greets a child, hugs them, and expresses delight over them, something profound is transacted and transferred into the soul of that child which shapes their identity and sense of worth and belonging.

2. Our deepest selves, our hearts, the core of our being, must be accessed and influence "indirectly" in a way that circumvents or goes deeper than the right side of our brains. That is because our core deepest "self" (seated in the right frontal cortex) operates on a faster brain cycle than our conscious thought and reasoning.

3. Therefore, our discipleship methods need to include forms of learning that reach people at a core level. Relational brain skills are transferred relationally at the speed of encounter and experiences. They are caught more than taught.

4. The core parts of our brain and hearts are accessed and influenced through:
   A. Desiring, welcoming, and practicing divine encounters with God – an "Immanuel Lifestyle". God's Spirit lives inside the human spirit of born again believers. God's Spirit also dwells upon believers when they are baptized by the Holy Spirit. An ongoing communion with the indwelling Christ is essential for personal transformation.
   B. Establishing secure and relational attachments with loving and healthy natural and spiritual families. Relational bonding at a mind, heart, and lifestyle level is essential for healing from trauma and maturing into wholeness.
   C. Positive emotional experiences transmit and transfer the life and energy of God's love.
   D. Interactive learning exercises with others help to exchange relational skills. Example:
   E. Teacher has incredible handshakes with each student
   F. https://www.youtube.com/watch?v=VctaUNJpT6U
   G. https://www.youtube.com/watch?v=O4buD-w9cj4
   H. Actions that have symbolic power (like baptism and communion).
   I. Visual, auditory and tangible aids.
      i.) These things also need to be nested in high joy environments. There are practical things we can also do to create those environments. More joy makes transformation amplify and accelerate.

TRANSFORMING FELLOWSHIP: 19 BRAIN SKILLS THAT BUILD JOYFUL COMMUNITY

by Chris Coursey

Introduction: The purpose of this book is to help the reader obtain the relational skills that produce sustainable transformation. These relational skills are tied to 19 brain skills. When these brain skills are developed a much higher quality of relational joy is the outcome. Unfortunately, relational skills are decreasing as a result of the amount of time people are spending in front of screens: television, smart phones, computers, movie, etc.

"Chesed" love (Hebrew word for covenant or bonded love) plus relational brain skills – the key ingredients for joy: "Relational brain skills are all relational in nature because at our core we have relational identities. Character is an expression of how we see ourselves in relationship to others. If training relational brain skills were a matter of sharing information, we would not need relationships to learn them. I will explain in detail how relational skills are learned and passed on to other people. This is the core of discipleship and fellowship. However, before we go into the details, here is the conclusion of the matter. Relational skills that build godly character can only be transmitted in the presence of "chesed", also known as "sticky love." Without chesed, the love that sticks us together, there is no lasting transformation. With some chesed, there is some transformation potential. Chesed without relational skills is a brutal and heartbreaking story of people who clearly care but cannot stop hurting one another. Relational skills without chesed are manipulative and even cruel. Education, authority, spiritual gifts, wealth, health, intelligence – none of these provide chesed or relational skills. No amount of chesed provides relational skills although without chesed we cannot learn these skills. Chesed is the kind of strong attachment to others that no matter what they do or how many times they do it we still want to be with them. We might call it love, but attachment is more like swallowing a fishhook than what we usually think of as "love". Chesed binds us together, and God is described as "chesed" 253 times in the Old Testament. In the New Testament, the word "agape" is used to translate "chesed". I Corinthians 13 is a good description of the sticky love known as chesed." ("Transforming Fellowship" page 11)

19 Brain Skills:

1. Share Joy – facial expressions and voice tone amplify, "We're glad to be together!"

2. Soothe Myself – Simple quiet: Quieting (shalom) after both joyful and upsetting emotions is the strongest predictor of life-long mental health.

3. Form Bonds for Two – Synchronize Attachments: When we can share a mutual state of mind that brings us closer and lets us move independently as well. We are both satisfied.

4. Create Appreciation – Healthy minds are full of appreciation: Appreciation creates belonging and changes stress to contentment.

5. Form Family Bonds – Bonds for Three: Family bonds let us share the joy built by the people we love.

6. Identify Heart Values from Suffering – The Main Pain and Characteristics of Hearts: Caring deeply can mean hurting deeply, but our deepest hurts hide our greatest treasures.

7. Tell Synchronized Stories – Four-plus (4+) Story Telling: When our minds work together our stories come together.

8. Identify Maturity Levels – We need to know where we are, what we missed and where we are going. Without a map we keep falling in the same holes.

9. Take a Breather – Timing When to Disengage: Skillfully take short pauses before people become overwhelmed. We read the non-verbal cues so we can build trust.

10. Tell Nonverbal Stories – The nonverbal parts of our stories strengthen relationships, bridge generations and cross cultures.

11. Return To Joy From The Big Six Feelings – We return to shared joy as we quiet distress. We stay in relationship when things go wrong. Big six feelings: 1.) sad, 2.) angry, 3.) afraid, 4.) ashamed, 5.) disgusted, 6.) hopeless.

12. Act Like Myself in the Big Six Feelings – When we find our design we will be life-giving, whether we are upset or joyful.

13. See What God Sees: Heartsight – Seeing people and events from God's perspective yields a life filled with hope and direction.

14. Stop The *Sark* (flesh) – False "Godsight" may seem true to us at the moment but leads to blame, accusation, condemnation, gossip, resentment, legalism, self-justification and self-righteousness. The *sark* requires active opposition.

15. Quiet Interactively – Skilled reading of facial cues allows us to operate at high energy levels and manage our drives without hurting ourselves or others.

16. Recognize High and Low Energy Responses: Sympathetic and Parasympathetic – Some people are at their best with activity and others with solitude. Knowing our styles and needs brings out the best in all our interactions.

17. Identify Attachment Styles – Our lives and reality need to be organized around secure love. Fears, hurts and emotional distance create insecure relational styles that will last for life unless we replace them.

18. Intervene Where the Brain is Stuck: Five Distinctive Levels of Brain Disharmony and Pain – Each of the five levels of brain processing react with a different kind of distress when it gets stuck. When we know the signs we will know the solutions.

19. Recover from Complex Emotions: Handle Combinations of the Big Six Emotions – Complex injuries from life leave us hurting many ways at once. We recover when we combine our brain skills and use them in harmony.

MATURITY SKILLS ASSESSMENT

No	Sometimes	Usually	Always	Infant stage Motivations and Regulations
				Infant stage **Motivations and Regulations**
				I have experienced strong, loving, caring bonds with mother/a woman
				I have experienced strong, loving, caring bonds with father/a man
				Important needs were met until I learned to ask
				Others took the lead and synchronized with me and my feelings first
				Quiet together times helped me calm myself with people around
				Important people have seen me through the "eyes of heaven"
				I can both receive and give life
				I receive with joy and without guilt or shame
				I can now synchronize with others and their feelings
				I found people to imitate so that I now have a personality I like
				I learned to regulate and quiet the "big six" emotions:
				Anger
				Fear
				Sadness
				Disgust
				Shame
				Hopeless/despair
				I can return to joy from every emotion and restore broken relationships
				I stay the same person over time
				I know how to rest

No	Sometimes	Usually	Always	Child stage Competency
				Child stage **Competency**
				I can do things I don't feel like doing
				I can do hard things (even if they cause me some pain)
				I can separate my feelings, my imagination and reality in my relationships
				I am comfortable with reasonable risks, attempts and failures
				I have received love I did not have to earn
				I know how my family came to be the way it is – family history
				I know how God's family came to be the way it is
				I know the "big picture" of life with the stages of maturity
				I can take care of myself
				I ask for what I need
				I enjoy self-expression
				I am growing in the things I am good at doing (personal resources and talents)
				I help other people to understand me better if they don't respond well tome
				I have learned to control my cravings
				I know what satisfies me
				I see myself through the "eyes of heaven"

No	Sometimes	Usually	Always	Adult Stage
				I have had a rite of passage into adulthood by the community
				I am comfortable relating to the same sex community
				I have a peer group where I belong
				I can partner with others
				My relationships are marked by fairness and mutual satisfaction
				I protect others from my power when necessary
				I protect my personal and group identity when boundaries are violated
				I live in a way that expresses my heart
				I have a diverse set of roles and responsibilities
				I make important contributions to my family and community
				I can bring two or more people back to joy at the same time
				I use my sexual power wisely
				I can proclaim my spiritual identity
				I can see others through the "eyes of Heaven"

No	Sometimes	Usually	Always	Pre-marriage Check List for Men
				I have a well-developed adult maturity
				My labors are productive
				I give life to others with style
				I have experienced life as:
				Brother
				Friend
				Priest
				Lover
				Warrior
				King
				Servant
				All of these together

No	Sometimes	Usually	Always	**Parent Stage**
				I have brought others to life
				I have an encouraging partner
				I receive guidance from elders
				I have peers that hold me accountable
				I have a secure and orderly home and community
				I can give without needing to receive in return
				I see my family through the eyes of heaven
				I include others in family activities
				I am present with my family
				I am protective of my family
				I am attentive of my family
				I am calming to my family
				I enjoy my family
				I comfort my family
				I help my children mature
				I can synchronize the needs of wife, children, family, work and church

No	Sometimes	Usually	Always	**Elder Stage**
				I have a community of people to call my own
				I am recognized by my community
				I have a proper place in the community structure
				I am valued and defended by the community
				I demonstrate hospitality
				I give life to the "familyless"
				I help my community mature
				I build and maintain the community identity
				I don't abandon when I disengage
				I share others feels but still know who I am and who they are
				I continue to be the same person when provoked or tempted
				I bear up well under:
				Misunderstandings
				Rage
				Contradictions
				I see some of what God sees in every situation
				I enjoy what God put in each and everyone
				I live transparently and spontaneously
				I build and rebuild trust

The LIFE Model of Redemption and Maturity

So hurt people wouldn't spend their lives simply recovering and "getting by," a small but dedicated group of pastors, counselors, prayer ministers, deliverance workers, abuse survivors, support people and parents looked, studied and prayed their way to a model that would guide us from birth to death—a LIFE model.

A growing number of books, tapes, videos, conferences and training seminars use aspects of the life model but its essentials are found in a small book called The Life Model: Living from the Heart Jesus Gave You.

This book has been translated in several languages. The LIFE Model is used around the world for trauma treatment, addiction recovery, community development, church design, child rearing and Christian missions.

The LIFE Model is, as its name implies, a model for life from conception to death. It is an idealized model, that is to say, it proposes what life should be like rather than describing what life on earth generally produces.

The LIFE model suggests that people need five things in order to thrive:

1. A place to belong
2. To receive and give life
3. The capacity to recover from things that go wrong (desynchronizations)
4. To mature as they get older
5. To live from their identities (hearts)

These elements develop when we share joy and sorrows together as natural and spiritual families in peaceful homes. The LIFE Model covers both our growth and recovery. These five elements apply whether we consider physical growth, emotional growth, family growth, community growth or spiritual growth. Taken in order from one to five, these elements are needed for strong and healthy human growth. Taken in reverse order, starting with living from our true identities, these same elements form an excellent diagnostic grid for a failure to thrive.

By understanding the causes for failures to thrive we can design a restoration process. The LIFE Model explains how to restore our identities as individuals, families and communities so that we live from a completely synchronized and authentic identity we call "the heart that Jesus gives us." This authentic identity is as much communal as it is individual.

Deep in the right hemisphere of every human brain is a control center that develops during the first two years after conception. This center will run our lives and bodies and, provided we develop a strong one, will see us through the tempests of life. We seek to train and restore this control center. With it we can regulate our emotions, act like ourselves and stay synchronized inside and out.

We become traumatized when the emotional intensity of life exceeds our capacity to maintain synchronization between the four levels of our control center. Thriving means building a strong control center through joyful attachment bonds that bring peace and return us to joy when we become upset.

We develop our identities by responding and resonating when we see the characteristics we possess expressed by an older and more experienced person. Identity is propagated like cuttings from live plants and not grown from seeds. This way of growing an identity by receiving the life passed on from one who went before is true for us at a physical level just as it is at an emotional and spiritual level.

What makes the LIFE Model a Christian model is a division between redemption and maturity. While most people will agree that not everyone matures correctly, some would say that all human beings could reach their full maturity by purely human means. Christians would say, "not without help." Some believe that everything needed for full human maturity is already contained within each person. Christians would say, "Something is still missing."

It takes a mutual effort between people and their God to fully live and experience life as it was meant to be lived. God clearly separates divine areas of responsibility from human areas of responsibility. Humans are responsible for maturity. God is responsible for redemption.

The LIFE Model is a profoundly Christian blueprint for wholeness for individuals, families, churches and communities across the lifespan.

The LIFE Model is a unifying approach to ministries of counseling, recovery, pastoral care, prayer ministry, deliverance, inner healing, child rearing, body life and health.

The LIFE Model is used internationally for substance abuse recovery programs. It has been widely used as a church model. Missions have adopted the model for the restoration of missionary children. Almost every major ministry that deals with trauma and abuse victims in the USA uses and distributes the LIFE Model as part of their teaching.

The theory behind this book was developed at Shepherd's House Inc. in California. Pastors, counselors prayer team members, lay leaders, people in recovery and an international advisory panel from many traditions and theoretical perspectives worked together to formulate this profoundly Christian view of life.

Where can I learn more about the Life Model?

www.lifemodelworks.org

Overview of the Life Model, downloads, handouts, resources in various languages, materials for sale, training, staff, events, contact information, newsletters, projects, donations, Shepherd's House Inc., current board membership and not-for-profit corporate information, maps of Life Model activities and a central search function can be located at this web site.

Joy Starts Here

Joy Starts Here: The Transformation Zone is arguably the most important book written on the topic on joy and could be the beginning of a joyful revolution, a new way of life for us all. The book includes 9 weekly Bible studies, assessments, joy building activities and group exercises. We recommend this book as a group study, or better yet for your entire church to use in their small groups.

THRIVE: Relational Brain Skills Training

THRIVE is intensive skill training for your nervous system and spirit. THRIVE is a brilliant and complete training program using brain science and the presence of Jesus to free you from fears and struggles that waste so much life. Down inside, you have always known there was something more to friendship, parenting, marriage, church or even counseling, than what you have seen. You have worked hard, tried the usual spiritual and counseling solutions but didn't thrive. THRIVE is the strategic solution for the training you missed growing up! With THRIVE you increase your capacity to handle distressing emotions and stay productive. The joy people at Life Model Works designed THRIVE for you, using the Life Model.

THRIVE applies the Life Model's 19 brain and character skills. THRIVE makes joy your foundation - spiritually, mentally and relationally. THRIVE lets you feel loved while you master difficult emotions. THRIVE helps you live in God's presence so you are transformed. THRIVE helps you stay connected with the people you love - even in painful emotions! THRIVE training includes international conferences, maturity retreats and Joy Rekindled Marriage Retreats where you live or training materials you can use at home.

CONNEXUS

Formerly Thriving: Recover Your Life, Connexus is an innovative and comprehensive life training program comprised of 3 different modules that will help you:

- Learn skills to engage God in order to grow spiritually
- Recover from painful addictions, trauma and attachment pain
- Learn to create community and healthy relationships around you
- Discover how to experience the presence of God in a way that heals
- Experience how God can heal the barriers that we put up in our relationships

One of the most unique and exciting elements of Connexus is that it brings people of all levels of maturity together to build a joyful healing community. This is one aspect of our program that you won't find anywhere else. Participants heal and grow by building joy in the context of secure, healthy relationships with God and others. As joy builds, they are better able to handle distress and increasingly able to live from their heart.

Connexus incorporates the latest advances in neuroscience with the Life Model concepts and the 19 relationship skills needed to thrive. This program is revolutionizing churches, recovery programs and other ministries all over the world.

Used by permission of E. James Wilder – joystartshere.com

THE LIFEBOAT IN YOUR BRAIN

19 Relational Skills that revolutionize your life, revitalize your marriage and reshape the world

By Chris Coursey
Used by permission of Chris Coursey

Imagine you are on a ship at sea when, suddenly, piercing sirens jolt you. A blaring voice over the loud speaker announces there is an emergency. Directions ensue: *Passengers must quickly reach the deck for a life-saving exit strategy.* Lifeboats are available to save you from the soon demise of the damaged vessel. Would you want a lifeboat?

Each of us has a lifeboat between our ears. The human brain is a three-pound, magnificent work of art that directs everything we say, think and do. In all its grandeur the brain dictates our decisions, runs relationships, and produces personal preferences. The brain tells us what to eat, when to go to bed and what to post on Facebook. Our brain is busily working at this very moment to keep us alive and interpret letters on this page.

When trained, the brain is a God-given instrument to sustain relationships, improve marriages, further friendships and create churches that change the world. Our brain is a personal lifeboat that works best with joyful relationships when people are glad to be together. This efficient little lifeboat relies on a select set of learned relational skills that enable us to respond to shifting, moment-by-moment circumstances in the best possible manner.

Life Model Works has identified nineteen relational brain skills that must be learned for optimal relational, personal, emotional, spiritual and mental health. Every one of us, ideally, develops these skills by the time we reach 3 years old. When the nineteen are not fully mastered, we feel inadequate. We cope with life in a painfully stunted sort of way. Something is missing. We may respond to people and circumstances rigidly. We make decisions out of fear and, deep down, believe there must be more out there, just beyond our reach. We feel comfortably numb or we relentlessly pursue activities to make us feel better, calmer and more secure. We feel distracted and discontent. Relationships are confusing or worse, abrasive. Who we are on the inside does not match our outside appearances. Simply, we do not express the life we dreamed was possible. We end up feeling empty, a shell of who we wanted to be.

At some point along the way our "relational ship" lost momentum, taking in water. For many of us we believe our current conditions are about as good as it's going to get. We lost hope and live each day as though getting by is the best we can do. We tread water and call this normal.

There is hope. The lifeboat between our ears can transform us to a confident, brilliant cruiser that sails the high relational seas with efficiency, style and grace. Young or old, we can train our brain to learn the nineteen skills. Whether we need a tune up or a makeover, there is no better time to start than today. Relational brain skills may be the best investment we can make in our lifetime.

The process of learning nineteen skills takes human interaction and time. When learned, the nineteen skills keep us engaged so our problems do not outgrow our relationships. We remain flexible during stress. We regulate our emotions while we interact in personal, meaningful ways. We tell stories that share our thoughts and feelings. People feel seen and valued. When learned, the nineteen form a resilient identity that gracefully endures under stress, fatigue and pain. We start to see joyful character that shines and suffers well during strain and distress. With each interaction relationships become the canvas to paint a masterpiece. Without these essential skills, something is missing in our lives.

I met a man in an airport who was missing something. The problem for him was he lacked the answer. His escalating emotions were spilling out, and spreading toxic material bystanders. I share this story in the new book, *Joy Starts Here: The Transformation Zone:*

We were standing in line to board an airplane when the announcement was made that our plane was full. Because this was the last flight, I knew we faced an overnight stay. One passenger in line suddenly lost it. In a rage he threw his bags and spewed profanities. His raging voice echoed in the terminal. Passengers scattered. This guy was no longer in relational mode. As I made my way over to the ticket desk, he walked around the terminal screaming at anyone in uniform. I could see his red face and his intense emotions were scaring people. By this time his eyes were bulging and he was sweating profusely. As he neared the ticket desk, I felt compelled to reach out to him. I knew this man was drowning. He needed some serious help returning to joy so I took a deep breath and walked up to him. For a moment I wondered if he would knock me out.

"You are really having a bad day, aren't you?" I asked affirmingly. "You are __ __ right I am having a bad day!" he fired back. We locked eyes for a few moments then I said, "Well, I am a pastor, a follower of Jesus and I would be honored if I could pray with you." I was pleasantly relieved when he muttered, "Ok, yeah, sure." Standing in the middle of the terminal we bowed our heads. I put my hand on his shoulder, we took a moment of quiet (skill two). Then, I invited Immanuel to share our distress and bring some vision (skill thirteen).

I noticed tears running down his face. "You see," he explained, "I have been traveling for medical help because I was recently diagnosed with serious cancer. This flight cancellation takes away my precious, limited time with my wife and daughters." For a few moments we shared sadness then he said, "Wait! I have to do something." He retraced his steps and apologized to every single airline employee he offended. After several minutes he returned. "I have been feeling like I need to get right with God," he told me. "I wonder if this whole ordeal is God speaking?" A sparkle of joy appeared in his eyes as his face muscles relaxed. The next morning I saw him boarding the flight with a smile and a brand new Bible under his arm.

Because of my learned relational skills I stayed anchored long enough to toss him a life preserver. He needed a lifeboat in the form of a trained brain who could stay connected with him even in the midst of intense emotions. His right hemisphere required another person, a mirror, to show him the way to Skill 2, Simple Quiet. All of us are taking in water. Some are used to the water while others are ready for change. Which one are you?

In an ideal world we would have the nineteen character skills because our environment had people who used the skills. Sadly, this doesn't always happen.

Joy is fundamental to the formation and expression of our character. Our character is molded through ongoing interactions with people who either have or lack the nineteen relational skills. Joy is the foundation to learn new brain skills that transform our relationships. Heck, joy even puts a smile on our faces. Joy refers to being glad to be together, we are the sparkle in someone's eyes. Joy is the wind in our relational sails. Learning new skills begins with joy.

Those of us who have the nineteen skills do not realize or remember how we gained the skills. Simply, the skills are used much like driving a car. We don't think about it. For this reason it is easy to misunderstand why everyone else does not simply respond like we do when upset or overwhelmed. We may even assume people lack motivation, faith, will power or should just stop making poor choices. "Get it together!" we might think, not realizing missing skills are at work.

We can learn the nineteen skills. Thanks to brain plasticity, experience reorganizes neural pathways in the brain. Experience, particularly joyful interactions with people who have the skills, propel us in mastering skills. Just think of someone you know who handles upset in a way that inspires you. What about a person who loses their cool at the drop of a hat? For too long nineteen skills have flown under the radar. There was no language, much less a training format to learn new skills. At Life Model Works we now have the language. We have the training structure. All we need is you.

Let's review the nineteen relational skills.

Skill One - *Share Joy*

Facial expressions and voice tones amplify, "We're glad to be together!"

Think about a time someone was glad to be with you. Their face lit up. Their body language, voice tone and words all conveyed, "Hey, I am SO glad you are here!" You feel seen and cherished. Their response made you feel special. Your heart rate increases. Your pupils dilate. Your face lights up. Here is joy.

Relational joy grows into an emotional state as it is shared with people who express warm delight to be together. Joy is contagious. Joy spreads interactively when shared and expressed with at least one other person. A wonderful mix of words and nonverbal signals allow joy to grow with each glance. Joy increases with every shared smile of the eyes. Joy creates a remarkable chemical cocktail that excites us for more.

Technically this nonverbal dance of warm voice tones, bright eye smiles and attuned body signals is described as right-hemisphere-to-right- hemisphere communication which amplifies our most desired positive emotional state. Relational joy is best conveyed face-to-face but voice tone is a close second.

We develop a strong bond with people who light up to see us. Skill One makes life, church, marriage, business and everything else better. Joy gives lovers fuel to endure, friends the strength to persevere and families the grace to recover. Ideally we return to joy from every unpleasant state the brain knows.

We have become so accustomed to breathing we rarely think much about it until smog, second-hand smoke or congestion from a cold interrupts us. We don't spend much time thinking about joy either until something happens. Our joy levels sink or we experience joy in a profound way such as a new baby. Thanks to dopamine messages are sent through cells to the brain telling us we need to breathe. Dopamine plays a key role for sustaining joy as well. Joy empowers, motivates and feeds us. We feel a reward when we share joy just as we feel satisfied during a favorite meal. Ideally joy leads to rest then serotonin recharges us for more joy.

If joy levels sink we are compelled to seek comfort from the same mechanisms that propel us to inhale after holding our breath. When our joy levels drop to dangerous levels we turn to BEEPS. BEEPS is an acronym for Behaviors, Experiences, Events, People and Substances that hijack the brain. BEEPS artificially regulates our feelings. Pseudo-joy leaves us empty.

We become weak when joy levels sink due to loss, pain and the absence of a familiar face to share our smiles. We feel depleted when our joy is met with anger, disgust or silence. Sinking joy consumes and destroys marriages. Our families substitute joy with activities, sports, movies, television, computers, busyness and endless distractions. When churches lose joy they focus on rules and become rigid. At this point people become numbers or problems to solve. Parents with low joy focus on behavior. Culture links joy with sex, shame, fear and skepticism. It does not take long to remember times in life when our joy was dashed due to rejection or ridicule. These moments hurt. Without Skill One we risk passing on the very patterns we despise.

As we remember, create, express and share joy, this positive state defines our personality. "Why are you so happy?" people wonder. The fun does not stop here. Joy has counterpart called Skill Two.

Resources for Skill One:

- Joy Starts Here: The Transformation Zone
- JoyQ Assessment
- 30 Days of Joy for Busy Married Couples
- Jesus In Mind: Talks on Kingdom Life
- THRIVE Skill Guides 52 weeks of training exercises
  - Mastering Joy and Rest

- o   Mastering Returning to Joy
- o   Mastering Applied Strategy

Training Opportunities:

- Connexus
- THRIVE 5-day Training
- Joy Rekindled Marriage Retreats

Skill Two - *Soothe Myself*

Simple Quiet - Quieting (shalom) after both joyful and upsetting emotions is the strongest predictor of life-long mental health.

Can you identify a time in your life when you were wrought with worry and dread? Intrusive thoughts robbed your peace. Maybe you felt misunderstood, even wrongly accused. Possibly you were concerned about paying the bills or worried about health issues. Your shallow breathing and tense body gripped you. You wondered if this riptide would ever end. When Skill Two is missing we do not effectively quiet our thoughts or body. We feel exhausted.

Relationships require a rhythm of joy and rest. We rest then cycle back to joy. We build joy and return to rest. This moment by moment interaction leaves us satisfied. Short moments of rest provide strength and stamina for more joy. We see this in infants who reflexively look away from interactions once they reach a peak of joy. They quickly return for more face to face joy, and the dance continues.

When synchronized, energy levels mutually climb and drop. Our brain knows these patterns and the fun feels natural. The lack of rest makes us overwhelmed. Alternating joy with rest prevents relational casualties.

Just think about a time you enjoyed a tasty meal with a friend. Each bite is savored as you synchronize your breathing, eating, tasting, swallowing and speaking. Your senses are pleased. Much like the result of your good meal and fellowship, Skill Two is a primary commodity that keeps relationships balanced. Skill Two releases serotonin on an "as needed" basis to recharge our relational battery. Serotonin leaves us content and peaceful. As a sunrise leads to a sunset, Skill Two follows Skill One to soothe our body and calm our mind. Joy and quiet are cyclical, each compliments the other.

Memories, language, talent, muscles and skills that are not used will atrophy. When it comes to relational skills, every generation can only transmit what they learn and use. As skills drop out generations spread undesirable traits such as abuse, pain, addictions and distortions. Regardless of intention and determination, we cannot give what we do not have. Skill Two diminishes when families and communities either do not allow or have not learned to rest. Without Skill Two we overwork, burn out, feel depressed, become lost in our devices, avoid states of quiet and push ourselves until something gives. We pass this deformity on and call it normal.

Skill Two is difficult to identify because replacement patterns are socially acceptable. We replace quiet and rest with BEEPS in the form of busyness, work, sex, music, iPhones, television and sugar. Who we are may be based on the things we do, the items we buy, the cars we drive, the places we work or clothes we wear. Synthetically calming our emotions and ignoring rest signals create strain and dysregulate the brain. BEEPS replace the natural ebb and flow families rely on. The inability to down-regulate emotions to rest and up-regulate positive emotions to joy lead to the largest risk of developing a mental illness in a lifetime. Skill Two, when absent, leaves us vulnerable to depression, anxiety, addictions, ADD, ADHD and a myriad of behavioral and personality disorders. We recognize the need for Skill Two when we fear slowing down, resist rest and surrender to the urge to disconnect in non-relational ways.

Skill Two is best learned by spending time with people who rest. Like all of the nineteen skills, Skill Two is relationally transmitted. With practice we may be pleasantly surprised to discover that rest and quiet feels enjoyable, even restorative. Small steps of quieting create a positive link that extends into our relationships. Rest is rewarding. Over time quieting begins to replace previously learned behaviors that replaced a genuine need for rest. Racing thoughts can be slowed. To-do lists can be written down instead of finished right now. Impulsive responses can be tamed. To varying degrees, yoga, silent retreats, the Sabbath and mindfulness exercises are some of the ways our culture embraces Skill Two.

Rest is a gift we give other people. As we demonstrate this skill we become experts at recognizing the need for rest. We allow others the freedom to rest. Breaking eye contact, low or high energy levels, overwhelm, loss of a relational mode, rising tension levels, even yawning can be signs that a breather is needed. With a bit of practice, quiet no longer threatens our busy lives, rather rest enriches productivity. Rest is one of the most productive skills we can practice.

Resources for Skill Two:

- Joy Starts Here: The Transformation Zone
- JoyQ Assessment
- 30 Days of Joy for Busy Married Couples
- Jesus In Mind: Talks on Kingdom Life
- THRIVE Skill Guides 52 weeks of training exercises
  - Mastering Joy and Rest
  - Mastering Returning to Joy
  - Mastering Applied Strategy

Training Opportunities:

- Connexus
- THRIVE 5-day Training
- Joy Rekindled Marriage Retreats

Skill Three - *Form Bonds for Two*

Synchronize Attachments - We can share a mutual state of mind that brings us closer and lets us move independently as well. We are both satisfied.

With Skill Three we feel safe and secure. We are free to be ourselves because the world is a safe place. We are no longer restrained by fear or the compulsion to conceal what we feel. Skill Three prepares us to engage the world with confidence, resilience, resourcefulness and creativity.

Skill Three refers to the delightful, interactive dance between two people who share and respect each other's signals and limitations. Expressions, feelings, thoughts and words reciprocate mutually and move rhythmically. In some ways Skill Three looks like a lively game of Ping Pong where one player serves the ball that soars over the net. In a flash the receiver returns the serve. If skillful, the two players volley and interact back and forth at high speeds until someone stops. Relationally this rest cycle allows both parties to catch their breath and start all over again. The fun continues within the range of expertise and ability each of the players possess. Ping Pong focuses on winning points whereas Skill Three aims to keep the relational volley in play with joy and rest. We respect each other's limitations and abilities to achieve mutual satisfaction.

Skill Three is the reciprocal sharing between two people that dynamically forms a mutual mind. We feel seen and understood. We are on the same page. This brain to brain coupling creates a cohesive mutual mind; we feel seen, valued and understood. We are connected. It feels as though you are the source of my joy. In reality *we are the reason for our joy.* When properly synched and executed early in life, the combination of shared thoughts, feelings and expressions provide lasting love and security. Our bond grows deeper with each new cycle of joy and rest. Skill Three, a bond between two people, provides the ideal foundation to learn the nineteen brain skills.

In some ways we have forgotten, missed, even lost the art of relationships. When relational skills disintegrate we no longer form strong, joyful, predictable bonds that mold our character, fashion our identity and build security. As far as the brain is concerned, we are the sum of our relationships. This may be good or bad news depending on our personal library of interactions. When relationships are a source of joy we enter each new relationship with wisdom and confidence.

The failure to form a healthy secure bond with someone results in deep-seated pain and detonated landmines that spread into each new relationship we encounter. Isolation, rejection and BEEPS hijack our reality instead of peace, security and joy. We can become better at preying than protecting, hurting instead of helping and killing instead of saving. At the least we become self-focused instead of people-focused. We want to win at whatever cost rather than play with integrity and maturity. Grudges, fear, resentment disconnectedness and self-centeredness alter the landscape of our decisions and values.

Skill Three is one of the more underestimated nineteen brain skills. From the onset of life Skill Three glues us to the person who loves, feeds, comforts, and protects us. Newborns, hours old, can recognize mother's scent compared with other moms. In the womb baby knows mommy's voice. This biological foundation for a strong bond with mom builds our brain and lays the framework for our identity, character, and view of the world. Problems that develop with Skill Three can lead to a devastating shift in how we relate to other humans. Because our personal reality as we know it is created by the people we are glued to, our deepest pain and greatest joys occur in loving, secure bonds. We are driven to connect, then reconnect again. The absence of connection creates some of the worst pain the human brain knows. We are built for human interaction anchored in joy.

A mutual exchange of verbal and nonverbal communication sheds light into the hidden recesses of our minds and our identities. Interpreting visual cues is one skill that takes practice and time. The power of a look, glance, smile and frown makes all the difference between love at first sight, a first impression, a vote, a successful business meeting, even the success of a marriage. We remember the joy of an embrace and the sting of a loss. Our identity expands with the introduction of each new joyful relationship.

Redemption is simply one joyful relationship away. Skill Three is the canvas where we develop relational intelligence and flexibility. Attunement, recovery and face to face interaction with others form a beautiful tapestry that builds our character, heals our wounds and increases our maturity. While family bonds at Skill Five will take our skills and growth to an entirely new level, the foundation established here anchors and sustains us throughout life.

Resources for Skill Three:

- Joy Starts Here: The Transformation Zone
- JoyQ Assessment
- 30 Days of Joy for Busy Married Couples
- Jesus In Mind: Talks on Kingdom Life
- THRIVE Skill Guides 52 weeks of training exercises
  - Mastering Joy and Rest
  - Mastering Returning to Joy
  - Mastering Applied Strategy

Training Opportunities:

- THRIVE 5-day Training
- Joy Rekindled Marriage Retreats

Skill Four - *Create Appreciation*

Healthy minds are full of appreciation. Appreciation creates belonging and changes stress to contentment.

What are you thankful for today? What makes you smile? Pause for a moment, and reflect on something you appreciate. What do you notice?

Appreciation is packaged joy. Appreciation is a gift we share anytime, anyplace, with anyone we encounter. Puppies, babies, sunsets, ocean breezes, colorful autumn leaves, a warm bath, a compliment, an unexpected surprise, a hug, a kind gesture and special memories with loved ones give us reason to be thankful. We call this gratitude. While enjoying special memories-in-the-making, we store, remember and share these moments. Appreciation gives birth to joy that spreads to people we encounter. We create appreciation with a compliment, "You look nice today!" and, "I appreciate your service, thank you." This simple gesture brings a smile.

Appreciation, when shared, activates our relational circuits, resettles our nervous system and releases a cocktail of bonding hormones so we feel connected and peaceful. We are in our best form when Skill Four permeates our interactions. The student of Scripture will discover frequent reminders to remember, appreciate, enjoy and meditate on the good stuff. "Be thankful" in both good times and bad. What are you thankful for today?

With Skill Four we feel better, lighter, stronger and safer. We know Skill Four is at work when laughter fills the air, people wear genuine smiles and hug. This warmth keep us connected, we feel seen and valued. Belonging is created by a simple compliment. Unfortunately, for many, appreciation does not fit with their learned responses. It is easy to think about, expect, even spread pain, distrust, anger, resentment and bitterness instead of joy. We expect the worst. This lens filters our views and guides our behaviors. The painful absence of Skill Four increases rejection, depression, overwhelm and despair. We all know someone who is grumpy, bitter and unforgiving. There is usually a story there. Appreciation is required to rewire the brain and restore vision for the downtrodden soul.

The lack of gratitude can lead to entitlement. Instead of "I like this about you" we think to ourselves, "she looks ugly in that dress" or "his voice really annoys me!" The glass is half empty. The human brain relies on the past to predict the future so experiencing rejection leaves us expecting, even creating rejection around us. Hurt people hurt people. Anger pushes others away while appreciation becomes the oil in the engine that runs our relationships. Skill Four brings us together. When we are used to creating rejection, lovers, family, peers and strangers become commodities instead of comrades. When the non-relational parts of our brain run our relationship, trust erodes. We evade intimacy. We no longer share our weaknesses nor do we give and receive joy. The presence of Skill Four is a game-changer for relationships, a direct reflection of what a healthy and stable marriage, family and community looks like. When appreciation levels run low bitterness springs up.

Bobby needed some serious appreciation.

Bobby spent much of his time at work isolated at his desk. All around him people busily and joyfully interacted with each other, but they did not include him. Without realizing it, Bobby's body language was pushing people away. He often appeared defensive and frustrated. His coworkers sensed something was wrong in Bobby but they respected his nonverbal signals that screamed, "Leave me alone! Quit talking! Get out of here!" People gave him space.

One day Bobby turned to a coworker and asked, "Why doesn't anyone talk to me? Everyone seems to interact, but they ignore me. What did I do wrong?" The coworker replied, "Bobby, to be honest, you give off signals that tell us you want to be left alone. You slam drawers. You grunt in frustration. You give us dirty looks. Your body language tells us to leave you alone, so we do." Bobby was surprised by his coworker's words but he decided to practice creating appreciation. Bobby began to reach out to his coworkers. "You look nice today Helen!" "Hey Curt, nice job on the project last week!" "Betty, I'm grabbing a cup of coffee, can I get you one?" Soon Bobby was fully engaged with his coworkers, interacting and building joy. Appreciation provided the opportunity for meaningful heart to heart connections.

As with any sport or musical instrument, exposure and practice trains the body and brain. The more we play an instrument, the better we become. If we did not grow up playing a sport or instrument, it may feel awkward and challenging to learn something new. Thankfully the brain has a novelty detector, and learning something new is very good! Being around people who use Skill Four provides a clear example of what appreciation looks and feels like. We enjoy interacting with individuals and groups who are well-versed in appreciation skills. Just think about someone who is good at appreciation, and someone who seems to be negative. Which example would you prefer? With practice and effort, appreciation becomes effortless.

Thanks to dopamine, learning something new builds memories, strengthens long term memories and helps us grow closer with people. In order to become a usable brain skill, appreciation must be practiced, enjoyed and shared on a daily basis. Thankfully, we can use appreciation on our own as well. Appreciation keeps us focused on what is important to keep us free from regrets and guilt. We restore appreciation when we ask, "What am I thankful for today?" We share appreciation when we express our appreciation. Start and end your day with appreciation and you will notice more energy, a more positive outlook and an increase in stamina to navigate hardship. Your health and relationships will thank you.

Resources for Skill Four:

- Joy Starts Here: The Transformation Zone
- JoyQ Assessment
- 30 Days of Joy for Busy Married Couples
- Jesus In Mind: Talks on Kingdom Life
- THRIVE Skill Guides 52 weeks of training exercises
  - Mastering Joy and Rest
  - Mastering Returning to Joy
  - Mastering Applied Strategy

Training Opportunities:

- Connexus
- THRIVE 5-day Training
- Joy Rekindled Marriage Retreats

Skill Five - *Form Family Bonds*

Bonds For Three - Family bonds let us share the joy built by the people we love.

Family bonds provide freedom to grow and explore the world. With this new skill we discover there is more than enough joy to go around. Thanks to Skill Three, the foundation for a house has been established. It is now time to increase. We are ready for a new surge in joy because a secure relationship with our primary caregiver, mom, sets the tone for joyful interaction with dad.

As long as the two-way bond with the mom is secure, infants readily turn their sights to dad with curiosity and a strong desire for connection. Babies become most interested in this third face who, up until about six months, has been in the back seat of the infant's focus and drives. There is no greater force than baby's need to bond with mom, so when a foundation is established securely, infant gravitates toward dad expecting more of the good stuff. This transition is most successful as mom stays present and joins the fun. Mom's face shines with affirmation while she observes baby and daddy build joy. Baby is keenly aware how well mom and dad delight in her.

Baby's brain is hard-wired for three-way bonds at seven months of life into the second and third year. Loving care from daddy from 12 to 18 months internalizes security for life. As baby feels safe, she longs to be included in this delightful dance of joy. Baby sees herself as an extension of this relationship that is now focused on "us." Family interactions become the playground for new skills. This three-strand cord, once established, is not easily broken. This family bond will shape baby's life and relationships for the rest of life.

Joy increases as our community expands. At 12 years old, children start their shift into adult maturity which begins a new stage of life. At this point children are more focused on their group identity than individual identity. Children want to be included in their "clan" and part of a bigger picture. Problems become "ours" to solve. The need for group belonging is deeply felt and this marks the time when children are most focused on peers. Depending on the quality of bonds that are established, new faces feel like an added bonus or a certain threat.

Tina needed some work on Skill Five.

Tina grew up in a tense home where she feared her mother's anger. Mom's anger kept everyone on edge and this painful disconnect left her feeling alone and overwhelmed much of the time. She did not fully understand how to relate to her father who was physically present but emotionally absent. As a teenager, Tina found relationships confusing and unpredictable. As long as she had a good friend to interact with, she felt safe but once other people joined the interaction, Tina became guarded, jealous and envious. Watching her friend interact with other people caused Tina to feel hurt and rejected. Group interaction was threatening.

As Tina began to look at her fear she realized a childhood pattern was at work and she wanted help. With the encouragement of a trusted church friend, Tina joined a women's group. At first this step was frightening, but over time Tina started to learn how rewarding group interactions could be. Joy levels increased. Tina began to make more friends and spend time with them in groups. For the first time Tina was excited for group interactions.

The prerequisite for a joyful, secure Skill Five is a stable Skill Three. While there is a significant learning curve, we learn from one relationship how to interact and grow into the next. Early life patterns shape how well family bonds form. What we learn in grade school prepares us for high school which prepares us for college, and so on. The same progression holds true for Skill Five. Will rejection or belonging set the tone for our interactions?

We recognize problems with Skill Five when we feel alone at work, church and within group settings. It seems threatening to relate with more than one person. Our comfort zone feels invaded. We may be guarded during gatherings and parties. Fear of rejection and anxiety may surface when we interact with other people. We may even count down the clock until it's time to leave. Computers, television, books and video games feel safer. Having one friend feels better than two or three so the motto, "two is company, three is a crowd" fits well with our internal responses.

Insecure bonds, divorce, death, broken families and early life experiences can scar our confidence and hinder our ability to develop Skill Five. Every child requires joyful three-way bonds between a mother and father. Three-way bonds provide the opportunity to express the best of ourselves, correct malfunctions and grow more joy.

Here is some good news for correcting Skill Five. Where biological family fails, spiritual family and the surrounding community can help us pick up the pieces for restoration. Trying to grow family bonds when unprocessed pain and unresolved ruptures hinder us can feel like stepping into a free fall at 15,000 feet. Because our brain uses the past to predict the future we tend to expect the worst when relationships go south. We can grow, nurture and develop a secure attachment with one other person (Skill Three) that provides strength and confidence to explore and strengthen a group bond. We can be delightfully surprised to discover how the addition of people into our network grows rather than drains joy.

Healing pain from disrupted bonds is not always easy but it happens when we turn to Immanuel (Skill Thirteen) for guidance and resolution. Processing painful events enables us to grow more joy, disarm fears and advance forward to connect with other people with confidence. We can join small groups, churches, sport teams, clubs, and organizations. These avenues become fertile ground to discover new ways to be ourselves in a group setting.

Resources for Skill Five:

- Joy Starts Here: The Transformation Zone
- JoyQ Assessment

Training Opportunities:

- Connexus

Skill Six - *Identify Heart Values from Suffering*

The Main Pain and Characteristic of Hearts: Caring deeply can mean hurting deeply. Our deepest hurts hide our greatest treasures.

Pain demands our attention. Left unchecked, pain steals our most valuable resources. For the limbic system of our brain, we are driven to fight, flee or freeze in order to avoid pain and the threat of pain. The survival circuit of our brain is most interested in preserving self. When pain goes unprocessed we learn to hide, mask and run from pain. Unless the relational parts of our brain actively shift this response, we rigidly avoid pain, even when the threat of pain is long gone. Pain that is not fully processed stays with us the rest of our lives.

The beauty of Skill Six is what it conveys: There is more going on than the pain we feel. Pain does not need to have the final word. Skill Six reveals something of value about the pain we experience. We ask, "Why do I hurt like this?" With a little exploration we discover the gold in our identities. Healing gains considerable traction as we find meaning in our hurts then begin to create a coherent narrative of our experience. After seeking, we discover a purpose that says, "There is something good in here that has been touched in a deadly way. I am more than my pain."

All of us have issues that particularly hurt or bother us, issues that show up throughout life. Looking at these lifelong patterns helps to identify the core values for each person's unique identity. As it says above, we hurt the more deeply we care. Should we stop caring?

If we hold truth as a high standard for character we are deeply troubled when people lie, deceive, and false advertise. Because our core values lead to deep pain we view these characteristics as liabilities not treasures. What things bother you? What has God placed within you that would cause you to be bothered by that particular issue? What inspires you? What gives you hope and makes you feel alive? The things that are important to us say something about what drives us. These things also reveal our tender places.

We do well to recognize our heart values and embrace the gifts God has uniquely given each of us to reflect aspects of His character. Would you leave a buried treasure untouched in your backyard?

Pain leads to clarity on the uniqueness of our identity. A failure to learn Skill Six reminds us we have not yet discovered the buried treasure.

One of the reasons Skill Six is not a household skill is because we are motivated to stop, fix and diminish the effects of pain. We cannot imagine there is something of value beneath our responses of what hurts us. When we hurt physically, we take aspirin. When emotionally or mentally damaged, we disconnect and turn to a variety of BEEPS. We neglect to find any value. The redemptive quality in pain is the reminder we are still alive. Pain serves a purpose and informs our nervous system that something is wrong and needs corrected. Just touch a hot stove and this reality quickly comes to a head.

We may not realize or embrace the point that God has brilliantly created each one of us uniquely in His image, a God who is both a suffering Servant and conquering King. Our identity is that precious treasure buried beneath painful experiences that distort and rob who God created us to be. It does not help that we live in a culture that pervasively floods us with cheap solutions, a culture that paints a glamorous portrait telling us who we are and what we really want. Infomercials tell us how to increase our comfort zones. There is a deluge of therapies offering to make us better, stronger, thinner, healthier and happier. The end result is misinformation. What would change if we started to look into the mirror that God provides? One that connects the dots of our wounds to a God-given set of values crafted into our DNA?

One of the most practical ways to develop Skill Six is to identify life-long patterns, moments where we experienced something that bothered us. These patterns show up throughout life, in our relationships, even in our major decisions. We can highlight sources of distress then prayerfully consider what our reactions say about us. What kind of person would be bothered by this? Why?

We can consider the non-negotiables that fuel, motivate and fire us up. What makes us zealous? We can ask people to share what they observe as our main pain (s) and heart qualities. Notice their responses. Barnabus encouraged, Paul fiercely valued truth, John loved, Jesus forgave, Peter jumped out of boats (passion). While these attributes demonstrate something essential within each person's character they also reveal qualities that caused pain, distress, even death. What does your pain say about you? How are these attributes expressed? In what ways do these qualities hurt?

Tim grew up believing something was wrong with him. As a child Tim felt a deep love and sadness for other people, particularly those who have suffered loss and hardship. Tim did not know what to do with these strong feelings but he felt vulnerable, even weak. He noticed how friends seemed to easily dismiss the needs of other people and yet, Tim could not shake the compulsion that he needed to do something in order to help people in need. He started praying.

Over time Tim began to embrace this "weakness" as he called it. Freedom and a newfound peace emerged in Tim's life. He discovered that compassion was a heart value for him, a precious characteristic that was his to share with the world. He no longer needed to fight or resist his gift. The more Tim embraced his need to show others compassion, the greater his peace. While Tim's gift over the years brought him a lot of pain, his gift has richly blessed his life and enriched his closest relationships.

Resources for Skill Six:

- Jesus In Mind: Talks on Kingdom Life
- THRIVE Skill Guides 52 weeks of training exercises

- o Mastering Joy and Rest
- o Mastering Returning to Joy
- o Mastering Applied Strategy

Training Opportunities:
- Connexus
- THRIVE 5-day Training

Skill Seven - *Tell Synchronized Stories*

4+ Story Telling – When our minds work together our stories come together.

Stories do more than captivate our listeners. Stories paint a picture how well our brain is functioning. When our brain is well trained, our capacity is high and we are not triggered by the past, our whole brain works together. Telling stories in a way that requires all the brain to work together is a simple test of how our brain is working as well as a clear method to train the brain.

Four-plus stories offer a glimpse into the workings of our internal world. Four-plus stories demonstrate secure bonds, grow relationships and share key brain skills. Four-plus stories are strategic, carefully crafted stories that require all four levels of the right-hemispheric control center to work together. When this happens the bonus of our words in the left hemisphere match our experience in the right. Words and nonverbal signals produce a coherent narrative. Telling and listening to stories brings people together, resolves conflicts, propagates brain skills and provides healthy examples of responses. Four-plus stories require time, practice, skill and synchronization. When emotional and spiritual blockage is resolved, our whole brain works together in a unified way. By carefully selecting stories we can test and train our brain's ability to handle specific aspects of life and relationships. We use four-plus stories to celebrate the special moments that leave our legacy.

Several ingredients make up a successful four-plus story. With eye contact, four-plus stories are to be shared at moderate emotion. Too much intensity overwhelms listeners. We want people engaged as they share our emotions and feelings. Four-plus stories are packaged in three formats, Return To Joy (Skill 11), Acting Like Myself (Skill 12) and Share Immanuel (Skill 13). Each story must illustrate a specific feeling for maximum efficacy. We show the authentic emotion on our face and in our voice. We rely on feeling words for emotions and body sensations. We use stories we have told before, and keep our stories concise. Stories improve with practice.

Now that you have the logistics, four-plus stories do not take place naturally unless family, friends and community spontaneously and frequently tell stories in everyday life. Unprocessed trauma, lack of examples, insecure attachments and few *stories of us* during childhood lead to difficulty with Skill Seven. We may simply be untrained to tell stories. Possibly we are too consumed with problems. We can be distracted by our own thoughts and feelings. Without practice it can be difficult to create a narrative using words to describe feelings and body sensations. It takes training to tell an autobiographical narrative, one where we are involved in the story. This step requires activation of the highest regions of the prefrontal cortex, what we identify as Level 4 in the right hemispheric control center. When the control center is working together, what we refer to as "synchronized," the left hemisphere creates coherent narratives with input from the right hemisphere. One of the signs of an insecure attachment is the inability to organize and create coherent stories from our history that flow in detailed, organized fashion.

The replacement of relational brain skills with technology and entertainment have created the urgent need for Skill Seven. We simply do not communicate like we used to. Computers, cellular phones, texting, tweeting and Facebooking minimize the frequency of face to face communication. It takes a relationally trained brain to use Skill Seven.

The human brain is a remarkable, efficient learning machine. With examples, practice and feedback, we grow new skills, strengthen weak skills and change unwanted patterns that hinder growth. In order to shift Skill Seven to the forefront of everyday life we must take time to notice our bodies. Sound strange? That's because we rarely notice our bodies until we discover something we don't like and want to change, or something is wrong that requires attention. Paying attention to our bodies is a key step in sharing the content of our minds. Our body is the canvas for our brain. "What is happening in me?" "How do I feel when I am joyful, angry, sad, hopeless, ashamed, disgusted and afraid?" "How's my breathing?"

We find words to describe these observations and sensations so others better understand our personal experience. We insert these details into a coherent narrative. A narrative that clearly conveys what it's like to be in "my shoes."

Like any good thing, four-plus stories must be shared with other people. Listeners help us gauge the effectiveness of our stories with suggestions and feedback. "You were smiling when you were talking about feeling sad." "I would have enjoyed hearing more how you felt when you perceived God was with you." We practice, we improve. Four-plus stories involve specific points to include so it helps to have the four-plus checklist nearby during practice. We write our stories then we share our stories using our senses and body. With practice, stories can be shared under two minutes but five minutes tends to be the starting point. Four-plus stories weave together our history with the present then prepares us and our listeners for the future.

Eric needed to work on his marriage. One of the difficulties Eric's wife expressed to him was his inability to communicate, to "share his heart." Eric felt like he was trying hard to be a good provider and a loving husband. Shouldn't his wife just know that he loves her?

After some thought and consultation with his prayer partner, he recognized something was indeed missing. After learning about Skill Seven from his prayer partner, Eric realized his father was "the silent type" and Eric was following his father's example. Along the way Eric developed a deep-rooted assumption that expressing himself was pointless, so why bother? It was time for change.

Eric began to practice four-plus stories with his prayer partner and eventually, his wife. Eric noticed a drastic shift in his marriage. Skill Seven became an avenue for joy as Eric used four-plus stories to highlight events from his day, share special moments from vacations, and convey the qualities he appreciates about his wife and marriage. Skill Seven became a foundational skill that improved Eric's ability to communicate, stay relationally connected and share joy. Resources for Skill Seven:

- THRIVE Skill Guides 52 weeks of training exercises
  - Mastering Joy and Rest
  - Mastering Returning to Joy
  - Mastering Applied Strategy

Training Opportunities:

- Connexus
- THRIVE 5-day Training
- Joy Rekindled Marriage Retreats

Skill Eight - *Identify Maturity Levels*

We need to know where we are, what we missed and where we are going. Without a map we keep falling in the same holes.

We want to identify our ideal level of maturity so we know if our development is impaired. Knowing our general maturity, our "baseline of operations," informs us what the next developmental task will be. Recognizing our immediate level of maturity from moment to moment reveals if we have been triggered into reactivity by something that just happened or if we encountered a "hole" in our development that needs remedial attention. Watching when our maturity level is slipping tells us when emotional capacity has been drained in us or others.

Scripture mentions six stages that define the ideal developmental roadmap for life. Unborn, infant, child, adult, parent and elder stage covers the full range of our potential for emotional, mental, physical and spiritual growth. At Life Model Works these six life stages have been carefully sequenced to bring clarity to the process of joyfully growing up.

We cannot give what we do not have. Skill Eight provides the framework for what happens when maturity is attained or stunted. Skill Eight offers clarity to develop earned maturity that matches our personal age and stage of life. When used, Skill Eight leads to joyful growth on an individual and corporate level. The following questions bring this useful skill to the forefront of our minds.

"Have you ever responded in a rigid, "childish" way that did not line up with your personal values?" "Do certain people, circumstances or emotions create strong reactions in you?" "Do you or someone you know respond like a small person in a big person's body? Under what conditions?" "Have you noticed times in your life when you or someone you know appeared relationally stunted in growth and development?" "Do you make decisions out of fear?"

We may not complete every life stage there is because everyone does not become a parent or an elder in their community. However, each of us, at the least, should aim to function at adult maturity. Each life stage ties specific tasks with needs. When undeveloped, we risk making decisions out of fear and developing a "pseudo-maturity" where we appear more mature than we really are. With each stage of growth we increase our capacity to care for ourselves and others. By identifying maturity we develop wisdom for growth. We also avoid passing on deformities and malfunctions. We correct problems. We increase our emotional capacity and build resiliency for life. We change unwanted generational patterns.

Skill Eight explains why we keep falling into the same holes, often in spite of attempts to do otherwise. Skill Eight offers clear steps for growth and recovery. Skill Eight suggests there is more to personal growth than making better choices, trying harder and having good intentions. Practice with Skill Eight fosters a clear understanding of personal and corporate maturity. This step prevents immaturity, so we avoid a fall-out or burn-out.

Skill Eight is misunderstood primarily due to the influence of British Rationalism and the persistent onslaught of messages that say more education, will power and better choices will fix what relationally ails us. Earned maturity develops joyful character that endures under strain. Maturity formation means *growing according to our needs and design.* Humans have needs that should be met at specific times. Just as inhaling when we should exhale produces problems, the same logic holds true emotionally and mentally. Timing for our needs determines whether I whither or flourish.

Church, business, education and society as a whole provides countless examples where educated, talented, successful, even godly leaders fall into immorality, greed and lust for power. Many confess with deep remorse to behavior contrary to their most cherished values. These moments may be chalked up as a mistake or a bad decision. In many cases more rules are added into the equation to prevent a similar mishap in the future. Without a clear understanding and application of Skill Eight we fail to recognize that developmental deficits, if addressed, could have prevented trouble. While a lake may be frozen, it takes only one weak spot to plunge us into the icy cold water. Weak spots in our maturity and character frequently appear during times of distress and pressure. Without systematic effort to correct weaknesses we risk relational plunges that leave us and others wondering, "What just happened?"

Personal maturity reflects the health and resources of our families and communities. Gaps and deficits that are not addressed are passed along like every unwanted pattern. There is a remarkable shortage of mature maps and guides within our communities. The lack of elders with earned maturity as well as missing multigenerational communities leave a gaping hole in the fabric of a family and community. For the church in general, it is easy to spiritualize maturity and miss the need for emotional maturity. Both are needed. We assume maturity is a natural progression from salvation or, just as insidious, we attribute maturity with one's value and self-worth. Subscribing to these beliefs create resistance to an honest assessment of maturity and create shame for those seeking to identify earned maturity.

We do well to assess the obstacles that keep us stuck. Unprocessed traumas and painful events stunt our maturity. "Do I need more mature people?" "Do I need healing in specific ways?" Acknowledging our weaknesses is the first step toward joyful change. We increase our maturity with an honest appraisal of our earned maturity. "Where in my character do I show weakness?"

Similar to the development of a house that starts from the foundation, we search for holes and unfinished tasks beginning with infant maturity. We fill gaps. We reinforce needs and tasks with the help of others who already have maturity, particularly where we lack it. All of us have something to give, and something to receive. We start to remove fears that hinder forward progress. We seek Immanuel's guidance to process traumas. (Skill Thirteen) We locate guides to encourage, pray and oversee our journey. We create belonging where the weak and strong mix. We increase our joy. Each step propels us forward. As we fill in gaps we explore next steps at child then adult maturity. Some steps require little effort while others a bit more. Maturity does not add to our value, rather, maturity enables us to express and share more of ourselves with the people we love.

Resources for Skill Eight:

- The Complete Guide to Living with Men
- Joy Starts Here: The Transformation Zone
- JoyQ Assessment
- 30 Days of Joy for Busy Married Couples
- Jesus In Mind: Talks on Kingdom Life
- THRIVE Skill Guides 52 weeks of training exercises
  - Mastering Joy and Rest
  - Mastering Returning to Joy
  - Mastering Applied Strategy

Training Opportunities:

- Connexus
- THRIVE 5-day Training
- Joy Rekindled Marriage Retreats

Skill Nine - *Take a Breather*

Timing When to Disengage – Skillfully take short pauses before people become overwhelmed. We read the non-verbal cues so we can build trust.

Have you ever felt overwhelmed by another person? "Settle down, you are too loud." "Get out of my face!" "Lower your voice!" "Back off!" Verbal and nonverbal warnings signal personal limits are not respected. By the time most people recognize overwhelm cues it is too late. We lose trust when people disregard our overwhelm signals. We avoid people who do not protect us from their intensity. When others accelerate and drive through the red lights of our personal space we become guarded. Teasing, bullying and violence occur when Skill Nine drops out leaving us violated and dishonored. Sustained closeness and trust requires us to stop and rest before people become overwhelmed and when they are tired. These short pauses to quiet and recharge take only seconds. Those who read the nonverbal cues and let others rest are rewarded with trust and love.

Skill Nine is the safety net for our interactions. Behaviors, sounds, facial expressions, words and responses can push us to the edge. These are moments we feel drained, hurt and run over. When limits are not respected our body cues are dismissed, minimized, unnoticed, even ignored. People who fail to attune with our limits do not increase our joy. All the brain-developing and relationship-building moments that create understanding and produce mutual-mind states require paired minds to stop a moment (pause) when the first of the two gets tired, near overwhelm or too intensely aroused. Those who disengage quickly, briefly and allow the other to rest, are rewarded.

Tender responses to weakness allow joy to increase. Family members who pause and "tone it down" when we show overwhelm signals give us the chance to catch our breath. Tickling is fun but damaging when pushed too much. The pause keeps interactions safe and joyful. When people fail to stop at the first signs of overwhelm a false peace becomes our "new normal."

The most common scenario of a Skill Nine failure is when the skill was not used with us so we do not use the skill in our relationships. When we or others fail to use emotional intelligence we may frequently hear "stop!" "back off!" "chill" "settle down!" when interacting, playing and communicating. We wonder why other people are so distractible, even fussy. When painful events go unprocessed our survival circuit may work too hard and we become more intense. At this point it will be difficult to regulate what we feel. The most vulnerable pay the greatest price. Bullies and violent offenders have not learned Skill Nine.

We learn Skill Nine because people use the skill with us. They relationally demonstrate how to pause when energy levels climb. They see our weaknesses but they protect rather than pounce. They let us rest.

The absence of Skill Nine tends to be the painful moments in our life. We turn to Immanuel (Skill Thirteen) and trusted friends (Skill Five) for support. Soon we start to search for signs that we are overwhelmed or overwhelming other people. We notice our body responses. We invite friends and family to offer suggestions in case we miss important cues. We ask, "Did I just overwhelm you? You looked overwhelmed." to update our minds about people and situations. We stay open to subtle cues in ourselves and others that were overlooked. We practicing noticing moments our relational engine is "in the red" and take some time to quiet. We keep our relational circuits on and notice when we relationally go dim in order to quickly return to our ideal state. Skill Nine prepares us for the more difficult brain skill, Skill Fifteen, Interactive Quiet.

Resources for Skill Nine:

- Joy Starts Here: The Transformation Zone
- JoyQ Assessment
- 30 Days of Joy for Busy Married Couples
- THRIVE Skill Guides 52 weeks of training exercises
  - Mastering Joy and Rest
  - Mastering Returning to Joy
  - Mastering Applied Strategy

Training Opportunities:

- Connexus
- THRIVE 5-day Training
- Joy Rekindled Marriage Retreats

Skill Ten - *Tell Nonverbal Stories*

The nonverbal parts of our stories strengthen relationships, bridge generations and cross cultures.

If you've ever been told by a parent, teacher or spouse, "Watch your tone!" or, "It's not what you said, it's how you said it!" you already know a little something about Skill Ten. In conversation, the content we convey is first assessed by *how* we say the words, while words are then assessed next in the process. (Hughes & Baylin, 2012) The brain processes nonverbal content faster than words so the nonverbal pieces of our conversations carry more weight in the brain than words alone. One UCLA study reported that 93% of effective communication is nonverbal. It has been said that 10% of conflicts are due to difference of opinion while 90% are due to the wrong tone of voice. Words, while weighty, have limitations.

Our brain relies on words and a vast collection of nonverbal signals to effectively communicate and attune with other people. Facial expressions, voice tone (prosody), body movements and the use of personal space contribute to the interactive dance we know as communication. If you ever visited a new culture where you did not speak the language, or enjoyed some good old fashion fun playing Charades, you practiced Skill Ten. Reading emails, text messages and Facebook postings give us words to read but no emotional content. This absence creates problems. Many misunderstandings have been caused by the lack of voice tone and facial expression. A number of problems have been caused by the lack of Skill Ten to help us read other people and correctly convey the emotional content of our minds.

If you receive an email from your boss that says, "I want to speak with you. Please come to my office now." This may be somewhat unsettling unless you can simulate what is happening in your boss's mind and have a secure bond. If your boss enters your office with a big, warm smile, high energy, a soft voice tone and open, inviting body language, you may have a more welcome response to these words and feel less guarded. The brain searches for emotional cues with every interaction. People feel seen, valued and understood when Skill Ten is present.

Our body is the canvas to expresses our deepest thoughts, feelings, desires, fears and our most prized memories. Skill Ten allows us to share our emotions and express the rich content of our minds through our face, voice and body. Skill Ten conveys our internal world, keeps us grounded, brightens our stories, anchors our relationships and creates mutual understanding in our interactions. Using a conglomeration of the limbic system, vagal nerve, anterior insula and more, our body informs us, often in compelling ways, when something is going on. The amygdala, part of the limbic system, what we refer to as Level 2 of the control center (Skill 18), detects a threat in 1/10 of a second. This response is much faster than the time it takes for our brain to create a conscious thought. (Hughes & Baylin, 2012) Skill Ten helps us use both our brain and body to bring clarity to our conversations and create mutual understanding in our relationships. Our face and body signal the quality of our day, an interaction, how rested we are and whether we enjoyed a recent meal. The brain and body have an intimate, interconnected relationship that improves with Skill Ten. We like it when our brain and body work together!

Skill Ten enhances our ability to interpret what we see on someone's face to know whether they are joyful, engaged, bored or up to no good. We improve our stories the more we use our face, voice, body language and personal space as part of the story-telling package. While we are accustomed to words as our primary way to communicate, our body actively engages the content of our minds to tell its story for others to view. This brings flavor to our stories. We notice the power of nonverbal messages when people ask, "I can tell by your face you are not well, so what's really happening?" and "You look upset, are you mad at me?" With practice we discover nonverbal stories are fun, engaging and invigorating. What's on your face today?

Resources for Skill Ten:

- 30 Days of Joy for Busy Married Couples
- THRIVE Skill Guides 52 weeks of training exercises
    - Mastering Joy and Rest
    - Mastering Returning to Joy
    - Mastering Applied Strategy

Training Opportunities:

- Connexus
- THRIVE 5-day Training
- Joy Rekindled Marriage Retreats

Skill Eleven - *Return to Joy from the Big Six Feelings*

We return to shared joy as we quiet distress. We stay in relationship when things go wrong.

The brain is wired to feel six unpleasant emotions. Fear, anger, sadness, disgust, shame and hopeless despair are each signals of something specific going wrong. We need to learn how to quiet each of these different circuits separately while maintaining our relationships. Training under these six emotional conditions covers the full range of our emotional distress.

We are designed for joy. Joy is our natural state. The longer we stay stuck in a negative emotion the weaker we become. A failure to learn Skill Eleven leaves us avoiding, side-tracking and disconnecting from the very emotions our brains are wired to feel. When people do not have Skill Eleven after the second year of life emotions stay unregulated. At this point we learn non-relational strategies to manage what we feel rather than quieting emotions back to joy. Relationships blow out. People justify their responses. People blame others for their upset and turn to BEEPS for comfort. Skill Eleven is a relational life-preserver for relationships.

Parents who have not learned Skill Eleven are unable to show children how to properly manage and quiet big feelings. Responses, usually anger and "behavior-management" typically shut down children. Power-plays intensify. Problems soon become bigger than the relationship. Friends and family do not resolve conflicts because who is right or wrong stays the focus. Rules and tasks steer people and conversations. Leaders end up avoiding situations that create specific emotions. We justify these responses and call them normal. No one considers the brain skill that returns us to joy and glad to be together states.

Marriages, families, communities, even cultures develop strategies to avoid certain emotions. Who do you know avoids a shame message? Who amplifies fear? Who stays stuck in hopelessness? Who avoids disgust? Who is a road-rager? Who is a people-pleaser? As we look at the relational landscape of our networks we start to see the urgency for Skill Eleven.

Resources for Skill Eleven:

- Joy Starts Here: The Transformation Zone
- JoyQ Assessment
- 30 Days of Joy for Busy Married Couples
- Jesus In Mind: Talks on Kingdom Life
- THRIVE Skill Guides 52 weeks of training exercises
  - Mastering Joy and Rest
  - Mastering Returning to Joy
  - Mastering Applied Strategy

Training Opportunities:

- Connexus
- THRIVE 5-day Training
- Joy Rekindled Marriage Retreats

Skill Twelve - *Act Like Myself in the Big Six Feelings*

When we find our design we will be life-giving - whether we are upset or joyful.

One crucial step to maintain our relationships when we are upset is learning to act like the same person we were when we had joy to be together. A lack of training or bad examples causes us to damage or withdraw from the relationships we value when we get angry, afraid, sad, disgusted, ashamed or hopeless.

Life throws curve balls. Unexpected problems plague our day. Plans change. Relationships create tension. Interactions produce stress. Work drains our battery. Disappointment of all kinds derail our relational train. At the end of the day, we are as good as our ability to manage what we feel. How well we navigate upset determines the level of trust and closeness we create with others. Do we stay relationally connected? Do we isolate? Do we attack? Our reactions always tell story.

Skill Twelve equips us to live relationally and respond gracefully as we navigate upset, pain, fatigue, distress, misunderstanding and loss. Our emotional brain must learn to feel unpleasant feelings and stay engaged, relational, kind, caring and attentive to the people close to us. Avoiding upset is impossible. The greater question becomes, "How well do I respond when I feel upset?" Odds are high every one of us has some work to do.

We learn Skill Twelve because people stay connected with us during upset. We learn that negative emotions do not have the final word. Helpful examples and our shared experiences give the resources to navigate upset. We internalize examples then carry them with us. A trained brain need not fear distress. Skill Twelve connects us together as we express the best of ourselves and repair as necessary when things go wrong.

Skill Twelve gives us the freedom to be ourselves under constantly changing circumstances. This consistency creates safety and inspires others.

Resources for Skill Twelve:

- Joy Starts Here: The Transformation Zone
- JoyQ Assessment
- 30 Days of Joy for Busy Married Couples
- Jesus In Mind: Talks on Kingdom Life
- THRIVE Skill Guides 52 weeks of training exercises
  - Mastering Joy and Rest
  - Mastering Returning to Joy
  - Mastering Applied Strategy

Training Opportunities:

- Connexus
- THRIVE 5-day Training
- Joy Rekindled Marriage Retreats

Skill Thirteen - *See What God Sees: Heartsight*

Seeing people and events from God's perspective yields a life filled with hope and direction.

Hope and direction come from seeing situations, ourselves and others the way they were meant to be instead of only seeing what went wrong. This spiritual vision guides our training and restoration. Even forgiveness flows from seeing people's purpose as more important than their malfunctions and makes us a restorative community instead of an accusing one. Through our hearts we see the spiritual vision God sees.

Without Skill Thirteen people become problems to solve, commodities for personal interests, and enemies to envy. With Skill Thirteen we discover God sees more to a person and situation than our limited vision allows. We are reminded that God is with us, even when fears and feelings say otherwise. We look to God for clarity. We find comfort.

Skill Thirteen reminds us the beggar on the street has a story, our persecutors need forgiveness and humanity longs for love. We ask for vision, "Lord, what do you see in this frustrating situation?" We pray, "Lord, help me see my child/spouse/friend with your eyes at this moment." We check our reality with, "Lord, how do you see this painful moment from my day?" We open the door for answers and perspective outside our limited scope.

Skill Thirteen tells us there is more going when pain, inconvenience and upset disrupts our day. We discover what is important. Skill Thirteen inserts perspective and restores our peace during strain and hardship. Skill Thirteen works for moments of upset but should be used as a lifestyle. We watch a beautiful sunset and sense that Immanuel here, orchestrating this moment. Heart vision guides our faith and restores our relationships.

Resources for Skill Thirteen:

- Share Immanuel booklet
- Joy Starts Here: The Transformation Zone
- Whispers of My Abba
- JoyQ Assessment
- 30 Days of Joy for Busy Married Couples
- Jesus In Mind: Talks on Kingdom Life
- THRIVE Skill Guides 52 weeks of training exercises
  - o Mastering Joy and Rest
  - o Mastering Returning to Joy
  - o Mastering Applied Strategy

Training Opportunities:

- Connexus
- THRIVE 5-day Training
- Joy Rekindled Marriage Retreats

Skill Fourteen - *Stop the Sark*

False "Godsight" may seem true to us at the moment but leads to: blame, accusation, condemnation, gossip, resentment, legalism, self-justification and self-righteousness. The sark requires active opposition.

This Greek work (also rendered sarx) refers to seeing life according to our view of who people are and how things should be. This conviction, that I know or can determine the right thing to do or be, is the opposite of heartsight. (Skill Thirteen) For the sark, people become what they have done (the sum of their mistakes) or what we want them to become for us. Blame, accusations, condemnation, gossip, resentment, legalism, self-justification and self-righteousness are signs of the sark.

Skill Fourteen is a fundamental skill to establish interactions where people feel seen and valued. Skill Fourteen prevents spiritual abuse. We think before we speak and we see some of what God sees. All of us have been convinced we knew the right thing to do. "If only people listened to me the results would be good!" we said or thought. Possibly we made a judgment about someone that guided our thoughts and behavior. We treated someone according to their appearance, mistakes or reputation. We may feel like someone views and treats us according to a mistake or malfunction we committed. In either scenario Skill Fourteen is missing.

Possibly we were on the receiving end of someone who knew what we should say, do or think. Their motivations may have been good but they were convinced their wisdom and expertise would solve a problem. "If you do this, everything will work for you!" "I know what you should do, listen to me..." We may have felt the person was pushing an agenda or simply failed to fully engage, hear or see us. We may have felt there was no attunement or peace in the strategy. Something was off. Previous experience, maybe our gut, told us otherwise.

One of the more sinister aspects of our disrupted ability to know the right thing to do or say occurs when a person uses Scripture to bring death instead of life. Someone believes they hear from God or know how to apply the Bible to a given situation that leaves us feeling run over, misunderstood, even ostracized.

One of the wisest men to walk the earth said, "To everything there is a season, a time for every purpose under heaven; a time to be born, and a time to die; a time to plant, and a time to pluck what is planted; a time to kill, and a time to heal; a time to break down, and a time to build up; a time to weep, and a time to laugh; a time to mourn, and a time to dance..." (Ecclesiastes 3:1-4, NKJV) How can we tell what time it is? Stopping the Sark starts with turning to God for guidance.

There are two kinds of knowing. One synchronizes with God and His Spirit. This attunement brings wisdom, peace and clarity. The other knowing is that which seems right but in the end does not bring life.

Resources for Skill Fourteen:

- Joy Starts Here: The Transformation Zone
- JoyQ Assessment

- 30 Days of Joy for Busy Married Couples
- Jesus In Mind: Talks on Kingdom Life
- THRIVE Skill Guides 52 weeks of training exercises
  - Mastering Joy and Rest
  - Mastering Returning to Joy
  - Mastering Applied Strategy

Training Opportunities:

- Connexus
- THRIVE 5-day Training
- Joy Rekindled Marriage Retreats

Skill Fifteen - *Quiet Interactively*

Skilled reading of facial cues allows us to operate at high energy levels and manage our drives without hurting ourselves or others.

Using the ventromedial cortex that is part of Level 4 of the Control Center together with the intelligent branch of the parasympathetic nervous system allows us to control the upper end of arousal states. Instead of taking us all the way to quiet/peace, this type of quieting allows us to operate at high levels of energy and quiet just enough to avoid going into overwhelm. This system controls aggressive, sexual and predatory urges so we can avoid harmful behaviors.

Skill Fifteen prevents some of the more violent, aggressive tendencies a human can develop. Skill Fifteen keeps us from going over the top during fits of anger, fear, excitement, sex and arousal. Based on early life experiences, particularly with the father between 12 and 18 months, we learn to regulate fear and control the two types of aggression, "hot" and "cold" responses. Interactive quieting training helps us resist acting on impulses (hot) or premeditating revenge (cold). Sadly we have no shortage of tragedies where Skill Fifteen was missing in students at schools who turn violent, with disgruntled workers in the workplace and all aspects of society.

As mentioned in Skill Nine, tickling is a common experience that stays fun as long as overwhelm cues are respected. When pushed beyond our ability to manage intensity, the brain's evaluation center at Level 2 quickly shifts into "Bad and Scary" mode. Now our brain suspends its highest levels of processing. The moment turns traumatic.

Skill Fifteen is best learned when the father plays tickling and wrestling games, including "I'm going to get you" and interactive facial fear experiences to identify fear signals. Skill Fifteen can be practiced later in life by going on extreme adventures such as backpacking. During THRIVE Training carefully designed exercises are crafted to effectively train Skill Fifteen. These training exercises are both impactful and delicately balanced so people practice the skill in a safe environment. Caution must be exercised, our most painful experiences arise from moments people lack this skill.

The brain region responsible for Skill Fifteen oversees real time updates and predicts negative outcomes. This part of Level 4 calms the fight/flight/freeze response. When working correctly, we rapidly update a situation in "live time" to avoid going over the top. We can observe a person's face switch from fun to fear then alter our responses accordingly. With damage to this circuit or the lack of training, problems quickly arise.

While experience and genes play a role, we see some of the more severe personality disorders develop when Skill Fifteen fails in the developmental process, from Borderline issues, Disorganized Attachments, Sociopathic and violent personalities and more. Skill Fifteen is a trainable skill that must be trained when people have the skill and practice under careful conditions.

Resources for Skill Fifteen:

- THRIVE Skill Guides 52 weeks of training exercises
    - Mastering Joy and Rest
    - Mastering Returning to Joy
    - Mastering Applied Strategy

Training Opportunities:

- Connexus
- THRIVE 5-day Training

Skill Sixteen - *Recognize High and Low Energy Response: Sympathetic and Parasympathetic*

Some people are at their best with activity and others with solitude. Knowing our styles and needs brings out the best in all our interactions.

Joy, anger and fear are energy-producing emotions (sympathetic) while sadness, disgust, shame and hopelessness reduce our energy levels (parasympathetic). Tendencies to activate or shut down often become "pursuit and withdrawal" or "anger and tears" instead of healthy relationships.

When confronted with fear or shame, Parasympathetic responders respond with self-deprecating attacks on themselves. "I am such an idiot!" "I can't do anything right." "I am worthless!" Problems and feelings are about them, and these low-energy responders often deny they matter or have any intrinsic value. Parasympathetic responders often feel like door mats and, at some level. At some level they feel hopeless about life and relationships.

Parasympathetic, low-energy responders become possums who hide while Sympathetic responders attack. High-energy responders react to fear and shame with arousal and anger. They typically avoid these emotions by shaping the responses of other people through their anger, control or punitive responses. Blame, accusations and self-justification are common. We may hear phrases such as, "Who do you think you are?" and, "What's the matter with you?" We notice a knot in our stomach when we must work under or correct someone who runs their relationships this way. It is common for critical responses to dictate life and interactions with children, spouses and coworkers.

High-energy responders prefer hot emotions and avoid energy-draining emotions. Low-energy responders experience sadness as a more common emotion compared with anger or fear.

Correcting unwanted patterns starts with Skill Sixteen, which provides mutual understanding for our God-given differences. We extend grace through the delightful discovery that we are uniquely created. We become mindful that people are wired for high-energy activities in the form of worship, exercise, music, play, extreme sports and hobbies while others seek low-energy activities. Low-energy responders gravitate to slow, soft relaxing music, hot baths, quiet moments and environments low in stimulation. High-energy responders may become bored with what fuels low-energy responders. Likewise, low-energy responders become overwhelmed by some of what fuels high-energy responders. There is no right or wrong style.

Leaders are more efficient when they learn Skill Sixteen, they recognize individuals as high-energy or low-energy then offer opportunities that best suits preferences. Pastors may offer high-energy worship for Sympathetic responders or low-energy worship for Parasympathetic responders. Supervisors create a work environment that best suits the workforce and meets the client's needs. Couples reach understanding when they recognize energy response styles and foster a home environment to best match those needs.

Some people seek prayer activities in an environment where the room is quiet, lights are dim, music, if any, is slow. Others prefer to jog, bike ride, exercise, dance and play to feel connected in prayer. Looking at these differences brings Skill Sixteen to the forefront of our minds and relationships. Skill Sixteen leads to acceptance and mutual satisfaction. With Skill Sixteen we identify these distinctions and respond with appreciation for what sustains equilibrium and creates order for couples, families, churches, classrooms and the workplace.

Resources for Skill Sixteen:

- Keeping Your Ministry Out of Court
- THRIVE Skill Guides 52 weeks of training exercises
  - Mastering Joy and Rest
  - Mastering Returning to Joy
  - Mastering Applied Strategy

Training Opportunities:

- Connexus
- THRIVE 5-day Training

Skill Seventeen - *Identify Attachment Styles*

Our lives and reality need to be organized around secure love. Fears, hurts and emotional distance create insecure relational styles that will last for life unless we replace them.

Secure attachments bring joy, peace, resilience and flexibility as we mature. Insecure attachments come in three types. An under-active attachment pattern (dismissive) leads to underestimating the importance of feelings and relationships. This group usually thinks things are fine and no big deal. An overactive attachment style (distracted) leads to excessive intensity and an exaggeration of feelings, hurts and needs. This group is always feeling hurt or thinking others are upset when they are not. The third style is afraid to get close to the people they love and need.

Skill Seventeen builds joyful bonds and corrects bonds of fear. People respond to our weaknesses with tenderness so we grow. Relationships develop security with careful attunement, validation, comfort and responsive timing to needs so we feel seen and satisfied.

Skill Seventeen corrects unwanted, addictive behaviors with a new-found joy and peace. Because the pain that drives insecure attachments is the worst pain the brain knows, Skill Seventeen identifies unwanted patterns while Skill Eighteen brings the solutions to process pain.

Life and relationships are deeply rewarding when our attachments are secure and synchronized. Skill Seventeen adds clarity for motivations, corrects distortions, and replace fears with love. Skill Seventeen helps couples stay connected through the understanding that unwanted bonding patterns are present for a good reason. We begin to recognize urges and fears that drive our thoughts, decisions and relationships. We go to the source of our deepest cravings that drive our BEEPS.

Resources for Skill Seventeen:

- Jesus In Mind: Talks on Kingdom Life
- THRIVE Skill Guides 52 weeks of training exercises
  - Mastering Returning to Joy
  - Mastering Applied Strategy

Training Opportunities:

- Connexus
- THRIVE 5-day Training

Skill Eighteen - *Intervene Where the Brain is Stuck: Five Distinctive Levels of Brain Disharmony and Pain*

Each of the five levels of brain processing react with a different kind of distress when it gets stuck. When we know the signs we will know the solutions.

There are five levels in the brain when we count the four in the right hemisphere control center and add the left hemisphere as the fifth. By knowing the characteristics of each we know when one level got stuck and what kind of interventions will help. For instance, explanations help Level 5 but will not stop a Level 2 terror like the fear of heights.

We all know that gasoline to put out a fire is unwise. Relationally, we turn sparks into forest fires when we use the wrong solution to resolve pain. Skill Eighteen provides the wisdom and expertise to effectively solve problems so we reach peace.

Pain no longer needs to dominate our world. Skill Eighteen brings strategic solutions to our relational tool belt so we effectively process pain and protect our relationships. When Skill Eighteen is missing we speak when we should listen and try to fix problems using the wrong methods that exacerbate distress. It is all too common to rely on words and information to solve problems when only one of the five types of pain diminishes with more information. Skill Eighteen opens the door for freedom and flexibility with useful solutions that work.

Have you ever been stuck in a negative emotion when well-intentioned people tried to fix you without attunement? What about a time you were expected to do something but required a mature example?

Here is a story about Mike who tried to help his friend Susan.

Mike sat with his friend Susan who was feeling intense sadness over some difficult family relationships. Mike wanted to help Susan, so he gave her advice that she could apply to her situation. Mike believed his strategies, if followed, would help Susan better navigate her painful family dynamics.

Much to Mike's surprise, the more he offered his input, Susan's distress intensified. Rather than helping his friend, Mike was inadvertently adding gasoline onto a fire. At one point Susan turned to Mike and begged, "Can you stop trying to fix me? I don't need you to fix me Mike, I just want you to be here with me!" Mike was stunned by Susan's request. "Doesn't she want my help?" he wondered.

Mike bit his lip, and honored his friend's request. He sat in silence as Susan shared her grief. After a short time, Susan settled down and looked more peaceful. Susan expressed how much better she was feeling. She thanked Mike for being with her and said how much it helped her that Mike was able to stay present during her upset. Once calm, Susan asked to hear Mike's encouragement and advice for her family. Mike felt surprised but mostly relieved by Susan's response. He learned a valuable lesson that day about Skill Eighteen. His presence and love for his friend was more important than his advice during negative emotions.

As the story illustrates, there is no one size fits all for pain resolution and recovery. The pain of loss, fight/flee/freeze responses, negative emotions, immaturity and internal conflicts each require specific solutions.

Resources for Skill Eighteen:

- Joy Starts Here: The Transformation Zone
- JoyQ Assessment
- 30 Days of Joy for Busy Married Couples
- Jesus In Mind: Talks on Kingdom Life
- THRIVE Skill Guides 52 weeks of training exercises
  - Mastering Joy and Rest
  - Mastering Returning to Joy
  - Mastering Applied Strategy

Training Opportunities:

- Connexus
- THRIVE 5-day Training
- Joy Rekindled Marriage Retreats

Skill Nineteen - *Recover from Complex Emotions: Handle Combinations of the Big Six Emotions*

Complex injuries from life leave us hurting many ways at once. We recover when we combine our brain skills and use them in harmony.

Once we can return to joy and act like ourselves with the six big negative feelings taken one at a time, we can begin to learn how to return to joy and act like ourselves when the six are combined in various combinations. Shame and anger combine to form humiliation. Fear and hopelessness (with almost any other feeling as well) form dread. These combination feelings can be very draining and difficult to quiet.

Have you encountered a situation where your heart raced with fear? To make matters worse, something more insidious added pressure to your plate. You were afraid but you could not find a way out. No matter how hard you looked, there was no escape or foreseeable solution. You wanted to make a threat disappear but you lacked time and resources to throw at the problem. You felt small while circumstances and emotions were simply too big. Sound fun?

For many of us we feel this way when we face a deadline, lack funds to pay a bill, or encounter a health scare. There are no shortage of opportunities to feel a complex emotion. Every moment, painful or otherwise, can lead to joyful change.

I clearly remember a time I needed Skill Nineteen.

I was in Mexico and about to try parasailing for the first time. While standing on a small wooden dock in the ocean, I was waiting for my turn to be harnessed and yanked into the glorious blue sky when a group of fellow parasailers caused a commotion. I heard yelling and screaming. I braced myself. I watched people jump up and down while looking down at their feet. "What do they see that I don't?" I asked before concluding, "This does not look good!"

Because I did not speak Spanish I could not understand what the distressed people were saying or yelling. My body was tense. Adrenaline surged through my veins. My heart raced. I was afraid!

Due to the limited space on the platform, I noticed hopeless feelings merge with my fear. There was no escape. I was trapped. As my energy threatened to leave, fear kept me vigilant.

I was feeling dread, high-energy fear combined with low-energy hopeless despair. This perfect storm amps up distress to an entirely new level.

Skill Nineteen is a solution to circumstances where emotions combine and intensify. Because the brain is a natural amplifier, emotions escalate which makes processing an event more difficult. When we experience a high-energy emotion (sympathetic arousal) that partners with an energy-draining emotion (parasympathetic response), the effect is similar to pressing the accelerator and brake simultaneously in your car. If you value your car, you want to avoid this step. If we value our brain and relationships, we want to learn Skill Nineteen.

Back to my story. *I continued to assess the situation. I started to breathe and calm my body. I turned to God for deliverance, asking for peace into this most distressing moment. In my helplessness I asked God to intervene. I noticed some peace return. My breathing and body relaxed.*

People began laughing, appearing more playful than before. I watched as sea crabs moved away from the spacing of the platform. They disappeared. I felt thankful for the relief. Soon I was off parasailing and enjoying myself. I now had a great story to tell my friends.

Thankfully the above experience was short-lived. Without attunement this pain would have shifted to a deeper level of processing. (Skill Eighteen) Skill Nineteen keeps us grounded, relational and clear when emotional turbulence invades life and relationships. We remember who we are under intense conditions. We quiet big feelings. We stay relational.

Resources for Skill Nineteen:

- JoyQ Assessment
- THRIVE Skill Guides 52 weeks of training exercises
  - Mastering Applied Strategy

Training Opportunities:

- Connexus
- THRIVE 5-day Training
- Joy Rekindled Marriage Retreats

MISSION AS A WAY OF LIFE

What is a "Prayer, Care, Share Lifestyle"? What does it mean to be fluent in the gospel? What are some of the most effective ways to demonstrate and share the gospel with others? We will learn about:

1.) Relational love & servant evangelism – opening the hearts of others to the gospel,
2.) Prophetic evangelism: words of knowledge, words of wisdom, dreams, visions,
3.) Power evangelism: healing the sick, casting out demons.

Step One:

Know and believe the power of the gospel. Romans 1:16 Become gospel fluent, able to share the good news of Jesus Christ, God's grace, and the Kingdom of God anywhere with anyone. Faith comes by hearing and hearing by the Word of God. Romans 10:17

I am not ashamed of the gospel, because it is the power of God for the salvation of everyone who believes. Roman 1:16

Key Bible Verses: Romans 1:16, 10:17; 2 Timothy 1:8-12; Colossians 1:27-29; 1 Corinthians 9:16, 15:2; Revelation 14:6; Matthew 4:17, 4:23-, 13:1-52; Luke 10:1-23; John 6:29

1. Knowing and speaking the gospel (gospel fluency): Verbalizing, believing, and living the gospel is God's powerful way to save (reconcile, restore, heal) individuals, cities, and nations. The spoken Word of God is the means by which God creates, sustains, saves, heals, and delivers! Gospel words have power. It is gospel words that both created the church and proclaiming gospel words, especially to youth, poor, oppressed, and lost or unreached, is the purpose of the church – its mission. A true and powerful church must be gospel centered, gospel driven, and on gospel mission as a lifestyle.

   A. The good news story of what God **has** already done for Himself, individuals, and His family/bride.

      - Father, Son, Holy Spirit – God as Three yet One, a Loving God who created a family of sons/daughters who are being formed into a Bride for His Son.

      - Forgiveness of sins through Christ's shed blood and sacrificial death on the cross.

      - Ability to be in a right and intimately loving relationship with God through Christ.

      - Jesus is King and Lord – He is central and supreme. All things were made by Him, live through Him, and exist for Him.

      - The Kingdom of God is here!

      - Adoption into God's family as sons of God (gospel identity). Our very nature has been changed. We are a new creation.

      - God's mercy and grace are available through Christ.

   B. The good news story of what God **is** doing for Himself, individuals, and His family/bride.

      - Transformation into Christ's likeness through the power of the indwelling Christ and the ministry of the Holy Spirit. It is no longer we who live, but Christ who lives in us. Galatians 2:20; Romans 8:29

      - The forming, maturing, and purifying of Christ's Bride – the Church.

      - Being disciplined and trained to rule and reign with Christ into eternity.

   C. The good news story of what God **will** be doing for Himself, individuals, and His family/bride.

- He will be returning in visual form to the earth as King and Judge to rule the nations.

- Christ will have a Bride and family to fellowship and partner with into eternity.

- Christ will make a new heaven and a new earth.

2. Believing and being the gospel from the heart (gospel reality). Romans 10:8-10

   A. We are saved by grace through faith. Our work is to believe the gospel. Biblical belief or faith is not just intellectual assent. It is placing our whole lives into the hands of Jesus Christ. It is trusting Him at all levels.

   B. Christ's Life is lived through us in our inner most being, our heart or spirit.

   C. Christ's fruit comes into our spirit and flows out to others: love, affection, joy, gladness, peace, patience, kindness, gentleness, self-control.

   D. Christ's wisdom and revelation flow into and out of us to others.

   E. Christ's power flows through and out of us to others. This includes the gifts of the Holy Spirit.

3. Living in Christ-centered family/community as a lifestyle. The gospel is both taught and caught in close "organic" family/community. We can experience some forms of discipleship in organized formal strategies and structures. At the same time, we need to have informal, relational, and "organic" life-on-life to transfer the life and ways of Christ to one another.

4. Demonstrating and proclaiming the gospel to the lost through a Micro-Church Family.

   A. On gospel mission intentionally 24/7.

   B. Demonstrating the gospel in the six rhythms of life:

      - Story formation: What do they believe is God's story and what is their story/script? We want to give them a new and true story of God and how their life's story can be woven into God's story. We want ourselves and others to live their life story in light of the dominate story of God's life and purpose. Where is their story broken or off track?

      - Listening & sharing.

      - Celebrations (party)

      - Eating

      - Blessings: (work, education, health care)

      - Recreation: (rest, creative, play, interact with creation, restoration, rejuvenation).

   C. Identifying individuals and groups that our Micro-Church Family wants to reach with the gospel.

      - Friends and Family

      - Neighbors

- Co-workers
- Companies
- Specific people groups
- Foreign visitors, students, workers
- Interest groups

Step Two: Develop a "Prayer, Care, Share Lifestyle"

Jesus came to seek and save that which is lost. He does not want anyone to perish. Luke 19:10; 2 Peter 3:9 Every follower of Christ is called to be a missionary as a way of life. We are on a search and rescue team and get to reach out to others. Being on mission is a lifestyle and can be woven into our everyday rhythms of life. For example, everyone needs to eat. People long for fellowship over a meal. Simply inviting someone into your home and life for dinner will open up great possibilities in the kingdom. Sharing the gospel involves spiritual warfare, so always stay in the Spirit and utilize prayer and fasting. Praying in tongues throughout the day is also very powerful.

Prayer: Prayer is the most powerful force in all the world because it releases God to move. We have not because we ask not. James 4:3 There are few prayers more powerful than Luke 10:2, *"Ask the Lord of the harvest to send out workers into His harvest field."* We will endeavor to pray new people into the Kingdom of God, and also pray that God will add to our number, enabling us to multiply. We will strategically pray for those who are not yet in Christ. Prayer releases the Holy Spirit to convict unbelievers that they can get right with God. It unleashes the Spirit of wisdom and revelation causing blind eyes to see the glory of God. Ephesians 1:17-18 It moves people and circumstances to positively influence unbelievers. It brings us before Christ's face and keeps us focused on who we are and why we exist. Matthew 6:9-13. *"My house will be called a house of prayer for all nations."* Mark 11:17 Prayer moves God who moves the world. Pray specifically for a person bringing their name before God. Ask God for these five things to occur in their life:

- Pray that the Father would draw them to Jesus. John 6:44 Include fasting. Mark 9:27 *"This kind can come out only by prayer and fasting"*.
- Bind the spirit that blinds their minds. 2 Corinthians 4:4
- Loose the Spirit of adoption (sonship). Romans 8:15
- Pray that believers will cross their paths and enter into positive relationships with them. Matthew 9:38
- Loose the Spirit of wisdom and revelation on them so they may know God better. Ephesians 1:17

Care: Demonstrating the Love, Wisdom, Revelation, and Power of God

- Love & Servant Evangelism: The Word of God is very clear that unbelievers will know us by our love for each other and for the lost, even our enemies. God is love and when we evidence His love to others it opens their hearts to the gospel. Matthew 5:43-48; John 13:35 We were all hardwired by God to receive and give love. Everybody needs and wants love. Relational love and practical serving opens the hearts of others to the gospel. When we are with someone who hasn't placed their faith in Christ, it is important that we emit the love, affection, and joy of the Lord. That radiant light and love will be contagious.

  Take time to ask people about their life. Always send the signal of acceptance, affirmation, and affection. Never be judgmental.

- Personal Evangelism: Where were you born? Tell us about your upbringing.

  Ask about their present: Where do you live? What kind of work? What are your interests and hobbies? Family? Friends?

  Ask about their future: What are your dreams?

- Prophetic Evangelism: People also long to know who they are, where they come from, why they exist. Therefore, when we tell others what their identity is in Christ, how they are known in heaven, what God is thinking about them there becomes a powerful openness to the gospel. We call this prophetic evangelism. It involves: prophecy, words of knowledge, words of wisdom, dreams, and visions, etc. An example of this is when Jesus told Nathaniel who he was by revelation. John 1:47

- Power Evangelism: Often in Christ's life, He healed the sick and cast out demons. This demonstration of God's power revealed His love and opened the hearts to receive the gospel. We get to do the same. Matthew 10:8

There are several great places to meet and influence friends to become followers of Christ. Co-workers, neighbors, schoolmates, and relatives are some of the places to reach out. You could even start a DNA Group at work, meeting during your lunch break or after work. Build loving relationships with those who are not yet in Christ. They open their hearts to us because we have loved and served them. The gospel will flow out of us and affect their hearts, causing them to open and receive Christ for themselves. Listen to their life story and respond with affirmation, acceptance, and affection. Do not hesitate to operate in the gifts of the Spirit as well. Healing and deliverance should be practiced regularly. Matthew 10:7-8; Mark 16:15-18

Share: Building a Relational Bridge of Love to Share the Gospel

HOW TO SHARE JESUS WITH YOUR DNA GROUP'S PRIVATE WORLD

Adapted from information received from Ralph Neighbour, Jr.

Every DNA Group member has a "private world." The people in it fall into three categories:

1. The "People People": people I transparently share my feelings and thoughts.
   a. Family, Relatives
   b. Intimate friends
2. The "Machine People": people who *serve me* that I treat with courtesy, but are not privy to a personal relationship with me.
   a. Man who fixes my flat tire
   b. Lady who checks out my groceries
3. The "Landscape People": Those around me I say "Hi" to in passing but never speak to.

Thoughtfully write down all the people in (1) and (2) – people you relate to in a typical week, over and over: *(Typically, you will have no more than 8 names for each group. Use more paper if necessary.)*

THIS IS YOUR "PERSONAL WORLD" LIST:

THE "PEOPLE PEOPLE"	THE "MACHINE PEOPLE"
1._____	1._____
2._____	2._____
3._____	3._____
4._____	4._____
5._____	5._____
6._____	6._____
7._____	7._____
8._____	8._____

NOW, ADD UP ALL THE NAMES OF THOSE IN YOUR DNA GROUP: _____

THESE PEOPLE ARE YOUR PRIMARY MISSION FIELD!

The Holy Spirit's task is to confront every person *(no exceptions!)* with three facts: sin, judgment, and righteousness (John 16:8-10). God allows each person to choose how to respond.

Those who seek righteousness are called "a son of peace" in Luke 10:6, a term meaning *one searching for peace.* Examples: the Ethiopian Eunuch (Acts 8), the Centurion (Acts 10). Note how the Holy Spirit led Philip and Peter to them. You will also be led in the same way.

THIS IS A "RESPONSE PYRAMID"

Those searching for peace will be found at Levels 3, 4, and 5:

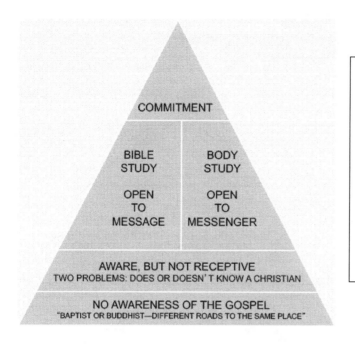

LEVEL 5: COMMITMENT

LEVEL 4: OPEN TO MESSAGE OF BIBLE

LEVEL 3: OPEN TO "BODY STUDY" (FRIENDSHIP)

LEVEL 2: REQUIRES TIME TO TRUST YOU

LEVEL 1: NEVER EXPOSED TO A CHRISTIAN

Prayerfully review all the names on your list and write the LEVEL you feel they are at now.

GOD WILL USE YOU IN A SPECIAL WAY AT ALL 5 LEVELS BY *WITNESSING*!

But you will receive power when the Holy Spirit comes upon you.

And you will be my **witnesses**, telling people about me everywhere, - Acts 1:8

Definition of a witness: "a person who sees or otherwise has personal knowledge of something."

Paul shared his witness twice, described in Acts 20 and 22. He shared four facts:

1. My life before I followed Christ.
2. How I became aware I needed Christ.
3. How I received Christ.
4. The results in my life.

You have a very personal witness! It is the first and most important thing about you that Jesus wants you to report to every person in your world. It should not be "preachy," just stating the true facts. And it should be short! In fact, one minute is the goal to share it. Thus, a sentence or two on each area is your goal.

HOW SHOULD YOU INTRODUCE IT?
"May I tell you the greatest thing that has ever happened to me?"
HOW SHOULD YOU COMPLETE IT?
"Perhaps this has also happened to you?"
WRITE OUT YOUR ONE MINUTE TESTIMONY:

1. **My life before I followed Christ:**

   _____

   _____

2. **How I became aware I needed Christ:**

   _____

   _____

3. **How I received Christ:**

   _____

   _____

4. **The results in my life:**

   _____

   _____

PRACTICE SESSION

Share this without reading it with each of your DNA partners.

Then share it with each person you listed who are on the previous page.

"May I tell you the greatest thing that has ever happened to me?"

"Perhaps this has also happened to you?"

A SIMPLE DIAGRAM TO HELP THE PERSON WHO RESPONDS WITH:
"No. How do I receive Christ into my life?"

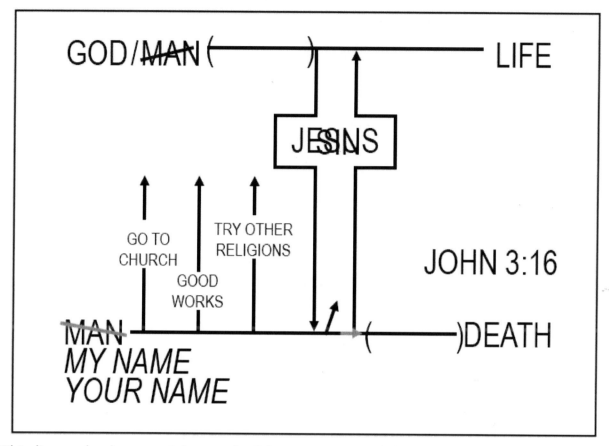

This diagram has been used thousands of times. You can easily learn to use it by practicing it with your DNA partners. It is valuable for these reasons:

- The seeker will have a full grasp of what this decision will mean. Too often, quick explanations have allowed people to "pray the sinner's prayer" so they can go to heaven, without realizing they must totally surrender their present life to Christ.
- It allows discussion about every element with the seeker.
- Do not proceed to the next element until you have agreement about the present one!
- Pause at any time there is strong disagreement and wait for the Holy Spirit to guide you. Sometimes you may need to delay the session until agreement is reached.
- Chase all "rabbits" that come up as you share. That means you "scratch the itch" rather than follow your own agenda.
- You can view free of charge three videos that review this chapter:

  https://youtu.be/E-NGWrDWFqs
  https://youtu.be/C5nfKUuKmhw
  https://youtu.be/55U2FHtKSFc

NOTES:

CHILDREN AND GENERATIONAL TRANSFER

Jesus made it very clear in His teachings that children are to have a very high priority in the kingdom. He is not willing that any of these little ones be lost. Matthew 18:14 *"Let the children come to me",* was one of Christ's highest values. Matthew 19:14 One of the highest privileges of a Micro-Church is to help children become lovers and followers of Christ.

Children in the Micro-Church Family?

- In a fragmented and mobile culture, children need the benefit of spiritual fathers and mothers, aunts and uncles, brothers and sisters, etc. When they connect relationally at the heart, the deepest needs of affection, belonging, identity, and affirmation get met. Children love Micro-Church Families as long as they aren't done like a strict religious program.

- Children can and/or should be included in almost every part of the Micro-Church Family gathering. The meals, times of praise, checking in, sharing, personal ministry, Bible study, outreaches are all opportunities for children to experience church life. In fact, they add a great deal of fun, love, entertainment, and excitement. Children keep things real. Besides all this, children are much more capable of ministry than we might imagine. They can enter in to praying for the sick, contributing during the sharing, and expressing compassion for those who are struggling.

- There are segments of time in a Micro-Church Family gathering when it may be best for a couple adult members to take the children to another part of the house and especially focus on the children, so that the other adults can share deep struggles and confess sin. During this time, age sensitive Bible study and training can occur, or kids can minister to and pray for each other, or they can enjoy recreation, games, crafts, etc.

- Since being in a Micro-Church Family is a 24/7 lifestyle, members of the Micro-Church Family should include the children in their lives outside the gatherings. Mentoring and relationship opportunities can be woven into everyday life.

Intergenerational Micro-Church Families?

- There is a notion that youth prefer being in groups with just youth, or that singles prefer only being with singles. This is often not the case. There is a rich exchange of life that occurs when people from different generations come together in a meaningful way.

- The keys to making intergenerational Micro-Church Families work are the same for more homogenous groups – humility, transparency, and the exchange of affection. When people are valued, received, and desired, able to give and receive life, great personal advances are made in people's lives.

- Fun, adventure, authentic relationships, and experiential learning are of utmost importance to GenXer's and Millennials. For the generations to connect, the older (and often more powerful due to their positions, education and finances) must regularly defer to the younger. That means the Micro-Church Family should include lots of hanging out time, goofing off, laughter and play. All generations need to find each other if the fullness of God's purposes are to be realized.

- Each generation has been created in such a way as to accent a kingdom value. Often, these values seem paradoxical and mutually exclusive. However, they are all complimentary if we will look more deeply into what each generation values. Those born after 1965 tend to lean toward relational intimacy, toward "being" more than "doing". Is that not a kingdom value? Those born before 1965 have a tendency to lean toward "doing" and desire to make impact. They really want to build something that lasts, and produce something of worth. Leadership, management, and discipline are highly valued because they enable the successful achievement of important goals. Is that not also a kingdom value? If we take a fresh look at the situation, we will realize that we all need each other. Mutual humility and respect are essential for actualizing the fullness of Christ. Let us submit to the Christ in one another.

NOTES:

HOW TO START A MICRO-CHURCH

What are the most important steps to starting a Micro-Church Family on Mission?

Who is the point person who will initiate the starting of the Micro-Church?

Do they have what it takes to be the kind of leader who can start, grow, and multiply the small spiritual family-platoon?

Introduction: Starting a Micro-Church Family is one of the most important ministries in the Kingdom. That is because it will result in people getting saved, receive a new identity, absorb Father's love, get healed, delivered, transformed, and empowered to fulfill their destiny. This level of Kingdom advancing purpose involves spiritual warfare. So get yourself prepared, and trust in the power of Jesus Christ. Remember, everything in the Kingdom is supernatural, especially starting a new spiritual family. Christ in you can do anything!

Here are a few things to have in order:

- Know what you are building and who you are building with. Be clear about your core values, vision, culture and general strategies.
- At least one person needs to function "apostolically". This does not mean they are an apostle. It means that they are going to be the key person who takes the initiative in vision casting, recruiting, gathering, unifying, and mobilizing the small family-platoon. They need to have enough of Christ's presence, "chesed" love, relational skills, heart, vision, values, culture and strategy to help ignite and sustain the family-army.
- Gather a core group of leaders, even if it's just one other person, who can walk with you in supportive unity. Make sure they are in unity of heart and mind, and in agreement with what kind of Micro-Church God has asked you to start.
- Identify your target group or geographic focus. For example, some Micro-Churches might be formed to reach the employees of a specific company. Some might be formed in a certain neighborhood. Some Micro-Churches might be started to reach university students.
- Some Micro-Churches might start out by just focusing on evangelism.
- Have the support and backing of a local congregation or church-planting family-of-churches. Problems will arise and you will need all the prayer, encourage, and support possible.

We believe that a successful strategy has to be Biblical and simple. We have formulated it in five easy to follow steps:

Five Steps to Forming a Micro-Church

1. **Pray**. Pray fervently with God's heart for the people you are reaching out to. Pray to meet people by "divine appointments." Pray until you can weep over people. Pray fervently. Fast and pray. Walk and pray. Ask God to let you see what He sees and feel what He feels. It is in the place of prayer that God will reveal the unfulfilled purposes and broken covenants for the people you are reaching. Pray for a man or woman of peace to open the door, the hearts and minds of people you are reaching. Pray for understanding and love of the culture. Pray for the word of the Lord to guide you and give you specific strategies to make disciples, train leaders and plant a church planting movement.

2. **Meet**. Meet people where they are. Hang out with those who don't know Jesus. Get outside the Christian bubble. Resist the temptation and emotional need to focus on team issues that absorb your time and energy. As you pray, trust God to give you strategies for meeting

people. Begin to build a network of relationships, what the Bible calls an oikos (literally a household). This network is the beginning of your future church plant. This network of relationships will become the future support system for those who accept Christ if they are disenfranchised by their family and friends. Build this network in faith that it will become a church for God in that place.

Meet the "felt needs" of people. That may be done by being a friend, listening, enjoying a similar recreation, teaching English, starting a medical clinic, launching a community development project, or starting a business that employs people. Discern the felt needs of people through prayer and asking questions. Allow local leaders to be "in control" of the process of determining their needs and the best way to meet those needs. Serve the people you are called to reach. Be careful not to impose your discernment of their needs and the best way to meet those needs on people. Let them tell you their felt needs and how they would like you to help meet those needs.

3. **Make**. Make Disciples. Invest in people's lives. Don't wait for them to pray a prayer to accept Jesus or say they want to follow Jesus to invest in them as people. Disciple making is another way of describing evangelism, and of building meaningful relationships. As you build those relationships, seek to discern what God has in His heart for each person.

   Jesus commanded us to make disciples. Disciple making is about introducing people to Jesus in such a way that they get to know him personally, and then learn to love and obey him. When it's the right time, teach people the seven commands of Jesus:

   A. Repent and believe
   B. Be baptized
   C. Forgive
   D. Give
   E. Pray
   F. Gather with others
   G. Make disciples of all nations

   H. Do not hesitate to tell new believers the cost of following Jesus. Emphasize the privilege of going to other nations so God's mission is part of their spiritual DNA.

4. **Gather**. Gather those you meet who are spiritually open with other seekers for fun, hanging out, enjoying common interests, prayer, and study of God's word. Focus on the words and stories of Jesus. Don't wait for them to say they want to become a follower of Jesus to gather people into a community of friends. Gathering around a meal with others is one of the best ways to build community. Jesus said that where two or three gather in His name, He is with them. This is church in its simplest, most essential form. Nothing more is needed to be church. There is more that can be done to contribute to growing a healthy, vibrant church, see Acts 2:42-47, but gathering people together is the beginning of planting that church.

5. **Multiply**. Plan for growth. From the beginning, train new believers to take responsibility for your meetings and outreaches. Stay in the background as much as possible to encourage others to grow and exercise their spiritual gifts. As soon as you reach 15-20 people, multiply. Start a new gathering. Give those you have been investing in assignments that will help you

discern their gifting's, strengths, and weaknesses. Build the community from the beginning, just like Paul did, by facilitating the development of indigenous leadership.

Obviously, the challenges of incarnational mission are more complex than represented here. But the greatest challenge of mission is to stay simple and focused in all our efforts. Mission that results in lasting impact is mission that focuses on changed lives, one person and one community at a time. We should dream big, but we must build small. And that means perseverance, courage, sacrifice and staying on task until God's Kingdom comes and His will is done.

NOTES:

NOTES:

RAISING UP LEADERS

God wants to saturate small towns, cities, regions, and nations with multiplying Micro-Church Families on Mission. This requires a proactive game plan for identifying, equipping, and mobilizing many Micro-Church planters and leaders. How do we make disciples who are leaders? How do we raise up leaders who raise up leaders?

Introduction: The kingdom is advanced through servant leaders. As go leaders, so goes the world. Therefore, identifying and training leader's needs to be one of our highest priorities. Let's grow in our understanding of who and what makes a Christ-centered leader. Then let's be deliberate and proactive in both making disciples and raising up leaders who make leaders.

Christ-centered Leadership:

Moses said to the Lord, "May the Lord, the God of the spirits of all mankind, appoint a man over this community to go out and come in before them, one who will lead them out and bring them in, so the Lord's people will not be like sheep without a shepherd." Numbers 27:15-17

He chose David his servant and took him from the sheep pens; from tending the sheep he brought him to be the shepherd of his people Jacob, of Israel his inheritance. And David shepherded them with integrity of heart; with skillful hands he led them. Psalm 78:70-72

Jesus went through all the towns and villages, teaching in their synagogues, preaching the good news of the kingdom and healing every disease and sickness. When He saw the crowds, He had compassion on them, because they were harassed and helpless, like sheep without a shepherd. Then He said to His disciples, "The harvest is plentiful but the workers are few. Ask the Lord of the harvest, therefore, to send out workers into His harvest field." Matthew 9:35-38

Here is a trustworthy saying: If anyone sets his heart on being an overseer, he desires a noble task. 1 Timothy 3:1

And the things you have heard me say in the presence of many witnesses entrust to reliable men who will also be qualified to teach others. 2 Timothy 2:2

Importance of Leadership: To the degree we value the glory of God and the love of our heavenly Father, is the degree to which we will learn and practice excellent leadership. Harassed and helpless people have no way of deliverance without compassionate and competent leadership. (See the article under Discovery & Discipleship Tools titled "Seven Key Paradigm Shifts" which describes the current leader development crisis and the corresponding solution.)

What is Leadership?

1. A leader helps someone move from where he is now to somewhere else, somewhere he/she would not go on their own.

   "Leadership is the art of mobilizing others to want to struggle for shared aspirations." *"The Leadership Challenge" by James Kouzes & Barry Posner.* Page 30

2. Leaders build bridges: a. from here to a better place, b. from the present to the future, c. from potential to fulfillment, d. from vision to experience.

What are the consequences of no or bad leadership?

Why is there such a lack of good leaders in the family, church, market place, community, civil government?

What are the three general parts of leadership? Matthew 28:18-20; Nehemiah

1. The leader established the direction.

2. They align the people in that direction.

3. They motivate and inspire them to move in that direction and to fulfill the vision.

What are the four special elements necessary to be a great leader?

1. Calling

2. Character

3. Competence

4. Culture: the "essence of Christ's life" emitting out of the heart.

What is the Source of all elements necessary to lead? John 15:5; Galatians 1:15

- Christ – Indwelling our hearts as King/Lord.

What are the five "C's" necessary to develop holistically as a great leader?

1. Christ
2. Community
3. Character
4. Calling
5. Competence

What are the five practices of exemplary leadership? When Leaders Are At Their Best They Effectively Do Five Important Functions: *Taken from "The Leadership Challenge" by James Kouzes & Barry Posner.*

1. They Challenge the Process – Leaders are pioneers who are not afraid to venture out and attempt something different and important. They confront the status quo with new ideas, values, vision, strategies, and goals. "They're willing to take risks, to innovate and experiment in order to find new and better ways of doing things. The leader's primary contribution is in the recognition of good ideas, the support of those ideas, and the willingness to challenge the system in order to get new products, processes, services and systems adopted. They are early adopters. The key that unlocks the door to opportunity is learning." *Page 10*

2. Leaders Inspire a Shared Vision – The capacity to see and help others see an exciting, highly attractive future for their organization. "They had visions and dreams that could be. They have absolute and total personal belief in those dreams, and they are confident in their (God's grace) abilities to make extraordinary things happen. Every organization, every social movement, begins with a dream. The dream or vision is the force that invents the future." *Page 11*

3. Leaders Enable Others To Act – Grand dreams only become realities through a group effort. "Leaders enable others to act not by hoarding the power they have but by giving it away. When people have more discretion, more authority, and more information, they're much more likely to use their energies to produce extraordinary results." *Page 12*

4. Leaders Model The Way Through Personal Example and Dedicated Execution. Leaders stand up and live out their core values and beliefs. "Leaders' deed are far more important than their words and must be consistent with them." *Page 13* "Leaders need operational plans. They must steer projects along a predetermined course, measure performance, give feedback, meet budgets and schedules, and take corrective action. Yet the personal-best cases we examined included very little about grand strategic plans and massive organizational changes; they sounded more like action adventure stories. They were about the power of little things piled one on top of the other until they added up to something big. Concentrating on producing small wins, leaders build confidence that even the biggest challenges can be met. In so doing, they strengthen commitment to the long-term future. *Page 13*

5. Leaders Encourage The Heart – Climbing to the top is arduous and long, and most all people are tempted to give up. "Leaders encourage the heart of their constituents to carry on." *Page 13* "Love – of their products, their services, their constituents, their clients and customers, and their work – may be the best-kept leadership secret of all." *Page 14*

What are the five kinds of power used to influence people?

1. Coercive
2. Reward
3. Positional
4. Expert
5. Servant

What Constituents Expectations of Leaders: Fundamental Credibility

1. Being Honest – The leader must be worthy of our trust.
2. Being Forward - Looking - "We expect our leaders to have a sense of direction and a concern for the future of the organization." *Page 23*
3. Being Inspiring – "We expect our leaders to be enthusiastic, energetic, and positive about the future.
4. Being Competent – We must believe that the leader is competent to guide us where we're headed.

"We may want certain people to be cool and objective, but we want leaders to articulate the exciting possibilities. Leaders don't just report the news; they make it. Leaders who are forward-looking are biased – biased about the future. They aspire to change the way things are and guide us to a better tomorrow. But this very admirable and desirable leadership quality means that leaders often become the target of those who propose an alternative future. Thus when a leader takes a position on issues – when that leader has a clear point of view and a partisan sense of where the country, community, or company ought to be headed – that individual will be seen as less believable than someone who takes no stand. Consequently – ironic as it might seem – by the very nature of the role they play, leaders will always have their credibility questioned by those who oppose them." *Page 27* "We place leaders in an awkward position. We demand that they be credible, but we also contribute to undermining their credibility by expecting them to focus on a clear direction for the future. Leaders must learn how to balance their personal desire to achieve important ends with the constituents' need to believe that the leader has other's best interests at heart."

Leadership Attributes:

1. Relational
2. Influence.
3. Vision
4. Empowerment
5. Personal responsibility
6. Decision-making.
7. Team-Building
8. Change or managing change
9. Culture. Organizational culture is the set of shared beliefs, values, and behaviors
10. Communication
11. Motivation
12. Persuasion
13. Creativity
14. Self-management
15. Integrity
16. Credibility
17. Trust
18. Modeling
19. Servanthood

What Leaders Do:

1. See The Vision.
2. Share The Vision.
3. Shift The Vision.
4. Show The Vision.
5. Sustain The Vision.

Leaders Inspire The Heart:

1. Leaders touch a heart before they ask for a hand. You can't move people to action unless you first move them in the heart. The heart comes before the head.
2. People don't care how much you know until they know how much you care. *Dr. John Maxwell*
3. To lead yourself, use your head; to lead others, use your heart. *Dr. John Maxwell*
4. People don't follow worthy causes, people follow worthy leaders who promote worthwhile causes. *Dr. John Maxwell*

The Law of Buy-In: Leader + Vision = Results

1. People buy into the Leader, then the Vision.
2. When followers <u>don't</u> <u>like</u> the leader or the vision, they look for another leader.
3. When followers don't like the leader <u>but they</u> do like the vision, they look for another leader.
4. When followers <u>like</u> <u>the</u> <u>leader</u> but not the vision, they change vision.
5. When followers like the leader and the vision, <u>they</u> <u>will</u> get behind both.

Being Before Doing:

1. Leadership is not just something you do; it's something you are. And that's one of the reasons good leaders have such strong magnetism. People are attracted to who they are.
2. All leaders desire results, but being must precede doing. To achieve higher goals, you must be a more effective leader. To attract better people, you must be a better person yourself. To achieve greater results, you must be a person of great character. A common problem occurs when a leader's real identity and the desired results don't match up. But when leaders display consistency of character, competence, and purpose, it makes a powerful statement to the people around them - and it draws those people to them.
3. If you desire to do great things with your life, then seek to become a better person and a better leader. Nothing great can be achieved alone. Any task worth doing requires the help of others. And if you want to attract good people, you've got to become a better person yourself. If you're willing to do that, then you will achieve outstanding results. *John Maxwell*

Your Identity as a Priest, Prophet, and King:

Too long have we Christians thought that we were supposed to be self-effacing, withdrawn milk toasts; we were not supposed to assert the glory of God; we were not supposed to walk with our heads high; we were not supposed to be what we were supposed to be --- kings, reigning with Him even now, in life; masters of our passions and our appetites, masters of sin, master of satanic insidious attempts to invade our territory, beating them off with royal flourishes, not condescending to scuffle with him in the dust, but bidding him to be gone in the Name of Jesus, rising to walk with dignity as those who are kings and reign in life by One, Christ Jesus. *Ern Baxter*
1 Peter 2:9-10

LEADERSHIP DEVELOPMENT: THE KEY TO PRODUCING ETERNAL FRUIT THAT LASTS

God blessed them and said to them, 'Be fruitful and increase in number, fill the earth and subdue it. Rule over....every living creature that moves on the ground.' Genesis 1:28

You did not choose me, but I chose you and appointed you to go and bear fruit – fruit that will last. John 15:16

The Objective of Leadership Development: The overall objective of leadership development is to help emerging leaders produce the maximum amount of fruit in their natural life time.

Producing Fruit That Remains: The Bible defines fruit in at least **TWO** ways. Fruit that refers to **Being** and Fruit that refers to **Doing.**

1. First, it is the character of Christ, the quality of our being. The Bible calls this the *fruit of the Spirit* in Galatians 5:22. The fruit of the Spirit is first and foremost internal in that it involves having a.) the mind of Christ, b.) and the heart of Christ. The quality of mind and heart will determine our outward actions, such as our relationships, behaviors, and lifestyles. Mind and heart issues involve core motives, attitudes, and desires, our worldview and way of thinking. *"No good tree bears bad fruit, nor does a bad tree bear good fruit. Each tree is recognized by its own fruit. People do not pick figs from thorn bushes, or grapes from briers. The good man brings good things out of the good stored up in his heart, and the evil man brings evil things out of the evil stored up in his heart. For out of the overflow of his heart his mouth speaks."* Luke 6:43-45

2. The second kind of fruit refers to the level of influence our life has on others and the world in which we live. Influencing others into Christ and His Kingdom could be referred to in terms of what we do outwardly to make impact. This kind of fruit is the calling and work God has assigned each believer. *"I am the vine; you are the branches. If a man remains in me and I in him, he will bear much fruit; apart from me you can **DO** nothing."* John 15:5   See also: John 15:1-17; Philippians 1:22; Romans 7:4; Colossians 1:10; Ephesians 2:10, 4:16

The Quality of the First Kind of Fruit Will Determine The Quality and Quantity of the Second Kind of Fruit! We minister from who we are!

Fruit Is Father's sons and daughters brought into Christ's likeness. Fruit is offspring. God placed within each person a desire to reproduce and multiply. Abraham, our father of faith, was taken outside by God and told to look into the heavens and count the stars. God said, *"So shall your offspring be."* Genesis 15:5 Jesus promised his disciples that they would be "fishers of men". In other words, he appealed to their desire to make eternal impact by producing spiritual sons and daughters. *"For the joy set before him Jesus endured the cross."* Hebrews 12:2 That joy was the ability to bring many sons to glory! Hebrews 2:10 Every son and daughter of God needs the awesome privilege of helping to be a part of spiritual "new birth" and ongoing spiritual parenting.

The great commission in Matthew 28:16-20 is an extension and clarification of God's dominion mandate to the human race, Genesis 1-2, and God's commission and blessing to Abraham in Genesis 12-17. (See also Galatians 3:14, 26-29; 4:6-7) The same blessing and commission given to Abraham has been passed on to all those brought to sonship through Christ.

Family Is The Kingdom Context In Which We Bring Forth New Birth and Spiritual Formation Using The Five C's Through the 4-D's: God is a Father, Son, and Holy Spirit – Family of Three Persons yet One God. As a Father and Son, God must build His kingdom relationally in the context of natural and spiritual family in order to be true to Himself. The most efficient, effective, and productive way to bear fruit in a person's life is for them to be an integral part of a spiritual family. It is in this close heart-to-heart connection that the maximum level of Christ's life gets transferred.

Fruit That Remains: In Matthew 9:16-17, we read of the necessity for new wine to be poured into new wineskins. The role of the new wineskin is to preserve the wine. An old inadequate wineskin is incapable of containing and preserving the wine. One's ministry impact will only remain into eternity if it is done within God's divine order, spiritual family. Healthy spiritual family is God's wineskin.

How We Obtain Fruit: Christ comes and dwells in our hearts by faith. As he forms himself in us, His life, love, wisdom and power flows from Him, through us, and out to others. Remaining, abiding, communing, fellowshipping with Christ is the key to bearing fruit. Christ brings us to the Father, and keeps on revealing the Father to us. The Father pours out His love into our hearts through the Holy Spirit. Father's Spirit tells our spirits we are sons, and He continually fills us with His life, love, affection and affirmation.

Eternal Judgment & Reward: We will be judged and eternally rewarded according to what level of fruit we have allowed Christ to bring forth.

Bible passages which refer to eternal judgment and reward: *"Produce fruit in keeping with repentance…The ax is already at the root of the trees, and every tree that does not produce good fruit will be cut down and thrown into the fire."* Matthew 3:10 *"For the Son of Man is going to come in his Father's glory with his angels, and then he will reward each person according to what he has done."* Matthew 16:27   See also: Luke 6:20-23; Matthew 12:33-37; Romans 14:10-12; Revelation 19:11-20:15

Helping People Reach Faith Goals in the Five C's is the Surest Way to Bear Eternal Fruit That Remains:

1. Helping Christ come into a person's heart by faith as their King.
2. Helping others connect deeply in unity of mind, heart, and lives with Christ's Body/Community/Family.
3. Helping others grow into Christ's character.
4. Helping others walk out Christ's calling.
5. Helping others develop Christ's competency in their life's calling.

Developing Leaders Who Develop Leaders In The Context of Multiplying Spiritual Kingdom Families That Are Connected To An International Apostolic Tribe Is The Most Effective and Efficient Strategy To Produce Fruit (Christ-like sons of God) That Lasts!

Flow Questions:

1. What is your level of motivation to produce eternal fruit that lasts, both "Being" and "Doing" fruit? What needs to happen to increase your desire to bear fruit?

2. Why is the "Being Fruit" (fruit of the Spirit/Christ's character) the essential foundation for producing "Doing Fruit" (tangible impact in the lives of others)?

3. According to John 15, what is the key ingredient to producing both kinds of fruit?

4. What level of commitment are you willing to make in order to produce the greatest quality and quantity of lasting fruit?

5. What role does prayer, fasting, and the supernatural power of God's Spirit play in producing fruit?

NOTES:

MULTIPLYING MICRO-CHURCHES

What makes something living is that it has the ability to reproduce? Every living thing can produce after its own kind. Micro-Churches need to start with the end in mind, which includes multiplying other Micro-Churches. We will learn about several ways to do this.

Introduction: What makes something living is that it has the ability to reproduce? Every living thing can produce after its own kind. Micro-Churches need to start with the end in mind, which includes multiplying other Micro-Churches. Every multiplication is a victory if it doesn't occur as the result of broken relationships or a split. Discuss and pray for the multiplication of the small spiritual family even at its beginning. When multiplication takes place be sure to celebrate. Allow for opportunities to maintain relationships with those who are sent out to start another Micro-Church Family. This is one important reason for weekly corporate worship celebrations. The timing of each multiplication is very important. Listen carefully to the voice of God, and the counsel of other seasoned leaders. If the multiplication is premature it will cause a strain on the family members. If it is "late", it will dwarf the growth of the family and prevent new people from being reached. There is a divine and often difficult tension when it comes to multiplication. This is also true when children leave home or get married. Rhythms of life can and should unleash greater grace. God is good, even during change, growth, and multiplication. Faith, love, and compassion for the lost needs to be our internal heart attitude. How we perceive multiplication is key. Is it a win or a loss? Let's view multiplication as a healthy kingdom reality and a sign of God's blessing.

There are several strategies that can be utilized to raise up leaders and multiply a Micro-Church Family:

- **Delegate responsibilities:** Have all the family members assume various responsibilities within the Micro-Church. Appoint and train assistant Micro-Church Leader(s).

- **Equip young believers to facilitate a DNA Group.** This will give opportunities to grow as caring servants – the foundation of leadership.

- **Send out a small delegation of the family to start another Micro-Church.**

- **Send out the Micro-Church leader to start another Micro-Church and have another member of the family fill that role.**

NOTES:

NOTES:

FINANCING MICRO-CHURCH PLANTERS AND TRAINERS

What God guides He provides! Jesus had a treasury, so did the Apostle Paul who frequently gathered and redistributed funds from the churches he planted and gave apostolic oversight. We call this their "war chest". It takes finances to underwrite a family and army. While we do not love, minister, or serve in order to receive a pay check, we do need to pay bills. We believe it is divine order to start with values & vision and the call of God on our lives. In other words, we start with our vocation. The word "vocation" means "voice" and refers to the call of God upon our lives. We follow Christ and His call first. We do our vocation whether we receive finances or not. That is because we are compelled by love. God foreordained us to do good works and placed these desires in our hearts. Ephesians 2:10 We want to fulfill God's destiny for our lives. Our occupation is the way we earn income in order to fulfill our vocation. This does not make our occupation any less important in the Kingdom, for everything matters to Jesus. Occupations are wonderful settings to advance Christ's Kingdom. The Apostle Paul received the call (vocation) to be an apostle. I Corinthians 1:1, Roman 1:1 On occasion, to support himself and bring credibility to the gospel, Paul had the occupation of tentmaker. Acts 18:3 Sometimes our vocation and occupation can be the same, or we can live bi-vocationally. The Bible clearly allows for receiving financial support for full time ministry. 1 Timothy 5:17-22; 1 Corinthians 9:7-18 There will be many creative ways to finance the call of God on our lives. God has given us a clear mandate to help raise up Micro-Church Planters and those who can train and multiply Micro-Church leaders. We believe that in most cases this level of leadership needs to receive a full-time level of income in order to free up the time availability of the laborer into the harvest.

Introduction:

God is raising up Micro-Church planters and those who can train and multiply Micro-Church leaders. I believe that in most cases, this level of leadership needs to receive a "full-time" level of income in order to free up the time availability of the laborer into the harvest. There are several possible sources for financial support. I would like to recommend two: 1.) income from the tithes and offerings of the members of the Micro-Church families, 2.) financial support from partners who capture the kingdom vision and values, and want to sow into God's purpose. Jesus had financial partners and so did the apostle Paul.

In my opinion, the most biblical and effective approach to funding one's missionary mandate is to develop partners. One of the best resources explaining the "why" and practical "how to's" for developing partners are the resources developed by Rob Parker. His book is entitled "The Fully Funded Missionary" - a biblically based, hope-filled guide to raising financial support. His training manual is outstanding, "Partnership Development For The Fully Funded Missionary".

Biblical rational:

These scriptures capture the heart of why I believe God is raising up apostolic type leaders who have the grace and gifts to start and multiply Micro-Churches and can train others to do the same.

Financing Apostolic Ministry: A Commentary on 1 Corinthians 9:1-14

A critical element in the development of the micro-church movement in the United States will be a change in our financial paradigm. In traditional church, money is given by church members to pay for such things as the building, salaries for the church staff, various programs, missions, etc. The disciple-making and Micro-Church planting movement offers an opportunity to reexamine Biblical values regarding the use of money for ministry.

Probably the most important single passage dealing with this topic is 1 Corinthians 9:1-18. The following is a commentary on these verses with a view to discerning principles for financing ministry. This article would be best read with your Bible open to the passage under examination. (Note: Gordon Fee's commentary, *The First Epistle to the Corinthians*, has been particularly helpful in this study.)

9:1-2. Paul: "You are asking if I really am an apostle. I will give you a clear answer to your question."

"With unexpected vigor Paul suddenly unleashes a torrent of rhetorical questions..." *Fee, p. 394* These questions give us a clue as to the context. Some within the Corinthians church were questioning if Paul was really an apostle. His implied answer, Of course I am!

9:3-6. Paul: "I have three questions that I will ask you. Your answers will prove that I am truly an apostle."

"In a series of cascading questions Paul plays variations on a single theme: his right to their material support, most likely his failure to take support has been used against him to call his apostolic authenticity into question." *Fee, p. 398-399* Their reasoning may have gone something like this. Apostles are supported financially. You are not receiving financial support from us. Therefore, you are not an apostle." Paul responds by saying, in effect, "Let me review for you the rights of an apostle and ask you (rhetorically) if this doesn't apply to me."

Paul lists **three rights of an apostle**. The word "right" (*exousia*) carries the idea of "appropriate authority." That is, these are things that are considered appropriate for an apostle.

1. Verse 4. *"Don't we have the right to food and drink?"* (v. 4) Implied answer: "Of course we do!"

2. Verse 5. *"Don't we have the right to take along a believing wife, even as the rest of the apostles, and the brothers of the Lord, and Cephas?* Implied answer: "Of course we do!" (Here we have a revealing glimpse into the actual financial practice of the New Testament church towards apostles.)

3. Verse 6. *"Or is it only I and Barnabas who must work for a living?"* "The implication is that the problem for the Corinthians is not simply that he took no support from them, but that he supported himself in the demeaning fashion of working at a trade. What kind of activity is this for one who would be an "apostle of our Lord Jesus Christ?" Paul's point of course is that he has the right not to (work), even though he rejected it." *Fee, p. 404*

9:7-14. Paul: "In order to validate the concept of financial support for apostles beyond a shadow of a doubt, I will give you four supporting arguments. I want you to be completely convinced about this."

1. Verse 7. **Arguments from everyday life**
   - "Who at any time serves as a soldier at his own expense? "Implied answer: "No one! And neither should apostles."
   - "Who plants a vineyard, and does not eat the fruit of it? "Implied answer: "No one! And neither should apostles."
   - "Who tends a flock and does not use the milk of the flock? "Implied answer: "No one! And neither should apostles."
   - "In everyday life one expects to be sustained by one's labors. So with the apostle. He should expect to be sustained from his 'produce' or 'flock' - the church owes its existence to him." (Fee, p. 405)

2. Verses 8 - 12. **Argument from Scripture**
   - "What Christians call the Old Testament was considered the Word of God by the Jews of the NT era, so an appeal to its words is an appeal to the authority of God himself." *Fee, p. 406*
   - "...when the plowman plows and the thresher threshes, they ought to do so in the hope of sharing in the harvest; that is, they should fully expect to share in the material benefits

of their labors. Paul thus applies the analogy of the threshing ox to yet another analogy from farming, both of which together make the point that he has the right to their material support." *Fee, p. 408-409*

- Note: Verse 11 leads us to a helpful question in deciding whom we should support financially. "Who is sowing or investing spiritually into my life?"

3. Verse 13. **Argument from the example of the temple**
   - "Both in Jewish and pagan temples the priests who served in making the sacrifices shared in the sacrificial food itself." *Fee, p. 412*

4. Verse 14. **Argument from the very words of Jesus**
   - Paul clinches the argument by referring to the words of Jesus Himself. Luke 10:7, Matthew 10:10 Whereas Jesus spoke this as a proverb, Paul has raised it to the level of a command. *"This is the way things are to be done regarding the financing of apostles."*

Comments on tent making. Martin Luther once remarked that the church is like a drunken horseman. Prop him up on one side and he falls off on the other. Nowhere is this truer than with church finance. In the traditional church environment, there have been many problems with money. Perhaps the most pervasive is that the concept of salaried church staff has resulted in perpetuating the clergy/laity divide.

As a result of reacting to the abuses, many in the house church movement are in danger of "falling off the other side." (This would validate the principle articulated by Jim Rutz: "The pendulum never stops in the middle.") The thinking is that if there are no full-time workers and everyone is a tentmaker, we will be kept safe from the development of "house church clergy." While this concern is understandable, this solution is both contrary to New Testament practice and is potentially a great hindrance to the work of the Kingdom.

Tent making: the exception to New Testament practice

As we have seen in the commentary above, both Jesus and Paul taught that the laborer is worthy of his wages. This teaching was implemented by the early church through the financial support of *"the rest of the apostles, and the brothers of the Lord, and Cephas"*. 1 Corinthians 9:5

In some situations, it was necessary for the apostles to support themselves through non-ministry work (ie, tent making). However, this practice is clearly the exception and not the rule. Paul chose this means of financial support in Corinth (Acts 18:3, 1 Corinthians 9:12, 15-18) so as not to be a hindrance to that church. In other words, the Corinthians church was so immature that they were unable to fulfill their normal obligation to Paul as the apostle. 1 Corinthians 3:1-3

However, even in Corinthians Paul received at least some of his support from the church - just not the church in Corinth. *"I robbed other churches, taking wages from them to serve you; and when I was present with you and was in need, I was not a burden to anyone; for when the brethren came from Macedonia, they fully supplied my need, and in everything I kept myself from being a burden to you, and will continue to do so."* 2 Corinthians 11:8-9

In Thessalonica, Paul also chose to make an exception to the normal pattern and support himself from non-ministry work. Again, the reason was because of the immaturity of the church. In this case, the Christians were lazy and Paul realized that he needed to show them how to work. *"For you yourselves know how you ought to follow our example; because we did not act in an undisciplined manner among you, nor did we eat anyone's bread without paying for it, but with labor and hardship we kept working night and day so that we might not be a burden to any of you; not because we do not have the right to this, but in order to offer ourselves as a model for you, that you might follow our example."* 2 Thessalonians 3:7-9

The more normal and mature church is modeled by the Philippians. Even after Paul had left town, they repeatedly sent him gifts. He points out that this is not so much to his benefit (God will supply all his needs) but for their profit. Philippians 4:15 - 19

Tent making: a potential hindrance to the work of the Kingdom

While there may be occasional situations where tent making is necessary because of the immaturity of a particular church, the work of the Kingdom would be greatly restricted if this became the normal practice for apostles. This becomes clear when we understand the farmer's mentality that Jesus displays in Luke 10:1-2.

In this passage, Jesus has just sent out 36 apostolic teams of two men each. While we might think that was a lot of teams for a fairly small region, Jesus' assessment is that they are only a "few", v. 2. So few, in fact, that He urges them to *"beseech the Lord of the Harvest"* to send more.

The Lord's motivation in all of this is the harvest. The harvest is ripe! The time is now! As every farmer knows, when the harvest is ripe, every available man hour must be freed up to bring that harvest in. Those that have been chosen to be apostles (sent ones) must be released to work from sun up to sun down. The idea that the majority of the workers would work all day making tents with only an hour or two at the end of the day to harvest the grain would have been appalling to the farmer. Perhaps there will be extenuating circumstances that will require a few workers to function like this. However, reducing every apostle (church planter) to tent making status would cripple the harvest workforce. By overreacting to the abuse and going to the opposite extreme, the church would play into the strategy of the Enemy.

Adopting the farmer's mentality: IT'S ABOUT THE HARVEST! Releasing thousands of full time apostles (skilled and gifted micro-church planters) is by far the best strategy for starting a million house churches in the U.S. in this decade. This can be accomplished if millions of believers come to understand the Biblical value of funding these apostolic harvesters. Instead of investing in church buildings, church programs and church staffs, believers will need to see the value of investing in those who are called to begin and nurture micro-church planting movements. This thoroughly Biblical concept must be once again understood, taught and practiced by the church.

NOTES:

Micro-Church Families on Mission

DISCOVERY AND DISCIPLESHIP TOOLS

It is important to develop humble, secure and sensitive hearts to the Holy Spirit and others, so that we can be ever-correcting problems and always growing. Therefore, we want to develop a positive and safe culture that enables self-awareness, assessment, repentance, and constructive debriefing. In addition, there are a number of simple discipleship tools that will help us to make disciples and raise up leaders.

DISCOVERY & DISCIPLESHIP TOOLS

5 MINUTE PERSONALITY TEST

Below are ten horizontal lines with four words on each line, one in each column. In each line, put the number "4" next to the word that best describes you in that line; a "3" next to the word that describes you next best; a "2" to the next best word, and a "1" by the word that least describes you. On each horizontal line of words, you will then have one "4", one "3", one "2", and one "1".

For example: One choice for the first line of words would be as follows:

3 Likes Authority 4 Enthusiastic 2 Sensitive Feelings 1 Likes Instructions

	L	O	G	B
1.	___Takes Authority	___Enthusiastic	___Sensitive Feelings	___Likes Instructions
2.	___Takes Charge	___Takes Risks	___Loyal	___Accurate
3.	___Determined	___Visionary	___Calm, Even Keel	___Consistent
4.	___Enterprising	___Very Verbal	___Enjoys Routine	___Predictable
5.	___Competitive	___Promoter	___Dislikes Change	___Practical
6.	___Problem Solver	___Enjoys Popularity	___Gives in to Others	___Factual
7.	___Productive	___Fun-Loving	___Avoids Confrontations	___Conscientious
8.	___Bold	___Likes Variety	___Sympathetic	___Perfectionist
9.	___Decision Maker	___Spontaneous	___Nurturing	___Detail-oriented
10.	___Persistent	___Inspirational	___Peacemaker	___Analytical
	___ TOTAL "L"	___ TOTAL "O"	___ TOTAL "G"	___ TOTAL "B"

Total up the numbers for each vertical column (L, O, G, B)

What does it all mean?

Now that you've taken the survey, what does it all mean? Each letter (L, O, G, B) stands for a particular personality type. The column with the highest score is your dominant personality type, while the column with the second highest number is your sub-dominant type. While you are a combination of all four personality types, the two types with the highest scores reveal the most accurate picture of your natural inclinations, strengths and weaknesses, and how you will naturally respond in most situations.

The four personality types can be likened to animals to make them easier to understand and remember. Below are complete descriptions of each one.

L = Lions

Lions are leaders. They are usually the bosses at work...or at least they think they are! They are decisive, bottom line folks who are observers, not watchers or listeners. They love to solve problems. They are usually individualists who love to seek new adventures and opportunities.

Lions are very confident and self-reliant. In a group setting, if no one else instantly takes charge, the Lion will. Unfortunately, if they don't learn how to tone down their aggressiveness, their natural dominating traits can cause problems with others. Most entrepreneurs are strong lions, or at least have a lot of lion in them.

Natural Strengths

- Decisive
- Goal-oriented
- Achievement driven
- Gets results
- Independent
- Risk-taker
- Takes charge
- Takes initiative
- Self-starter
- Persistent
- Efficient
- Competitive
- Enjoys challenges, variety and change
- Driven to compete projects quickly and effectively

Natural Weaknesses

- Impatient
- Blunt
- Poor listener
- Impulsive
- Demanding
- May view projects more important than people
- Can be insensitive to the feelings of others
- May "run over" others who are slower to act or speak
- Fears inactivity, relaxation
- Quickly bored by routine or mechanics

Basic Disposition:	Fast-paced, task oriented
Motivated by:	Results, challenge, action, power and credit for achievement
Time Management:	Lions focus on NOW instead of distant future. They get a lot more done in a lot less them than their peers. Hate wasting time; and like to *get right* to the point.
Communication Style:	Great at initiating communications; not good at listening (one-way communicator)
Decision Making:	Impulsive; makes quick decisions with goal or end result in mind. Results focused. Needs very few facts to make a decision.
In Pressure or Tense Situations:	The lion take *command* and becomes autocratic.
Greatest Needs:	The lion needs to see results, experience variety, and face new challenges. He needs to solve problems and wants *direct* answers.
What the Lion Desires:	Freedom, authority, variety, difficult assignments, opportunity for advancement.

O = Otters

Otters are excitable, fun seeking, cheerleader types who love to talk! They're great at motivating others and need to be in an environment where they can talk and have a vote on major decisions. The otters' outgoing nature makes them great networkers—they usually know a lot of people who know a lot of people. They can be very loving and encouraging unless under pressure, when they tend to use their verbal skills to attack. They have a strong desire to be liked and enjoy being the center of attention. They are often very attentive to style, clothes, and flash. Otters are the life of any party; and most people really enjoy being around them.

Natural Strengths

- Enthusiastic
- Optimistic
- Good communicators
- Emotional & Passionate
- Motivational & Inspirational
- Outgoing
- Personal
- Dramatic
- Fun-loving

Natural Weaknesses

- Unrealistic
- Not detail-oriented
- Disorganized
- Impulsive
- Listens to feeling above logic
- Reactive
- Can be too talkative
- Excitable

Basic Disposition:	Fast-paced, people oriented
Motivated by:	Recognition and approval of others
Time Management:	Otters focus on the future and have a tendency to rush to the next exciting thing.
Communication Style:	Enthusiastic & stimulating, often one-way; but can inspire & motivate others.
Decision Making:	Intuitive and fast. Makes a lot of "right calls" and lots of wrong ones.
In Pressure or Tense Situations:	The otter ATTACKS. Can be more concerned about their popularity than about achieving tangible results
Greatest Needs:	The otter needs social activities and recognition; activities that are fun, and freedom from details.
What the Otter Desires:	Prestige, friendly relationship, opportunity to help and motivate others, and opportunities to verbally share their ideas.

G = Golden Retrievers

One word describes these people: LOYAL. They're so loyal, in fact, that they can absorb the most emotional pain and punishment in a relationship and still stay committed. They are great listeners, incredibly empathetic and warm encouragers. However, they tend to be such pleasers that they can have great difficulty being assertive in a situation or relationship when it's needed.

Natural Strengths

- Patient
- Easy-going
- Team Player
- Stable
- Empathetic
- Compassionate
- Sensitive to feelings of others
- Tremendously loyal
- Puts people above projects
- Dependable
- Reliable
- Supportive
- Agreeable

Natural Weaknesses

- Indecisive
- Over-accommodating
- May sacrifice results for the sake of harmony
- Slow to initiate
- Avoids confrontation even when needed
- Tends to hold grudges and remember hurts inflicted by others
- Fears changes

Basic Disposition:	Slow-paced, people oriented
Motivated by:	Desire for good relationships and appreciation of others
Time Management:	Golden Retrievers focus on the present and devote lots of time to helping others and building relationships
Communication Style:	Two-way communicator; great listener and provides empathetic response
Decision Making:	Makes decisions more slowly, wants input from others, and often yields to the input..
In Pressure or Tense Situations:	The Golden Retriever gives in to the opinions, ideas and wishes of others. Often too tolerant.
Greatest Needs:	The Golden Retriever needs security; gradual change and time to adjust to it; an environment free of conflict
What the Lion Desires:	Quality relationships; security; consistent known environment; a relaxed and friendly environment; freedom to work at own pace

B = Beaver

Beavers have a strong need to do things right and by the book. In fact, they are the kind of people who actually read instruction manuals. They are great at providing quality control in an office, and will provide quality control in any situation or field that demands accuracy, such as accounting, engineering, etc. Because rules, consistency and high standards are so important to beavers, they are often frustrated with others who do not share these same characteristics. Their strong need for maintaining high (and oftentimes unrealistic) standards can short-circuit their ability to express warmth in a relationship.

Natural Strengths

- Accurate
- Analytical
- Detail-Oriented
- Thoroughness
- Industrious
- Orderly
- Methodical & exhaustive
- High standards
- Intuitive
- Controlled

Natural Weaknesses

- Too hard on self
- Too critical of others
- Perfectionist
- Overly cautious
- Won't make decisions without "all" the facts
- Too picky

Basic Disposition:	Slow-paced, task oriented
Motivated by:	The desire to be right and maintain quality
Time Management:	Beavers tend to work slowly to make sure they are accurate
Communication Style:	Beavers are good listeners, communicate details and are usually diplomatic
Decision Making:	Avoids making decisions; needs lots of information before they will make a decision
In Pressure or Tense Situations:	The beaver tries to avoid pressure or tense situations. They can ignore deadlines.
Greatest Needs:	The beaver needs security, gradual change and time to adjust to it.
What the Otter Desires:	Clearly defined tasks, stability, security, low risk, and tasks that require precision and planning.

ASSESSING OUR MICRO-CHURCH FAMILY

Instructions: Please use this assessment page as a way to continually improve the quality of your Micro-Church Family (MCF). Rate each area from 0 to 10 (0 means that this is not happening at all, 1 means that if we do this at all it needs a great deal of improvement, 10 means we are doing this in an exceptional and outstanding way) We realize that your individual answers are subjective, based on your perceptions. Therefore, it is important that the entire house church use this tool as a way to invoke positive dialogue, prayer, and growth. Debriefing helps us to be self-aware and keeps us on track. Are all four directions of God's love occurring in our MCF: Down, Up, In, Out?

Our Overall Life Together:

1. Every member of our MCF understands and wholeheartedly agrees with the core values, vision, and strategy of our local church. _____
2. Each person understands and is committed to the expectations and commitments involved in being a member of our MCF.
3. Every member of our MCF participates in all aspects of our life together. _____
4. Every member of our MCF is in a DNA Group. _____
5. Every member of our MCF feels like that have been adopted as a "son" by their heavenly Father, and a wanted and loved "son" in this spiritual family. _____
6. Each member of our MCF gives and receives the delight, affection, and affirmation from Father through the other members of the family. _____
7. We connect relationally in other situations and settings during the week outside our family/house church gatherings. _____
8. We regularly enjoy each other over meals, at play, informally and "organically". _____
9. Our MCF relationships and atmosphere/culture is positive, joyful, merciful, and enjoyable. _____
10. Our MCF helps people feel free to be themselves, while at the same time always encouraging growth into Christ's likeness. _____
11. When our MCF members cannot attend, they make sure to communicate with the family/house church leaders.
12. The members of our MCF like and enjoy one another as friends both inside and outside our gatherings.
13. Our leaders function as healthy spiritual parents who are used by Father to communicate and emit His love, delight, affection, truth, wisdom, and power. They declare and demonstrate Father's heart to us consistently. _____
14. Our assistant leaders are being prepared in every way to accept responsibility for leading another spiritual family/house church.
15. Our MCF has a clear and compelling mission to reach others for Christ in our community._____
16. We glorify, love, and minister to our heavenly Father through Christ by the Holy Spirit as a lifestyle
17. Whenever we come together we all practice Biblical praise and worship such as corporately thanking and praising God, songs, hymns, spiritual songs (singing new songs inspired by the Holy Spirit). _____
18. Whenever we come together, we all exuberantly and demonstratively express our appreciation and love to God (clapping, dancing, hands raised, bowing, kneeling, shouting, etc)

19. There is a freedom in our MCF to bring glory and pleasure to God versus the fear of man, pride, self-consciousness, religious duty, and inhibitions. _____

20. We use the Word of God (like the Psalm) as our guide to help us minister to the Lord together. _____

21. We utilize musical instruments and other audio/visual aids to enhance our ministry to the Lord._____

22. We all practice the gifts of the gifts of the Holy Spirit to minister to the Lord like praying in tongues. _____

23. We have learned to "wait on the Lord" and to be "led by the Holy Spirit", so that we are sure to give God what He desires. _____

24. Every member of our MCF gives tithes (at least 10% of income) and offerings to the Lord through our local church.

God loves and ministers to us through His Spirit & Word:

25. Each person in our MCF is being trained to teach the Word of God for at least 10 minutes with discussion, question and answer time, and strategies for practical applications. _____

26. The objective Word of God is our authority for how we think, believe, feel, make decisions, and act in every area of life. _____

27. We individually and corporately practice listening to God's voice from His Holy Spirit to our human spirit(s). After we receive confirmation from the Word of God and our spiritual family, we obey God's voice as best as we can. _____

28. We practice the gifts of the Holy Spirit like prophecy, tongues with interpretation, words of knowledge, etc. _____

29. We enjoy and experience the manifest presence and glory of God when we are together. _____

30. We often have a couple of our adult family members train our children in the Word of God and kingdom lifestyle in a way that is age relevant to them. _____

We love and minister to one another:

31. Each person is viewed as both a disciple of Christ and as an emerging or actual leader. Therefore, each person regularly sets goals using the 5 C's (Christ, Community, Character, Calling, Competence) using the 4 D's (Dynamics of Transformation: spiritual, experiential, relational, instruction). _____

32. We have a culture and practice of regularly praying for each other, even doing inner healing and deliverance when necessary.

33. Our MCF "fellowships in the light" meaning that we practice sharing our inner conversations, confess our sin, and live transparently before one another and God. _____

34. Each member of our MCF is in a DNA Group for accountability, discipleship, and outreach. _____

35. Our MCF culture and atmosphere is positive, loving, safe (nonjudgmental), merciful, peaceful, open, joyful, even fun a lot of the time.

36. Our MCF freely and easily shares what is going on in their lives, relationships, hearts, work, finances, etc. _____

37. Our MCF are discovering their callings and spiritual gifts and are encouraged to practice their gifts in the safety of their spiritual family. _____

38. We celebrate the Lord's Supper (communion) on a regular basis.

We love and minister to those who don't yet know, love, and follow Christ:

39. Each member of our MCF has identified, befriended, and served someone who isn't in Christ. _____

40. We regularly pray together for those who aren't following Christ and in His kingdom. _____

41. We have set specific goals and made clear plans for doing outreach and mission to particular person, neighborhood, business, etc. _____

42. We regularly pray to the Lord of the Harvest for laborers (leaders) and for unsaved individuals.

43. Each of our MCF members has a clear sense of calling and is using their spiritual gifts and talents to reach our community for Christ. _____

BEING A DISCIPLE, MAKING A DISCIPLE

Name: _____	Matthew 28:18-20, Mark 3:13-15, Colossians
Date: _____ _____	1:27-29, Matthew 7:24-27, Romans 8:28-30
DNA Group: _____	2 Peter 1:3-11, I Corinthians 15:45-49, John 14:15 Scripture: _____

What Does It Say? (write scripture)	What Does It Mean? (My own words)	Because I Love, I Will Obey! ("I will...." Statements)
		I will....
		I will....
		I will....

Coaching Questions to Ask

CHRIST	COMMUNITY	CHARACTER	CALLING	OTHER
When did Jesus become more than a word to you?	How are you getting along with the other folks in the Discipleship Intensive?	What three things are you most thankful for?	At this point, what do you sense is your God-given purpose?	Tell me one good thing that has happened since we last spoke?
How have you experienced the love of God?	What relationships add stress to your life? What's happening?	What would you do if you knew you could not fail?	What is something you think God wants you to do?	How much of the Bible have you read? Studied?
Tell me about a spiritual turning point in your life?	What relationships are sources of strength in your life?	Which of your habits irritate you most?		How do you learn new things?
When have you felt closest to God? What was happening at that time?	How's your relationship with your spouse? Parents? Children?	What fears are you fighting?		How can I pray for you?
What areas of frustration do you feel about your relationship with God?	Are there any unresolved conflicts in your circle of relationships?	If the devil was attacking you, where would he find you most vulnerable?	What do you want to get out of this Discipleship Intensive?	What are you doing to rest or have fun?
How is your relationship with Christ right now?	When was the last time that you spent time with a good friend?	What are the most persistent negative thoughts you deal with?	What are your spiritual gifts? What spiritual gifts do you wish you had?	When did you feel closest to God this last two weeks?
How is your time with God? How do you connect?	What other kinds of relationships do you need in your life?	If you could change one thing about yourself, what would it be?	What do you most enjoy doing? And what do you do best?	Tell me about a turning point in your life
What are you reading in the Word right now?	With whom can you be totally this last week?	What is one thing you really like about yourself?	What do you daydream about?	
What is God showing you in your reading of the Word?	Who has had the most influence on your spiritual life?	How have you served others this last week?	What would you be willing to exchange your life for?	
Where is the enemy getting to you?	How are your relationships with unbelievers?	What's one challenge or fault you've overcome?	What are you consistently complimented for?	
Where or how are you experiencing the power and presence of God?	What would your spouse say about your state of mind, spirit, energy?	Where does anger crop up in your life? What seems to trigger it?	What kinds of things were you good at as a child and how did it make you feel?	

CHRIST	COMMUNITY	CHARACTER	CALLING	OTHER
Where do you find yourself resisting God these days?			What have others told you that you are good at doing?	
Are you sensing any spiritual attacks from the enemy right now?			What do you want to be able to do 3 months (6, 12) from now that you are not doing now?	
How are you practicing the spiritual disciplines?				
Which spiritual discipline most needs to be developed? Any plans?				

DIAGRAM ASPECTS OF EQ

	Recognition	Regulation
Personal Competence	**Self-Awareness**	**Self-Management**
	Self-confidence	Getting along with others
	Awareness of your emotional state	Handling conflict effectively
	Recognizing how your behavior impacts others	Clearly expressing ideas and information
	Paying attention to how others influence your emotional state	Using sensitivity to another person's feelings (empathy) to manage interactions successfully
Social Competence	**Social Awareness**	**Relationship Management**
	Picking up on the mood in the room	Getting along well with others
	Caring what others are going through	Handling conflict effectively
		Clearly expressing ideas/information
	Hearing what the other person is "really" saying	Using sensitivity to another person's feelings (empathy) to manage interactions successfully

DISCOVER YOUR SPIRITUAL GIFTS INVENTORY

I. UNDERSTANDING YOUR GIFT POTENTIAL

A. The investment of the enemy.

    1. Satan will spend years depositing insecurities, doubt, mediocrity, fear, etc. to undermine our potential of flowing in the gifts of the Spirit.

    2. He labors in vain! Continual encounters with the Father and an eager desire to be His vessel will lead us to overcoming all inhibitions. This will render Satan totally ineffective!

B. The investment of the Father.

    1. God sees us uncontaminated. He knit us together in our mother's womb. From our beginnings, He formed us to be powerful and effective. Certain gifts lay dormant and undiscovered, while others will be given by the Holy Spirit as we walk with the Lord. We must begin to see ourselves as God sees us. The Holy Spirit will reveal our true identity! (Spiritual DNA)

    Jeremiah 1:5 – Before I formed you in the womb I knew you, before you were born I set you apart;

    Psalm 139:13-14 – For you created my inmost being; you knit me together in my mother's womb. I praise you because I am fearfully and wonderfully made; your works are wonderful, I know that full well.

    Galatians 1:15 – But when God, who set me apart from birth and called me by His grace,

    2 Corinthians 4:7 – But we have this treasure in jars of clay to show that this all-surpassing power is from God and not from us.

    2. Let us tap into our investments and unleash our anointing.

II. TALENTS VS. GIFTS

A. Quibbling over the distinction between gifts and talents has little value in discovering what gifts we have. It would be odd for God, who made us, not to "build into" some of us natural talents that would later be used as gifts. On the other hand, neither should we be surprised when the Holy Spirit gives gifts to make up for a lack of natural ability.

B. For those with spiritual gifts that intersect with natural talent, there is always the temptation to minister in the power of the flesh. If this is the situation, we must be careful not to produce "Ishmael's" with the natural ability God has given us (Galatians

4:23). We must wait upon the Lord to use our natural talent with supernatural results. Natural talent, after all, won't last long. But those who have learned to trust in God and are strong in the Lord will live forever (Luke 8:18).

C. For those who are gifted in areas where they have no talent, fear of failure can paralyze the spiritual gift. But if we are obedient to the Spirit's low-risk promptings, God will confirm the gift in us with power, and our confidence in God will grow. (If pride grows as well, God will let us fall to remind us where the power comes from.) Those who excel in gifts where they have no talent bring glory to God and remind everyone just how gracious He is.

D. Do not be afraid to make mistakes when stepping out in the gifts. To be used by God we must be willing to get past our insecurities and take personal risks. It is our faith (trust, assurance) that convinces us to yield to the gifts. Great faith gets great results. Our ability to excel in the gifts is directly proportionate to our faith.

Romans 12:6 (NIV) – If a man's gift is prophesying, let him use it in proportion to his faith.

I would rather have one Peter willing to get out of the boat, than a thousand disciples allowing fear of the unknown to keep them from walking on water. With humility comes wisdom. God will not abandon us concerning the gifts, but will walk us through to maturity.

III. BODY BUILDING -- WE NEED EACH OTHER

1 Corinthians 1:4-9 (NIV) – I always thank God for you because of His grace [Greek: charis] given you in Christ Jesus. For in Him you have been enriched in every way... Therefore you do not lack any spiritual gift [charisma] as you eagerly wait for our Lord Jesus Christ to be revealed. He will keep you strong to the end, so that you will be blameless on the day of our Lord Jesus Christ. God, who has called you into fellowship with His Son Jesus Christ our Lord, is faithful.

1 Corinthians 14:12 (RSV) – ...Since you are eager for manifestations of the Spirit, strive to excel in building up the church.

1 Timothy 4:14 (NIV) – Do not neglect your gift...

IV. DESIRE THE GIFTS OF THE SPIRIT!

1 Corinthians 12:29-31 (Phi) – As we look at the body of Christ do we find all are His messengers, all are preachers, or all teachers? Do we find all wielders of spiritual power, all able to heal, all able to speak with tongues, or all able to interpret the tongues, you should set your hearts on the best spiritual gifts.

1 Corinthians 12:31 (NIV) – ...Eagerly desire the greater gifts.

V. THE GIFTS IN FULL CONCERT

A. There is nothing more chaotic than the abuse of spiritual gifts. God intends for the body to function in harmony. To accomplish this, we must pray that wisdom, love, and humility be intertwined with all our efforts to yield to the gifts.

Ephesians 2:21 (Phi) – In Himeach separate piece of building, properly fitting into its neighbor, grows together into a temple consecrated to the Lord.

Ephesians 4:16 (Phi) – For it is from the head that the whole body, as a harmonious structure knit together by the joints with which it is provided, grows by the proper functioning of the individual parts, and so builds itself up in love.

VI. THE 20 SPIRITUAL GIFTS IDENTIFIED BY PAUL – *1 Corinthians 12:1 (RSV) – Now concerning spiritual gifts, brethren, I do not want you to be uninformed.*

Romans 12:4-8	1 Corinthians 12:4-11	1 Corinthians 12:27-30	Ephesians 4:7-12
Prophecy	Prophecy	Prophecy	Prophecy
Serving			
Teaching		Teaching	Teaching
Exhortation			
Giving			
Leadership			
Compassion			
	Healing	Healing	
	Miracles	Miracles	
	Tongues	Tongues	
	Interpretation	Interpretation	
	Wisdom		
	Knowledge		
	Faith		
	Discernment		
		Apostleship	Apostleship
		Helps	
		Administration	
			Evangelism
			Pastoring

VII. SPIRITUAL GIFTS IN BRIEF

ADMINISTRATION is a gift that provides insight into other people's spiritual gifting, as well as natural talent, which puts people who want to minister in a particular way together with those who need just this ministry. These are "well connected" advisors in the body. (Septuagint uses same word in Proverbs 24:6 & 11:14.)

Additional Info: Administration is the divine enablement to understand what makes organizations or projects function and the ability to plan and execute procedures that increase effectiveness. Administration is a serving gift. Administrators should serve in humility and wisdom, always seeking to coordinate the gifts and ministries of others for the common good. Different from leadership, administration works with the details that bring the overall vision to a successful completion.

APOSTLESHIP is the ability to communicate across cultural barriers and plant churches where there is no knowledge of the gospel. It is usually accompanied with a distinct calling and a miraculous lifestyle. Apostles establish the government of God. In Greek (apostolos) "a sent one", or "a messenger", a Missionary.

Additional Info: Apostleship is the divine enablement to start a church or ministry and to have the authority to oversee its development and spiritual growth. New Christians look to apostles for leadership and wisdom. Paul and John warn of false apostles; therefore, this is considered a continuing gift needed in the church. The gift of apostleship is given to the church today for its instruction, correction, and nurture. This gift is seen most often in missionaries and church planters.

COMPASSION transcends both natural human sympathy and normal Christian concern, enabling one to sense in others a wide range of emotions and then provide a supportive ministry of caring and intercessory prayer. Also called the gift of Mercy.

Additional Info: Compassion/Mercy is the divine enablement to feel genuine empathy for individuals with problems and to transfer this compassion into deeds which reflect Christian love. Saints with a gift of mercy are usually less judgmental and give unconditional love. Paul states in Romans 12:8 that mercy is to be exercised cheerfully. They may have difficulty giving "tough love" if they become emotionally involved. It is important to seek discernment and let God do His work in people.

DISCERNMENT is the heightened ability to read or hear a teaching, to encounter a problem, or to consider a proposed course of action, and then determine whether the source behind the teaching, problem, or action is divine, merely human, or satanic. This will be a much needed gift near the End of the Age.

Additional Info: Discerning of Spirits is the divine enablement to know with assurance whether certain behavior purported to be of God is in reality divine, human, or Satanic. The gift of discernment is concerned with truth and error even if motives are pure. The operation of the gift of discernment will give approval to teaching and preaching that brings fresh truth from God. The discerning individuals work well with intercessors but need to be careful to distinguish between personal taste and true discernment.

EVANGELISM is a special ability to lead unconverted persons to a saving knowledge of Christ. The person with this gift has the wisdom to know when, who, and how to call the rebellious into the Kingdom of God. Evangelists are the spiritual "obstetricians" in the church.

Additional Info: Evangelism is the divine enablement to effectively communicate the message of Christ to unbelievers that they respond in faith. The word evangelism stems from a Greek root meaning "to proclaim the good news". All Christians are called to be Christ's witnesses, but the gift of evangelism is given to some to endow them with an unusual capacity to lead others into a saving relationship with Jesus. Evangelism may take the form of public speaking or one to one witnessing. Saints with this gift need to be careful to respect other areas of ministry.

EXHORTATION is the gift of being able to encourage others by well-timed and wise counsel. This gift builds the Body of Christ by helping new, young and adolescent disciples to turn from sin and believe in the power of the Holy Spirit. Also called the gift of Counseling, or the gift of Encouragement.

Additional Info: Exhortation, or Encouragement, is the divine enablement to reassure, strengthen, and affirm those who are discouraged or wavering in their faith. This gift enables one to help others to develop ways of growing spiritually. This gift is usually exercised in private conversation although it may be sometimes exercised publicly. Those exercising this gift need to be watchful for feelings of superiority or the desire to dominate. It will be important to respect the dignity and integrity of others even when they are discouraged.

FAITH as a gift is an extraordinary confidence in God that is unshakable by situations, pain, apparent failure, or ridicule. This gift strengthens the individual and other believers (by example) to endure persecution and wait upon the Lord.

Additional Info: Faith is the divine enablement to trust God's will and act on it with belief in God's ability and faithfulness. The Christian who possesses this gift of the Spirit has a supernatural conviction that God will reveal His power in response to the prayer of faith. The gift of faith takes Biblical principles, and under the inspiration of the Holy Spirit, applies them to the current situation. The common way this gift is exercised is through prayer. This saint with this gift should be careful never to put down others for a lack of faith.

GIVING empowers one in a sensitive way to detect material or financial needs and meet those needs with Spirit inspired generosity. Recipients of help from Christians with this gift have a clear sense that God has provided, not man.

Additional Info: Giving is the divine enablement to contribute material resources to the work of the Lord with liberality and a cheerful heart. The gift of giving empowers one to understand the material needs of others and to meet those needs generously. Often the one possessing this gift will discover that his giving harmonizes with the prayers of those needing help. This gift requires wisdom for there is Godly timing involved, a time not to give, ways to give, and what to give. Those with a gift of giving typically give much more than a normal tithe.

HEALING is a "sign gift" which enables one to function as an instrument of God's healing grace in the lives of hurting people. The gifts of healings (double plural in the Greek text) include miraculous healing of the body, the mind, the emotions, and relationships.

Additional Info: Healing is the divine enablement to be God's agent or human intermediary through whom God will restore health. In scripture, we are encouraged to place faith in Christ's ability to heal. This gift applies to all healing God chooses to perform...physical, emotional, and inner healing. Some look upon this gift as a specialized part of the gift of miracles, although scripture lists them separately. The function of this gift doesn't do away with God's healing through natural means such as diet, rest, doctors, or medicine. The saint with this gift should place his faith in God's power and leave the results to Him. Pride and self-deception are things to guard against.

HELPS enables one to assist people in routine ways that are supernaturally enhanced by the anointing of the Holy Spirit. The helped person has the impression that they have been touched by God. Those with this gift should be highly esteemed in the Body.

Additional Info: Helps is the divine enablement to attach spiritual value to the accomplishment of practical and necessary tasks which support the body of Christ. In Acts the Christian community chose Spirit-filled laymen with wisdom to serve the temporal needs. The gift of helps/service usually leads one to supply temporal services to the Christian community. Helps and service lead to a kind of ministry to others that relieves them of burdens and enables them to better serve. People with this gift have a difficult time saying "no" and can get burned out if they are not careful.

KNOWLEDGE is an ability to remember Scripture or have it supernaturally quickened, or to know a fact or truth about a person or situation revealed directly by the Holy Spirit.

Additional Info: Knowledge is the divine enablement to accumulate and analyze information effectively. This gift is needed to effectively mediate the grace of God to human need. Many in the body who have this gift are at home with research and sometimes have a low need for people, depending upon the other gifts they have. This gift is often mixed with the gift of teaching. The Greek term is two words translated "word of knowledge" or "the ability to speak with knowledge." This gifting also needs to guard against pride.

LEADERSHIP in the Greek is actually "he who provides leadership in giving aid". These go first and lead by example, so that others are motivated to follow. (1 Corinthians 11:1) Those with the gift of leadership are quick to identify problems and show by doing how to minister to those in need.

Additional Info: Leadership is the divine enablement to instill vision, to motivate, and to direct people to accomplish the work of ministry. A leader usually sees the big picture. They are motivators and are usually outspoken and make wise plans. An active strong leader may have difficulty delegating. A Godly leader will listen for God's directions and listen to others. They need to guard against manipulating others to get what they want.

MIRACLES is another "sign gift" where the gifted person is able to cast out demons, show a supernatural sign to unbelievers, or perform a public healing-- all to the glory of God. Those with this gift will be humble, broken people, full of the fear of God.

Additional Info: Miracles is the divine enablement to be God's agent to perform powerful acts which are perceived to have altered the laws of nature. Miracles were used in the New Testament to draw people to God or sometimes to simply meet human need (Acts 19:11). In America people are turning to an interest in the supernatural. Many have pulled away from this gifting because of its abuse, but this is still a powerful gift to touch people for Jesus. In Mark 16:20, miracles were to confirm the word with signs following. The church needs this gifting in this generation.

PASTORING is the ability to "shepherd" an individual or community of Christian believers. This gift is a special empowering to lead people into green pastures, steer others away from danger, fight off predators, and bind up wounds. Those with this gift have "big shoulders" spiritually, and are not afraid to jump into people's problems.

Additional Info: Pastoring is the divine enablement to lead, care for, and nurture individuals/groups in the body of Christ as they grow in faith. The gift of shepherding is not limited to clergyman; some saints who possess the gift of shepherding perform the vital ministry by feeding and guarding others in Christian discipleship. In John 10:1-18, Jesus says that the shepherd sacrifices for his sheep; he goes before them and he protects them. Saints with this gift like people and gain satisfaction in helping encourage people to mature. A Godly shepherd will desire to help people grow and not make them dependent upon the shepherd.

PROPHECY is speaking what God wants said with clarity, creativity, and power. It is also called the gift of Preaching. The primary ministry in this gift is not prediction, but in confronting people with the truth about God and man -- with conviction and repentance as the result.

Additional Info: Prophecy is the divine enabling to proclaim God's truth with power and clarity in a timely and culturally sensitive fashion for correction, repentance, or edification. This is a divinely anointed utterance from God given as an immediate message to certain members of the body or the whole body. Some characteristics of many who exercise this gift are independence, boldness, bluntness, openness to truth, sober, and little mercy. This isn't an easy gift to exercise due to the fact that the response is often unsympathetic to the message. If you receive this gift, be careful about the following traits: lack of sympathy and sensitivity, pride, judgmentalism, and discouragement. Christian prophecy will be orderly, positive, and edifying to the church. Prophecy will bring inspiration but never new revelation.

SERVING is a gift which expresses the love of Christ by taking care of lowly or time-consuming tasks to allow others to be more effective ministers. Those with this gift seek no recognition, but will be exalted by God Himself at the End of the Age.

Additional Info: Service is the divine enablement to attach spiritual value to the accomplishment of practical and necessary tasks which support the body of Christ. In Acts the Christian community chose Spirit-filled laymen with wisdom to serve the temporal needs. The gift of helps/service usually leads one to supply temporal services to the Christian community. Helps and service lead to a kind of ministry to others that relieves them of burdens and enables them to better serve. People with this gift have a difficult time saying "no" and can get burned out if they are not careful.

TEACHING is the ability to understand and communicate the Christian faith so as to make the truth clear to others. The result of this gift is the equipping and maturing of others in the body of Christ so that they will grow in grace and be more effective disciples.

Additional Info: The gift of teaching equips one to impart truth to others in a relevant way so that the gospel can be understood and applied to life. Teachers bring clarity and unity. Through them, we receive help, edification, truth, and life. They exhibit good communication skills, are usually organized, and are good listeners. Some have an inward struggle with the desire to study in lieu of prayer and relationships. Guard against being rigid, impatient, more interested in facts than people, and being too detailed. A good teacher (even in lifestyle) is learner-oriented as well as content-oriented.

TONGUES enable some Christians (1 Corinthians 12:30) to praise God either in another language not learned (Acts 2) or in ecstatic utterance which is not an earthly language (1 Corinthians 14). In either case, one's prayer is directed to God, not to other people (1 Corinthians 14:2). This is separate from one's personal prayer language as it relates to the baptism of the Holy Spirit.

INTERPRETATION OF TONGUES is required if speaking in tongues is exercised publicly in a loud voice. This gift allows one to declare to others the intent or meaning of the public ecstatic utterance, so that the entire Body is built up.

WISDOM is special illumination that enables one in a specific instance to grasp divine insight regarding a fact, situation, or context. This gift is useful in directing the Body in what to do next; in making God's will known.

Additional Info: The divine enablement to apply knowledge effectively. The saint with this gifting is given the ability to discern a situation and share the wisdom of God for clarification and encouragement. All Christians may receive wisdom when in need of it, but when the gift of wisdom is operating, wisdom is given for a specific issue in a relevant fashion. A gift of wisdom often helps discern the root of the problem. All wisdom given is for God's glory.

Spiritual Gifts Inventory – Questions

(Read all instructions on the answer sheet following the questions before beginning)

1. I feel empowered to stand alone for Christ in a hostile, unbelieving environment.

2. Often I have a burning desire to speak God's word when I know it will not be well received.

3. I seem to have insight on when people are ready to give their lives to Christ.

4. I have a heart to help Christians who have lost their way.

5. I love to meditate on the patterns of God and His ways, and speak to others of such things.

6. I enjoy serving others so that they, in turn, may perform their ministries.

7. I can identify with weakness and temptation so as to encourage people to repent and believe.

8. I give to others in such a way that they won't feel as if they owe me anything.

9. Other Christians have imitated me when I have led the way in serving the needs of others.

10. I often am overcome with emotion for the person I am praying for.

11. God sometimes prompts me to pray for the total healing of others in body, mind, and emotions.

12. I find it easy to believe that God can miraculously alter circumstances if we pray.

13. I often speak in tongues.

14. I have interpreted tongues so as to help others worship God without confusion.

15. Sometimes God gives me an insight into the proper course of action others should take.

16. God often quickens Scripture to my mind that is useful for the moment.

17. I have an extraordinary confidence in God and an ability to embolden others.

18. I usually detect spiritual truth from spiritual error before fellow-believers.

19. The Spirit often leads me to do a simple thing for someone that touches them deeply.

20. I can serve others by organizing and harnessing their gifts to solve a particular problem.

21. I often think that God is calling me to be a missionary.

22. My words often bring conviction to others, leading to repentance.

23. I find it easy to ask people to believe in and commit to Christ

24. I tend to be patient with Christians who are making slow spiritual progress.

25. I think it is very important to use words accurately and in context.

26. I believe my ministry in life is to be humbled before men by being obedient in service.

27. I have a special gift of helping others get "reset" emotionally, mentally, and spiritually.

28. I believe God has given me the ability to make and share money.

29. I am willing to "go first" when it comes to meeting the needs of others.

30. I believe that God wants to reach out to people by using me to share in their suffering.

31. I am irritated when the physical pain of others is overlooked or ignored.

32. I believe God wishes to use me to publicly cast out demons.

33. Praying in tongues has been meaningful to me in my personal prayer life.

34. When others have prayed in tongues, I felt that I understood the meaning of their prayer.

35. Other Christians seek my advice when they are uncertain of their direction.

36. God has made me aware of a deep need in someone that they were careful to hide.

37. I am not moved from my personal belief in the truth by ridicule, apparent failure, or pain.

38. God has often used me to encourage others to accept difficult, but Biblical teaching.

39. People often try to give me glory for helping them, which I am able to direct to God.

40. I can recognize talents and gifts in others, and find ways of using these for God.

41. I desire to learn another language, culture, or religion so that I could be a better witness.

42. Ridicule or rejection for speaking forth the truth, by family or friends, does not affect me.

43. I tend to conclude my vocal witness with an appeal for others to become Christians.

44. God has shown me sources of sound teaching and rich fellowship, and I guide people to such.

45. I get troubled by "testimonies" which contain false teaching or unsound advice.

46. I often recognize ways that I can minister to others indirectly without speaking or teaching.

47. I can challenge others without making them feel condemned.

48. I have strongly sensed the Spirit leading me to give money to a specific person or cause.

49. Obeying Christ *now* is my passion in life. It is not about mere words, but deeds.

50. Sometimes God gives me a taste of other people's pain.

1 Corinthians 12:4 (KJV) – Now there are diversities of gifts, but the same Spirit.

51. Often I have a strong sense that God wants to heal someone through my prayers or words.

52. I believe God will use me to speak forth a miracle when the situation looks most hopeless.

53. I often feel compelled to speak forth aloud in tongues in a public meeting.

54. I feel that God wishes to use me to build the fellowship with the interpretation of tongues.

55. God uses me to dispel confusion about God's will with supernatural insight.

56. I often find I know things that I have never learned, which are confirmed by mature believers.

57. I am totally convinced God will fulfill His word even if He is not doing so yet.

58. I often sense when people are moved by the Holy Spirit, evil spirits, or by their own flesh.

59. In the church, I gravitate to undone work, even if unpopular.

60. People often look to me for guidance in coordination, organization, and ministry opportunities.

61. Strange customs, cultures, and unusual behavior don't offend me or my faith.

62. I love to find creative ways to confront people with the truth of God.

63. I minister better to the spiritually "unborn" than baby, adolescent, or mature believers.

64. God has shown fruit in my life in the effective discipling of other believers.

65. I love to learn Biblical principles from my studies and then share them with others.

66. I don't mind helping others, even if they are undeserving or do not express appreciation for my help.

67. People will take correction from me because I make it clear that I am on their side.

68. I strive to seek ways to give to others without calling attention to myself.

69. God has given me an ability to "rally the troops" in giving aid to others.

70. Sometimes I feel so much love for others that I am at a loss for words.

71. Through prayer, God sometimes helps me to impart physical healing to others.

72. I believe that if we trusted God more, we would see dramatic, public miracles.

73. I never publicly speak forth in tongues unless I strongly believe it will be interpreted.

74. When I hear others speak in tongues, I am compelled to explain the meaning.

75. My advice to others has led them into mature Christian living.

76. God has given me words to say in witnessing situations that surprised even me.

77. I seem to be less "shakable" than most Christians.

78. I sometimes get the sense that what I am reading or hearing is divinely inspired.

79. God often supernaturally enhances my service to others.

80. I have a knack for, and enjoy, helping people in the Body of Christ work together toward a common goal.

81. I feel God might use me to bring the gospel to people who have never heard.

82. I am more interested in saying the right thing than making people feel good.

83. I'm troubled when salvation is not emphasized.

84. I feel that I am responsible to help protect weak Christians from dangerous influences.

85. I reflect on my own life experiences so I can help others grow and assist with their own expectations.

86. I would rather work in secret than have my work recognized publicly.

87. The Spirit gives me the ability to call forth the best that is in others.

88. Everything I own is Christ's, and I make this clear to others I encounter.

89. I can motivate others to obey Christ by the living testimony of my life.

90. I have a desire to visit prisons and rest-homes in order to minister comfort and hope.

91. When I pray for someone's healing, I check to see if it really happened and continue to pray until it does.

92. The Holy Spirit leads me to pray for impossible things that really come true.

93. I usually know when a message in tongues is about to be given, even if I'm not the one who speaks it forth.

94. My interpretations of tongues are confirmed by mature believers.

95. God uses me to bring clarity to other believers when they are uncertain what to do.

96. I often know about a real problem another person is hiding through a layer of deception.

97. My hope in God, against all odds, is inspiring to others.

98. God has used me to warn others of the danger of a certain teaching.

99. I cannot stand idly by while things go undone.

100. People come to me when they need help in desperate situations, and I know people who can help.

1 Corinthians 12:31 – Be ambitious for the higher gifts.

Questions 101-120 are a self-rating of true God-placed desire to exercise a particular gift in your own life. These desires (or *dreams*) must not contain any "vain imaginings" that allow self to come before God. Any fantasies of self-glory must be repented of before the gift will be actuated by the Holy Spirit because God will not share His glory. We should use our imaginations to think about *how to give God the glory* if/when the Holy Spirit gives us an increased measure of a particular gift. In any case, dreams and desires can be useful clues to the reality of a latent gift. Rate your relative agreement from 0 to 5.

101. I dream of being a missionary to some group of people who have never heard the gospel.

102. I dream of God speaking through me in a powerful way.

103. I dream of winning many souls to Christ.

104. I dream of discipling others by serving them as Pastor.

105. I dream of teaching God's Word so as to help others in the way of faith.

106. I dream that I will experience the presence of God by serving others.

107. I dream of speaking words of hope that God will confirm in others by the Holy Spirit.

108. I dream of being used of God to meet someone's financial or material need.

109. I dream of being first to lead the way in finding new ways to minister to others.

110. I dream that God will use my emotions to feel His feelings for others.

111. I dream of being used by God to radically heal hurting people.

112. I dream that God will use me to perform awesome miracles.

113. I dream of speaking to the body of Christ through messages of tongues.

114. I dream of publicly interpret tongues so that the Body may be edified.

115. I dream of being used of God to help people know what God's will is.

116. I dream that God will give me the knowledge needed to help at just the right moment.

117. I dream that I will be stronger than others when persecution comes.

118. I dream that I could help those who are confused about teachings, spirits, and events.

119. I dream that God would anoint my every move as I give help to others.

120. I dream of coordinating the gifts of others so that they will be at their best in Christ.

What gifts are lacking among the believer's you know? You may be surprised at how differently people perceive these needs. This can be a useful clue as to what problems God *wants you to solve* by allowing the Holy Spirit to give you grace. What requirement has God put on your heart to meet? On questions 121-140, rate from 0 to 5 the relative intensity of need in the Body of Christ *from your perspective*.

121. We need more people to take what we have and go out as missionaries.

122. We need more prophets in the Church to preach against sin and of the coming judgment.

123. We aren't spending enough time trying to win souls to Christ.

124. We need more people who are willing to take care of the spiritually newborn and young.

125. We need more, and better teaching.

126. We lack people willing to serve the brethren and outsiders.

127. We need more exhortation and encouragement to do the right things.

128. We have un-met, real financial or material needs among us.

129. We need someone to take the first step in starting a new initiative to help others.

130. We lack compassion for the hurts, pains, and struggles of people.

131. We need more believers with the true gift of healing in the Church.

132. We, or unbelievers, need to see a miracle.

133. We need more speaking in tongues to build up the individual believers.

134. We need interpretation so that we can be obedient to Scripture concerning public tongues.

135. We need wisdom from above to know what God would have us do next.

136. We need the gift of divine knowledge to make up for man's deficiencies.

137. We need more examples of faith that have stood the test of adversity.

138. We lack discernment in identifying unclean spirits, the flesh, and false teaching.

139. We need to stop talking and start really helping people in practical ways.

140. We need someone to direct the spiritual gifts of our group more effectively.

Gifts Inventory Results for *(Name):* _____

For this test to be valid, please do not respond on the basis of what you think you ought to say, but rather on the basis of your interest and experience. Do not let modesty hinder you from answering honestly. Fold back the gifts key below along the dotted line before answering the questions. Answers are scored on a scale of 0-5.

0 The statement is not relevant to my experience, or not true of me

1-Not quite zero, but close   2-Only a slight response

3-Medium or moderate response   4-Greater than average response

5-Strong agreement with statement

					I DREAM OF	WE NEED	SPIRITUAL GIFTS	TOTALS
1	21	41	61	81	101	121	A	
2	22	42	62	82	102	122	B	
3	23	43	63	83	103	123	C	
4	24	44	64	84	104	124	D	
5	25	45	65	85	105	125	E	
6	26	46	66	86	106	126	F	
7	27	47	67	87	107	127	G	
8	28	48	68	88	108	128	H	
9	29	49	69	89	109	129	I	
10	30	50	70	90	110	130	J	
11	31	51	71	91	111	131	K	
12	32	52	72	92	112	132	L	
13	33	53	73	93	113	133	M	
14	34	54	74	94	114	134	N	
15	35	55	75	95	115	135	O	
16	36	56	76	96	116	136	P	
17	37	57	77	97	117	137	Q	
18	38	58	78	98	118	138	R	
19	39	59	79	99	119	139	S	
20	40	60	80	100	120	140	T	

After responding to all statements, expose the key and write each gift next to the appropriate letter above.

Next, add the scores in each horizontal line and place the total in the far right column. Since some people tend to respond more conservatively than others, the important thing is the relative scores. Highlight the *five highest gifts*, taking note of the highest value. Fill out the Ministry Gifts Information sheet provided and turn in to your facilitator.

Romans 12:6 (NEB) – The gifts we possess differ as they are allotted to us by God's grace [charis], and must be exercised accordingly.

1 Peter 4:10 (TEB) – Each one, as a good manager of God's different gifts, must use for the good of others the special gift he has received from God.

2 Timothy 1:6 (NIV) – For this reason I remind you to fan into flame the gift of God...

Luke 19:12-27 – (Read from the NIV the parable of the talents.)

The gift definitions and questions in the Spiritual Gifts Inventory are based in part on K. C. Kinghorn's *Discovering your Spiritual Gifts,* A. Jordan's *Spiritual Gift's Outline,* integrated with our expanded studies on each gift. The gift table and test format are derived from Kinghorn's *Gifts of the Spirit.*

-     **(Fold Paper Back Here)** -

A = Apostleship, **B** = Prophecy, **C** = Evangelism, **D** = Pastoring, **E** = Teaching, **F** = Serving, **G** = Exhortation, **H** = Giving, **I** = Leadership, **J** = Compassion, **K** = Healing, **L** = Miracles, **M** = Tongues, **N** = Interpretation, **O** = Wisdom, **P** = Knowledge, **Q** = Faith, **R** = Discernment, **S** = Helps, **T** = Administration

EMOTIONAL INTELLIGENCE DIAGRAM

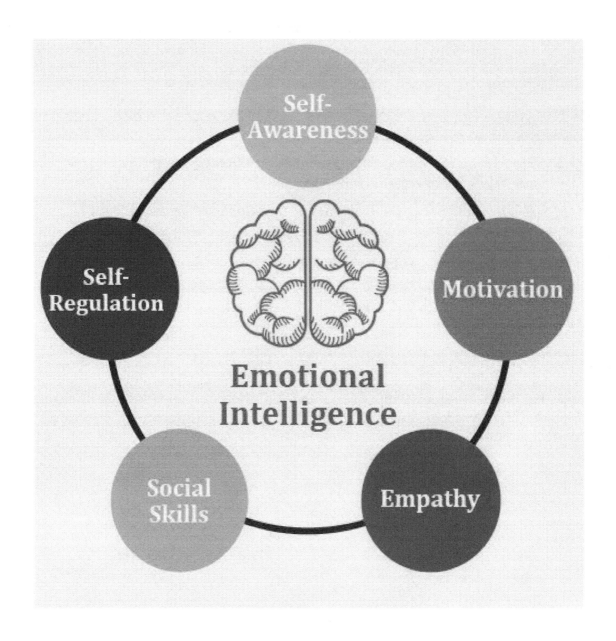

FAITH GOALS – 5-C'S WITH 4-DYNAMICS OF TRANSFORMATION

Leadership Development Using 5 'C' Goals through 4 Dynamics of Transformation

Dynamics ▶ Goals ▼	Instructional	Relational	Experiential	Spiritual
Christ				
Community				
Character				
Calling				
Competence				

Micro-Church Families on Mission

If we are to build the whole person, our leader development design must strongly be:

•Spiritual. We must bring our emerging leaders face-to-face with God through prayer, fasting, meditation in the Word of God, forgiveness, reflection and encounters with the Holy Spirit.

•Relational. Healthy leaders are built in a context of genuine relationships with other people who are their mentors, coaches, role models, leaders, teachers, friends, and spiritual mothers and fathers.

•Experiential. Leader development is a hands-on experience. People learn by doing, especially when they are challenged. Pressure is also essential in the formation of a leader.

•Instructional. The teaching of the Word of God must be practical, relevant and engaging.

To build healthy leaders, all Four Dynamics of Transformation must be strongly present; none can be neglected, all have the highest priority. This is the true challenge of Christian leader development — to design and cultivate transformational cultures of leader development.

Praying the 5C's

CHRIST

1. Father, Your Word says that the greatest commandment is to love You with all our heart, mind, soul and strength. Let this fullness of love and commitment to You be present in _____'s life. Convict him/her when thoughts or actions contradict this priority. Help him/her to get rid of any heart affection that would take him/her further from You.

2. Jesus is the author of eternal salvation for all who believe. Let _____ have strong trust in the effectiveness of the death and resurrection of Jesus Christ and reject every other means including good works as a foundation for redemption.

3. Father, may _____ express his/her trust in You daily for provision of everything he/she needs, knowing that You are faithful to care for him/her. Let his/her attitudes, words and actions reflect a deep faith in Jesus Christ in every practical life issue.

4. Father, let the power of the Holy Spirit be upon _____'s life today. Help him/her to seek the leading and empowering of the Holy Spirit for every decision and action.

5. Father, let the love of Jesus Christ flow like a fountain in _____'s that overflows in witness to others. Let him/her be bold share Jesus with others and with genuineness and sensitivity.

6. Lord, our lives in You are built up as we devote ourselves to the things that feed our life in You. Please help _____ to build consistency in his/her prayer life. Let him/her maintain a heart of praise and find ways to praise You in every situation. Let him/her be committed to giving, and regular times of fasting, solitude, spiritual rest. Please help him/her do this out of a heart to know You and not as a way to earn Your approval or the approval of men.

7. Father, Jesus told us to seek first the Kingdom of God. Help _____ to understand what this means in his/her daily life and future plans. Please give grace to _____ to put Christ and His kingdom above every personal ambition. Let him/her submit every decision, action, relationship, and motivation of heart to the authority of the Lord Jesus.

8. Just as Jesus took up His Cross, let _____ be deliberate in taking up his/her cross daily. Let him/her live the new life in Christ and count the old ways of sin and flesh dead. Please give him/her the grace and wisdom to see the opportunities to die to self as the pathway to greater identification and fellowship with the Lord Jesus Christ.

9. Father, Jesus said that when we obey You, You make Your abode with us and manifest Yourself to us. Please let _____ experience Your indwelling presence a reality and not just a theological truth. Let him/her daily experience fellowship with the Lord Jesus by the Holy Spirit. Let him/her learn to be sensitive to the Spirit's voice affirming his/her identity as a child of God.

10. Father, Your unconditional love is what we crave so desperately. Please reveal the depth of Your love to _____ and let him/her know that nothing can separate him/her from Your love.

Whatever _____'s background was please cause him/her to develop a deep security in Your unfailing love.

11. _____ is a soldier in Your army. Let him/her submit to You and resist every attempt of the enemy to ensnare him/her or stop Your work in his/her life. Cause her to know Your voice and recognize and reject the lies of the enemy.

12. Father, please give _____ eternal perspective. Let him/her keep his/her sights on things of eternal value especially in times of suffering. Let the rewards of eternity be motivation for him/her to endure to the end.

13. Father, You made us for relationship with You. Please lead _____ into deep and life-changing experiences of You in prayer and daily abiding. Don't let him/her be content with doctrinal knowledge only, but give him/her passion and faith to expect You to reveal Yourself in powerful manifestations.

14. You desire to communicate with Your people. Help _____ to overcome every obstacle to a consistent daily prayer time. Protect _____ from the sense of condemnation and discouragement that comes up in the battle to be consistent.

15. Father, please draw _____ to Yourself in times of difficulty and suffering. Let him/her draw strength from You and not turn away to self-reliance or self-pity. Let the fires of adversity teach _____ to look to Your Word and trust You always.

16. Let Your Word be _____'s delight and constant meditation. Cause him/her to go beyond reading for knowledge for sermon ideas, but let the Word of life water his/her spirit and reveal Jesus. Let every false religious idea be washed away by truth.

17. Father, hear _____ as s/he makes his/her prayer to You. You are the God who hears and answers so that our joy can be full and that the Name of Jesus can be glorified. Teach him/her to pray the prayers You love to answer.

18. Father, You are a jealous God and You deserve one hundred percent from Your people. Please expose every connection to the occult and every idol of the heart so that _____ can repent and be free. By Your Spirit, empower _____ to love You with his/her whole heart, soul, mind and strength.

COMMUNITY

1. I pray that _____ will be merciful, kind, patient, that he/she doesn't boast, isn't proud and isn't easily angered according to the description of love in 1 Corinthians 13. I pray that he/she keeps no record of wrong and learns to listen well. In dealing with the church let him/her not quarrel but be kind and able to teach. When dealing with others outside the church let _____ bless and show mercy.

2. I pray that _____ keeps malicious gossip away from family and home. May he/she not let any unwholesome talk come out of his/her mouth but only what is helpful for building others

up. Don't let bitterness, rage, anger, brawling, and slander, along with every form of malice come into his/her life in dealing with others.

3. May _____ be teachable, listening to complaints and ideas from home and church when they respectfully appeal. Help him/her not to show self-pity but respond positively to healthy correction without blame-shifting. Help him/her keep in mind that there are blind spots in his/her spiritual vision that he/she can't see with out others' help. Let him also be humble toward others outside the church, forgiving them and praying for them.

4. Work with _____ to have his priorities in order as husband/wife first and father/mother next and leader third. May _____ 's example help train the body on healthy balance of family and calling as a church leader. Give him/her favor to encourage all team members to have a balanced healthy family. Make his family a big witness of God's blessing to the world to the glory of God.

5. Use _____ as the leader of his home to teach his family how to set money aside for the Lord and be an example for his children. May he/she teach the body to give. Let him/her show from Jesus' words that is more blessed to give than to receive, correcting errors and misconceptions about giving and getting. May he/she bring a balance to the body about the stewardship of money. Let him/her be an example of integrity to other leaders.

6. Help _____ to forgive people when they have wronged him/her. Help him/her not to take revenge, but to bless and not curse. Let _____ not be overcome with evil but overcome evil with good. Let the peace of Christ rule in his/her heart since as members of one body we were called to peace.

7. Lord, let _____ show no partiality or exclusiveness. May he/she be completely humble and gentle and be patient bearing with others in love and making every effort to keep peace. May he/she be willing to associate with the members of that may be looked upon as less popular. Let him/her help those who are new believers or weak in the faith.

8. May _____ do nothing out of selfish-ambition or in competition with other leaders, but let him/her in humility consider others better than him/herself. May he/she not look only to his/her own interests but also to the interests of others, and promote peace.

9. I pray that _____ with his/her would be willing to graciously share feedback and ideas about vision with those in appropriate authority and ultimately submits to them whether or not he/she agrees.

10. Father, as Your word says that others will know we are Your disciples by our love for one another, I pray _____ will show Your heart through their words and deeds to those around them—glorifying You by putting others first and extending Your grace, mercy and forgiveness.

11. With a heart of a shepherd—Father I ask that _____ would be able to discern error. Let him/her in a spirit of meekness boldly bring forth Your words of guiding truth, enabling others to take heed and be set free from the snares of lies and deceptions.

12. I ask Father that _____ would be given insight and wisdom in looking after his/her household. Let _____ nurture and instruct those You have placed in their care. Let their home be recognized by others as a place where You dwell by the Spirit.

13. Father I pray that _____ would contend earnestly for the truth. Let him/her place You and Your word first in all matters and stand for purity and holiness. Let him/her be one who walks uprightly and steadfast, yet is apt to serve and teach others. Let him/her not serve for his/her own gain but for Your glory and the building of Your church.

14. Father Your word teaches us that we must bridle our tongues and that we should edify and encourage each other that we speak no guile. I pray that _____'s words will be seasoned with grace and truth and You would use them to encourage and edify those that cross their path.

15. Lord, I ask that _____'s house be filled with Your Spirit and that _____ will guide and rule over the affairs of the house well. Father we know that our leaders are to watch over the flock with a shepherd's heart of love and not as a hireling looking for personal gain. I ask You, Father to impart Your wisdom and character into _____ that he/she would look upon those in their house and others whom they minister to as Your sheep and keep a diligent watchful eye for their well being. Let _____ be able to say as Jesus did— "I have kept those the Father has given me."

16. Father, enlarge the borders of _____'s heart let him/her take pity upon the poor and needy. Open his/her eyes to see Your glory in all mankind as they are all created in Your Image. Give him/her the desire and ability to put others above self. Guide _____to be hospitable, always willing to lend or help while expecting nothing in return but to see You glorified.

17. Father, let _____ be diligent in the work place that You have provided. Bless the works of his/her hands and cause him/her to know that in the workplace he/she is serving You. Help _____ submit to those over him/her as though it were You Yourself. Please watch over that motive and let him/her have a pure humble heart of obedience to You, not seeking self-promotion or causing others to stumble through hypocritical ways. Let _____ treat coworkers with respect and compassion - even serving them as though they were over him/her.

18. Father, I pray _____ will not isolate him/herself from other believers but will come together and function as a part of the body of believers and grow in You together with the church family. Let _____would not just come and sit, but actively seek to serve, build up, pray, worship and follow hard after that which You would have them to do. Let it not be out of duty, but out of genuine love for You, Father, and for the brethren.

CHARACTER

1. Father, please develop true meekness in _____. Help him/her to have a close relationship to You to where the meekness of the Lord Jesus is revealed in his/her walk with You and relationships with others. Let _____ keep a teachable attitude before You and others all through life.

2. Lord, teach _____ the meaning of godly authority under the headship of Jesus Christ. Help him/her recognize and walk in servant leadership. Help him/her avoid the snares of manipulating to please authorities and misusing his/her own authority for personal gain, recognition or self-affirmation.

3. Cause _____ to maintain a joyful attitude in the good times and in bad times. Help him/her to find joy in knowing You and being loved by You. Let him/her be a thankful person, recognizing and appreciating the small tokens of Your love as well as the dramatic answers to prayer.

4. Give grace to _____ to be able to persevere with courage in times of adversity. Let him/her yield to Your work of developing endurance in times of stress, knowing that ultimately all things are working for good.

5. Father, please let _____ remember that he/she is a picture of the love and character of Jesus Christ to the world around him/her, as well as to the brothers and sisters in Christ. Please give wisdom so he/she will avoid every snare of the enemy to exploit his/her weaknesses to bring reproach on the name of Christ.

6. Please cause _____ to walk in truth and uprightness in all his/her daily life and decisions. Root out all areas of insecurity that would give rise to lies and deceit for purposes of self-protection.

7. Father, please build faithfulness and integrity in _____. Just as You are faithful to Your word, cause _____ to be true to his/her word. Let him/her be cautious about his/her commitments and careful to fulfill the promises s/he makes.

8. Let Your purity be revealed in _____'s conduct and dress. Please convict his/her heart concerning anything whether word, deed, or appearance that is unclean or would be a poor testimony to Your holiness. Please let him/her do this from the heart and not out of desire for an outward appearance of holiness.

9. Father, please work a heart of contentment in _____ so that s/he resist materialism and covetousness. Cause him/her to be responsible with finances and avoid debt and excess. Let his/her delight be in You and the riches of Your love and grace as s/he trusts You for daily needs.

10. Give _____ the determination and wisdom to manage his/her own life well. Let him/her learn to use time, finances and every other resource wisely, knowing that it is a stewardship from You.

11. Since the Word says if we are not faithful in money issues we won't be faithful with the true riches, please guide _____ in matters of finances. Make him/her a cheerful giver and keep him/her free from greed and covetousness. Let him/her maintain self-control in spending and avoid debt snares. Let him/her be responsible to pay bills and consider every possession a blessing from You to steward wisely.

12. Father, let _____ live according to Your principles of faith and honest labor. Keep him/her from falling prey to the lure of gambling and dishonest gain and all "get-rich-quick" scams.

13. Please let the character qualities of patience and self-control be visible in _____'s speech and relationships. Give him/her grace to be deal with others with gentleness. Let him/her avoid contentions and not be easily angered. If there are tendencies toward impulsive behavior or hasty words, let him/her yield to the transforming power of the Holy Spirit who desires to replace every fleshly attitude with the fruit of the Spirit.

14. Father let _____ be so secure in Your love for him/her that he/she can affirm others and freely and publicly give credit to others without feeling threatened or diminished.

15. Please let _____ maintain self-control in care of his/her physical body. Let him/her use good judgment in eating, proper rest, and personal fitness. Let this not become an obsession but an expression of his/her understanding that our bodies belong to You.

16. Lord, so many even in the church are bound with various addictions. Please keep _____ from every form of bondage including drunkenness and all additions.

17. Father, give _____ the strength to overcome temptation in every form. Don't let him/her be deceived or get careless as to the power of sin and the evil one. Let him/her live submitted to the Lordship of Jesus Christ and resist the devil. Let him/her be assured that no temptation or test is too strong for him/her to overcome by Your strength.

18. Father, may _____ have the maturity to take responsibility for his mistakes, decisions and actions. Keep him/her from blaming others or looking for excuses. The enemy works in darkness so don't allow him/her to hide or cover up sin or mistakes. Let him/her know that You are his/her Father and will not reject him/her when he/she comes to You with honesty and repentance.

CALLING

1. Lord, give _____ a hope that burns inside him/her, a hope that goes beyond what he/she sees, a hope that believes and trusts that he/she has a destiny and a purpose in You. Grant him/her grace to believe when there seems to be no hope.

2. Heavenly Father, give _____ insight into Your heart toward fellow believers. Allow him/her to hear Your voice concerning others, and give him/her the words to speak life into others.

3. Father, with growth and maturity comes the authority we have in You. Would You grant _____ the grace to yield and bend to Your breakings. Allow him/her to fully submit him/herself to You so that You *can* trust them with Your authority.

4. Father, as _____ steps out in faith in his/her ministry would You keep his/her eyes focused on You. Would You grant him/her divine alignment with Your Holy Spirit. Keep his/her ears sensitive so they hear Your voice, Your direction. Keep him/her from the traps of the enemy. Let his/her ears be closed to negative comments that the enemy would try to use to harm or to end his/her ministry.

5. Lord Jesus, would You keep _____ on track with the vision You have given him/her. Guard him/her from getting caught up with the daily requirements of the

position/ministry to where he/she loses the big picture. Give him/her a fresh perspective of the vision You have given him/her. Let his/her motivation be straight from You.

6. Father, as _____ pursues his/her life in You, would You grant him/her grace to pursue You in all things and in all times. No matter the circumstances, would his/her pursuits be towards You. Keep him/her from the temptations of following personal goals and/or dreams. Keep his/her eyes and heart focused on You.

7. Father, teach _____ how to regularly take time away to reflect on his/her life. Reveal to him/her how You are using situations and people in his/her life to form and shape him/her into the man/woman of God You've designed him/her to be! Teach him/her to recognize that it's You who has created these situations so that he/she can grow and mature. Keep him/her from falling into bitterness, resentment or anger over situations in his/her life.

8. Father, keep _____ from the mindset of self-sufficiency. Keep him/her soft and pliable, and willing to learn from others who have gone before. Give him/her the grace to boldly seek out mentors who can impart wisdom and understanding into his/her life and ministry.

9. Lord, as _____ seeks You and submits to You daily, would You bring more and more clarity to him/her concerning Your purpose and call upon his/her life. Father, as he/she keeps his/her eyes and heart focused upon You, as he/she willing lays down his/her life for the sake of others, and as he/she seeks wisdom from others, would You grant him/her divine insight and clarity into Your purpose for his/her life. Keep showing him/her the next step to take in order to fulfill Your plans and purposes.

10. Father, grant _____ confidence in his/her calling and ability to express the vision so others can benefit and enter in so that Your purposes will be fulfilled.

11. Do that deep work of heart that enables _____ to know and do the work of ministry at the level You have him/her now – free from selfish ambition and pride.

12. Father, help _____ develop a heart to embrace what You are doing throughout the earth as it relates to his vision.

13. Bring the rich love of God for Your church to _____'s heart that he/she will follow after his/her calling in order to meet the needs of the church.

14. Allow honesty of heart to examine the fruitfulness of _____'s ministry in order to confirm and adjust the direction and emphasis of his/her calling.

15. Father, stir up willingness in _____ to operate in his/her gifts as he/she understands them now, and to choose to grow in depth.

16. Keep _____'s heart free from identifying too strongly with his/her ministry successes, and give the willingness to explore what ever else You would have for him/her to do.

17. Break off the power of fear and fear of man, and let _____ keep his/her heart in all diligence so he/she knows the joy of Your heart in his/her obedience to You.

18. Give _____ the strength and tenacity needed to stay focused on the specific call of God in his life, so he/she can resist seeking the easy affirmation from other things that come along.

COMPETENCE

1. Father, I pray that _____'s understanding of the Bible as Your infallible Word will increase. Open his/her heart to a deeper knowledge and certainty of this in Jesus' name.

2. I pray that _____'s knowledge of the Bible will increase. I pray that he/she will be able to comprehend and understand with clarity the things that he/she learns from Your word.

3. Father, I pray that _____ will have a hunger to learn and understand more about the historically-accepted doctrine of the church. Help him/her to understand how this will increase his/her leadership skills.

4. Father, I pray that _____ will understand by the Spirit the importance of interpreting the Scriptures soundly. Help him/her to make this a priority in his/her life. Please give him/her Your grace for this.

5. I pray that _____ is careful to guard his doctrine and that of those for whom he is responsible. Let him/her accept this responsibility with humility and diligence.

6. Father, please help_____ to rightly divide the Word of truth at all times. Help him/her to determine in his/her heart to believe, obey, and teach the entire Bible and not just certain parts. I ask for Your grace for this in Jesus' name.

7. I pray that You will give _____ the wisdom to separate important Biblical issues from minor ones. Help him/her to understand the importance of this in leading people further into Your kingdom.

8. Father, in Jesus' name, give _____ a hunger to not just read the Scriptures but to experience and share their life-changing power. Let him/her not be satisfied with just reading and knowing Your word in his/her head but to desire to experience the truths of it in every aspect of his/her life.

9. Father, I pray that You will teach _____ to rely more and more on the Holy Spirit to illuminate the Word of God to his/her heart. Increase his/her sensitivity to the Holy Spirit's direction and guidance in this area in Jesus' name.

10. Father, Your Word is meant to be understood and obeyed. Please guard _____ against the snare of spiritualizing Your Word or making it more complicated than it is meant to be. Guide _____ into the literal plain meaning and context of a passage. Let his/her heart be to help people know You and not draw attention to his/her teaching gifts.

11. Father, Your Word is life to us as we hear and obey. Give _____ the anointing to teach and the skills to present the Word in a positive and engaging manner.

12. Father, let _____ have a godly zeal for truth and the boldness to confront doctrinal error and cults that would ensnare Your people. Let him/her be gentle but uncompromising in contending for the faith that once for all delivered to the saints.

13. Father, when Jesus taught the Word it was understandable and practical. Please give _____ the ability to make the concepts of the Word of God relevant and practical so Your people can know how to apply it in everyday life. Protect him from the snare of pride and the temptation to appear deeply spiritual by speaking in terms few can understand.

14. Father, Your Word applies to our situations today just as in every other time. Please help _____ avoid looking to psychology, or current social trends as solutions to the problems of people today. Let _____ see the Word of God as the final authority on every subject it addresses.

15. Let _____ be forever a student of the Word of God. Guard him/her from the mistake of studying about the Word rather than studying the Word itself. Let the Word be his/her constant delight.

16. Give _____ the wisdom to be patient with others when their convictions on minor issues are different. Let him/her resist the temptation to take a harsh stand on minor issues or look down upon a brother or sister with a sincere but different conviction.

17. Father, cause _____ to develop the daily habit of looking to You through Your Word for every situation, whether great or small. Let Your Word be his/her daily food and not something merely to base sermons on.

18. Father, give _____ the openness and humility to include his/her life experiences in You as he/she ministers. Let him/her see the value in sharing victories and mistakes to encourage and warn others.

Simplified 5C Indicators

A leader who is strong in **Christ:**

1. Trusts Jesus for his eternal life
2. Is secure in Christ's love
3. Enjoys inward fellowship with Jesus
4. Surrenders to Jesus by putting His Kingdom before his own personal ambitions
5. Turns more deeply to God in times of suffering, drawing peace and strength from Him
6. Has a healthy fear of God
7. Avoids idols or any form of the occult
8. Trusts Jesus in everyday life
9. Meditates regularly on God's Word
10. Submits to God's Word as the final authority
11. Is not content with a purely academic knowledge of the Scriptures, but seeks to experience its life-transforming power
12. Has received their identity in Christ as a son of God.

A leader who is strong in **Community:**

1. Forgives those who have wronged him
2. Is kind to others
3. Encourages others
4. Prays for others
5. Is good at working with people of different backgrounds or personalities
6. Is a generous giver
7. Does not gossip
8. Participates in the life of the local church
9. Leads his own family well
10. Genuinely cares for his followers
11. Is a healthy follower
12. Accepts healthy correction without self-justification

A leader who is strong in **Character:**

1. Is joyful
2. Is trustworthy
3. Is humble
4. Is resilient, bouncing back well from setbacks
5. Is slow to anger
6. Is not given to drunkenness
7. Refrains from lust, sexual immorality or pornography
8. Is not greedy
9. Stewards financial resources well
10. Recognizes others for their accomplishments without personally taking credit

11. Does not blame others when things go wrong, but takes responsibility for his own decisions and actions

A leader who is strong in **Calling:**

1. Is not content with the status quo, always striving for God's highest
2. Has a vision that is not limited to his own local community, but extends to God's work in the nations
3. Seeks the approval of God for his ministry rather than the approval of people
4. Loves to learn and grow
5. Seeks out relationships with mature leaders to learn from them
6. Takes initiative
7. Does not exploit or use people for his own ambition
8. Possesses spiritual authority that is recognized by others
9. Casts a compelling vision for the future
10. Inspires others to grow so they can fulfill their calling from God

A leader who is strong in **Competence:**

1. Thinks creatively
2. Is willing to take risks
3. Is good at critical thinking
4. Learns from failure and mistakes
5. Builds leaders
6. Positively influences people over whom he has no direct positional authority
7. Is decisive
8. Involves others in decision-making as appropriate
9. Communicates effectively
10. Listens to others well
11. Builds relational networks with those outside his own group
12. Interprets the Scriptures soundly
13. Leads meetings effectively

Indicators of the 5C's with Their Biblical Basis

According to our "ConneXions" Model, a healthy Christian leader knows God (Christ), was formed and lives in supportive and accountable community (Community), has integrity (Character), knows the purpose of God and presents it with clarity, passion and credibility (Calling), and has the capacity to think and act effectively in leading the people in the accomplishment of this purpose (Competencies) – and he is continually growing in all five areas (the "5Cs").

These areas of deep change in a leader's life are nurtured through the "Four Dynamics of Transformation" (the "4Ds"):

- Spiritual Dynamics – including prayer, worship, reflection, meditation in the Word;

- Relational Dynamics – including encouragement, accountability, examples, mentors, coaches;

- Experiential Dynamics – including learning by doing, challenging assignments, and pressure;

- Instructional Dynamics – the teaching of the Word of God in an engaging and interactive way, integrating doctrine into the context of life, experiences and relationships.

When all 4Ds are strongly present in a training design, spiritual life is nurtured, relational capacities are strengthened, character is developed, calling is clarified and deep capacities to think and act are built.

The following specific indicators for each of the 5Cs provide:

- A clear path for evaluating one's own leadership. (For an online evaluation tool that uses this model – the 5C Checkpoint tool – please go to: www.5CCheckpoint.com)

- A clear goal for designing training.

- A clear way to evaluate training – both the training itself and its effectiveness.

- As a basis for prayer for emerging and existing leaders.

"**Christ**" refers to the leader's spiritual life. Jesus' first great commandment is to: "Love the Lord your God with all your heart and with all your soul and with all your mind and with all your strength." (Mark 12:30).

A leader who is strong in Christ:

1. Trusts Jesus for his eternal life. (Mark 16:16; John 17:3; 20:31; Romans 3:28; Galatians 2:16)

2. Receives and is secure in Christ's love. (John 15:10; 17:26; 1 John 4:16-18)

3. Recognizes that without Christ he can do nothing of eternal value. (John 15:5)

4. Enjoys continual inward fellowship with Jesus by His Holy Spirit and is consistently guided by Him. (John 14:21-23; 17:3; Romans 8:14; 2 Corinthians 3:18; Ephesians 5:18; Philippians 2:1; 1 John 1:3)

5. Surrenders his life to Jesus, putting His Kingdom before his own personal desires and agendas, and submits to Jesus' authority for his beliefs and decisions. (Matthew 6:33; 7:13-14, 21; Romans 10:9; 12:1-2; Revelation 14:4)

6. He turns more deeply to God In times of difficulty and suffering, drawing peace and strength from Him. (2 Corinthians 1:3-11; 12:1-10; 2 Thessalonians 3:5; Hebrews 4:16; 1 Peter 1:6-9; 4:12-19)

7. Enjoys the Presence of God. (John 17:3; 1 John 1:1-3)

8. Has a healthy fear of God. (1 John 4:18; Romans 8:15; Hebrews 2:14-15; Romans 11:20-22; 2 Corinthians 5:9-11; Philippians 2:12-13; Hebrews 4:1; 12:28-29; 1 Peter 1:17; 2:17; Revelation 19:5)

9. Avoids idols and every form of the occult. (Exodus 20:3-4; Deut. 18:9-13; 1 Corinthians 10:14-22; Galatians 5:20)

10. Passionately worships God. (John 4:23-24)

11. Occasionally withdraws from people and responsibilities to spend time alone with God. (Luke 4:1-2, 42-44; 5:15-16; 6:12; 9:18, 28; 11:1-2; 22:39-40; Ephesians 5:19-20; Colossians 3:16; Matthew 6:1-18; Exodus 20:8-11; Mark 6:31)

12. Prays consistently. (Matthew 6:6-13; 7:7-11; Mark 14:38; Ephesians 6:18; 1 Thessalonians 5:17)

13. Has his prayers answered. (John 15:7; James 5:16; 1 John 5:14-15)

14. Deliberately takes up his cross daily, treating the old life as dead, and walking in new life in Christ. (Romans 6; Ephesians 4:22-24; Colossians 3:9-10)

15. Is engaged in spiritual warfare, resisting the enemy. (Luke 10:19; Ephesians 4:27; 6:10-12; James 4:7; 1 Peter 5:8-9)

16. Talks about Jesus in day-to-day conversation. (Colossians 4:5-6; Philemon 6; 1 Peter 3:15)

17. Demonstrates in his attitudes, words and actions that he trusts Jesus in his everyday life. (Matthew 6:25-34; 2 Timothy 4:18; James 2:14-16)

18. Lives for eternal reward, not blessing in this life. (Matthew 6:19-24; Acts 20:24; 2 Corinthians 4:18; Philippians 1:21-23)

19. Loves the Word of God. (Psalms 119:97, 127, 165, 167)

20. Believes that the Bible is the true Word of God. (Psalms 12:6; 119:86, 160; John 17:17; 1 Thessalonians 2:13; 2 Timothy 3:16; 2 Peter 1:20-21)

21. Meditates regularly on God's Word. (Psalms 1:1-3; Romans 12:2; Ephesians 5:26)

22. Relies on the Holy Spirit to illuminate the Word of God. (John 16:13; 1 Corinthians 2:10-13)

23. Submits to the biblical revelation as the final authority on every subject it addresses. (Isaiah 8:20; Matthew 24:35; John 10:35; Galatians 1:8)

24. Looks to the Word of God for direction and answers to his daily questions. (Joshua 1:8; Psalms 1:1-3; Matthew 4:4; 7:24; James 1:22)

25. Carefully guards his own doctrine and that of those for whom he is responsible. (Acts 20:28; 1 Corinthians 15:1-2; 1 Timothy 3:9; 4:16; 2 Timothy 1:13-14; 3:14-17; 4:5; Titus 1:9; 1 John 2:24-25; 2 John 9)

26. Is not content with a purely academic knowledge of the Scriptures, but seeks to experience and share its life-transforming power. (Psalms 119:11; Proverbs 4:20-22; John 5:39-40; 6:63; Ephesians 5:25-27; 1 Thessalonians 2:13; 2 Timothy 3:16-17; James 1:18; 1 Peter 1:23; 1 John 2:14)

27. Has their very identity established in Christ and has received the revelation of "sonship" as a beloved adopted child of Father. Romans 8

"**Community**" refers to the leader's relationships with others. Jesus' second great commandment is to: "Love your neighbor as yourself" (Mark 12:31). This includes four kinds of relationship – in marriage and family, in the church, with other leaders, and with people in the world.

A leader who is strong in Community:

1. Loves others as himself, treating them as he would like to be treated. (Matthew 7:12; 22:39; Romans 13:8-10; 2 Peter 1:7; 1 John 3:16-18)

2. Is not self-seeking, considering the good of others before his own. (Romans 12:10; 15:1; 1 Corinthians 13:5; 2 Corinthians 11:29; Philippians 2:3-11)

3. Forgives those who have wronged him, keeping no record of wrongs; is not resentful. He blesses those who curse him, turning the other cheek rather than defending himself. (Exodus 20:13; Matthew 5:10-12, 21-26, 38-41; 6:14-15; 18:21-35; Romans 12:17-21; 1 Corinthians 6:7; 13:5; Ephesians 4:32; Colossians 3:13)

4. Is merciful, kind and courteous. (Matthew 5:7; 1 Corinthians 13:4; Galatians 5:22; 2 Timothy 2:24)

5. Gives affirmation and support to strengthen others. (1 Corinthians 16:17-18; 2 Timothy 1:16; Ephesians 4:29; 5:4; Colossians 3:16; 1 Thessalonians 5:11; James 3)

6. Prays for others. (Ephesians 6:18-20; James 5:16)

7. Is a generous giver and acts hospitably to all, especially the stranger and the needy. (Proverbs 14:31; Matthew 6:1-4; Acts 20:35; 2 Corinthians 8:9; 9:7; Ephesians 4:28; 1 Timothy 6:17-19; Romans 12:13; 1 Thessalonians 5:14; 1 Timothy 3:2; James 1:27)

8. Is unprejudiced and inclusive toward others. (Romans 12:16; 14:1; Galatians 5:20, 22; Philippians 2:2-3)

9. Is good at working with different people, recognizing and adjusting to their various backgrounds, cultures and personalities. (1 Corinthians 12:21-22; Galatians 3:28)

10. Thinks and acts interdependently with others. (Proverbs 15:22; 1 Corinthians 12; Ephesians 4:1-16)

11. Allows other believers the freedom to determine their own convictions on minor issues. (Romans 14; 1 Corinthians 8:1-13)

12. Does not engage in malicious talk or gossip. (2 Corinthians 12:20; Ephesians 4:31)

13. Does not start unnecessary conflict; when conflict occurs, he prayerfully and actively seeks to resolve it, working always for unity. (Matthew 5:9; Romans 14:19; Galatians 5:20, 22; Ephesians 4:1-4)

14. Meets regularly with other believers to fellowship, worship, share the communion of the bread and cup, pray and study the Scriptures. (Acts 2:42; 1 Corinthians 11:23-34; 14:26; Hebrews 10:25)

15. Shares his life as well as his teaching with those to whom he ministers. (Mark 3:14; 2 Timothy 3:10)

16. Leads and manages his own family well. (1 Timothy 3:5, 12)

17. Treats his spouse, parents, children and/or siblings with self-giving love and respect. (Exodus 20:12; Ephesians 5:22-33; 6:1-3; Colossians 3:18-21; 1 Timothy 3:4-5; Titus 1:6; 1 Peter 3:1-7)

18. Fulfills his vocational responsibilities faithfully and effectively, obeying his leaders from the heart and not with "eye-service." If he is the leader, he genuinely cares for his followers. (1 Timothy 3:5, 15; 5:17; 1 Peter 5:2; Ephesians 6:5-9; Colossians 3:22 – 4:1)

19. Is a healthy follower. (Romans 13:1; Hebrews 13:17)

20. Graciously shares ideas and feedback with those in appropriate authority and ultimately submits to them from the heart, with respect, whether or not he agrees (unless it involves disobedience to God). (Genesis 33; Ruth 1:16-17; Esther 3 – 7; Nehemiah 2:3-8; Dan. 1; Romans 13:1-7; 1 Thessalonians 5:12-13; Hebrews 13:17; Acts 5:29)

21. Seeks feedback and accepts healthy correction without self-justification, self-pity or complaint. (Proverbs 9:8-9; 2 Corinthians 7:10; Philippians 2:14)

22. Questions others when appropriate and gives correction discreetly and tactfully. (1 Timothy 5:1-2; Philemon)

Emotional Intelligence:

23. Is self-aware, knowing how he feels and how his emotions and actions affect the people around him. (Proverbs 21:2; Romans 12:3; Galatians 6:3)

24. Manages his own emotions well. (Proverbs 15:28; 1 Corinthians 9:24-27; Philippians 4:8-9; Titus 1:8; Hebrews 4:15; James 3:2)

25. Is aware of how others feel. (Matthew 9:36; Romans 12:15; 1 Peter 3:8; 1 John 3:17)

26. Is able to manage the emotions of others. (Proverbs 12:18; 17:2; Galatians 5:19-23)

"**Character**" refers to the leader's personal integrity.

A leader who is strong in Character:

1. Is committed to obeying the Bible. (Matthew 7:24-27; Acts 20:27; 2 Timothy 3:16-17; James 2:14-26)

2. Is joyful – thankful to God and positive toward life. (Romans 12:12; 1 Corinthians 13:6-7; Galatians 5:22; Ephesians 5:20; Colossians 3:15; 1 Thessalonians 5:16; Titus 1:8)

3. Is truthful and honest; not lying, cheating or stealing. He pursues what is right above what is expedient or popular. (Exodus 20:15-16; Matthew 5:8; Ephesians 4:25, 28; Colossians 3:9)

4. Is faithful and trustworthy, keeping confidences and following through on responsibilities and commitments. (Proverbs 25:13; Matthew 5:33-37; 2 Corinthians 1:18; 8:11; Galatians 5:22; 1 Timothy 3:11; James 5:12)

5. Is humble – not overbearing, rude, proud or boastful. Doesn't let power or status go to his head. (Matthew 5:3-5; 1 Corinthians 13:4-5; Ephesians 4:2; 1 Peter 5:5-6)

6. Exhibits patience and self-control; is not impulsive. (Galatians 5:23; 1 Timothy 3:2-3; Titus 1:7; 2 Peter 1:6)

7. Perseveres during adversity, without complaining or arguing, with hope resting in God. (2 Corinthians 1:9-10; Philippians 2:14; 2 Timothy 4:5; James 5:10-11; 2 Peter 1:6)

8. Is resilient, dealing well with setbacks and bouncing back from failure or defeat. (Proverbs 24:16; Romans 8:31-39; 1 Peter 1:6-7)

9. Is tenacious, without being stubborn or unteachable. (2 Corinthians 4:16-17; Hebrews 13:5-6)

10. Is flexible, good at varying his approach with the situation. Takes ideas different from his own seriously, and occasionally changes his mind. (Proverbs 9:8-9; Exodus 18:23-24)

11. Is slow to anger, responding proactively rather than reactively. (1 Corinthians 13:5; 1 Timothy 3:2-3)

12. Is not given to overeating, drunkenness or addictions. (Galatians 5:21; Proverbs 23:2; Ephesians 5:18; 1 Timothy 3:3; Titus 1:7; 2:3)

13. Refrains from lust, sexual immorality, pornography, profanity, immodesty and all forms of impurity. (Exodus 20:14; Matthew 5:27-30; Romans 13:13; 1 Corinthians 6:13-20; Galatians 5:19-21; Ephesians 5:3; Colossians 3:5; 1 Timothy 5:2; 1 Peter 3:3-5; 4:2)

14. Is not greedy, covetous, jealous or envious but is content with what he has. (Exodus 20:17; 1 Corinthians 13:4; Galatians 5:20-21; 1 Timothy 6:6-10; Proverbs 30:8; Acts 20:33-35; Ephesians 5:3; 1 Timothy 3:3; Titus 1:7; 1 Peter 5:2)

15. Stewards resources well, exercises self-control financially, and is not irresponsible with debt. Does not gamble. (Proverbs 13:11; 22:7; Romans 13:8)

16. Takes responsibility for his own physical care, well-being and fitness. (1 Corinthians 6:20; 1 Timothy 4:8)

17. Guards himself. Avoids spreading himself too thin, dealing well with the tensions between work and family. (1 Timothy 4:6; 1 Corinthians 9:25; Ephesians 5:16; 1 Timothy 3:2; 2 Peter 1:6)

18. Does not take advantage of his authority, using it for personal gain. (Acts 20:30; 2 Corinthians 7:2; 12:14-18; Philippians 2:6; 1 Peter 5:3)

19. Recognizes others for their accomplishments without personally taking the credit. (Romans 16:3-4, 6-7; 2 Corinthians 1:11)

20. Does not blame others when things go wrong, but takes responsibility for his own decisions and actions. (Genesis 3:12; Philippians 2:14)

21. Is appropriately transparent, willing to admit ignorance or struggles. Doesn't hide mistakes. (Luke 22:42; 2 Corinthians 1:8-11; 12:1-10; James 5:16; 1 John 1:8-10)

22. Has a good reputation. (1 Thessalonians 4:12; 1 Timothy 3:7; 1 Peter 3:16)

"**Calling**" refers to the leader's vision and purpose in God. Calling includes six core realities:

- God does everything with clear purpose.

- Everyone has individual purpose given by God.

- God calls certain individuals to be organizational leaders. They must be clear about their personal calling.

- Churches and ministries have a corporate calling from God.

- Our personal callings integrate with the corporate calling of our church or ministry.

- Leadership primarily means "movement" so every leader must understand and communicate the vision God has for those whom he leads.

A leader who is strong in Calling:

1. Serves God zealously out of a strong sense of destiny and divine purpose. (Jeremiah 1:5; Romans 12:11; 2 Timothy 1:9)

2. Has a passion for the highest, always striving to grow, to solve, to build, to overcome – always pressing on to fulfill God's purposes, with hope for the future, believing that things can be improved and problems can be solved, and seizing new opportunities. (Philippians 3:12-14)

3. Faces reality, in order to deal with the real problems and the real opportunities. (Mark 7:5-8)

4. Engages deeply with the people and world around him. (Matthew 9:36; Luke 19:41-44; Acts 17:16; Romans 12:15; 2 Corinthians 11:28-29)

5. Has a vision that is not limited to his own local community, but extends to God's work in the nations. (Acts 1:8; Colossians 1:23; Isaiah 49:6)

6. Has an increasingly-clear understanding of his own motivated abilities and God's will for his life. (Romans 12:2; Philippians 1:9-10)

7. Stays focused in his calling, setting priorities well, distinguishing clearly between important and unimportant tasks, and avoiding the distractions of other opportunities. (Colossians 4:17; 2 Timothy 4:5, 10)

8. Has a vision that comes from God and not his own ambition. (Jeremiah 14:14; 23:16; Acts 20:30; Galatians 5:20; James 3:14; 4:13-16)

9. Is motivated by vision from God rather than the mere requirements of position. (1 Peter 5:2)

10. Seeks the approval of God for his ministry rather than the approval of people. (Matthew 6:1-2, 5, 16; 23:5-12)

11. Does not compromise his calling out of fear, or pressure from others. (Jeremiah 1:4-8; Matthew 10:32-33; Luke 14:26; Acts 20:18-24; Philippians 1:14, 27-28; 1 Timothy 4:12-14; 2 Timothy 1:6-7)

12. Regularly and prayerfully reflects on his life, recognizing that God uses people, events and circumstances to prepare him for his ministry. (Romans 8:28; Ephesians 1:11)

13. Exercises the gifting of God, while seeking to grow in them. (Romans 12:3-8; 1 Peter 4:10-11)

14. Loves to learn and grow, intentionally exploring a variety of ministry opportunities, including ones that require him to stretch. (Proverbs 8:17; 15:14; 18:15; 19:8, 20; 23:12; Ephesians 4:15-16)

15. Seeks out relationships with mature believers and leaders to learn from them. (Romans 16:13; 2 Timothy 3:14)

16. Pursues further learning of the Word of God. (Psalms 119; Matthew 15:6, 9; Hebrews 5:11-14)

17. Evaluates the fruitfulness of his ministry in order to discern and confirm his calling. (2 Corinthians 13:5)

18. Serves at a level of authority appropriate to his gifting, maturity and favor. (Luke 16:10, 12; Romans 12:3; 2 Corinthians 10:12-18)

19. Takes initiative, not waiting to be asked to act or take responsibility. (Proverbs 6:6-8; 30:27; Matthew 25:14-30)

20. Selflessly pursues his own calling as a means to build up the church and not to promote himself. Does not exploit or use people for his own ambition. (Matthew 20:25-28; 1 Corinthians 9:19-23; Ephesians 4:12; Philippians 1:24-25)

21. Possesses spiritual authority that is recognized by others. (Matthew 9:8; Acts 16:2; 2 Corinthians 10:18)

22. Casts a compelling vision for the future. (1 Peter 3:15)

23. Inspires others to grow and take action to fulfill their calling from God. (Romans 15:14; Ephesians 4:12, 16)

"**Competence**" refers to the leader's capacities to think and act. The following "master competencies" cover a wide range of thinking and acting capacities, and provide the leader the ability to understand and then respond well to the challenges and opportunities of life and ministry.

A leader who is strong in Competence:

Thinking

Thinking holistically:

1. Sees the big picture, recognizing how each part relates to the whole. (1 Corinthians 3:1-10; Ephesians 4:16)

2. Is aware of the broad external environment, spotting problems, opportunities and trends early on. (1 Chronicles 12:32; Matthew 16:3; Ephesians 5:16)

3. Can create order out of large quantities of information. (Ecclesiastes 12:9; Matthew 13:37-40; Galatians 5:14)

Embracing ambiguity:

4. Embraces ambiguity and uncertainty, recognizing the opportunities they create. (Proverbs 26:4-5; Philippians 2:12-13)

Integrating Science and Art:

5. Thinks creatively, consistently generating new and innovative ideas, appropriately challenging the status quo and willing to take risks. (Exodus 35:31-32; Matthew 13:52; 14:29; Acts 10:19-21, 25-29; Ephesians 2:10)

6. Is good at systematic and critical analysis, probing beneath the surface. (1 Samuel 16:7; 1 Kings 3:16-28; 4:29-34; John 7:24; Acts 15:13-21; Colossians 2:23)

Thinking about thinking:

7. Continually reflects and evaluates. (Proverbs 14:15; Ephesians 5:15; Galatians 6:4)

Learning from mistakes:

8. Learns from failure and mistakes. (Proverbs 14:4; 26:11-12; Luke 22:32; 1 Corinthians 10:11; 1 John 1:9-10)

Acting

Building leaders:

9. Identifies emerging leaders. (Mark 3:14; Acts 16:1-2)

10. Personally builds leaders, coaching and mentoring them. (Mark 3:14-15; 2 Timothy 3:10-17)

11. Gives challenging assignments to those he is building. (Genesis 22:1-2; Matthew 10:5-10; 28:18-20; John 6:5-6; 2 Corinthians 2:9; 8:8)

12. Cares for the leaders around him. (Philippians 2:25; 4:10-19; 1 Corinthians 16:15-18; 2 Corinthians 7:5-7; 2 Timothy 1:16-18)

Team building:

13. Is a good team builder, bringing together people with different personalities and strengths. (Romans 12:3-8; 1 Corinthians 12)

14. Empowers others, giving them both responsibility and authority, along with much encouragement. (Matthew 10:1-20; 1 Timothy 1:3; 4:12)

15. Provides accountability for others with regular and constructive feedback. (Matthew 6:30; Luke 9:10; 10:17-20; Acts 14:27; 15:4, 12; 21:19)

16. Recognizes and rewards others for their work, celebrating accomplishments. (Exodus 12:42; Esther 9:26-28; Acts 11:18; 1 Thessalonians 5:12-13)

Leading change:

17. Leads change successfully. (Exodus 3:8; 15:13, 17; Numbers 27:15-17; Nehemiah 2:17-18; Matthew 28:19-20; Acts 26:16-18; Romans 12:1-2; Colossians 1:13; 1 Peter 2:9)

18. Understands the culture of the organization (shared beliefs, values, attitudes, actions, language) and intentionally shapes it in the right direction. (Ephesians 4:16)

19. Is able to positively influence people over whom he has no direct positional authority. (Luke 2:46-52; Acts 9:20-22; 2 Corinthians 3:1-2)

Strategizing:

20. Translates the broad vision into specific strategies. (Mark 16:15; Acts 1:8)

21. Creates actionable goals, plans, structures and systems. (Exodus 18:13-26; 2 Chronicles 3; Acts 6:1-6; 1 Corinthians 16:1-4)

Managing:

22. Manages his own life wisely, including his time. (Ephesians 5:16; Colossians 4:5)

23. Manages people well. (Exodus 18:13-26; Nehemiah 3; Acts 6:1-7)

24. Effectively mobilizes resources, including finances. (1 Chronicles 29:1-9; 2 Corinthians 8-9)

25. Stewards organizational resources responsibly. (Proverbs 31:10-31; Matthew 25:14-29)

26. Understands and implements healthy organizational governance. (Acts 14:23; 15:2; Titus 1:5; 1 Peter 5:1)

27. Possesses the necessary knowledge and skills for his particular role and responsibilities. (Proverbs 22:29)

Decision making:

28. Is decisive, analyzing choices and making timely decisions, without unnecessary delay. (Joshua 24:15; Psalms 119:60; 1 Kings 18:21; Matthew 21:28-32; Galatians 2:4-5, 11-14; Revelation 3:15-16)

29. Involves others in decision-making as appropriate. (Exodus 18:13-26; Acts 6:1-6; 15:1-21, 25)

Problem solving:

30. Deals with problems early, before they become out of control. (Matthew 5:25; Acts 15:1-31; Galatians 1:6-9)

31. Defines problems accurately, getting to the heart of the issue. (Acts 8:18-25; 9:26-30; 13:5-12; 16:16-18; Romans 14)

Communicating:

32. Communicates with clarity. (Mark 1:22; Luke 2:47; 4:22, 32; 1 Corinthians 14:8; Colossians 4:4)

33. Communicates with passion. (Isaiah 58:1; Jeremiah 20:9; Hos. 8:1; Amos 3:8; Acts 4:20; 14:14-18; 20:30-31; 1 Corinthians 9:16; 2 Corinthians 2:4; Philippians 3:18)

34. Communicates with credibility. (Acts 17:2; 18:4; Ephesians 6:19; Colossians 4:6; 1 Timothy 4:11-16; 1 Peter 3:15)

35. Actively listens to others. (Proverbs 18:13; James 1:19)

Negotiation:

36. Negotiates well, trading-off and working towards solutions that are best for everyone. (Acts 15:36-41; Galatians 2:9-10; 1 Corinthians 10:23-24)

Networking:

37. Networks with others, initiating and nurturing numerous positive relationships. (Romans 16; Colossians 4:7-17)

38. Builds relational networks with those outside his own group. (Acts 10; 18:24-26; 19:1-7; Romans 14; Ephesians 4:1-6)

Leading meetings:

39. Leads meetings effectively, creating opportunities for participation while maintaining focus. (Acts 15:14-30; 1 Corinthians 14)

40. Has extensive and accurate knowledge of the Bible. (1 Timothy 1:7; 2 Timothy 2:2)

41. Interprets the Scriptures soundly. (2 Timothy 2:15; Titus 2:8)

42. Is knowledgeable about the church's history and its established and historically-accepted doctrine. (1 Timothy 4:6; 2 Timothy 1:5, 13; Titus 1:9)

43. Teaches the Word of God in a positive and engaging way. (Philippians 1:7; 1 Timothy 1:3; 4:1-3; 2 Timothy 4:2; Titus 1:9)

44. Is practical and relevant in his teaching. (1 Timothy 1:5; 4:7; Titus 2:1-2)

45. Gently and effectively corrects those who are in doctrinal error, including the cults. (Philippians 1:7; 2 Timothy 2:16-18, 24-26; 4:2; Titus 1:9; Jude 3)

46. Actively engaged and effective in Christian ministry work, including leading others to Christ, discipling new believers, spiritual warfare, discerning and responding to the presence of the Holy Spirit, etc.

Scriptures Depicting the 5C's

CHRIST	COMMUNITY	CHARACTER	CALLING	COMPETENCY
James 1:5	Proverbs 27:17	Acts 12:21-23	Galatians 1:15	1 Corinthians 12:7-11
Ephesians 3:20	Acts 4:42-47	1 Timothy 3:1-7	Ephesians 3:7-12	Romans 12:3-8
Philippians 2:1-7	1 Corinthians 12:12 & 27	1 Timothy 4:7, 12	Luke 1:39-43	Ephesians 4
John 15:1-5	Galatians 6:10	Titus 2:7-8	Mark 1:16-18	2 Corinthians 3:5
John 5:39-49	Mark 3:34-35	Galatians 5:22-23	John 21:15-19	2 Corinthians 8:7
2 Peter 1:3-4, 8	1 John 1:6-7	Proverbs 25:28	Galatians 1;1	Exodus 28:3
1 Corinthians 3:10-15	1 Timothy 5	Luke 16:10	Jeremiah 1:5	Exodus 31:1-6
Philippians 4:13, 19	2 Timothy 1:16	Ephesians 4:2	Isaiah 6:8	Exodus 36:2. 8
1 John 1:6	Ephesians 4:3	Romans 12:9f	Matthew 16:24	Colossians 1:28-29
Ephesians 1:3	Proverbs 3:29-30	James 1:2-4	Genesis 12:1-3	2 Timothy 2:15
Philippians 3:7-11	1 Samuel 12:23	2 Corinthians 6:3-10	Acts 9	Galatians 2:1-2?
1 John 3:24	Philippians 1:7	Titus 2:11-14	1 Samuel 3:4	Acts 18:24-28
Philippians 1:21	Ephesians 2:19-20	Job 1:1, 9	Joshua 4:12	Titus 1:9
Ephesians 6:10	Matthew 27:55-56	Psalm 78:72	1 Timothy 4:12	Acts 6:3
Hebrews 12:2	Proverbs 27:6, 9	Psalm 86:11	1 Timothy 6:12	1 Kings 3:28
Matthew 10:1	1 John 1:3	Romans 5:3-4	John 3:16	2 Timothy 3:16-17
John 17:20-26	2 Timothy 1:2, 5	Proverbs 27:21	Mark 4:19-20	2 Timothy 4:2
Colossians 3:1-4	2 Timothy 3:10	Proverbs 31:10	Acts 4:29-31	1 Peter 3:15
Galatians 2:20	Exodus 17:12	Luke 22:25-26	Ephesians 2:10	Ezra 7:6
Colossians 1:18, 27	1 Chronicles 18:17	Joshua 1:6-9	Acts 13:1-3	Psalm 78:72
John 12:33	Acts 9:25	1 Peter 1:6-7, 12-13	2 Timothy 1:9	Proverbs 22:29
1 Corinthians 8:5	Hebrews 10:24, 33	1 Peter 5:2-3	Exodus 3:4	
2 Corinthians 12:9	Ephesians 4:12-16	2 Peter 1:5-8	2 Kings 2:1-18	
Deuteronomy 8:12-14, 17	John 13:34-35	Proverbs 8:13	Psalm 78:70	
Psalm 62:1-2	Proverbs 15:1-2, 23	Proverbs 29:23	2 Timothy 4:5	
Joel 2:12-13	Proverbs 17:9	Deuteronomy 1:17	Romans 8:29-30	
Exodus 33:13-14				
2 Samuel 22:33-37				
Psalm 73:23-24				
Romans 8:26-27				

FIVE ESSENTIAL CITY REACHING STRATEGIES

Advancing Christ & Christ's Kingdom in Cities & Regions

When the Body of Christ initiates the five essential Christ-centered and Biblical strategies in a city, three kingdom realities are unleashed
– revival, restoration and transformation, which then advance Christ's Kingdom!

Local
International
Cross-cultural
Missions

Marketplace
Compassion Ministries

Father's House of Prayer
24/7 Worship & Prayer

Micro-Churches
-Inner Healing
-Deliverance
-Relational Discipleship
-DNA Groups (2's & 3's)

Corporate Training &
Equipping
-Worship
-Bible Training
-Life Training
-New Believers
-Discipleship Training
-Leadership Training
-Children's Ministry

FROM PRAY TO GO

From Pray to Go: CATALYZING A CAMPUS CHURCH-PLANTING MOVEMENT

PRAY	REACH	WIN	TRAIN	GO
Gather believers to pray regularly on your campus	Ask God to show you who to invite to an exploratory study topic or passage in the Bible for non-believers lasting 3-6 weeks. Informally see if they might be interested.	Love your friends enough to present even the hard truths of the gospel to them.	Intensive 14 day foundational discipleship material, one-on-one meeting daily for the first two weeks with new believers…	Encourage each campus church to begin to focusing on a specific unreached student populous and send out two students to build relationships and start an explore study.
Get the mind and heart of the Lord and pray as a campus missionary team.		Consistently challenge to application and trying God out at His Word.	Meet as a house church, not an exploration study utilizing the 5 Ws and modeling.	Multiply by having them begin the process all over again from reach to go.
Begin to pray specifically for lost friends by name.	Ask God to show you what passage to use: CCN has a number of studies written up to model how you might approach this.	Build relationship outside of study times. Follow-up individually.	Continuing discipleship and 3E studies, accountability, worship and prayer.	Mentor students through each step of the way: while continuing to meet for training and accountability, worship and fellowship.
As possible, gather campus ministries to pray together and cast vision.		By the end of the study, clearly present the gospel and call for commitment. Often times this will happen as a product of God's Word by the Holy Spirit as natural progression of application.	One on one mentoring through issues and areas of healing/deliverance as they surface.	As leaders emerge that may be called to work with CCN more closely get them connected with area leadership…
Host early morning prayer throughout the week.	Formally invite them and set up a meeting place and time. Be praying for them by name leading up to the study.			
Call a day or meal of fasting and prayer. Host all-night prayer.	Host the study in a home/campus environment— facilitate the discussion but let the Bible speak for itself.	Trust the Holy Spirit to guide and move.	As soon as they are ready within the first two weeks, go with them to share their faith with their friends.	Encourage all students disposed to this to go through the full 7 modules and be certified to train in them.
Prayer walk the campus… spiritually map the campus demographics.				
714 prayer– gather at 7 am and at 7:14 join campuses all over the nation praying 2 Chr 7:14 over your school and the nation.	Allow dissent, discussion and expect "non" churched responses… Come with the attitude of a fellow learner.	Lead those that are ready to the Lord, fully explaining repentance and the commitment they are making to give Jesus their life.	As their friends come to the Lord, the new believer repeats the process he/she has just come through and you transition into a more purely train the trainer approach… meeting with your core that are now pastoring their friends and have their own campus churches meeting– modeling and mentoring.	Send teams cross cultural to other campuses and other nations.
In short pray and obey.	Lead and challenge consistently to application.			
Ask God to show you the person of peace in your midst and build real relationships with the lost around you by hanging out with them.	Pass out index cards for people to submit questions they have and any prayer requests.	Baptize them as soon as possible– pool, fountain, tub/ Explain/pray for Holy Spirit baptism. Break generational curses, command blessings, cast out any demonic that presents.		Network all leaders in the area together for equipping and worship events-- fellowship, area conference calls, etc.
	Model simple prayer that is talking to God.	Begin meeting as a campus church.	Continue to partner with the larger Body on campus for unified prayer and outreach.	
ACTIVATION RESOURCES: "Pray" activation summation Campus Prayer Shield Summary and materials.	**ACTIVATION RESOURCES:** "Reach" activation summation Model 3D studies for non-believers	**ACTIVATION RESOURCES:** "Win" activation summation	**ACTIVATION RESOURCES:** "Train" activation summation Seven module discipleship training curriculum, 3D studies.	**ACTIVATION RESOURCES:** "Go" activation summation Training team certification Full-time CCN associate

Activation Summation

Pursue God's Presence and His Purposes for your campus.

Rally believers on campus to join in a corporate campus prayer initiative.

Allow God to speak and lead: Spend time listening to Him.

Yield to the Holy Spirit's leading.

Pursuing God's Presence and Purposes

- ☐ Meet with your core team to begin to pray regularly seeking God's face... several times a week. ☐Stand on His promises found in His Word. Pray Scripture back to Him.
- ☐ Write down what He tells you—keep a team journal of what God is saying. ☐ Begin to pray specifically for people you know who are lost.
- ☐ Psalm 24, Luke 10:2, Jeremiah 33:3, Jeremiah 29:13

Rallying a Campus Prayer Initiative

This really is not as difficult as many people think. #1 it is God's work! We just join Him. One thing almost every ministry and believer can agree on the need for prayer. This is an easy point to unite the Body of Christ around in concept. Your campus just needs someone to rally them in action... so why not you and your team?

- ☐ ☐Contact other campus ministries and believers you know to begin to pray together once or twice a week at first. Keep it simple and approachable. God will do the rest.
- ☐ ☐Pick a time and place and begin meeting. Regardless of numbers stick to it. Try a time no one has a legitimate conflict with (and beauty sleep doesn't count): EARLY MORNING PRAYER! As other groups emerge, begin to host different days until each morning is covered.
- ☐ ☐Eventually you may have someone to facilitate each day of the week and you can simply let the campus know the Body of Christ is gathering to pray each morning for God to move.
- ☐ ☐Join a nationwide movement of college students in 714 PRAYER: Meet to pray at 7am and at 7:14 pray 2 Chronicles 7:14 over your campus, city and nation. Campuses all over America are beginning to do this. Pray into the areas covered by this verse: Intimacy with the Lord, Identity—that the Body would know and be who they are called to be in Christ, Humility, Repentance and Accountability, Healing and Revival
- ☐ ☐Your group doesn't need to be long—just focused. Where 2 or 3 are gathered: concentrate on having the RIGHT people there to start with, the numbers will follow later.
- ☐ ☐Organize campus-wide concerts of prayer and periodic All-Night Prayer. Host one or two larger events a semester—soon other groups will step up and you can do more. Do be afraid of starting small—just start! Acts 4:29-31. Prayer walk your campus: Genesis 13:14-17

Allow God to Speak and Lead

This may seem like a no-brainer, but it is easy to get caught up in the activity of praying and loose the purpose of prayer. Prayer is the place of learning God's ways. Spend time corporately waiting on the Lord and trusting Him to speak through Scripture, through promptings, through visions or pictures. Don't be afraid of silence. Learn to make time for it intentionally so together you can hear what God is saying. As a prayer facilitator, ASK the people in your groups what they are sensing from the Lord. It is amazing because often after a time of waiting when people share, you begin to see a theme of what God is saying. Watch for themes or repeated insights that emerge. And YES you can hear the voice of God: in John 10:27 Jesus says "My sheep hear My voice, and I know them, and they follow Me..." God's voice sometimes sounds a lot like our thoughts. Don't be afraid to listen—simply make sure all what you hear or sense, individually and corporately, agrees with what you read in the Bible. If you are not sure: test it out by studying it out and asking God to show you from His Word in the Bible. Trust Him—He wants you to hear Him even more than you do!

Yield to the Holy Spirit's Leading

When God speaks as you pray, obey! Allow the Holy Spirit to rearrange your plans or even throw them out and give you new ones. There is nothing wrong with having a plan, but always be sensitive to the Lord to make sure He is still going where you thought He was leading. Prayer not about an activity. It is about a relationship between you and Jesus. As He speaks and you step out in obedience to put feet to your prayers, there is the opportunity for heaven to invade earth and God to demonstrate His Word in your midst! Prayer is an adventure with Jesus that prepares the way for Him to move in your situation and circumstances.

Contact Michele for further resources: songsofthebride@yahoo.com

Compiled by Michele Perry, CCN

Activation Summation

Real relationships that reflect Who Jesus is as you hang out with the lost.
Engage the person(s) of peace in authentic friendship that is honest about your faith.
Ask God to move. Ask your new friends to participate with you in a seeker study.
Choose your place, passage and time.
Host the study times.

Real Relationships Reflecting Jesus

- Hang out where the lost are. Get involved in campus activities doing what you already love to do... then you have common ground already to start on. You just be you loving Him.
- Be intentional about watching to find the person(s) of peace that are potentially receptive to the message of Jesus, have relational connections, have a reputation (good or bad!) and are seeking.

Engage the Person(s) of Peace in Intentional Relationship

- Do stuff together—invite them over for dinner and movies. Do what you both love to do.
- Serve your new friends... be very purposeful in building real relationship that is authentic. Be real and honest about your faith from day one. And don't be afraid to have a bad hair day or let your friends see you struggle. That just makes you touchable and open.
- Speak normal English—when topics of faith come up resist the urge to revert to "Christianese". The lost want to know about a faith that touches them where they live not one they have to learn a new language to understand.

Ask God to Move... Ask Your Friends to Participate

- Pray for your friends daily by name. Ask God to speak to them and show you how to pray effectively for them. Trust the Holy Spirit to guide you. Romans 8
- Construct a custom invite for your friend based on what you know of their needs. You can tell them you are hosting a spiritual discussion for those who don't identify with church. You can share with them it's for people who want to learn in a friendly, laid back, home, beach, _____environment.
- Tell them it is only an hour (and honor them by sticking to the time commitment!).

Choose Your Place, Passage and Time

- Set a time you all can meet each week for a period of 3-6 weeks.
- Host the study in your home, dorm, library, coffee shop—where ever facilitates open discussion. Ask God to show you what passages of Scripture to use
- Pick passages that appeal to who your friends are or which highlight the life and uniqueness of Jesus or passages that personally have changed your life.
- Pray and prepare studying the passage and writing out questions ahead of time you can use in facilitating discussion. Print out the passage you are studying so everyone will be on the same page.

Host the Studies

- Set your group's ground rules the first time you meet. This actually sets people at ease because now they know what to expect. 1. Be open to spiritual growth and applying what you learn. 2. Choose to be curious and ask questions. 3. Answer questions that are asked from the text. 4. Be cool with each other and treat eachother with respect.
- Introduce the symbols you are looking for in the passage: Question mark (questions), Light bulb (insight, understanding, an AHA!), Arrow (application) : ?, 7,
- Take the passage you are studying and look at one verse or sentence at a time. Ask if anyone has any question marks. Don't answer the questions yourself—turn it back ot the group and guide them to get answers from the text. Ask for if anyone has any lightbulbs, then arrows.
- Don't be afraid in closing to share briefly from your life how God made Himself real to you and that He will make Himself real to them too. Telling them going to Jesus and inviting Him to act is how to have faith. Challenge them to step out and try out God's Word.
- You can pass out index cards for your friends in the study to write out questions THEY have about God. This can help even in discerning what passages to choose to study.

Contact Michele for further resources: songsofthebride@yahoo.com   Compiled by Michele Perry, CCN

Activation Summation

Water the seed, watching for "teachable" moments
Invite your friends to follow Christ.
New believer's discipleship intensive...

Water the Seed, Watching for Teachable Moments

- ☐ Continue to water the seed of God's Word through real intentional relationship.
- ☐ Watch for the things that seem to touch your friends' hearts. Pay attention to the things that are important to them when you are studying Scripture together. Pray for God to talk more to your friends about the things that are on their hearts.
- ☐ Pray regularly for God to guard the seeds sown in your friends' hearts—to prepare the soil of their hearts and to protect the truths of His Word He is planting there so the seed will not be stolen, scorched or strangled.

Invite Your Friends to Follow Christ

- ☐ Sometimes coming to this point will happen naturally in the course of the study or relationship as you are open and real about your relationship with Jesus and how amazing He is and as you discuss the passages. If it does, go with it and don't be shy.
- ☐ Practice cutting "Christianese" out even of your story (aka your testimony). Practice telling your story to other members of your team and have them play the role of the seekers who know no "Christianese" and will ask you to explain what you mean by phrases like "come to faith, got saved, etc."
- ☐ When the time is right and as you pray for your friends and are watchful, you will know because God will LET you know: set a time to talk with them and share a clear, concise invitation to follow Jesus.
- ☐ Keep the Gospel potent—don't be afraid to let Who Jesus is confront in love the sin patterns and speak into the struggles where your friends live. You are not inviting them to accept a fire insurance policy—you are inviting them to give their lives to Jesus so they are no longer their own and He's the One in charge of their lives. You are inviting them to the greatest adventure we could ever have. You inviting them to a relationship with One that will never fail them, leave them or take advantage of them. You are inviting them to LIFE and life more abundantly and life that will never end.
- ☐ If they are not ready or want to think it over or outright say no, while it may break your heart, realize it isn't about you. Keep praying and respond as God shows you. If they say yes, lead them to talk to Jesus and in their own words repent (choose to do life God's way, not their own) and commit their life to Him. (Romans 3:23, 5:6-8, 6:23, 10:9-10; Ephesians 2:8-10; Acts 2:38 may be helpful passages)

New Believer's Discipleship Intensive

- ☐ Welcome them to the family! Tell them there are some basic things to help them get started and you'd like to commit to meet with them for one hour a day for the next 14 days to make sure they get the right start in their new life in Jesus (CCN has materials to help you do this!)
- ☐ Make sure they have a Bible
- ☐ Baptize them as soon as possible after making their decision. Explain water baptism is something Jesus asks us to do (Acts 2:38) and is a powerful way to publicly say you are following Jesus. It is also picture of your old way of life being buried under the water and when you come up out of the water, coming up in your new life following Jesus. Find a pool, a fountain, even a bath tub will do in a pinch.
- ☐ Pray with them to receive the baptism of the Holy Spirit (Acts 2:38)
- ☐ Break off generational curses (Gal 3:13) and command the blessings of Abraham (Deuteronomy 28:1-3) As things come up in the context of discipleship (issues, wounds, past involvement with the occult, sin patterns, ungodly beliefs—things that give the enemy access to their lives), pray through the issues and where appropriate, break the power of the demonic and cast it out. (CCN has further resources on this process in the new believer's discipleship intensive).
- ☐ Coach them in sharing their story with their friends—after the two weeks go with them and pray as they meet with their friends and THEY share their story. When their friends come to Jesus, mentor the new believer in repeating these steps with their friends. As they begin to meet with and pastor their friends another campus church is born.

Contact Michele for further resources: songsofthebride@yahoo.com

Compiled by Michele Perry, CCN

Micro-Church Families on Mission

Activation Summation

Transition from being a seeker study to being a campus church
Real life, real world, real time reproducible discipleship...
Activate those you are mentoring into God's Word... DO the stuff together!
Invest in those you are serving.
Nth factor multiplication...

Transition from Being a Seeker Study to Being a Campus Church

- As people in your study come to faith in the Lord and are going through the 14-day new believer intensive begin to meet not as a seeker study but a campus church. Begin to incorporate worship and more prayer and study passages on what it means to follow Jesus, including things like giving and service.
- Use the same discussion method using the symbols of a ?, 7, ☐ to study Scripture passages together. Model for them what it means to be a campus church planter. Begin thinking and praying like a mission team. Go through the New Believer Intensive as a group... as their friends begin to come to Lord mentor them through now leading someone else or a small group through the same process.
- Practice the 5 W's: Welcome, Worship, Waiting (on the Lord), Word, Works

Real Life, Real World, Real Time Reproducible Discipleship

- Make sure all the methodology that you are using is simple and reproducible. For example, not everyone would likely be able to give a sermon, but everyone can facilitate a discussion.
- Authenticity and accountability: it is important that as you study and grow and live life together there is loving accountability to actually be transformed by God's Word and His Spirit not just be informed about them.
- Live life together and use real life as your classroom in mentoring others how to follow Jesus—after all that's how HE trained His disciples.
- For additional resources, CCN has some helps on their website, *www.campuschurch.net*, and is in the process of developing comprehensive studies that take you from precepts of the faith to leadership material.

Activate Those You are Mentoring into God's Word

- Don't just talk about Scripture—GO DO IT! And do it together. Ask God how best to help those you mentor apply His Word and walk it out in life.
- Have planned application times, which means if you are studying together what it means to do outreach and hear the voice of God: GO, wait on the Lord as a team and then do what He says and watch Him move!

Invest in Those You are Serving

- Take time to meet one on one regularly and really pour into those you are serving. Really get to know their heart and what makes them tick. Look for the gifts in them you can encourage and draw out. Watch for possible pitfalls or weaknesses you can walk with them through.
- Allow people to grow in the pace of God's grace for them. Some may come from harder pasts and have more to deal with before they are ready to fully step out and lead a group: be sensitive to how you can challenge them to the point they can handle it and help them grow one step at a time.

Nth Factor Multiplication

- Think missionally from day one—not just how can you be equipped but who are you reaching out to? What specific unreached student groups has God given you connection with or laid on your heart? What is His strategy for reaching them?
- Begin praying and sending twos and threes out from your group to begin the process of planting a campus church in some of these unreached groups God has shown you to focus on.
- Don't add to your numbers—multiply exponentially by reproducing and sending people out. Stay in touch as a core team and as a church plant trainer continue to train them as they start to train others.
- Network the campus churches together for larger campus wide times of prayer and worship.

Contact Michele for further resources: songsofthebride@yahoo.com   Compiled by Michele Perry, CCN

Activation Summation

Grow in Christ, in community and in connection to the lost. Outreach, service, mission and Kingdom transformation...

Grow in Christ, in Community and in Connection to the Lost

- ☐ Grow in Christ individually and corporately. Make knowing Jesus and relationship with Him a priority for everyone in your campus network.
- ☐ Grow in community—plan times of just plain fun and fellowship. Summer picnics, winter sledding— times to get to know one another and even to which to invite lost friends.
- ☐ Practice being a Biblical community of faith—when one is in need, serve; when someone's is grieving weep with them, when someone rejoicing celebrate with them. Be intentional about building community.
- ☐ Grow in connection to the lost and the larger community: ask God how He would have you connect either through involvement or service or even just hanging out.

Outreach, Service, Mission and Kingdom Transformation

- ☐ Be bold in your outreaches. Where possible try to work with other campus ministries. As a campus church have open air worship on campus and as God leads, open air preaching.
- ☐ Prayer walk as a team and take time for onsite intercession: hold prayer meetings on campus.
- ☐ Find out what needs to be done on campus and offer to help get it done. Find practical ways to serve the people around you: how about homemade cookies in the dorms at finals or midterms? Or hosting a trash pick-up day? These times are great community building times for your campus church as well.
- ☐ Use service as an opportunity to be witnesses to Jesus practically and in words as well.
- ☐ As soon as possible, take your team "cross cultural" to another campus in the area and begin to plant a church network there too.
- ☐ Plan a regional mission trip or even an international one to another campus overseas for 3 weeks in the summer.
- ☐ Be involved in local missions as well... partnering with existing ministries to serve them is a great way to connect to the larger regional Body of Christ and to get to put feet to your faith and practice what you study.
- ☐ Continually keep the big picture of God's Kingdom coming and His will being done in and through your lives like it is in heaven.
- ☐ Ask the Lord what things He wants to see change on your campus and then ask Him what part He has for you to play in the process.
- ☐ Get involved—as God directs run for student government, join up with clubs and groups, intentionally develop relationships all with the larger picture focus of God moving, lives coming into the Kingdom and God's Spirit coming and transforming your campus, your city and your nation.

CAMPUS CHURCH NETWORKS:

Visit us online at *www.campuschurch.net* and find out more how to connect with us!

Vision: Every campus, every nation for Christ.

Mission: To fulfill the Great Commandment and the Great Commission in this generation through initiating and cultivating church planting movements on every campus around the world.

Contact CCN: info@campuschurch.net or (408) 252.5500 x146

Contact Michele with CCN: songsofthebride@yahoo.com

Contact Michele for further resources: songsofthebride@yahoo.com   Compiled by Michele Perry, CCN

KINGDOM LIFESTYLE PLANNING WORKSHEET

(See following page)

Relationship w/Father, Son & Holy Spirit

Facetime w/God 7x/week:
Adoration ___
Confession ___
Thanksgiving ___
Supplication (prayer) ___
Forgiveness ___
Hear:
Word ___
Spirit ___
Obey ___
Fruit of the Spirit ___
Wisdom of the Spirit ___
Revelation of the Spirit ___
Power of Spirit ___
God's Love to others ___

Relationship w/Natural Family

Family Facetime w/God ___
Kingdom:
Values ___
Mission ___
Vision ___
Culture ___
Strategies ___
Divine order in marriage/family ___
Love language practiced ___
Marriage/family unity ___
Culture of honor ___
Culture of submission ___
Family meals ___
Family communication ___
Family conflict resolution ___
Family play & recreation ___
Parenting skills ___
Children obeying from the heart ___

Relationship w/ Spiritual Family

Unity of mind around values vision, culture, strategies ___
Unity of heart ___
Unity of lifestyle ___
Love, honor & submission to leadership & other family members ___
Active in MCF ___
Active in DNA ___
Making disciples ___
Active in corporate worship ___
Active in family-of-churches (Rock Tribe) ___
Utilize spiritual gifts ___
Regularly pray for leaders & others ___
Tithe & offerings ___
Gospel mission is way of life ___

Relationship w/Myself

Body:
Exercise ___
Healthy Eating ___
Rest ___
Soul:
Mental health ___
Yielded will to Christ ___
Emotions ___
Fruit of Spirit ___
Mind of Christ ___
Motives of Christ ___
Character of Christ ___
Inner healing is way of life ___
Mercy over judgement ___
Faith in God ___
Wisdom & revelation ___
Spirit:
Rev of identity as "son" ___
I live from heaven->earth ___
Ongoing sense of Father's love ___
Evid. sonship in daily life ___
Intimate union w/Christ ___
Conscience clean ___
Fear of the Lord ___
Intuition sanctified ___
Obedient heart ___
Sensitivity to HS leading ___
Discernment of spirits ___
Level of spiritual passion ___
Fruit of spirit operative ___
Power of HS flows thru me ___
Life Skills:
Time management ___
Money management ___
Relational intelligence ___
Emotional intelligence ___
Rest & recreation ___

Relationship w/Neighbors & Coworkers

Prayer, care, share lifestyle ___
Gospel fluency ___
Reach out to neighbors ___
Life reveals the gospel ___
Seek 1st the Kingdom of God ___
Relationships:
Friends ___
Relatives ___
Boss ___
Coworkers ___
Strangers ___
Internationals ___
Children & Youth ___
Poor ___
Disciple making:
Family ___
Individuals ___
DNA Group ___
Coworkers ___
MCF ___
Neighbors ___
Serving attitude ___
Integrate gifts & calling ___
24/7 ___

Holy Spirit's Current Emphasis 1 - 10
1 = Not a top area of focus right now
5 = Growing conviction-pay attention
10 = Top priority: Set faith-goals now!

Weekly Planning Sheet

TIME	SUN	MON	TUES	WED	THUR	FRI	SAT
12:00							
1:00							
2:00							
3:00							
4:00							
5:00							
6:00							
7:00							
8:00							
9:00							
10:00							
11:00							
12:00							
1:00							
2:00							
3:00							
4:00							
5:00							
6:00							
7:00							
8:00							
9:00							
10:00							
11:00							
12:00							

Discipleship Questions: Pray, Hear, Obey

1. How are you known in heaven? Rehearse God's vision for your life.

2. How are you seeking Christ & His Kingdom first, living from heaven to earth? Are you having daily Facetime with God? When & Where? (Pray, Hear, Obey Lifestyle)

3. In which of the five relational categories is the Holy Spirit most focusing upon? What specifically is the Holy Spirit dealing with in your life?

4. What is God saying to you? How will you obey God's voice?

5. Who are you reaching for Christ? How are you reaching them? (Prayer, Care, Share Lifestyle)

6. What area of your life is the Holy Spirit upgrading? Is there any sin (commission and omission) which you need to confess to your DNA group in order to get free?

   Are you concealing any sins or problems?

7. Who are you currently discipling?

Faith goals for this coming week:

Write two or three faith goals you wish to reach this week:

Strategy and plans:

How do you plan to reach these faith goals (where, when, how, with whom)?

What is your strategy?

What will be the results of reaching your faith goals?

LEVELS OF EFFECTIVE LEARNING

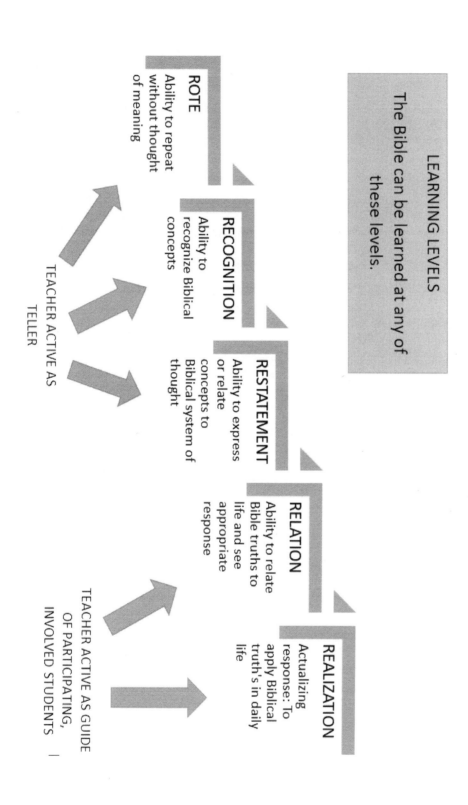

LEARNING LEVELS

The Bible can be learned at any of these levels.

ROTE
Ability to repeat without thought of meaning

RECOGNITION
Ability to recognize Biblical concepts

RESTATEMENT
Ability to express or relate concepts to Biblical system of thought

RELATION
Ability to relate Bible truths to life and see appropriate response

REALIZATION
Actualizing response: To apply Biblical truth's in daily life

TEACHER ACTIVE AS TELLER

TEACHER ACTIVE AS GUIDE OF PARTICIPATING, INVOLVED STUDENTS

LIFE MODEL SMALL GROUPS

By Michael Sullivant

The "Interchangeable Parts" of a Life Model-Based Small Group:

These life-giving activities or "parts" are initially thought of as "interchangeable" in nature. They may vary according to the particular need discerned and the "flow of life" in terms of their order, time frames and whether to include them or not into any given small group gathering. This list provides a "menu" that leaders can choose from to plan a gathering or series of gatherings. **These groups will succeed to the degree that they are viewed and experienced as circles of genuine Jesus-centered friendships and not a church program. Programs do not love people. God and people love people. LM-based group activities can help inspire, empower, inform and support the experience of God's** *chesed* **authentic** *koinonia* **within the context of a community of Christ-followers.** The primary underlying goal is to unveil, strengthen and reinforce our *new identity* in Christ as individuals and a *shared new way of life* as a Jesus community. **These small groups specialize in creating informal (totally unscripted) and non-formal (interactive) joy-filled learning environments that are hard to facilitate in larger congregations.** On the front end of such initiatives, people tend to think, "What are we going to do all those hours?" After the groups start to *hum*, people tend to think, "We need more time to do all these things!"

- *Informal* fellowship with refreshments and light healthy foods - create an "open house" feel
- Gracefully migrate into the *non-formal* interactive portion of the group time - facilitate life-giving activities such as:
  - Turn on relational circuits
    - Breathe YHWH as prayer
    - Tap the vagus nerve
    - Do the surprise and calm exercise
    - Yawn side to side
  - Share simple gratitudes and joyful anticipations
  - Engage in an *Interactive Gratitude* together and share it with the group or triad
  - Answer *Curiosity Questions* with vulnerability (We all long to be known and to know others without the fear of rejection. I have formulated a list of such questions as a start.)
  - Sing together
    - Simple acapella worship songs
    - Worship videos
    - Lead worship songs with guitar or piano
  - Recall/share a "Golden Memory" - a moment in life when you felt like your truest self, God's presence, God's goodness or beauty, deep joy and/or "this is the way life was meant to be" feeling.

- o "Listen on God's behalf" to a group member share their life journey. Respond with curious and clarifying questions and personal prayer with laying on of hands. Welcome, but don't force, vulnerability. (This can be done in the triads if need be.)
- o Read printed out brief transformational Scripture passages and engage in spontaneous sharing of questions, insights and possible applications. Especially utilize personal and corporate "new identity" passages.
- o Watch a 6 minute thebibleproject.com video and discussing it together. (This is an amazing free resource on YouTube. No need to reinvent the wheel.)
- o Break down into triads to:
  - Look others in the eyes for 5-7 seconds at a time
  - Practice other brain-skill exercises
  - Share about unresolved pains - failures, injustices or traumas
  - Practice Immanuel prayer (once it is carefully explained, taught and modeled)
  - Share pressing needs and intercede for each other
- o Share Immanuel testimonials
- o Put someone in the "hot seat," lay on hands and pray God's blessings down upon them and share inspired thoughts and words
- o Share in the *Lord's Supper* together - do this in various creative ways (Exodus feed/serve others)
- o Practice being *Alone Together* - find a corner or private space indoors/outdoors to meditate on a Scripture passage, listen to what God might be saying, do an interactive gratitude, craft a prayer, write in a journal and then come back to share what you experienced with the group or triad.
- Have a dinner party
- Have a game day/night
- Have a "Fabulous Movie" night
- Take a nature hike to observe God's beauty as a group
- Take a road trip to a special destination
- Help group members with a home project too big for one family
- Go on a retreat to do these things more intensively and to rest and play together - long unplanned hours together are a *hidden strategy* of discipleship in the gospels. Jesus and the 12 spent many hours traveling and camping out together.
- Function as a ministry team
  - o Serve the needy together
  - o Offer prayer to others beyond the group
  - o Take on a service project
  - o Take a mission trip together
- Make several commitments outside of the gathering times
  - o Watch all thebibleproject.com videos
  - o Read Jesus Calling every day - everyone gets on the same page
  - o Pray the Lord's Prayer at noon every day
  - o Gather in pairs or triads to foster deeper partnerships in Jesus

    ○Support one another in any crisis

• When groups become too large to facilitate in one place, pray and invite people to "hive off" and form a new group. Then plan some ways to keep these 2, 3, 4 groups organically connected. **This strategy works best if the people involved see themselves as on a longer journey together as friends in Christ and who support one another to discover and do the Father's will in all the seasons of life.**

MODELS FOR LEARNING

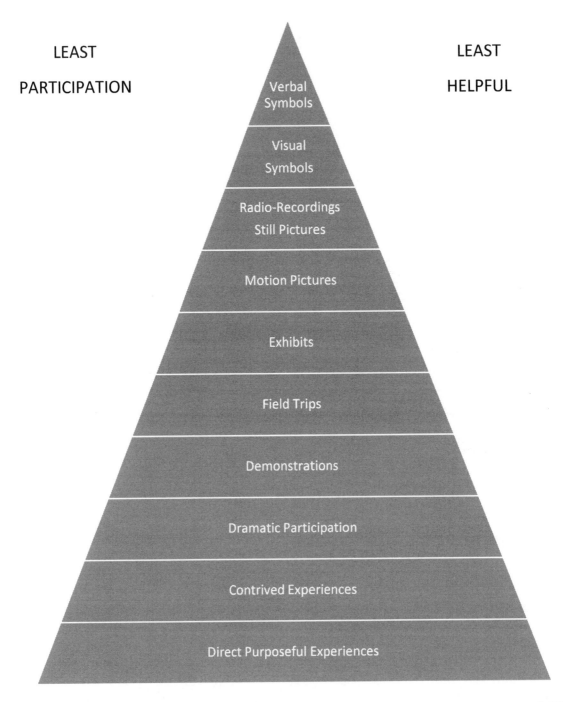

LEAST
PARTICIPATION

LEAST
HELPFUL

Verbal
Symbols

Visual
Symbols

Radio-Recordings
Still Pictures

Motion Pictures

Exhibits

Field Trips

Demonstrations

Dramatic Participation

Contrived Experiences

Direct Purposeful Experiences

MOST
PARTICIPATION

MOST
HELPFUL

OSV & CLARIFYING EXPECTATIONS FOR MCF'S

Becoming A Member Of a "Micro-Church Family"

By Dr. Timothy Johns

Acts 2:42-47, 4:32-37; Luke 10:1-24; Matthew 6:33, 28:18-20

Welcome: Your Father in heaven loves you, and so do we! You can become His son or daughter through Christ by the Holy Spirit. God is One, yet reveals Himself in Three Persons, Father, Son, Holy Spirit: a Family of One. Because of this, Father builds His Kingdom relationally through natural and spiritual families. Every person who has placed their faith in Christ and been indwelt with His Spirit is a child of God and a part of His universal Family – The Church. At the same time, we are to connect deeply with a local spiritual family so that 1.) we can help one another become like Christ, 2.) we can work together to advance Christ's Kingdom in this community and the nations. We would be thrilled if Father led you into our spiritual family. There are two ways you can know if you have been called into this Micro-Church Family. One, in your mind and heart you come into unity with the values, vision, strategy, and leadership of a family-of-churches we call a "Jesus Tribe". Two, you sense in your spirit/heart that the Holy Spirit is placing you into this family and the leadership believes the same thing. In other words, there is an objective standard of determining family membership based in agreement around the Person of Christ, The People of Christ, and The Purpose of Christ as it has been given to the leaders of your Jesus Tribe. There is also a subjective witness of the Holy Spirit to you and the other family members that Father has joined you to this spiritual family.

Introducing our Jesus Tribe (Family-of-Churches) and Micro-Church Families on Mission:

Because unity of head, heart, and "hands" (reaching out together) is so essential to advancing Christ's Kingdom in our community, we must all understand and agree upon Biblical core values, vision, and strategy. These are all written out for you to research and pray about. We will discuss the Biblical core values, vision, and strategy of our Jesus Tribe in a face-to-face orientation time, so that we can process in more depth what we are to be and do in Christ.

One of our five strategies to advancing the Kingdom of God in our Micro-Church Family is to help each disciple of Christ become a vital member of a "small spiritual family". This is the best Biblical strategy for 1.) helping you become like Christ. Roman 8:29; 2 Corinthians 3:18, 2.) training you to help others become like Christ. Matthew 28:18-20, 3.) "organically" and relationally expanding the Kingdom of God in our region and the nations Matthew 6:10, 33. Jesus, who focused His training on twelve disciples Mark 3:13-19, Moses, who gathered the Israelites in groups of tens Exodus 18:13-27, and the Holy Spirit led early church which met house-to-house Acts 2:42-47, 20:20; Roman 16:5, all modeled the necessity of discipleship and missions through small groups. In the traditional or institutional church organizations, people can too easily "hide" in the larger meetings and programs. Personal issues of heart motives, mental and emotional struggles, and day-to-day kingdom living tend to be neglected in "religious" settings that do not promote transparent, heart-to-heart, covenant family relationships. This Micro-Church Family hopes to serve the whole body of Christ (including local churches) by encouraging, teaching, and modeling prayer, evangelism, and discipleship within the context of covenant families (house churches).

What Is a Micro-Church Family?

Definition: A Micro-Church Family is made up of at least five people but no more than twenty-five (one of whom is a qualified leader and the other one is an apprentice leader). They connect around the Lordship and Person of Christ and His manifest presence and glory as both a lifestyle and in a gathering at least once a week. They connect in deep loving relationships for the purpose of enabling one another to be radical disciples of Christ, reach the lost, advance the Kingdom of God in all areas of life in their cities/communities, and multiply more covenant families. Christ, God's manifest presence and glory, spreading the love of the Father by the Holy Spirit, and the advancing of Christ's Kingdom are the passions and missions of a Micro-Church Family (MCF's).

1. MCF's are a spiritual family – people connected covenantally heart-to-heart around Christ in order to advance His kingdom and help each person become like Christ. I Corinthians 4:15-17; Ephesians 3:14

2. MCF's are a group of friends unified around Christ's love and mission. Matthew 11:19; John 15:12-17

3. MCF's are a healing community that prays for the sick, counsels the confused, carries out inner healing, sets people free from curses and demonic bondage, and creates such an atmosphere of acceptance and love that rejection and insecurities are displaced automatically over time. James 5:16; Matthew 10:1,8

4. MCF's are a training and equipping center, a safe setting for people to practice leadership, management, preaching, teaching, creative ministry, spiritual gifts, and all forms of servanthood. Matthew 28:18-20

5. MCF's are a missionary team and spiritual army – a flexible, spontaneous, organized platoon capable of reaching those who do not follow Christ and are not in a spiritual family. They are dedicated to seeking and saving the lost, delivering people from demonic bondage, doing justice, and serving youth, poor, widow, orphan, and alien. Luke 19:10; Ephesians 6:10-18

6. MCF's are a lifestyle of deep, intentional, meaningful relationships that connect any time and place with an ultimate goal to reach lost people, and transform communities through Christ and the Kingdom of God. Acts 2:42-47, 4:32-35.

Important Perspective:

The starting and multiplying of MCF's must occur under Biblical heart motives and core values in order to receive the full enabling presence and power of the Holy Spirit. It takes the supernatural Life of Christ to sustain Christ-centered relationships. It is almost as if a warning label should be attached to any document which tries to explain or instruct people about covenant families. **Warning: Do not attempt to start, grow, or multiply covenant families (house churches) as another church program or evangelistic strategy. Covenant Families will only work to the**

degree each individual and the group as a whole have died to themselves and are governed and empowered by the indwelling Lord, Jesus Christ, and His Word by the Holy Spirit.

One more key point must be made regarding the reason for writing down the purposes, expectations, and commitments of MCF's. All of the contents included in this overview should be understood as instructions on **"how to love God and people in a way that advances Christ's Kingdom."** It should **not** be viewed as a rule book or religious document that has to be mechanically applied. **This overview is to help coach people into a lifestyle of loving relationships**. Every expectation or recommendation has Biblical wisdom and truth, with the ultimate intention that the greatest amount of Christ's love gets spread to the most people in the highest quality way in the least amount of time. Because people are suffering and dying, our mission is time sensitive.

Truth exists for love. So many people come from dysfunctional families and/or unhealthy churches (or no church background at) that it takes clear teaching and constant coaching to help people walk in God's ways of truth and love combined. Most people have very little understanding as to the etiquette of relationships and group life within the context and government of a healthy spiritual family. The "spirit" of this document is to promote the life and love of Christ within individuals and covenant families, and should in no way be used legalistically, so that people are judged or rejected. MCF's should be the safest, most loving, life-giving settings on earth. But true safety involves accountability and discipline along with unconditional affection and love, just like a healthy family. **Bottom line, MCF's should feel as much like heaven on earth as possible!**

The key to advancing the Kingdom of God on earth is for laid-down lovers of Christ to exchange the life of Christ between each other in the context of covenantally connected Christ-centered relationships. Because the Kingdom of God involves coming under the Lordship of Christ in every sphere of life, those in the covenant families learn to submit to the Christ in one another and assist each other to follow Christ completely.

Perspective on Shifting Into a Biblical Paradigm of Kingdom Life Together:

For MCF's to be viewed and experienced as the primary context for church life, it will take a significant paradigm shift in the hearts and minds of God's people. Being in a true "Book of Acts" house church is really a major shift of perspective, values and lifestyle. Usually this does not occur unless there is 1.) high degrees of discontentment, dissatisfaction, and internal and external pain and pressure, 2.) high degrees of promise and pleasure that come from both the manifest presence of Christ and authentic covenant love between the members, 3.) a willingness to make the sacrifices necessary to reach the lost and transform communities.

Commitments and expectations of MCF members:

These commitments and expectations should be presented in writing and discussed with each *person at the beginning of their involvement in the Micro-Church Family.* They should also be reviewed regularly with all the members. Clear expectations helps people know how to come into unity with the Person, People, and Purpose of Christ. Skilled leadership and spiritual "parenting" plus clear expectations create a safe and secure setting for people to mature in Christ.

One becomes a member of our Jesus Tribe by becoming a son or daughter of Father through Christ by the Holy Spirit and becoming an active member of a Micro-Church Family. **Remember: These commitments and expectations are not rules and regulations. They are to be used as helpful guidelines and principles which enable us to love Christ, one another and unbelievers more effectively. Here is what we aspire to be and do:**

1. We are **committed to experience the freedom in Christ, and to help others do the same.** We are sincerely seeking to know God through Christ unto the end that others become born again Christians, Spirit-filled, real disciples of Christ, being transformed into His likeness. By joining the covenant family, we are inviting the leaders and other members to help us follow Christ and grow into Christ's likeness.

2. We are **committed to being of "one heart and mind" with one another** Acts 4:32. To the best of our ability, we strive to understand and submit to the values, vision, strategies, and expectations of the leaders of their covenant family, the local elders, and the leadership team of our "Jesus Tribe".

3. We are **committed to participate weekly in the corporate life and activities** of the covenant family, and regularly attend the regional celebrations and training. We honor and worship God and help advance His Kingdom by giving tithes and offerings through our local church i.e. "store house".

4. We are **committed to grace affirmation**: (Unconditional Love, Agape Love) Colossians 3:5-14 "I will choose to love you, up build you, and accept you, my brothers and sisters, no matter what you say or do. I will choose to love you in whatever form you come. There is nothing you have done or will do that will make me stop loving you. I may not agree with your actions, but I will love you as a person and do all I can to hold you up in God's affirming love."

5. We are **committed to honesty**: Ephesians 4:25-32 "I will not hide from you what I feel about you or coming from you, good or bad, but I will see, in the timing of the Spirit, to deal openly and directly with you in a loving and forgiving way so that you are affirmed when in need, and so that our frustration with each other does not become bitterness. I will try to mirror back to you what I am hearing you say and feel. If this means risking pain, realizing it is in *"speaking the truth in love that we grow up in every way into Christ who is the head"* Ephesians 4:15, then I will take the risk. I will try to express this honesty in a sensitive and controlled manner and to meter it, according to what I perceive the circumstances to be."

6. We are **committed to openness**: Romans 7:15-25 "I will try to strive to become a more open person, disclosing my feelings, my struggles, my joys and my hurts to you as well as I am able. The degree to which I do so implies that I cannot make it without you. This is to affirm your worth to me as a person. In other words, I need you!"

7. We are **committed to prayer and fasting**: Matthew 6:9,16-18; 2 Thessalonians 1:11-12 "I commit to pray for you in some regular fashion, believing that our caring Father wishes His

children to pray for one another and ask Him for the blessings we all need. I will not be merely a passive listener. Rather, I choose to be a spiritual participant, willing to enter into your situation and prayerfully helping to shoulder your burden."

8. We are **committed to sensitivity**: John 4:1-29 "Even as I desire to be known and understood by you, I commit to be sensitive to you and your needs to the best of my ability. I will try to hear you, see you, and feel where you are and to draw you out of the pit of discouragement or withdrawal. I will earnestly avoid giving "simplistic" answers to the difficult situations you may find yourself in."

9. We are **committed to availability**: Acts 2:43-47 "Here I am if you need me. Anything I have-- time, energy, insight, possessions--is at your disposal, if you need it, to the limit of my resources." I will open my heart, my home, and my life to help you become more like Jesus.

10. We are **committed to confinement & boundaries**: Proverbs 10:19; 11:9,13; 12:23; 13:3; 15:4; 18:6-8 "I will keep whatever is shared within the confines of our Micro-Church family in order to provide the atmosphere of trust necessary for openness. I understand, however, that this confidentiality does not prohibit my MCF family leader from sharing either verbally or in written form any pertinent information with the elders of our local church. I understand that our MCF family leaders function under pastoral/elder oversight, having delegated authority as an extension of the pastoral care ministry of our local church elders. As a result, our MCF leaders are accountable to the elder(s) of the local church family, who are themselves accountable to others in ministry and the Chief Shepherd, Jesus Christ, my Lord." Hebrews 13:17

11. We are **committed to accountability and confession of sin**: Ezekiel 3:16-21; Matthew 18:12-30; James 5:16 "I commit to growth, maturity and discipleship using the Bible and other equipping materials that each of the MCF's in our spiritual family are progressing through as part of their equipping times, and in doing so will make myself accountable weekly to my accountability DNA partner in the MCF. I give you the right to question, confront, and challenge me in love when I seem to be falling in any aspect of my life under God--family, devotions, general spiritual growth, etc. I trust you to be in the Spirit and led of Him when you do so. I need your correction and reproof so that I may ever better fulfill God-given ministry among you. I will try not to be defensive." Proverbs 12:1,15; 13:10,18

12. We are **committed to following the Biblical process of conflict resolution**. Matthew 18, Galatians 6:1-5 We will not triangulate, gossip, or slander our brothers or sisters in Christ. We will deal with offenses with truth and love. Disagreements or conflicts should in no way divide our hearts or justify a breech in relationship or closing

13. We are **committed to time regularity**: Hebrews 10:25; Luke 9:57-62 "I will regard the regular time which my MCF family spends together weekly as time under the disciplining hand of Jesus in our midst. I will not grieve the Spirit or hinder His work in the lives of my brothers and sisters by my absence, except in an emergency. By His permission, and through prayer alone, will I consider being absent. If I am unable to attend for any reason, out of consideration I will call my covenant family leader in order that the covenant family members may know why I am absent, will be able to pray for me, and will not worry about me."

14. We are **committed to outreach**: Matthew 25:31-46 "I will find ways to sacrifice myself for those outside our Micro-Church family and our local church in the same way that I have committed to sacrifice myself for you, my brothers and sisters. I will network in prayer and relationships with my fellow MCF family members to evangelize and disciple unbelievers or unchurched friends outside of the MCF meeting during the course of its life. I will do it in Jesus' Name so that others are added to the Kingdom of God in His love."

15. We are **committed to serving and giving time, talents, gifts, and finances** to the purpose of advancing the kingdom in our community and the nations. "I will give tithes, offerings, first fruits to the Lord through our local church and "Jesus Tribe" in order to provide the resources necessary to fulfill our mission." 2 Corinthians 9:6-15

RARE LEADERSHIP HANDOUT

The Brain Science Revolution – 2 Distinct Processors!

- ➢ Left-Brain Functions (Slow Track – 5 Cycles/sec.)
  - ○ Conscious Thought
  - ○ Problem-Solving
  - ○ Getting Work Done
  - ○ Isolation
  - ○ Management
- ➢ Right-Brain Functions (Fast Track – 6 Cycles/sec)
  - ○ Attachment (Supra-Conscious Emotion)
  - ○ Belonging/Identity
  - ○ Relating w/ Joy
  - ○ Engagement
  - ○ Leadership
- ➢ When your right-brain works well, your left-brain works better too
- ➢ When the right-brain leads, the left-brain follows automatically
- ➢ When the left-brain leads, you lose your mind and so do others!
- ➢ The brain is fueled by joy and joy is relational

Key Right Brain Issue – Emotional Capacity

- ➢ Measured by the size of your right orbital prefrontal cortex
- ➢ Your Joy Bucket!
- ➢ When its full you can do the RARE habits
- ➢ It gets emptied by unresolved pains in our lives – Psalm 139's "way of pain" – our sins, sins against us, traumas (A & B)
- ➢ It gets replenished by gratitude in the presence of God and His representatives

Filling Your Joy Bucket – GAMES (Exercise 1)

- ➢ G – Gratitude
- ➢ A – Anticipation of joy
- ➢ M – Memories
- ➢ E – Entertainment/Eating
- ➢ S - Singing

2 Leadership Paradigms

- ➢ Common Paradigm – Reason + Choices Bring Transformation – Accountability => Productivity
- ➢ Uncommon (Rare) Paradigm – Belonging + Identity Bring Transformation – Authenticity => Productivity

- Left-Brain Leaders – focus on getting results – they use people to get work done
- Right-Brain Leaders – focus on building belonging – they build groups that get things done

Defining Leadership

- Leadership is creating engagement (right-brain) in what matters (left-brain)
- Problem 1 – People don't know what matters
- Problem 2 – People are motivated by Shame, Anger, Disgust, Sadness, Anxiety, Despair
- Rare Leadership is creating engagement with joy in what matters

3 Types of Leaders (Exercise 2)

- Fearful Leaders (Possums) – hide their weaknesses and disappear when hardship comes
- Predator Leaders (Wolves) – scan for weaknesses and use it for their gain
- Protector Leaders (Elephants) – scan for weaknesses and looks for ways to help people grow

Habit 1 – Remain Relational

- Your right-brain (fast track) has an On/Off switch
- On/Off Checklist
  - I want to make a problem, person or feeling go away
  - I want to fight, flee or freeze
  - I feel like it's your fault when I hurt your feelings
  - I listen with my answer running
  - I don't want to make eye contact
  - I would rather just handle problems myself
  - People are a bother and just get in my way
- How to Flip the Switch On (Relational Circuits (RC's)
  - Curiosity – helps you attune
  - Appreciation of Another
  - Kindness – deeds and actions (childlike)
- "Envelope" Conversations when you need to confront a problem
  - Keep the relationship more important than the problem – if possible
  - Not all relationships make it – (Gottman's "Bids and Responses" Observations)

Habit 2 – Act Like Yourself

- The Problem of Putting on Masks – "hypocrite"/actor
  - Takes so much energy to manage a false image
- Anatomy of a Stronghold
  - The world wounds us
  - The devil lies to us
  - The flesh makes vows in reaction
  - Strongholds form to block love (3 directions)

Habit 3 – Return to Joy

- ➢ The 4 Story Elevator – pain processing pathway
  - o Attachment – Lights up when someone is *personal* with me
  - o Assessment – Good, bad or scary
  - o Attunement – Reads the person
  - o Action – Act like myself (Identity/Joy Center) or put on a mask (stuck elevator)
- ➢ How to Return to Joy
  - o Validate the emotion
  - o Comfort by making the problem smaller (Immanuel is with us)
  - o Recover by experiencing joy on the heels of the disruption and rewire your brain

Habit 4 – Endure Hardship Well

- ➢ Suffering well means maintaining the 3 skills below when in adversity:
  - o Remaining relational
  - o Acting like yourself
  - o Returning to joy
- ➢ Immature people don't suffer well

5 Stages of Maturity

- ➢ Infant – My job is to let you know I'm upset. Your job is to figure out why and fix it.
- ➢ Child – My job is to tell you what I want. You job is to make it happen.
- ➢ Adult – Can remain relational, act like myself, return to joy from upsets, endure hardship and practice the first 3 skills
- ➢ Parent – Helps children learn RARE skills
- ➢ Elder- Helps a community learn RARE skills

Orphan vs. Son

THE HEART OF AN ORPHAN		THE HEART OF SONSHIP
See God as Master	IMAGE OF GOD	See God as loving Father
Independent/self-reliant	DEPENDENCY	Interdependent/acknowledges need
Live by the love of law	THEOLOGY	Live by the Law of Love
Insecure/lack peace	SECURITY	Rest and peace
Strive for the praise, approval and acceptance of man	NEED FOR APPROVAL	Totally accepted in God's love and justified by grace
A need for personal achievement as you seek to impress God and others, or no motivation to serve at all	MOTIVE FOR SERVICE	Service that is motivated by a deep gratitude for being unconditionally loved and accepted by God
Duty and earning God's favor or no motivation at all.	MOTIVE BEHIND CHRISTIAN DISCIPLINES	Pleasure and delight
'Must' be holy to have God's favor, thus increasing a sense of shame and guilt	MOTIVE FOR PURITY	'Want to' be holy; do not want anything to hinder relationship with God
Self-rejection from comparing yourself to others	SELF-IMAGE	Positive and affirmed because you know you have such value to God
Seek comfort in counterfeit affections: addictions, compulsions, escapism, busyness, hyper-religious activity	SOURCE OF COMFORT	Seek times of quietness and solitude to rest in the Father's presence and love
Competition, rivalry and jealousy toward others success and position	PEER RELATIONSHIPS	Humility and unity as you value others and are able to rejoice in their blessings and success
Accusation and exposure in order to make yourself look good by making others look bad	HANDLING OTHERS' FAULTS	Love covers as you seek to restore others in a spirit of love and gentleness.
See authority as a source of pain; distrustful toward them and lack a heart attitude of submission	VIEW OF AUTHORITY	Respectful, honoring; you see them as ministers of God for good in your life.
Difficulty receiving admonition; you must be right so you easily get your feelings hurt and close your spirit to discipline	VIEW OF ADMONITION	See the receiving of admonition as a blessing and need in your life so that you faults and weaknesses are exposed and put to death
Guarded and conditional; based upon others' performance as you seek to get your own needs met	EXPRESSION OF LOVE	Open, patient and affectionate as you lay your life and agendas down in order to meet the needs of others
Conditional and distant	SENSE OF GOD'S PRESENCE	Close & intimate
Bondage	CONDITION	Liberty
Feel like a servant/slave	POSITION	Feel like a son/daughter
Spiritual ambition; the earnest desire for some spiritual achievement and distinction and the willingness to strive for it; a desire to be seen and counted among the mature	VISION	To daily experience the Father's unconditional love and acceptance and then be sent as a representative of His love to family and others
Fight for what you can get!	FUTURE	Sonship releases your inheritance!

Heart of Serving Son/Daughter in an Apostolic Tribe vs. Heart of a Slave/Hireling/Organizationally Attender

The Heart of a Son/Daughter:	The Heart of a Slave/Hireling/ Organizational Attender:
1. They have identified their spiritual fathers and their family. They hold their spiritual father's heart and work as their own. a. They identify first corporately, then as an individual b. They think and act in terms of responsibilities versus authority or position.	They tend to their own things such as ministries and activities. a. They are ambitious and desire to begin their calling prematurely, often independently. God will give them the opportunity to seize what He wants to give us (i.e. He will allow us to gain our inheritance prematurely.) b. They are willing to settle for God's good vs. perfect will c. They think in terms of rights and privileges.
2. They use languages of "us", "we" and "our" because they are family oriented.	They use the language of "me" and "my" because they think in terms of their ministry, job, etc.
3. They honor leadership and cover the nakedness of their spiritual fathers and mothers. Sons do not delight in the nakedness of a leader. a. If we listen to accusations, we undermine our cause. b. They guard the way they speak to each other. c. They cover nakedness, not sin. d. The difference in motivations will show up under pressure	They trade in the coinage of revealed flesh; their wage is discovering nakedness. a. They press for equality and level speech. b. They are offended by nakedness. c. Differences in Noah's sons' responses. d. Can't discern between intimacy and familiarity.
4. They naturally honor the chain of command. a. A good soldier takes orders from any officer. b. They recognize real authority, and they also recognize the lack of real authority.	They are unwilling to honor authority selective about whom they yield to. a. Test of a hireling's heart; ask them to submit to someone they don't 'witness to'. b. They are often confused. c. They continually need re-definition of authority and roles because it isn't in their heart to submit.
5. Secure sons/daughters don't focus on loyalty, but the joy of working together.	They focus on loyalty and reveal insecurity, need of position, desire for privilege.
6. They share inner conversations (doubts, fears, insecurities, anxieties, weaknesses, etc.)	They share only what they want you to know.

7.	They always entreat their father and come with open hand for input.	They carry offenses against leaders. a. They cultivate rejection and mistrust. b. They engage and fuel gossip and slander.
8.	They have generational vision (spiritually and naturally) a. They want to share life with fathers together down to third and fourth generation. b. They are willing to sow life into training next generation of leaders vs. pursuing their own glory.	They are self-focused. "My ministry" vs. kids/grandkids in the spirit. a. Talk about finding his own truth and discovering their own ministry and calling. b. Always wants 'pay offs' and to pick and choose involvement. c. Won't produce Isaac and Jacob.
9.	They bond new and weak people to the whole family.	They bond new and weak people to themselves.
10.	They focus on the welfare of the people. a. Conversations and time involvements reflect caring for the whole flock.	Unfathered people tend to focus on appearance: meetings, numbers, events, success, and 'who I know'. a. The leaven of the Pharisee's is 'to be seen of men...' Matthew 6 b. Negative manifestations: a critical spirit.
11.	They can be secure to accept and welcome confrontations and change. (Heb 12:1-15) a. They respond to discipline. b. Their trust is obvious to see.	Confrontations and correction offends. a. Reveals levels of mistrust b. Independent contractors – outside ministries. Put steel walls around who you let them touch.
12.	They have 'puppy feet' (i.e. you can see their potential for growth)	Already appears to have matured by themselves and has no seed of parental impute. a. Agenda: what he/she will add to you vs. what you can add to them.
13.	Time, energy, finances, gifts, talents and affections are generously given to further the kingdom purpose. This is due to a full and grateful heart. Out of the heart comes the issues of life.	Resources are given conservatively and not necessarily cheerfully.
14.	Because of a keen sense of 'ownership' doesn't hesitate to carry out small, mundane or 'dirty' jobs when no one is noticing. Like cleaning the buildings or taking out the trash.	Avoids the dirty, hard and hidden jobs.

Comparisons between the Orphan and the Child of God

The Orphan

I will not leave you as orphans...John 14:18

Feels alone. Lacks a vital daily intimacy with God. Is full of self-concern.

Anxious over felt needs: relationships, money, health. "I'm all alone and nobody cares. I'm not a happy camper."

Lives on a succeed/fail basis. Needs to "look good and "be right". Is performance-oriented.

Feels condemned, guilty and unworthy before God and others.

Has little faith, lots of fear, lots of faith in himself: "I've got to fix it."

Labors under a sense of unlimited obligation. Tries too hard to please. Burns out.

Rebellious. Resists authority. Heart is hard. Is not easily teachable.

Defensive. Can't listen well. Bristles at the charge of being self-righteous (thus proving the point).

Needs to be right, safe secure. Unwilling to fail. Unable to tolerate criticism. Can only 'handle' praise.

Excessively self-confident or self-loathing. Discouraged, defeated. Lacks spiritual power.

Tends towards an 'I can do it myself!' attitude. Is strong-willed, driven.

Unbelieving effort. Relies only on his gifts to get by in ministry.

The Child of God

But He has given us the Spirit of sonship and by Him we cry, 'Abba, Father!' Romans 8:15

Has grown assurance that 'God is really *my* loving heavenly Father.'

Trusts the Father and has a growing confidence in His loving care. Is being freed up from worry.

Learning to live in daily, conscious, partnership with God. Is not fearful.

Feels loved, forgiven and totally accepted because Christ's merit really clothes him.

Has a daily *working trust* in God's sovereign plan for her loving, wise and best. Believes God is good.

Prayer is the first resort: "I'm going to ask my Daddy first. Cries, "Abba, Father!"

Has strength to be submissive. Has a soft, broken and contrite heart. Is teachable.

Open to criticism since she *consciously* stands in *Christ's* perfection, not her own. Is able to examine her unbelief.

Able to take risks and even fail, since his righteousness is in Christ. Needs no 'record' to boast in, protect or defend.

Confident in Christ and encouraged because of the Holy Spirit's work in her.

"I can do all things through Christ who gives me strength!"

Trusting *less* in self and more in the Holy Spirit – a daily, conscious reliance

Scriptural references on becoming a spiritual son/daughter:

Romans 8:15-17

Hebrews 2:10-18

Galatians 3:26 – 4:7

John 1:10-13

Luke 15:11-32

1 John 3

MODELBRIEF

SUMMARY OF THE CONNEXIONS MODEL OF LEADER DEVELOPMENT

THE 5C GOAL OF LEADER DEVELOPMENT

According to our ConneXions "5C" model, a healthy Christian leader knows God (Christ), was formed and lives in supportive and accountable community (Community), has integrity (Character), knows the purpose of God and presents it with credibility, clarity and passion (Calling), and has the necessary gifts, skills and knowledge to lead the people in the accomplishment of this purpose (Competencies) – and he is continually growing in all five areas.

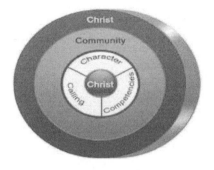

Too often, in leader development, we only focus on the last of these "Cs." When a young man or woman goes to Bible school to become a leader, what is addressed? Competencies! Perhaps some token attention is paid to the other four elements, but for the most part, our attention to "leader development" is given in the area of competencies such as Biblical knowledge, how to preach, how to counsel, etc. Competencies are essential but not sufficient in developing healthy leaders. Consequently, we have many "disconnections" in our leaders today.

As necessary as competency development is, it is not sufficient to ensure that the leader's life will result in truly positive influence or an enduring legacy. Many leaders may accomplish much but never amount to much! According to Robert Clinton, over 70 percent of leaders who successfully climb the ladder of leadership influence do not finish well. Some dramatically fail, precipitating public scandal, while the majority of leaders who lose their influence just fade quietly into obscurity. They fall short because in their outwardly successful lives there is a disconnection between the development of leadership competencies and the development of leadership character. The lack of character is a frequent cause for leaders failing to fulfill their true potential; and this lack of character can be traced to a lack of Christ and community in the lives of the leaders.

Significantly, a recent 14-nation research project found that the prime reasons for early and painful return from missionary service (in both older and younger sending countries) were not related to inadequate formal training in missions. The project found that the prime causes were clustered around issues related to spirituality

character and relationships in the life of the missionary. In other words, it is usually not a lack of competencies that undermines missionaries; it is inadequacies that occur in the other areas that are to blame. These are areas frequently not addressed in preparation – Christ, community and character (no doubt calling was not specifically addressed by the research or else we suspect it would have shown up, too).

In the ConneXions model, we deal with the whole leader, not just his head. Our ultimate goal is the holistic transformation of the Christian leader into the mature image of Jesus Christ.

THE 4D PROCESS OF HEALTHY LEADER DEVELOPMENT

If we accept that healthy Christian leadership includes all 5Cs, and not merely academic capacity, it is immediately clear that building such a leader is easier said than done. It is not sufficient merely to send someone to a seminar or to give him a book on leadership to read. Leader development is highly complex and very little understood. Consequently, in many (perhaps most) organizations, it is essentially left up to chance. We pay lip service to it, but devote little time to this endeavor. The small efforts at leader development that are made are often haphazard and not part of any overall cohesive strategy. Apart from sending young people to Bible school, usually we simply hope that the leaders will somehow raise themselves up! When asked what his leader development strategy was, one leader said, "You just have to let the cream rise to the top." In other words, "We have no intentional strategy for leader development; we're just hoping for the best!"

As a result, many times, efforts at leadership building focus on courses and curriculum – the content. Not much time is spent on developing an appropriate *process* of development, which includes context as well as content.

Jesus' method of building leaders is summarized in Mark 3:

He appointed twelve – designating them apostles – that they might be with Him and that He might send them out to preach and to have authority to drive out demons. (Mark 3:14-15)

In this simple but profound statement, we have a distillation of how Jesus built leaders. In short, Jesus created a *transformational context* around His emerging leaders:

☐ A *spiritual* environment, involving relationship with God (with Himself, as well as with the Father through prayer).

☐ A *relational* web, involving relationship with a mature leader (Himself), and relationships with others (the community of the disciples).

☐ An *experiential* context, involving challenging assignments, pressure and a diversity of learning opportunities.

Then, in that transformational context, He instructed them – the *content* of development.

In a nutshell, that was how Jesus built leaders. Thus, context + content = the process of leader development.

Traditionally, we are more likely to seat our emerging leaders in neat rows behind desks and lecture them interminably in our attempts to build them. We are often very strong in our content but weak in the context we create for leader development.

Usually, in leader development design we have focused mostly on instruction. However, we must give significant attention to all four of the "dynamics of transformation." These are the 4Ds:

- ☐ Spiritual
- ☐ Relational
- ☐ Experiential
- ☐ Instructional

This is how lives are changed! When all 4Ds are strongly present in a design, spiritual life is nurtured, relational capacities are strengthened, character is developed, calling is clarified and deep leadership capacities are built.

This was also the practice of the early church:

They devoted themselves to the apostles' teaching and to the fellowship, to the breaking of bread and to prayer. (Acts 2:42)

They were "devoted" to all four dynamics:

- ☐ The apostles' teaching – instructional
- ☐ Fellowship – relational
- ☐ The breaking of bread – experiential
- ☐ Prayer – spiritual

The author has asked hundreds of Christian leaders around the world, from a wide variety of cultural backgrounds, these questions, "How were you built? What were the influences that formed and molded you as a leader? What made you the leader you are today?" Almost invariably, the answers include such things as parents, role models, examples, mentors, sufferings, responsibilities, rejections, failures, challenging assignments, etc. It is rare that someone will mention a course, and when they do, it is often the teacher who personally impacted their lives and not so much the content that they remember.

This should not surprise us, since an honest study of the Gospels will reveal that Jesus did exactly this with His disciples. His strategy was not merely instructional; He also created a transformational context of leader development, including spiritual, relational and experiential elements.

This is not to devalue content. We must have strong content; indeed, instruction is one of the four key dynamics of transformation of the ConneXions model. However, by itself, content is not sufficient. To build lives we must design transformational contexts that are strong spiritually, relationally and experientially.

To illustrate this, consider the following example. Suppose we want to build evangelists. We could begin with an *experiential* component by simply sending them out to share the Gospel with unbelievers. "Just go and do it!" Will that work? Will they learn anything about evangelism? Certainly they will!

Now let's include a *relational* dimension by sending them out with experienced evangelists who they can watch and who will watch them and encourage and correct them. Clearly this will work even better.

Now let's add a strong *spiritual* element by having our emerging evangelists join with intercessors before going out. They will pray and cry for the lost, entering into God's burden for those without Christ. Then, when they go out to evangelize they are also to look to God for help, asking Him who to go to, and waiting upon Him inwardly for the right words to speak. This will work better still!

Finally, let's give them some *instruction* – a good interactive course on the meaning and nature of evangelism, studying God's plan of salvation, a simple way to share the Gospel and one's own testimony, some common objections to the Gospel and how to respond, etc. Now we're building strong evangelists!

This simple example demonstrates the power of designing learning experiences that give strong attention to all four dynamics of transformation – the 4Ds. This is how lives are changed; this is how leaders are built!

Just as we must intentionally build all of the 5Cs (Christ, Community, Character, Calling and Competencies) in the leader's life, so we must design processes of leader development that include all four dynamics of transformation (Spiritual, Relational, Experiential and Instructional). None can be neglected!

This is a brief summary of the ConneXions model of healthy Christian leader development – building the 5Cs through the 4Ds!

FURTHER INFORMATION

For our complete models, please see: *Healthy Leaders: SpiritBuilt Leadership #2* and *Building Leaders: SpiritBuilt Leadership #4* by Malcolm Webber.

LeaderSource SGA

2601 Benham Ave.

Elkhart, IN 46517

Tel: +1 574 295 4357

Fax: +1 574 295 4673

Email: info@leadersource.org

Website: www.leadersource.org

Seven Paradigm Shifts

THE CURRENT LEADER DEVELOPMENT CRISIS

For the last 20-30 years, there has been a great deal of focus around the world on evangelism and church planting.

Some of the contributing reasons for this have been:

- The sovereign outpouring of the Holy Spirit.
- The Lausanne International Congress on World Evangelization (1974).
- Amsterdam '83 (and since): Billy Graham's International Conference for Itinerant Evangelists.
- The AD2000 Movement: "A Church for Every People and the Gospel for Every Person by AD 2000."
- Advances in research creating widely-used resources especially focusing on Unreached People Groups, such as *The World Christian Database and Joshua Project*.
- Proliferation of "world evangelism plans" – there have been over 1000 new ones in 30 years!
- Multiple major prayer initiatives focusing on evangelism.
- Considerable missions mobilization of local churches, especially focusing on Unreached People Groups.
- The rise of dynamic evangelism efforts from the Majority World.

The fruit of this has been profound:

- Tens of thousands of people are coming to Christ *each day* around the world.
- Thousands of new churches are planted *every* week.

We should thank God for this spectacular growth!

However, there has not been corresponding attention given to *leader development* during this time. Consequently, today we have a deficit of Christian leaders in the existing churches, with new churches being planted all the time! *An increasing deficit*!

In addition to this crisis of *quantity* of new leaders, we also face a crisis of *quality* of existing leaders.

Clearly, our traditional methods of leader development simply have not delivered either the quantity or quality of leaders that today's churches need.

It would be careless and irresponsible for us to simply rejoice in the great harvest of souls that is happening today in many parts of the world, without addressing the issue of leader development. We should remember the Welsh Revival of 1904-06.

During the Welsh Revival, tens of thousands of people came to Christ, the churches were filled with people praising God and entire towns were transformed. Many bars were emptied. Men and women who used to spend their money on getting drunk were now giving it to help their churches, buying clothes and food for their families. Stealing and other offences diminished so that, more than once, a magistrate came to court and found there were no cases for him to deal with! Men, whose language had been filthy before, learned to talk purely. It was observed that not only did the coal miners put in a better day's work, but also that the pit ponies turned disobedient! The ponies were so used to being cursed and sworn at that they simply didn't understand when orders were given in kind, clean words! The dark tunnels underground in the mines echoed with the sounds of prayer and hymns, instead of foul language, nasty jokes and gossip. People, who had been careless about paying their bills or debts, paid all they owed. Others forgot their quarrels and forgave one another. Much of the nation of Wales was shaken by God's mighty power, and, from this revival, many other nations were impacted.

However, today, at the start of the 21st century, Wales is one of the most secular countries in Europe – a mere 100 years later!

We can learn from this, and from other historical revivals, that unless there are healthy leaders who are capable of leading God's people to maturity, within a generation or two much of the harvest will be lost!

We are in a crisis of leader development. Our traditional methods of leader development have not delivered either the quantity or quality of leaders that we need, and unless this is addressed, in a generation or two much of today's glorious harvest will be lost.

We need a new paradigm of leader development. It's time for some "lateral" thinking!

VERTICAL AND LATERAL THINKING

Vertical thinking begins with a single concept and then proceeds with that concept until a solution is reached. Lateral ("sideways") thinking refers to thinking that generates alternative ways of seeing a problem before seeking a solution.

Vertical thinking is like digging a hole deeper and bigger, to make it a better hole. But if the hole is in the wrong place, then no amount of improvement is going to put it in the right place. No matter how obvious this may seem to every digger, it is still easier to go on digging in the same place than to start all over again in a new place. Vertical thinking is digging the same hole deeper; lateral thinking is trying again somewhere else.

A missionary friend of ours in Central America watched this played out quite literally. After spending a long time stubbornly digging a deeper and deeper hole in one location trying to find water (vertical thinking), the well diggers finally moved to *another spot* and struck water almost immediately (lateral thinking).

THE PRINTING PRESS A NEW PARADIGM

From AD 450 to 1450, Bibles were all hand-written manuscripts ("manuscript" comes from the Latin for "handwritten"), the heritage of monks. From the eleventh century, each abbey and monastery had its own "Scriptorium," where work was done copying or creating, decorating or binding. A single manuscript would take weeks, with a monk hand-copying the manuscript and working nine hours a day.

Imagine this today in the face of the church growth we're experiencing – tens of thousands of new Bibles are needed every day!

In the time of the monks, what would have been a vertical-thinking response to the crisis of rapid church growth? Employ more monks! Write faster! Of course, this would never have worked. They needed a new paradigm.

Enter Gutenberg, a lateral thinker! Johannes Gutenberg took two previously unconnected ideas: the wine press and the coin punch. The purpose of the coin punch was to leave an image on a small area such as a gold coin. The function of the wine press was, and still is, to apply force over a large area to squeeze the juice out of grapes. Gutenberg took many coin punches and put them under the force of the wine press so that they left their image on paper. The resulting combination was the printing press and movable type (ca. 1450). This began a revolution!

This relates directly to our current leadership crisis around the world. We need a new paradigm of leader development. We cannot keep building leaders the same way while merely trying to do it faster and on a larger scale. More of the same will not do! *We need to transform the way leaders are built*. We need a new paradigm.

SEVEN KEY PARADIGM SHIFTS

There are seven key paradigm shifts that address the current crises of leader quantity and quality.

1. A new goal.

Traditionally, our primary goal has been academic capacity. This is reflected in the central role of the academic degree in determining a leader's ministry qualification.

In the new paradigm, we focus intentionally on *building the whole person*. Of course, the healthy Christian leader needs strong biblical knowledge, but, by itself, this is not sufficient. The clear goal of leader development must be the development of the whole person – spiritual life, relational capacity, marriage, character and vision, as well as ministry knowledge and competencies. Our goal is not mere information, but transformation! We must build *healthy* leaders.

2. A new process.

If we shift our goal from academics to building the whole person, it is immediately apparent that we need a new process. A purely academic process (desks, lectures, books and exams) will not effectively build spiritual life, character and practical ministry capacity. Many seminaries and Bible schools have recognized this and are complementing their classroom agendas (information) with a variety of intentional spiritual, relational and experiential dynamics (transformation).

In the new paradigm, we implement a holistic process that gives strong and balanced attention to four dynamics:

- *Spiritual*. Experiential union with Christ is the center of a truly transformational process. We must bring our emerging leaders to God!

- *Relational*. Emerging leaders need more than lecturers; they need daily relationships with mature leaders, role models, examples, spiritual mothers and fathers – in the context of normal daily life and ministry. In the encouragement, support, challenge, teaching, discipline and accountability of these relationships, character is built, marriages are strengthened and spiritual life is nurtured.
- *Experiential*. Leaders learn by doing and not only by listening to lectures. They are transformed through the fires of suffering and pressure, and are stretched by challenging assignments.
- *Instructional*. The teaching of the Word of God – in an engaging way, and woven into the ongoing daily realities of life, family and ministry – is central to healthy leader development.

All four of these dynamics will be strongly present in an effective leader development process.

3. A new design.

Traditionally, we have rarely given much thought to leader development design; we have simply perpetuated tradition, teaching as we were taught. Jesus, however, designed an extraordinary collage of diverse learning experiences for His emerging leaders.

In the new paradigm, we learn how to design learning experiences as Jesus did. Leader development is a rather chaotic, complex and multifaceted experiential collage of diverse people, relationships, influences, assignments, tasks, responsibilities, duties, deadlines, opportunities, pressures, crises, blessings, sufferings, rejections, successes, mistakes, etc., that all work together to build the emerging leader. Thus, an effective leader development process is not a neat series of courses but a fiery immersion in real-life, real-time experiences, reflecting the complicated and fundamentally difficult nature of Christian leadership, bringing deep heart issues to the surface to be dealt with, and compelling the participant to look utterly to God for success.

4. Leaders building leaders.

Jesus came to the earth to do three things:

- To die on the cross for the sins of humanity.
- To proclaim the Kingdom of God and reveal the Father, through His words and works.
- To build a team of emerging leaders.

And that's all He did! So we know that building leaders is one of the central things that healthy leaders do.

Thankfully, we do not have to die on the cross for humanity's sins, since Jesus has accomplished that once and for all. We must, however, embrace the other two responsibilities. While we have focused on proclaiming the Kingdom and revealing the Father – that is, doing the "ministry stuff" – we have rarely, however, embraced personal and systematic responsibility for building leaders. Instead, we have sent our emerging leaders off to the "experts" in the remote academic institutions, hoping that they would do it for us. We have been too busy with leadership to build leaders!

We need to reconnect the two – leaders do ministry work *and* they build leaders at the same time. In the new paradigm, leaders embrace personal responsibility for leader development as a core part of what it means to be a leader. This shift alone has the potential to address both issues of *quality* (as mature leaders impart the vision, passion, courage and strategic perspectives of leadership) and *quantity* (as every leader takes personal responsibility to build leaders).

5. Churches building leaders.

Biblically, the primary unit of leader development is the local church or cluster of churches. It is not the disconnected academic institution.

In the new paradigm, just as leaders personally embrace their God-given responsibility to build leaders, so local churches embrace their God-given responsibility to build their own sons and daughters. This shift also has the potential to address both crises of quality and quantity. Some of the benefits are:

- **Multiplication.** The inherent limitations of the institutional approach will be lifted, the church-based approach providing a model that can be multiplied virtually endlessly with every local church or cluster of churches providing a learning environment for their emerging leaders. If every local church would build only one or two new leaders, the quantity crisis would be over!
- **Holistic development.** The learning process becomes considerably more effective since the local church provides the spiritual, relational and practical context for the development of the whole person.
- **The right people receive training.** The emerging and existing leaders who need training the most are those who are already engaged in ministry and cannot leave their work for years at a time to go and study in a distant institution. In the traditional approach, we consistently train the wrong people.
- **Flexibility.** When it comes to leader development, "one size" does not fit all. Around the world, leaders from a vast variety of cultures, backgrounds, experiences, education levels, etc., need to be built. Our approaches must be flexible and customizable. In addition, in many countries, the environment is rapidly changing around the church, again requiring flexibility in our approaches to leader development.
- **Self-support.** The local church provides the financial support for the learning process, thus maintaining both responsibility for and control of the development of its own emerging leaders. To be truly self-governing, the community must be self-supporting.
- **Security in restricted countries.** In restricted countries, educational institutions are often not viable due to their size, visibility and the ease with which they can be closed down. Church-based learning communities, on the other hand, can be small, easily-hidden and pervasive.
- **Ongoing, lifelong leader development.** The training is not limited to a certain period of time, but continues throughout the emerging leaders' lives. Leaders are built over lifetimes!
- **Effective evaluation.** Members of the local community who know the emerging leader and who work with him on a daily basis are the very best ones to help him both establish goals for his development and evaluate his growth toward those goals.

6. Church planting through leader development.

Jesus' vision was for hundreds of thousands of churches are around the world in every people group. He did not, however, personally plant any! Instead, He built leaders and those leaders then turned the world upside down. We have done it the other way around, by multiplying evangelistic efforts and planting many churches and then trying to address the need for leaders.

In the new paradigm, healthy leader development is raised to the same level of priority and focus as church planting. This is the only way we will plant and grow sustainable churches.

7. The centrality of the Person of Jesus Christ in Christian leadership.

For many years, Christian leadership training consisted essentially of courses related to biblical knowledge – Old Testament Survey, New Testament Survey, Systematic Theology, Biblical Ethics, Church History, etc. Of course, this did not prepare the students very well for the practical demands of life and ministry. To meet this need, new and more practical approaches to leader development have grown in popularity, often consisting of business models of leadership or motivational, "success" anecdotes of basketball coaches, football stars and wealthy businesspeople.

However, when Jesus described His own leadership, His entire focus was on His inner union with the Father:

> *The Jews were amazed and asked, "How did this man get such learning without having studied?" Jesus answered, "My teaching is not my own. It comes from him who sent me..." (John 7:15-16; cf. Acts 4:13)*

> *I am telling you what I have seen in the Father's presence... (I have) told you the truth that I heard from God... (John 8:38-40)*

> *...the Son can do nothing by himself; he can do only what he sees his Father doing, because whatever the Father does the Son also does. (John 5:19)*

> *...it is the Father, living in me, who is doing his work. (John 14:10)*

In the new paradigm, union with Christ, the cross, suffering, holiness and dependency on the Holy Spirit are at the center of all our leader development. The Person of Jesus Christ is the Beginning and the End of all Christian leadership and leader development.

> *Abide in me, and I will abide in you. No branch can bear fruit by itself; it must abide in the vine. Neither can you bear fruit unless you abide in me. I am the vine; you are the branches. If a man abides in me and I in him, he will bear much fruit; apart from me you can do nothing. (John 15:4-5)*

SUMMARY

In summary, these are the seven key paradigm shifts to transform the way leaders are built:

1. A new goal – the healthy Christian leader, not just academic achievement.
2. A new process – holistic development, transformation and not just information.

3. Intentional design – a collage of diverse learning experiences, not simply perpetuating traditional courses while teaching (lecturing) as we were taught.

4. Leaders build leaders – leaders taking personal responsibility for leader development, rather than only fulfilling ministry responsibilities themselves while delegating leader development to others.

5. Churches build leaders – the primary unit of leader development is the local church or cluster of churches, and not a disconnected academic institution.

6. Church planting through leader development – the emphasis on building leaders must be raised to the same level of priority and focus as evangelism and church planting if we are to plant and grow sustainable churches.

7. The centrality of the Person of Jesus Christ in Christian leadership. Union with Christ, the cross, suffering, holiness and dependency on the Holy Spirit (John 15:4-5) must be at the center of all our leader development. The Person of Jesus Christ is the Beginning and the End of all Christian leadership and leader development.

This is how we can build Christian leaders who will, once again, turn the world upside down!

FURTHER INFORMATION

For our complete models, please see: Healthy Leaders: SpiritBuilt Leadership #2 and Building Leaders: SpiritBuilt Leadership #4 by Malcolm Webber.

LeaderSource SGA
2601 Benham Ave.
Elkhart, IN 46517
Tel: +1 574 295 4357
Fax: +1 574 295 4673
Email: info@leadersource.org
Website: www.leadersource.org

MODEL BRIEF

A Letter from an Emerging Leader (How Leaders Are Built)

" I am an emerging leader. You are an existing leader. I'm so grateful that God has placed you in my life. I really need you!

First, please teach me the Word of God – because the Truth is life. The Truth can change my thinking. It can transform my life. But I need you to teach me with the anointing and conviction of the Holy Spirit; not only with words, but with conviction and power.

However, please don't simply teach me; I need you to share your life with me. Don't teach me only theoretical ideas; be transparent with your life. Tell me about your experiences of God, about the victories you have seen, and about the failures you have had. Your hopes, your disappointments, your joys, your frustrations – share it all with me.

In addition to instructing me, please genuinely engage with me in my life. I need to know that you really care about me, that your intention is not merely to train me to do certain things and then send me out as a foot-soldier in your army. Please don't use me. I need to know that you love me and are committed to me. Express this commitment to me in a variety of ways. When I do things well, affirm me. When I make errors, hold me accountable; with love and gentleness, correct me.

Please give me responsibilities; responsibilities that are appropriate to my maturity. Some should be mundane tasks to build servanthood in my life. But also give me important things that increase my vision and help clarify my calling. Carefully design these responsibilities so they stretch me and force me to learn, to grow, and to look to God for success.

As I fulfill those responsibilities, don't leave me alone; be with me and encourage me. And not only you; please build other relationships around my life. Encourage other mature brothers and sisters in the church to embrace me as their spiritual son. Help them know how to engage with me in practical and meaningful ways in my life. In their lives I'll see what it means to be a mature believer. I'll see it. Not only will you teach me about it; I'm also going to see it. I've got to see it!

I need to see marriages that, while not perfect, are healthy. In a little while I'm going to be married. I need to know what it means and how it works. You taught me that the husband should love his wife as Christ loves His church. Because of the Presence of the Spirit upon your teaching, I was moved and touched by it; I was so moved I wept when I saw this in the Scriptures. But I still need to see it in life. I must see it. I've got to see it in lives around me.

I need those people also to walk with me in life. As I'm going through experiences, responsibilities and pressures, I must know that I'm not doing it my myself, but there are others who are with me, committed to me, affirming me, encouraging me, and praying for me. In their lives I will see how to endure. I know I need to endure; you taught me this well. But I need to see it. I need to be with you when you go through some terrible fiery sufferings. I'll watch you endure. That's how I'm going to remember. That's how I will really get it.

So please take me with you sometimes. Let me watch you as you do leadership stuff. I love your teaching, but I need to see you actually do it!

As I walk with you and as we do things together, I will learn more deeply what it means to be a leader. I will watch you as pray for the people you are serving, and when you weep for them. I will be with you when you are patient with people. I will be with you when you correct those who are wrong. That's how I will learn to do it myself.

As you look at my life, help me see the purpose of God for me and give me assignments. Continually look for opportunities to put me to work. Never allow me to be passive. Don't let me sit at a distance and be quiet. Draw me out saying, "Hey, come on my son! Look at the vision of God. Look at what God's doing, and what you can be and do in Him. Come on!" Affirm the calling I've got on my life. Affirm that God has given me a wonderful purpose. Always be in front of me saying, "Come on! You can do it!" When I respond, "No, I can't!" tell me, "Yes, you can." Affirm me.

Challenge me. Then send me off to go and do it, with others around me.

Please intentionally connect with me and others around me – with ministry partners and teams. Wisely connect with me and other people who complement how God made me. Sometimes you should intentionally connect me with people with whom you know I will have conflicts. And we'll start to get into little disagreements, and some sparks will fly. And then I'll feel bad. I'll notice that you have been watching me during these conflicts, and I'll feel as if I have let you down. But then I will see that you are not upset. You will reach out to me with care and love. You'll say, "Hey, come on! Let's dig into this. There are some bad things in your life, aren't there? And this relationship, this circumstance, has brought up the worst. So, lets' dig it out now."

In the past, I was afraid to let anyone touch those deep inner things, but you've built a strong relationship. I know you are for me, I know you are committed to me. So, cautiously, I will open up a little bit. And you'll pray with me and look over some of the pains in my life. We'll face it together. Gently you'll encourage me to forgive those who have wronged me. You'll help me understand this conflict that I had in the relationship – that the relationship didn't cause the issues in my heart; it simply gave them an opportunity to be exposed. As you work with me through this, I will understand more how God deals with me in the struggles of life. He allows me to go through the fire. I'll remember that you taught me about this from Peter's first letter; now I know it in my life. Other spiritual mothers and fathers will gently nurture this transparency and honesty in my life.

In dealing with all this, submitting myself to Truth, submitting myself to God, through these deep, nurturing, caring, accountable relationships, in the midst of the challenges, complexities and pressures of life, God will change me. I'll find myself freer. I'll realize that I'm learning the true nature of the Christian life. I'm learning what the nature of leadership is. Not just the doctrine. Not just some "eight points" that someone says is important. But I'm really getting it. I'm seeing it. I'm being changed. I'm being changed by the Truth of the Word, in the power of the Spirit, in the midst of a loving, nurturing, accountable family, going through the deep, challenging experiences of life. I'm finding God.

I'll see Him in your life, and in the lives of the others who are around me, committed to me. I'll learn how to pray, because I watch you pray. I'll watch you worship God. In this way I'll learn what it means to worship God. I'll see in the Word the wonderful revelation of how I'm made just to worship Him. I will understand this. And then I'll do it, because you will encourage me to do it. I'll know how to do it because I have seen you do it. As I do it, I'll be changed even more by the Spirit. I'll come to know Him. I'll learn how to turn my heart to Him, to find Him, to see Him, to know Him. I'll know God. And I'll have good doctrine about God too.

I'll learn what it means to be a friend because I have friends. They will love me and remain committed to me even when I act ugly. They will always be there for me. They won't reject me. You will be there for me. Then I'll start to realize what you've been teaching me, that God says He will never reject me. What you taught me about Hosea will start to make sense to me – that even though Hosea's wife was not faithful, he remained faithful to her. And God said to His people, "That's how I treat you. I will never abandon you." I will remember when you taught me – at that time my heart rejoiced, and again there was such a beautiful presence of god that I wept in the teaching. But now I'll see it more clearly, more richly, because I see you do it. I understood the Scriptures, but I wasn't sure what it looked like in life. How would it work? I had many questions. But now you have answered my questions, not just in your teaching but in your life. Because I see it, now I know. I thought I knew it, and in a way I did. But now I really know it, it has changed me.

In all the difficult times, I will not be alone; you will be there with me. I know that I only need to give you a call. If I come over and knock on your door, you'll be there for me. And not only when I come after you, but you will come after me too, and hold me accountable. Even at times when I want to run, when I want to hide, you won't let me. Not in a dominating way, but with affirmation, you will reach out to me. You'll say "Come on! Let's face the issues, let's face this stuff together. You can rise above it. Together let's cry out to God. In the midst of the difficulty and pressure, together let's look to God, to see His hand in your life.

I will learn what it means to work with people, by watching you. I'll learn how to work with nice people. I'll learn how to work with difficult people. I'll learn what it means to have a healthy marriage, because you will intentionally invite me to see what really happens in marriages. And when I think I have found my wife, you will help us. You will also connect us with mature couples, and they will share their lives and struggles transparently with us.

I'll find that all the junk and worldliness that used to be in my life will drop off. I'll be changed in this loving community around me, as we walk together in the experiences, sufferings and challenges of life. God will build true holiness in my life, making me a man of integrity – because you have worked deeply with my life. You were not content with superficial things. You created experiences for me that gave me the opportunities to show what was really in my heart. Then when all that was there came out, you were there fro me, helping me to understand it according to the Truth of the Word of God, helping me to submit to Him, to give it to the Lord, and genuinely receive His grace – not just know about His grace, but actually receive it. Something changed in me; inwardly, in my heart, genuine integrity was born. I know I'm not perfect. I know I'm not going to be perfect, because when I look at you I don't see perfection. So I know it's going to be no different for me. But I know I'm going to do well, because I have seen it in your life.

I want to be like you. As I see the way that you seek God for your purpose and the destiny of the church, as I watch you do that, my heart will be gripped, because I see your heart gripped. I'll see your passion for the lost, reflecting Jesus' heart, my heart will be changed.

I'll watch as you look at all the complicated things around you, all of the complexity of what's happening in your life and ministry. I'll see you are not overwhelmed. But you respond to this complexity with brokenness and a deeper looking at the Face of God. I'll see you do that. I'll be watching you. I will se how you are able to look at all that complicated murky stuff and then make a decision and say, "Here is where we are going to go." By the leading of the Spirit, you establish a clear direction. That will affect me. I'll remember that for the rest of my life. I will learn how to do the same thing myself, without even realizing that I'm learning this. I will find myself in complicated situations and my first response will be

to look at God – because that's what you did. I've seen you do it many times. So without even thinking about it, I will do the same things. Somehow your abilities to think strategically and make decisions will have rubbed off on me. I'll have developed this capacity to think. Not only to think, but also to act. I'll have seen you do it. I'll have watched you so many times where a lesser man or woman would have been paralyzed by indecision. But you took the responsibility. You didn't take the easy way out. You took the responsibility in spite of the complexity and, at times, the cost. I'll have seen you do that numerous times. I didn't realize that as I was watching you, somehow it affected me too. Now I'll do the same thing, because through your teaching you have changed me. By bringing me to God again and again in so many different ways, you have changed me. By your example and your interaction, you have changed me, as you walked with me through the difficulties and challenges of my life.

Then I will notice that you've given me opportunities where I can serve others in the same way – where I can be to them what you have been to me.

One day, suddenly, I will realize that people are looking to me for leadership. And I will recognize that God has been raising me up to lead and serve His people. Through other lives around me, through His Presence, by His Word, in the experiences of life, God has changed me, prepared me, built me. I know I'll never be perfect, but now I can do it. I can lead. I've been built – well built."

FURTHER INFORMATION

For our complete models, please see: *Healthy Leaders: SpiritBuilt Leadership #2* and *Building Leaders: SpiritBuilt Leadership #4* by Malcolm Webber.

LeaderSource SGA
2601 Benham Ave.
Elkhart, IN 46517
Tel: +1 574 295 4357
Fax: +1 574 295 4673
Email: info@leadersource.org
Website: www.leadersource.org

Father – Jesus – Holy Spirit

Tribe – Big T

The entire Body of Christ in heaven and earth

Tribe – Middle T

Large group of believers who are held together by common values, vision, culture, strategies and ways of thinking and perceiving reality. E.g. Roman Catholics, Anglican, Pentecostal, Evangelical

Jesus Tribe – Little T

Spiritual families-of-families that are in unity of mind, heart and lifestyle around God Himself, kingdom, core values, vision, culture, strategy and Christ's delegated church government like an APEST leadership team. Like the Rock International "Tribe"

Local church families led by a plurality of elders in unity with & in submission to a trans-local APEST teams

Micro-Church Families connected to other Micro-Churches & in unity & submission to local elders.

DNA Groups/Ekklesia Groups (2's & 3's) in unity with & submission to a Micro-Church family

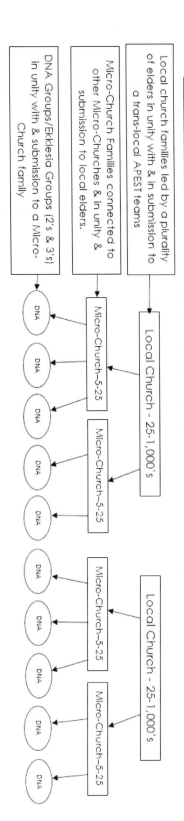

THE VIRKLER GRID

	Apostle	Prophet	Evangelist	Pastor	Teacher
Heart Passion	For the whole	For inspirational creativity	For the harvest	For people	For truth
Main Gifts	Ability to lead, organize, develop, build and expand	Creative abilities, sense of timing & rightness	Ability to be persuasive	Loves people and heals their hurts	Ability to research and present clearly
Emotions	Less emotional, more structured	Quite emotional-both ups and downs	Highly invigorated, intense	Very sensitive	Less emotional, more structured
Goal	See things organized and running smoothly	Experience the creative flow	Persuade others to see what he sees	For people to be healthy, safe and cared for	Truth clearly communicated and assimilated
Judges others by	Their ability and willingness to fit in	Their ability to experience or appreciate the creative flow	Their ability to influence	Their ability to be sensitive and concerned for people's needs	Their ability to discern and clearly express truth
Influences others by	Helping them to see their value and place in the overall picture	Edification, exhortation, comfort	Enthusiasm, excitement, dynamism	Warmth, love and acceptance	Helping them understand and grow
Value to organization	Gets everyone working together as a team; is a good troubleshooter	Gives creative expression, spirit encounter, sense of divine timing and destiny	Convinces and excites people about moving in a certain direction	Ensures that people's heart needs are met; provides warmth, happiness and contentment	Provides continuous clear, practical training for all who enter the organization
Overuses	Abusing power, authority; insensitive to people	Living only out of intuition without validation	Selling things not worth selling	Becoming mushy, weak, too flexible	Leaving no place for intuition; to analytical
Under Pressure	Meets with others to seek resolution	Retreats to be alone	Becomes more invigorated and passionate about what he has to sell; may become dishonest	Reaches out with more warmth and understanding	Does more research
Fears	Loss of authority structure, organization	Not being able to capture the intuitive creative flow	Not being able to convince	Disunity and discord, brokenness and emotional destruction	Not being able to pass on progress to the next generation

A Comparative Analysis of the Foundation Offices of Ephesians 4:11

Dangers: If we do not offer balanced fivefold ministry, the church will gravitate toward one or another extreme:

- The Evangelist tends to build a church focused exclusively on winning the lost, minimizing discipleship.
- The Prophet tends to build a legalistic church.
- The Teacher tends to build a theological church.
- The Pastor tends to build a social church.
- The Apostle tends to build a super-organized church.

Used by permission of Mark Virkler - http://www.cwgministries.org/

NOTES:

RECOMMENDED READING AND RESOURCES

Apostles & Apostolic Ministry

The Permanent Revolution by Alan Hirsch & Tim Catchim

The Gift of Apostle by David Cannistraci

Christ

Jesus Manifesto by Frank Viola & Leonard Green

Community

True Fellowship by Art Katz

Life Together by Dietrich Bonhoeffer

Disciple-making & Spiritual Parenting

Contagious Disciple Making by Paul & David Watson

Revolution of Character by Dallas Willard

You Have Not Many Fathers by Mark Hanby

Authentic Spiritual Mentoring by Larry Kreider

The Cost of Discipleship by Dietrich Bonhoeffer

DNA Groups

DNA Groups by Dr. Timothy Johns

Ekklesia (Church) & Church Planting

Ekklesia by Ed Silvoso

Church Planting Movements by David Garrison

Church Planting: The Next Generation by Kevin Mannoia

Evangelism

Radical by David Platt

The Art of Neighboring by Jay Pathak & Dave Runyon

The Celtic Way of Evangelism by George Hunter

That None Should Perish by Ed Silvoso

Gospel Fluency by Jeff Vanderstelt

Face Time with God

Secrets of the Secret Place by Bob Sorge

The Secret to the Christian Life by Gene Edwards

The Spirit of the Disciplines by Dallas Willard

Ministering To the Lord by Roxanne Brant

Joyful Journey: Listening To Immanuel by James Wilder, Anna Kang

Family & Tribes

Spiritual Family as the Emerging Apostolic Paradigm by Dr. Timothy Johns (Doctoral Dissertation)

Covenant Relationships by Keith Intrater

Financing & Funding Ministry

The Fully Funded Missionary by Rob Parker

Partnership Development for the Fully Funded Missionary by Rob Parker

The Key to Everything by Jack Hayford

The Treasure Principle by Randy Alcorn

Forgiveness & Mercy

Total Forgiveness by R T Kendall

How to Stop The Pain by James Richards

The Bait of Satan by John Bevere

Gospel of Grace

Destined To Reign by Joseph Prince

The Prodigal God by Timothy Keller

God without Religion by Andrew Farley

The Ragamuffin Gospel by Brennan Manning

The Gospel In Ten Words by Paul Ellis

The Normal Christian Life by Watchman Nee

The Cure by John Lynch

Unfiltered Grace by Joe Langley

Healing & Spiritual Warfare

They Shall Expel Demons by Derek Prince

The Essential Guide to Healing by Bill Johnson & Randy Clark

What Everybody Ought To Know About Healing by Paul & Lynn Crawford

The Healing Breakthrough by Randy Clark

Christ the Healer by F. F. Bosworth

Holy Spirit

The Anointing by R T Kendall

Holy Spirit I Hunger For You by Claudio Freidzon

Inner-healing & Deliverance

Prayers That Heal the Heart by Mark Virkler

How to Cast Out Demons by Doris Wagner

Kingdom

The Unshakable Kingdom and the Unchanging Person by E. Stanley Jones

Rediscovering the Kingdom by Myles Monroe

Kingdom Principles by Myles Monroe

Applying the Kingdom by Myles Monroe

The Power That Changes the World by Bill Johnson

Last Days (Eschotology)

Surprised By Hope by N.T. Wright

Leadership

Rare Leadership by Marcus Warner & Jim Wilder

The Leadership Challenge by James Kouzes & Barry Posner

Leaders Who Last by Dave Kraft

Building Leaders by Malcolm Webber

Making of a Leader by Robert Clinton

The 21 Irrefutable Laws of Leadership by John Maxwell

The Making of a Leader by Frank Damazio

Values-Driven Leadership by Aubrey Malphurs

Life Model

Living from the Heart Jesus Gave You by James Friesen & James Wilder

Joy Starts Here: The Transformation Zone by James Wilder, Chris Coursey

Transforming Fellowship: 19 Brain Skills That Build Joyful Community by Coursey, Chris M.

Marketplace

Anointed For Business by Ed Silvoso

Marketplace Miracles by Rick Heeren

Transformation: Change the Marketplace and You Can Change the World by Ed Silvoso

Marriage & Family

The Meaning of Marriage by Timothy Keller

Micro-Churches & Missional Communities

The Global House Church Movement by Rad Zdero

Houses That Change the World by Wolfgang Simpson

Stetzer, Ed. *Planting Missional Churches.*

Launching Missional Communities by Mike Breen & Alex Absalom

Starting a House Church by Larry Kreider

Missions & Missional Communities

Perspectives on the World Christian Movement by Ralph Winter

Miraculous Movements by Jerry Trousdale

Parenting

Loving Our Kids On Purpose by Danny Silk

Shepherding a Child's Heart by Tedd Tripp

Spiritual Protection for Your Children by Neil Anderson

The Key to Your Child's Heart by Gary Smalley

Prayer & Fasting

Prayer That Brings Revival by David Yonggi Cho

Understanding the Purpose & Power of Prayer by Myles Munroe

Shaping History through Prayer & Fasting by Derek Prince

Break Through Prayer by Jim Cymbala

Rees Howells Intercessor by Norman Grubb

Prayer Evangelism by Ed Silvoso

Prophetic & Hearing God's Voice

4 Keys to Hearing God's Voice by Mark Virkler

Prophetic Etiquette by Michael Sullivant

Revival

Hosting the Presence by Bill Johnson

When Heaven Invades Earth by Bill Johnson

Lighting Fires by Randy Clark

Defining Moments by Bill Johnson

True Stories of the Miracles of Azusa Street by Tommy Welchel

They Told Me Their Stories by Tommy Welchel

Revival Fire by Wesley Duewel

Ablaze For God by Wesley Duewel

Sonship - Daughtership

Spiritual Slavery to Spiritual Sonship by Jack Frost

Order of a Son by Mark Hanby

Abba's Child by Brennan Manning

Experiencing Father's Embrace by Jack Frost

Agape Road by Bob Mumford

Resources

Verge - www.vergenetwork.org

DNA Groups - http://wearesoma.com/wp-content/uploads/2014/10/1-FINAL-FINAL-FINAL-DNA-Booklet.pdf

DNA Groups - https://www.youtube.com/watch?v=gEtTZ7Pjhdc

Value of DNA for men - https://www.youtube.com/watch?v=ulN1_y5jo2M

Value of DNA for women - https://www.youtube.com/watch?v=dS_odxY1tj8

Missional Church Network - http://missionalchurchnetwork.com

ABOUT THE AUTHOR

Dr. Timothy Johns is a business man and church planter. He is the founder and leader of the Rock Tribe, an international family of churches in the USA and three other nations. Tim also started and leads Rock Solid Urban Impact and All Nations College. His life focus has been to create healthy spiritual families that are effective in making disciples and raising up leaders that advance Christ's Kingdom in every sphere of life. He has produced many resources to help emerging APEST leaders start and multiply small Micro-Church Families (Missional Kingdom Families). (APEST – Five-fold ministry gifts like apostles, prophets, evangelists, and teachers).

Since the 1970's, Tim has helped to plant and multiply hundreds of small spiritual families, and effectively trained others to start and lead life-giving, disciple-making micro-churches. His father's heart, contagious love, affection, and joy have helped others learn how to create the culture necessary for sons/daughters of Father to become like Christ. Tim has been a keynote speaker at numerous churches and conferences. He also consults with church leaders, helping them to improve evangelism and discipleship in the context of small missional communities.

Tim received formal training with three earned degrees: Bachelors of Arts (Tarkio College), Masters of Divinity (Fuller Theological Seminary) and Doctorate of Ministry (Regent University). He has served as an ordained pastor in the Presbyterian denomination and with the Vineyard. He helped raise up a church-planting movement in the 1980's called Grace Ministries. In the 1990's those church plants merged into the International House of Prayer, Vineyard, or became Independent.

Tim's passion is the Person of Jesus Christ and the Kingdom of God. He longs to reveal Father's heart to all people. His mission is to inspire Christ's Church to be a catalyst of the Holy Spirit which proclaims the gospel, makes Disciples of Christ, and transforms cities for the glory of God. He believes God is radically changing the understanding and expression of Christianity in this generation by merging three supernatural realities: Revival, Reformation of the Church, and Transformation of culture.

Tim and Janet have enjoyed 43 years of marriage, raised two married children who are Christ-loving leaders, and six beautiful grandchildren. They live in Northern Colorado where they are planting micro-churches in the Rocky Mountain region and giving oversight to the Rock Tribe Family-of-Churches and its compassion and educational ministries.

For More Resources:

www.JesusTribes.com

www.micro-churches.com

† Jesus
⊤ribes

Jesus Tribes – a catalyst for igniting relational love and joy in all seven areas of cultural influence: marriage & family, church, marketplace, media, education, arts, social & civil services.

Jesus Tribes offers consultation, training conferences and resources on how to start and multiply Micro-Church Families on Mission.

www.JesusTribes.com

All Nations College – A College of Family of Faith University

All Nations College is offering an accredited BA ministry degree in:

- "Micro-Church Planting"
- Cross-cultural Missions Leadership
- Wilderness Ministry Leadership
- Market Place Leadership

www.AllNations.College